The medical revolution of
the seventeenth century

The medical revolution of the seventeenth century

Edited by

ROGER FRENCH *and* ANDREW WEAR

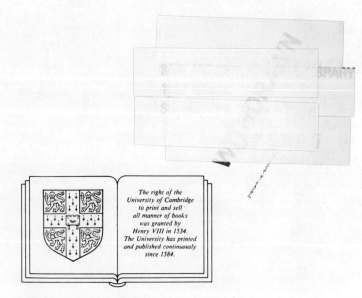

The right of the
University of Cambridge
to print and sell
all manner of books
was granted by
Henry VIII in 1534.
The University has printed
and published continuously
since 1584.

CAMBRIDGE UNIVERSITY PRESS

Cambridge

New York   Port Chester

Melbourne   Sydney

Published by the Press Syndicate of the University of Cambridge
The Pitt Building, Trumpington Street, Cambridge CB2 1RP
40 West 20th Street, New York, NY 10011, USA
10 Stamford Road, Oakleigh, Melbourne 3166, Australia

First published 1989

Printed in Great Britain at the University Press, Cambridge

British Library cataloguing in publication data

The medical revolution of the seventeenth century.
1. Europe. Medicine, 1600–1750
I. French, Roger II. Wear, Andrew
610'.94

Library of Congress cataloguing in publication data

The medical revolution of the seventeenth century/edited by Roger
French and Andrew Wear.
p.   cm.
Includes index.
ISBN 0-521-35510-9
1. Medicine–Europe–History–17th century. I. French, R. K.
(Roger Kenneth) II. Wear, A. (Andrew)
R484.M433 1989
610'.9'032–dc19   88–28521 CIP

ISBN 0 521 35510 9

Contents

Contributors

L.W.B. Brockliss, *Magdalen College, Oxford*

Harold J. Cook, *Department of the History of Medicine, University of Wisconsin Medical School*

Andrew Cunningham, *Wellcome Unit for the History of Medicine, Department of History and Philosophy of Science, Cambridge*

Peter Elmer, *Harlaxton College, University of Evansville, British Campus*

Roger French, *Wellcome Unit for the History of Medicine, Department of History and Philosophy of Science, Cambridge*

Johanna Geyer-Kordesch, *Institut für Theorie und Geschichte der Medizin, Münster*

Anita Guerrini, *Program in History of Science and Technology, University of Minnesota*

David Harley, *Wellcome Unit for the History of Medicine, Oxford*

John Henry, *Science Studies Unit, Edinburgh*

Roy Porter, *Wellcome Institute for the History of Medicine, London*

Andrew Wear, *Wellcome Institute for the History of Medicine, London*

Acknowledgements

We would like to thank the Wellcome Trust for its generous support of the conference, at Corpus Christi College, Cambridge, which gave rise to this book.

Introduction

How did medicine fare in an age of revolution? The aim of the editors in calling for contributions to this volume was to show that medicine in the century approximately from 1630 to 1730 did not exist as an activity unrelated to others, whether intellectual or social. But more than this, the aim was to go beyond putting medicine into a 'context' of political, religious and social change, and explore the dynamics that changed the nature of medicine, given the major movements of the time in these other activities and in medicine's substrate, natural philosophy. It was not, after all, until the seventeenth century that the revived classicism of the medical renaissance of the previous century was successfully overturned.

The question of how medicine fared in an age of revolution becomes necessary because it has been given less attention by historians than it deserves. This is partly because the giant figure of Newton has previously focused attention on natural philosophy, so that, for instance, discussions of William Harvey have often been related to the 'scientific revolution' rather than to the medicine of the time. Over the last half century too, historiographical trends have tended to express the relationship of medicine, religion and politics in terms of the persuasive puritan-and-science thesis. Both of these approaches too readily identify medicine with 'science' and ignore medicine's specific characteristics and development. It is time to look anew at medicine in the period, and the detailed studies in this book will help redress the balance.

The book as a whole tries to characterize seventeenth-century medicine and to show how it was open to external forces of change. Perhaps the greatest of these forces, as appears from these chapters, was that deriving from the relationship between medicine and religion. Given that our topic is the seventeenth century, and partly in England, the interest of the authors of these chapters in this theme is not surprising. Religion was a system of belief, supported by law, that expressed its dominating presence in many areas of life ranging from ordinary family relationships to politics and civil and national wars, and which, of course coloured most of the intellectual life of Europe as a whole.

A thread common to a number of chapters is that the new natural philosophy (of the 'scientific revolution') appealed to those who found in it some answer to the sectarian struggles in religion: More and Cudworth (in John Henry's chapter), the eirenicists of varied background (described by Peter Elmer) and the latitudinarian Arminians and their successors in Holland (in the chapter by Roger French). In contrast, those at either extreme of the religious spectrum might see these men of the middle ground as doctrinally lax to the point of atheism, a charge also often laid against medicine. These themes touch on the much discussed 'protestant ethic' question and that of the place of medicine in puritan millenarial thinking, and Elmer provides us with a revision of recent scholarship. He shows that those in the main stream of puritan thought did not always press for reform in medicine and they were frequently deeply conservative, as is shown when they attacked any competition that was offered to university-trained physicians. He challenges the association made by recent scholars of puritanism with reform in medicine by looking at the careers of thorough-going puritans who were also physicians. His conclusion is that the reformist call to replace Galenic doctrines with a more Christian and iatrochemical medicine came from radical sectarians as well as from advocates of religious toleration. These believers in eirenicism came from a variety of religious positions ranging in England from central Anglican to radical, and were united by an interest in hermetic theories.

Roger French's chapter discusses the fate of the greatest medical discovery of the age, the circulation of the blood, in a society dominated by the urgencies of political and religious disputes. It is argued that the spread of the doctrine was due less to its own momentum, or truth, than to its congruence with the political, religious and medical ideas occupying the minds of its potential recipients. This chapter also looks at how these recipients were grouped together, and what effect this might have had on their adoption of the doctrine; in other words how a consensus of opinion upon a doctrine might be reached. For medical doctrines do not change historically by remaining the property of an individual.

Medicine and religion naturally interacted too where they had common ground, and nothing did they have more in common than the human soul. The soul was man's immortality in the next world, while in this it was the form of the body, and the body its instrument. Natural philosophy and religious doctrine had long since worked out an accord on this central issue, but at a time when doctrine and philosophy were both undergoing radical changes new accords were needed.

The broadest of these changes in philosophy was made as the century moved from revolution to enlightenment. The soul as form, the user of the instrumental body, was in seventeenth-century medical thought physiologically active and in two, if not three, parts. Particularly in England, man was held to share the lower of the two souls (or the lower two of the three) with animals. But on the continent the followers of Descartes entirely denied that animals had a soul, and reduced man's rational, immortal soul to consciousness or thought, which played no part in the working of the body save in voluntary motion. By now, in an enlightened age, the soul was above all rational. Loss of rationality, madness, could be explained as possession of man's immortal principle by the Devil, but increasingly it came to be seen as a medical problem. Again we are in the middle ground between religion and medicine, and we find that the kind of explanation of madness varied as the religious sects varied. Just as much that was new in natural philosophy and medicine was welcomed by those who were weary of sectarian struggles, so the tone of enlightenment thinking was opposed to the earlier religious enthusiasm. In the second half of the seventeenth century many people saw God as the giver of laws of nature rather than of the divine Providence of the earlier century. The soul was a rational faculty rather than a vehicle of divine inspiration. The new intellectual climate was rational, optimistic and deistic. The medical theory that followed upon this climate was largely mechanical (with important exceptions) in following such laws of nature. John Henry shows, however, in providing a careful analysis of the relations between medicine and religion in the writings of the Cambridge Platonists Henry More and Ralph Cudworth, that the interactions of medicine and religion were not always equal in both directions. He points out in his chapter that most English theologians ignored the intellectual and ethical problems posed by medicine. Although the physicians' business involved authorities that were ultimately pagan and a materialism that was potentially heretical, a formal and perfunctory obeisance to religion and a defence built of technicalities often prevented theological attack. However, the possibility of dispute remained, because the materialist basis of medical treatment could always be interpreted as being in conflict with the religious belief that illness was God's punishment, and that healing lay in the hands of God (as Christ had healed). The church developed the position of compromise that the means of cure (herbal remedies) although material, were God-given and efficacious only through the particular exercise of God's power.

Debate between the two professions, church and medicine, could also centre specifically on the soul, the principle of both mortal and immortal life. Harvey, for example, had the soul flowing into and enlivening the blood; but in the anti-Aristotelianism that followed, the successors of such a doctrine might seem as making the soul – and indeed life – depend upon the circulation of the blood, thus appearing to establish that the soul depended on matter, if not indeed that the soul was itself material. Such a monism was often proposed as a solution to the problems of dualism, but its secular nature is unmistakable. As John Henry points out, not all theologians remained silent. His analysis shows how the Cambridge Platonists, More and Cudworth, tried to combat the atheism implicit in medical theories by emphasizing the role played by immaterial substance: in man and animals, the soul, responsible for mental events. The close relation that existed in these areas between medicine and religion is expressed by their conclusion that the immaterial soul – which uniquely among man's attributes was both physiological and spiritual – was philosophically necessary, and that, indeed, matter could not act or move without the agency of the soul.

The concept of a soul that was both physiological and spiritual also had very practical consequences. Madness after all was often regarded as an affection of the soul, whether a loss of rationality or demonic possession. So madness like the soul itself was of interest to both physicians and the clergy. David Harley's discussion of mental illness, magic and the Devil in Northern England brings out clearly the pluralistic nature of the explanations of madness current in the society of the time. The laity, for example, often blamed a third person, the witch, when accounting for madness, and they used counter-magic and the services of cunning-folk to combat her. In contrast, the godly and the ministers of the 'old' dissent, those who had undergone the full rigours of persecution immediately after the restoration, emphasized the responsibility of the afflicted person for his or her madness. God or the Devil had to be responsible, they argued, and the power of both was such as to prevent countervailing medicines from taking effect. The remedies proposed reflected the tradition of providentialism of the earlier seventeenth century and consisted of intense self-examination to discover what sin or error had brought about the demonic possession or divine retribution. In addition, the mad person would be helped by the prayers and fasting of the minister and congregation (methods used also in physical illness).

Different again, Anglicans (and increasingly in the eighteenth century, the dissenters) saw madness in naturalistic terms, and resorted to the remedies of the physicians, often justifying their action by referring to the 'superstition' of the catholics in their practice of exorcism of the possessed. These differing approaches are brought to life in Harley's detailed case-study of Richard Dugdale, the Surey Demoniack.

Newton, that 'stupendiously Great Man' in the phrase of George Cheyne, had great influence over medical thinking. His work provided a model for physicians to attempt medical *principiae*, setting out mathematical and mechanical systems of physiology and therapeutics in opposition to chemical or older systems. Anita Guerrini points out that Newtonian physicians such as Pitcairne, Cheyne, Keill and Mead were a closely knit group (although not always in agreement) who used the fashionable new learning to build up fashionable and lucrative practices. By following the career of George Cheyne, Guerrini shows how a Newtonian physician moved from a highly mechanical and mathematical treatment of the body to one in which spirits came to provide the motive forces of action. This lessened the determinism of human action implicit in his earlier view, and led him to become a friend of the enthusiast, John Wesley. Cheyne's change of heart was based on Newton's own development of a theory of ether. A developing Newtonianism then, allowed less for a reductionist approach to medicine than at first seemed likely. It also shows how medicine varied with its underlying natural philosophy, and how this in turn – Newton's perception of spiritual forces at work in the universe – was closely related to religion.

In a different context and country, Johanna Geyer-Kordesch describes how a newly rationalized religion and natural philosophy (partly deriving from Newton) could be seen to denude the world of subjectivity and emotion, and how passions and imagination – traditional attributes of the soul – were no longer acceptable and real entities in the world of the new reason. As she puts it, the definition of 'disease' in enlightened terms not only ameliorated the idea of witchcraft, but also disempowered the idea of divine inspiration. The concept of 'natural' events drew boundaries: within the gates the objectively recognizable and its symptoms; without the gates, the inexplicable relationships of possession, divine will and the believer. Geyer-Kordesch argues that experimental knowledge came to represent unquestionable *authority*. This of course puts such knowledge into the sphere of social relations, an insight that most contemporary students of natural philosophy were unaware of, even when they were condemning the pernicious effect of following the authority of past authors. But not everyone accepted the claim of the new experimental natural philosophy to extend its boundaries in this way. Just as in England religious enthusiasts before 1660 had believed in the value of personal inspiration within the spiritual soul, so the pietist revival in Germany after 1670 consciously resisted the rational world of the mathematical and mechanical philosophers. It was this movement that produced Stahl, the focus of the animist revival that restored the physiological attributes of the soul.

This book addresses not only the question 'What changed in medicine?', but also 'How did it change?' In two of the following chapters we shall see how different individuals like Sydenham and Hecquet perceived the world in different ways (and so how medicine 'changed' from one individual to another). Andrew Cunningham penetrates the historical reputation of Sydenham to discover how the practice of the 'English Hippocrates' was founded on the politics and religion of the interregnum, and how in the changed circumstances of the restoration Sydenham's frustrated political and religious ideals were channelled into a research programme whose aim was to replace traditional medicine with a medicine based on experience. Cunningham also describes how Sydenham's political views barred him from gaining a rich clientele; the result was that he was obliged to look after large numbers of poor and relatively anonymous patients, and in turn that his attention came to be focused not on the patient but on the disease. In so doing, Sydenham defended an experiential method as basic as trial and error against the theory- and patient-orientated method of the faculty.

The mechanism that was such a feature of the later part of the century was received more sympathetically by those of some religious convictions than of others. Just as Hogelande (in French's chapter) found a metaphysical identity between predestination and mechanism of the Cartesian kind, so Laurence Brockliss shows that in the case of Hecquet, Jansenist theology could be sympathetic to a later kind of mechanism. Brockliss makes the interesting suggestion that the rather fatalistic and polarized view of the Jansenists of Port-Royal-des-Champs was shared by the French mechanists, along with a common social origin and a feeling of belonging to a persecuted minority. Hecquet's mechanism was of course as much his as that of a group, and it seems individual to him that he adopted a mechanism of solids partly to attack current theories of physiological fermentation.

At the practical level the case of Hecquet shows how in medicine the committed Christian and the physician could come together. In the sixteenth and seventeenth centuries it was by no means unusual for clergymen to practice medicine, to which their book learning, as well as the traditional association of healing and charity with religion, often led them. Established physicians, like John Cotta, frequently objected to the encroachments of ministers into their preserve. Hecquet typified the Christian physician by his charitable medical practice among the poor, and by his belief in the need for piety and prayers by the physician to seek divine efficacy for the material treatment.

Other chapters explore how groups as well as individuals might come to accept a doctrine. The role of the disputation in academic groups is touched on in French's chapter, and Harold Cook explores how professional bodies that included physicians (the College of Physicians and the Royal Society) had commercial and professional as well as intellectual needs to accommodate changes in medicine and philosophy. He highlights the relationship between institutional rivalry and competing theoretical positions in medicine in his account of the complex skirmishing between Galenic physicians, Royal Society virtuosi physicians, chemists (who nearly founded a rival society of chemical physicians), apothecaries and empirical virtuosi. He shows how empiricism (in the sense associated with Boyle and natural philosophy in the Royal Society) might be viewed as being uncomfortably close to empirical or quack practice in medicine, the two having the same emphasis on remedies. In contrast, the traditional university-educated physician stressed the study of nature's principles, and practised a medicine that was also preventive, and based on advice about diet and regimen. Such physicians looked down on the purely commercial matter of providing remedies. Cook discusses how anxiety over what appeared to be the attempt of the virtuosi such as Robert Boyle to change 'physic' (the traditional College view of a theoretically based medicine) into 'medicine' (based on remedies) generated a spate of acrimonious literature. Clearly the new natural philosophy produced violent reflex action in some College traditionalists, and these in turn provoked corresponding responses from the new philosophers. Naturally some of this may be seen simply as self-interested rhetoric. Such rhetoric had a history indeed, that went back to Galen and before and which had been presented as an attempt at protecting the patient (the learned physician, of course, did not suffer) by asserting the superiority of learning over experience, which was labelled as charlatanism. However, the claims of experience over theory were the claims of the new knowledge over the old, and the rhetoric that had satisfied generations of physicians in their perennial quarrels with empirics would not do so well now that in this, the battle of the ancients and moderns, the opposition could not be represented merely as ill-bred quacks: it now included the respectable, the noble and the royal, together with a whole battery of new philosophies all proclaiming the virtues of experience. At the same time, traditional learned medicine also felt threatened by the apothecaries and an incipient Society of Chemical Physicians, who both marched under the banner of experience. The traditional members of the College of Physicians clearly had to politicize their learning. Roy Porter's chapter discusses the other side of the coin. The early Royal Society had a direct interest in medicine. From the correspondence of the Society's secretary, Henry Oldenburg, and other sources, Porter depicts a lively commerce in medical information amongst the Society's followers and correspondents. Monstrous births, large breasts, remedies for plague and other diseases, faith healers – such as Valentine Greatrakes, the 'stroacker' – and the relationship between environment, health and disease were all discussed. What emerges is the very public nature of medicine where laymen and practitioners felt equally capable of observing and assessing medical matters. Porter also shows how the Society and especially Oldenburg were selective in what was published and tried to get first hand, precise information, and impressed upon correspondents the need for critical assessment and the avoidance of exaggeration. It is in this way that the Baconian ideals of the Society were conceived and put into practice, combining, the Fellows hoped, both experience and truth in the formation of the Society's new descriptive natural philosophy. If the latter was seen by some physicians as dangerously close to empiricism, which if accepted would mean the end of learned medicine, they were right – but from the wrong perspective. The new medicine being shaped – by people such as Sydenham, the Royal Society Baconian empiricists and Newtonian physicians – from the old medicine, from a new iatrochemistry and from a recent natural philosophy, was no mere quackery but a new learned medicine. The classical renaissance of the sixteenth century gave way to the enlightenment of the eighteenth. This indeed is the medical revolution of the seventeenth century.

Finally, these studies of change are complemented by Andrew

Wear's contribution in which he argues that some elements of medicine in fact remained relatively unchanged. Much of the theory and practice of medicine was influenced by doctor-patient relationships and the need for doctors (and empirics) to produce a type of medicine that was intelligible to their patients. In this sense the learned physician and the quack had some things in common, and Wear argues that when change occurred it could be ascribed at least as much to the commercial developments of the medical market-place as to the rhetoric of medical theories and the pressures exerted by the success of the new natural philosophies.

Medicine in this period was part of culture, both learned and popular, and its practitioners ranged from village wise women to university-trained physicians. Being so centrally situated in society its changes naturally reflected the great changes that occurred in religion, natural philosophy and politics. Although historians of modern medicine have convincingly argued that modern medicine is greatly influenced by social pressures – one has only to think of the economics of medical care and the ethical problems posed by medical technology – it is the case that medicine in the period under discussion was more strongly connected to the main intellectual and religious movements of its day than it is now. This volume, by exploring the dynamics of the changes in medicine, should help to show the integral place of medicine in the general history of the seventeenth and early eighteenth centuries.

1

Medicine, religion and the puritan revolution

PETER ELMER

INTRODUCTION

The first major critique of orthodox medical practice in England was composed as early as 1585 by the Paracelsian, Richard Bostocke, yet no attempt to implement a programme of medical reform took place until the 1650s – the years of the so-called 'puritan revolution'. Not surprisingly, many historians have for some time assumed that the well-documented opposition to medical orthodoxy in the middle decades of the seventeenth century must have been related to some extent to the political and religious upheavals of these years. In particular, it has become widely accepted that the beliefs and values associated with the puritan movement were largely responsible for the promotion of reform, not just in medicine and natural science, but in all aspects of early modern English society. In the words of R.F. Jones, 'the Puritans were out to reform not only Church and State in their narrow connotations, but almost everything else'.[1]

Since Jones's statement, the 'puritanism–science hypothesis' has undergone numerous refinements and, in the process, attracted large numbers of adherents. In particular, the work of Christopher Hill has established beyond reasonable doubt the vogue for new attitudes to science and medicine in revolutionary England, and in 1975 Charles Webster published what is certainly the most thorough and persuasive account to date of the 'puritanism–science' connection in *The Great Instauration*.[2] In what follows, I should like to stress that I take issue

---

[1] R.F. Jones, *Ancients and Moderns: A Study of the Rise of the Scientific Movement in Seventeenth-Century England* (Gloucester, Mass., 1961), pp. 87–8.

[2] C. Hill, 'The Medical Profession and its Radical Critics', in Hill (ed.), *Change and Continuity in Seventeenth-Century England* (London, 1974), pp. 157–78; C. Webster, *The Great Instauration: Science, Medicine and Reform, 1626–1660* (London, 1975). For background information relating to the 'puritanism-science' debate, see C. Webster (ed.), *The Intellectual Revolution of the Seventeenth Century* (London, 1974), pp. 12–22.

with Dr Webster and others only in so far as their suggestions impinge upon the movement for medical reform in seventeenth-century England. And in particular, I should like to concentrate (though not exclusively) upon those medical reformers who took their cue from the theories and beliefs of the continental iatrochemists whose chief standard bearers were the towering figures of Paracelsus and J.B. van Helmont.

The argument which I will attempt to develop in the course of this chapter is that, in the light of recent research into the nature of puritanism, the subject of medicine and medical reform provides a particularly *inapplicable* example for those who seek to justify the 'puritanism–science hypothesis'. It is, I believe, inapplicable for two main reasons. First, because the arguments of Webster and others greatly overstate the incipient radicalism of puritanism. And secondly, because such arguments vastly exaggerate the extent to which puritanism can be seen, at least after 1640, as a single religious movement held together by a common set of goals, ideals and beliefs.

With respect to the first point, I would suggest that especially relevant here is the work of Nicholas Tyacke and Robert Ashton who have both argued that pre-revolutionary puritanism was not so much a movement of radical opposition, as a conservatively motivated ideology on the defensive, responding that is to the radical initiatives of Laudian Arminianism.[3] As I shall try to show, if one extends this concept to puritan social and medical thought, one finds little evidence before 1640 to support the view that puritanism operated as a catalyst for innovation in the medical profession.

With regard to the second point, this seems to be as good as admitted by Dr Webster and those of similar viewpoint who, aware of the deep divisions within post-1640 puritanism, nonetheless refuse to accept that such disunity might in fact invalidate the concept of a homogeneous movement of puritan social, scientific and educational reform. To state therefore, as Dr Webster does, that the writings of the English Paracelsians were framed in a religious context which was 'thoroughly congenial to a Puritan audience' is, I believe, simply to avoid the real problems posed by the diversity of religious opinion in

[3] R. Ashton, *The English Civil War: Conservatism and Revolution, 1630–1649* (London, 1978), pp. 98–126; N. Tyacke, 'Puritanism, Arminianism and Counter Revolution', in C. Russell (ed.), *The Origins of the English Civil War* (London, 1973), pp. 119–43; N. Tyacke, 'Science and Religion at Oxford before the Civil War', in D. Pennington and K. Thomas (eds.), *Puritans and Revolutionaries* (Oxford, 1978), pp 73–93. See also the criticisms of John Morgan, 'Puritanism and Science: A Reinterpretation', *The Historical Journal*, XXII (1979), 535–60.

England during the middle decades of the seventeenth century.[4] Indeed, as Dr Webster himself and others before have noted, the greatest support for medical reform in England came not from the ranks of orthodox puritans (that is, those who favoured the retention of a disciplined state church run on strictly Calvinist lines), but rather from the radical sectaries (of various denominations) who were united in their opposition to the tyranny of any state church.[5]

I would not wish to suggest, however, that the underlying religious motivation for the promotion of medical reform in England was simply sectarian in character. Although there seems little doubt that the cause of medical reform did hold a peculiar fascination for the radical sectaries of the period, it would be wrong to underestimate the divisions, frequently bitter, which existed between the various sects. Moreover, it would also be entirely wrong to ignore and omit the substantial contribution made to the cause of medical reform, before, during and after the revolution, by those of Anglican persuasion. Consequently, any attempt to account for a religious factor in the medical reform movement must include some reference to Anglican physicians such as Robert Fludd, Thomas Browne, Thomas Vaughan and George Thomson, who were often as keen as their sectarian counterparts in promoting the new medicine.[6]

In order to account for the existence of such disparate elements in the English medical reform movement, I shall argue that the essential thread of religious belief which runs through the writings of the reformers was primarily non-denominational in tone and was characterized by what one might best describe as the spirit of eirenicism. Broadly speaking, eirenicism can be defined as the belief in the principle of religious reconciliation and reunification, which was to be attained through the pursuit of peaceful methods. It was, I shall argue, the one consistent factor which united the iatrochemical reformers, and was largely a product of the hermetic foundations of the new medicine which, in the words of Frances Yates, so often promoted an 'effort to avoid doctrinal differences, to turn from them to the exploration of nature in a religious spirit'.[7] Accordingly, it should be possible

---

[4] Webster, *The Great Instauration*, p. 282.
[5] *Ibid.*, pp. 280–4, 497; see also P. Rattansi, 'Paracelsus and the Puritan Revolution', *Ambix*, XI (1963), 24–32; K. Thomas, *Religion and the Decline of Magic* (London, 1971), pp. 270–1, 372–7; C. Hill, *The World Turned Upside Down* (London, 1972), pp. 231–46.
[6] I remain highly sceptical of the idea that Anglican involvement in hermetic and Paracelsian natural philosophy can be explained by reference to 'the less practical and more esoteric' aspects of these beliefs; see Webster, *The Great Instauration*, p. 282.
[7] F. Yates, *The Rosicrucian Enlightenment* (London, 1972), p. 227.

to dispense with the notion that an ill-defined puritanism lay at the heart of the movement for medical reform in England, whilst at the same time maintaining the underlying significance of the English revolution as a key phase in the history of English medicine and medical thought.

RELIGION AND MEDICINE BEFORE 1640

Before looking in detail at the literature of the 1650s, I should like to re-state some general (and probably very familiar) points relating to the traditional interaction of religion and medicine in England before 1640. These are of the utmost importance when one considers the demands made by the reformers with respect to the medical status quo, especially since it was so often the religious content of traditional medicine (or rather the lack of it) which provoked the anger of the reformers. This is evident in three main respects. Firstly, in the atheism and antichristianism implicit in the doctrines of the Roman physician Galen. Secondly, in the reluctance of many Galenists to contemplate or interfere in those areas of medical practice traditionally reserved for the theologian or cleric (for example, the physical attributes of the soul; the origin of plague; witchcraft). And thirdly, in the strict observation and protection of the professional integrity of the Collegiate physicians, particularly in as much as this excluded all outsiders, including clerics, from the legal pursuit of a medical career. The effect in all three cases was to deprive traditional medical practice and theory in England of any religious content, something to which the Paracelsian and Helmontian physicians were intrinsically opposed.[8]

Prior to 1640, however, it is extremely difficult to find examples of individuals, regardless of their religious backgrounds, criticizing the medical authorities on the grounds listed above. This was undoubtedly a reflection of social convention which puritan physicians and apologists seem to have upheld in much the same way as their Anglican opponents. A good example of this deep-seated reverence for conformity and the maintenance of order in the medical profession can be found in the writings of the puritan physician James Hart.[9] Hart, along

[8] See especially P. Kocher, *Science and Religion in Elizabethan England* (New York, 1969), chs. 12–14. For a recent appraisal of the role of the Royal College of Physicians in regulating the practice of medicine in London, see H.J. Cook, *The Decline of the Old Medical Regime in Stuart London* (Ithaca and London, 1986).
[9] J.F. Payne describes Hart as 'a strong puritan, an appellation which he adopts more than once in his writings'; *Dictionary of National Biography* (hereafter referred to as *D.N.B.*), xxv, p. 60.

with his Northamptonshire colleague John Cotta, was one of the most outspoken defenders of medical privilege and orthodoxy. He was particularly critical of all those who attempted to subvert the rights of the trained and qualified physician. Amongst those singled out for special condemnation, however, were members of the church who according to Hart neglected their parochial duties and 'doe wrongfully and injuriously, both contrary to the Law of God and man, intrude upon another weighty profession'.[10]

Hart went on to refute the suggestion that Christ might be used as 'a proofe to maintain this lawless intrusion', and in a display of typical pre-revolutionary puritan zeal, he chastized all subversive meddlers who dared to encroach upon the livelihood of another. Clearly such actions were interpreted by Hart as conducive to social anarchy for 'God is the God of order, not of confusion, and never did allow of this confused Chaos of callings'. Significantly, in a later work on the same subject, Hart cited the arguments of the leading puritan theologian William Perkins to the effect that vocational pluralism was inconsistent with the spiritual duties of the priest.[11]

It should be stressed that Hart's reaction to medical intruders, quacks and 'poor vicars' was fairly typical of the conservatism of the medical profession in general, and was echoed in the writings of numerous seventeenth-century English physicians. Similar arguments, for example, were employed at an earlier date by Hart's Northamptonshire colleague, John Cotta, who may well have shared the former's sympathy with the puritan cause.[12] Certainly the similarity of their intellectual and medical concerns is very striking. Cotta, like Hart, opposed clerical intrusion into the realm of medicine on the grounds of religious and scriptural authority (citing St Paul to the effect that all men should 'walke within his owne calling, and not be busily

---

[10] J. Hart, KAINIKH, or the Diet of the Diseased (London, 1633), pp. 12–13.

[11] Ibid., p. 14; J. Hart, The Arraignment of Urines: wherein are set down the Manifold Errors and Abuses of Ignorant Urine-monging Empirickes (London, 1623), sig. A4r. For a further example of Puritan opposition to 'practising' clergymen, see The Winthrop Papers, 1498–1628 (Mass. Hist. Soc., Cambridge, Mass., 1929), pp. 306–7.

[12] J. Cotta, A Short Discoverie of the Unobserved Dangers of Severall Sorts of Ignorant and Unconsiderate Practisers of Physicke in England (London, 1612). According to A. Vian, Cotta acquired a considerable practice in Northamptonshire through the patronage and influence of Sir William Tate, a leading figure in the well-established Puritan movement of that county (cf. Hart's dedication of KAINIKH to Edward Montagu, Baron of Boughton, a puritan associate of Tate); D.N.B., XII, p. 1213. Montagu and Tate were also members of the puritan circle centred on Sir Richard Knightley, whose son-in-law and Tate's cousin, Sir Euseby Andrew, was a patient of Cotta. See W.J. Sheils, The Puritans in the Diocese of Peterborough, 1558–1610 (Northampton, 1979), pp. 13, 100, 103, 107, 110–12, 117; J. Cotta, 'The Poysoning of Sir Euseby Andrew . . . from the original ms.', in Tracts . . . relating to Northamptonshire (Northampton, 2nd ser., 1881).

stragling in others'). And to those who objected that there were not
sufficient physicians to serve the whole community, Cotta invoked the
twin arguments of divine providence and the preservation of the social
order. Under no circumstances, therefore, might any man seek help
from an unqualified or unlicensed physician, for

God, and nature, and law have tied and allotted men to seeke meanes, and those
meanes confined to certaine set bounds and limits, that men may still in all things
according to the law of mortalitie, be ever in this life subject unto casualties, oft for
their triall, sometime for their punishment, or else for a further decree and secret
purpose of the Divine providence, so and to such ends so ordering.[13]

It is just possible that the conservative reaction of physicians like
Hart (and possibly Cotta) may have been too extreme even for the
Anglican authorities. Hart for example had attempted in the 1620s,
without success, to publish a tract on the subject of 'the lawlesse
intrusions of PARSONS and VICARS upon the profession of Phisicke'. A
manuscript edition of this work was subsequently inserted into the
British Library's copy of Hart's *The Anatomie of Urines* (1625) with a
note stating that this work 'was intended to be printed with the others:
but could by noe means bee licensed'. Hart seems, however, to have
persisted with his campaign against the intrusive clergy, an indication
perhaps that in the eyes of this puritan at least, the Anglican authorities
were displaying an appalling laxity in their function as the regulators
of the medical profession outside London. The true nature of the
puritan zeal for medical reform may thus be glimpsed in the work of
the arch-conservative Hart who in 1633, just seven years prior to the
meeting of the Long Parliament, was able to lament that

although this injury hath heretofore, both out of the pulpit, and by the pen of the
learned been spoken against . . . *yet hath all this as yet produced no reformation.*[14]

[13] Cotta, *A Short Discoverie*, pp. 88–9. According to the astrologer William Lilly, Cotta's attack
on 'practising' divines was intended as an oblique assault upon the Anglican minister and
medical practitioner Richard Napier. Cotta's opposition to clergy-physicians might therefore
constitute a veiled puritan protest against Anglicanism in general. See W. Lilly, *Mr William
Lilly's History of His Life and Times* (London, 1715), pp. 53–4; M. MacDonald, *Mystical
Bedlam: Madness, Anxiety and Healing in Seventeenth-Century England* (Cambridge, 1981),
pp. 22–5, 30–2, 70.

[14] Hart, *KΛINIKH*, p. 13 (my emphasis); cf. Charles Webster's assertion that opposition to
monopolies, including that of the physicians, 'was one of the few issues which united puritan
opinion', *The Great Instauration*, p. 256. Although it would be wrong to suggest that puritan
clergymen never combined the functions of priest and physician, it was nonetheless very rare
for such ministers to practise both professions simultaneously. John Burgess is a case in point;
see *D.N.B.*, VII, p. 311. Richard Baxter, who pursued both careers for a short time in the 1640s,
later apologized profusely for this embarrassing intrusion claiming that it was 'necessity' that
'forced' him to practise medicine. In his autobiography he states: 'yet at last I could endure it no
longer . . . so that . . . I procured a godly, diligent physician to come and live in the town
[Kidderminster] . . . and never meddled with it more'; J.M. Lloyd Thomas (ed.), *The
Autobiography of Richard Baxter, Being the Reliquiae Baxterianae Abridged from the Folio
(1696)* (London, 1925), p. 78.

The reaction of physicians such as Hart to any attempt to undermine
the professional integrity of the doctors in early Stuart England was
paralleled by the equally fierce opposition of the medical authorities to
the proponents of heterodox opinions in medicine, especially those
propounded by the iatrochemists. And as with the problem of medical
intruders, religious argument played a large part in the debate which
followed between the conservatives and the would-be reformers. The
Paracelsians, for example, deliberately emphasized the Christian origins of the hermetic art of healing. Great stress was placed upon the
apocryphal text from Ecclesiasticus ('Honor the Physition with the
honnor due unto him, for the most High hath created him . . .'), and the
anti-Christian sentiments of Galenism were mercilessly exposed as
irrefutable evidence of the erroneous nature of traditional medicine. A
new emphasis upon the Bible as a source of natural wisdom is also
evident in the writings of the English Paracelsians, knowledge which
was generally believed to complement the evidence gleaned from that
other book of God, 'the Book of Nature'.[15]

The new alliance of religion and medicine, implicit in the magico-
chemical tradition of Paracelsism, also achieved practical expression
in the hermetic concept of the 'priest–physician'. The idea that God
created the physician and imbued each doctor with the sacred gift of
healing was widely interpreted by the Paracelsians as a sign of divine
favour which God reserved only for those worthy of the office. As a
result, Paracelsian epistemology emphasized the divine source of much
medical wisdom and the pious character of the recipient of that
knowledge who practised medicine for the good of all mankind.
Needless to say, gnosticism of this kind ran completely counter to
orthodox scholastic teaching concerning the origin and nature of
human learning. In sharp contrast to the Paracelsian insistence upon a
direct covenant between God and the physician, the Galenist rendered
the passage in Ecclesiasticus to support the view that it was 'physick' or
nature, and not the physician, that was the particular object of divine
munificence. In theory, therefore, all men, whether good or bad, might
practise the healing art, for as the Galenist James Primrose explained,
'God is wont to blesse such meanes, in regard of the covenant which he
hath made with nature'.[16]

---

[15] For the Bible as a source of medical knowledge and the inspiration for reform, see, for example,
    the opposition of the Helmontian Noah Biggs to phlebotomy on the scriptural grounds that the
    blood was 'the seat . . . chamber and magazine of life'; N. Biggs, *Mataeotechnia Medicinae
    Praxews. The Vanity of the Craft of Physick* (London, 1651), p. 162.
[16] J. Primrose, *Popular Errours or the Errours of People in Physick; first written in Latine by
    J. Primrose . . . translated into English by Robert Wittie* (London, 1651), p. 49. For the
    Presbyterian Wittie, see above pp. 30–1. Thomas Tymme, John Evans and possibly Francis
    Anthony would all seem to fit the Paracelsian stereotype of the priest–physician.

The threat to scientific and medical orthodoxy posed by Paracelsism is clear enough in the light of the radical epistemology which underlay the new medicine. Any attempt to integrate natural and theological concerns was certain to arouse suspicion and hostility in orthodox circles which taught, as a matter of principle, that the study of the creation was largely irrelevant to the higher goal of religious salvation. Though nature undoubtedly reflected the glory and omnipotence of its Creator, there was nothing divine as such in the study of the natural world; hence the traditional separation of science and theology, material and metaphysical, body and soul, which characterized early modern scholasticism and which was left unscathed by the onset of Baconianism. Knowledge of natural things, though impaired by the Fall, was not perceived as irrevocably lost since it might of course be retrieved through the arduous process of reason and study. Knowledge of God and personal salvation on the other hand was quite unrelated to the former which it eclipsed in every respect, and was thus reserved to the acknowledged expert in this field, the theologian.[17]

In early seventeenth-century England, there can be little doubt that this fundamental dichotomy in learning was implicitly accepted by the great majority of educated men, including those of the medical profession. The latter in particular were careful to observe the distinction between body and soul, just as in return they demanded of the religious authorities protection from clerical intruders. It is hardly surprising therefore that the activities of Paracelsian propagandists in pre-revolutionary England should have excited criticism, and in the process initiated a debate in medical circles which would continue into the restoration. The major issue of contention was clearly the tendency of the Paracelsians to conflate religious and medical concerns – to bridge the gap, as it were, between heaven and earth – and so blur the traditional divisions of early modern society and thought. In practical terms this meant a far greater desire on the part of the Paracelsian to investigate medical phenomena which might be associated with the operation and function of the soul, as well as generally enlarging the scope of medical research to encompass the study of diseases hitherto neglected by the Galenists.[18]

A good example of this trend was the tendency of the Paracelsian and Helmontian to ascribe natural causes and to prescribe physical

---

[17] Cf. Paul Kocher's view that 'long before Francis Bacon came to preach the separation of science and religion, theology itself split apart the twin continents of natural and supernatural knowledge', *Science and Religion in Elizabethan England*, p. 37.

[18] See, for example, the claim of the Paracelsian I.W., which intimated that gout, dropsy, leprosy and epilepsy were all curable despite the failure of the Galenists to prescribe successfully in such cases; I.W., *The Copie of a Letter* (London?, 1586), sig. B7v.

remedies in cases of suspected witchcraft.[19] Whereas Galenic physicians tended on the whole to diagnose 'supernatural' causes (and thus
prescribe 'supernatural' remedies) in such cases, the Paracelsian,
whilst not necessarily arguing against the existence of witchcraft *per
se*, was far more likely to proffer naturalistic explanations and optimistic prognoses. In the process, many Paracelsians attracted even greater
opprobrium and did nothing to dispel the accusation, frequently
levelled against them, that they were themselves diabolically inspired.
This belief was itself founded upon the widely held view that systems
of thought such as Paracelsism and hermeticism attempted to raise the
level of human understanding far beyond those limits originally
proscribed by God. As the puritan William Perkins observed,

> when a man resteth not satisfied with the measure of inward gifts received . . . but
> aspires to search out things as God would have kept secret . . . hence he is mooved to
> attempt the cursed art of Magick and witchcraft . . . that by working wonders, he may
> purchase fame in the world.[20]

To those who shared Perkins's notion that God had reserved certain
knowledge from the mental capacity of man, and also conceived of the
world in Aristotelian terms, it would have seemed completely logical to
denounce Paracelsian devices such as the weapon-salve as the work of
the Devil. Such thinking clearly formed the basis of the Buckingham-
shire cleric William Foster's attack on Robert Fludd. It can also be
discerned in the frequent denunciations by orthodox Galenists of the
Paracelsian belief in universal medicines or elixirs. John Cotta for
example intimated that the *aurum potabile* of the Paracelsian Francis
Anthony was in fact the work of Satan, since any drug which made all
others redundant was clearly 'out of the order and rule of all things
created by God'. Steeped in the conventions of orthodox learning and
science, Cotta could not fail to conclude therefore that such cure-alls
were 'in reason impossible, in nature monstrous, so in religion most
impious'.[21]

The irreligious implications of Paracelsism were everywhere apparent with Paracelsus himself frequently denounced as an agent of the
Devil (see for example below, p. 30). These views were shared by

[19] I have discussed this phenomenon in more detail in my 'Medicine, Medical Reform and the
    Puritan Revolution' (University of Swansea, Ph.D. thesis, 1980), pp. 87–94, 282–331.
[20] W. Perkins, *A Discourse of the Damned Art of Witchcraft* (Cambridge, 1608), p. 11. John
    Cotta expressed the view (probably typical of the medical profession before 1640) that some
    diseases were so obscure and difficult to diagnose that it was hopeless to expect a cure since to
    do otherwise would be 'impatience of those bounds which God hath set to limit the curiosity of
    man'; J. Cotta, *The Triall of Witchcraft* (London, 1616), p. 8.
[21] W. Foster, *Hoplocrisma Spongus: Or, A Sponge to Wipe away the Weapon-salve* (London,
    1631), pp. 8–9; J. Cotta, *Cotta Contra Antonium* (London, 1623), pp. 5–6.

Anglican and puritan alike, one of the fiercest attacks before 1640 emanating from the pen of the puritan physician James Hart. Taking up the cudgels on behalf of Foster in his debate with Fludd, Hart derided all aspects of Paracelsian medicine. He poked fun at Paracelsus for his fanciful claims concerning longevity (Paracelsus died at the age of forty eight), rejected much in the Paracelsian corpus and defended the belief in witchcraft which he clearly felt to be under attack from the Paracelsians. Aware of the iconoclastic implications of Paracelsian medicine, Hart thus expounded the view that,

if imagination do all (as the Paracelsians held), our witches and wizards are mere ignorant fooles, let them but turn Paracelsists, and by their strong imagination they may bring any mischiefe to passe which they had purposed, and not be liable to the law. What need they be so beholden to the divell, as to sell themselves to be his slaves, if these operations may so easily be effected. *But if this should come to passe, then the Divell would have nothing to doe.*[22]

NEW MEDICINE AFTER 1640

Evidence from the pre-revolutionary period in England clearly suggests that overt support for the new medical philosophy was minimal, denounced as it was by both Anglicans and puritans. The unorthodoxy implicit in Paracelsism was sufficient to deter most from open espousal of its wider goals even if, as is generally recognized, chemically prepared medicines were slowly accepted by medical authorities. After 1640, however, with the collapse of Laudian censorship and central authority in England, the ideas of the Paracelsian reformers were rapidly publicized. Broadly speaking, the objectives of the reformers were twofold. First, they wished to destroy the monopoly of the College of Physicians in London, and thus open the practice of medicine in the capital to all who claimed the ability to heal (regardless of formal qualifications). And secondly, they wanted to transform the whole basis of medical practice itself; that is to replace the outdated, ineffective anti-Christian doctrines of the Galenists with those of the various new schools of iatrochemical medicine. In both cases I shall argue that the puritan establishment of this period made little contribution to the cause of reform, and was on the whole positively hostile to the aims and activities of the reformers.[23]

[22] Hart, *KΛINIKH*, pp. 360, 362–3 (my emphasis).
[23] The arguments of the medical reformers of the revolutionary period have been widely discussed. See, for example, C. Hill, 'The Medical Profession and its Radical Critics'; C. Webster, 'English Medical Reformers of the Puritan Revolution: A Background to the Society of Chymical Physitians', *Ambix*, XIV (1967), 16–41. Needless to say, not all those who supported the first aim (deregulation of the medical profession) were necessarily drawn from the ranks of those who supported the latter (iatrochemistry).

It is not difficult to appreciate why support for the medical reformers in the struggle with the College authorities was largely drawn from
the ranks of the radical sectaries. The restrictive and elitist practices of
the College were all too obviously on a par with the oppressive,
monopolistic powers wielded by the puritan state church. A shortage
of physicians in London as well as in the country at large meant that for
the great majority of the population, especially the poor, there was no
official source of medical care. The great variety of illegal practitioners
and quacks who swarmed over the land in this period provides ample
evidence of the lack of medical facilities available to the poor. Quacks
such as the infamous William Trigge thus gained great notoriety
during the 1640s because of their charitable work with the destitute, in
much the same way as the 'mechanick preachers' of the sects braved the
scorn of the puritan establishment by preaching to all who would
listen. They also shared, of course, the common tag of 'unlearned
ignorance' in their respective callings. In these circumstances, it is
hardly surprising that those who wished to democratize the practice of
medicine were more often than not equally vocal in their support for
religious freedom and liberty from oppression.[24]

Well known in this respect are the works of Nicholas Culpeper,
though his radical religious and political leanings have tended to
escape closer scrutiny.[25] Culpeper's familiar assertion that medicine
was a blessing of God which should be made available to 'all Estates
and conditions of Men' might thus be compared with the thoroughly
democratic stance which he adopted towards religious and political
reform. Indeed, in the political sphere there is some evidence (much of
it admittedly circumstantial) to associate Culpeper and his work with
the Leveller movement in politics. Not only was Culpeper an advocate
of civil marriage, describing his wife as 'all his time . . . at her own
disposing, *enfranchised, free-born* from her Wedding Day', but he also
espoused the cause of extreme republicanism in the astrological tract
Catastrophe Magnatum (1652). In this work, Culpeper showed more
than just a passing interest in the Leveller myth of the Norman Yoke,
and it is just possible that he moved in the same circles as the Leveller
leader William Walwyn who, it will be remembered, took up the

---

[24] For Trigge, see J. Cook, *Unum Necessarium* (London, 1648), pp. 61–3. In a petition of 1648,
Trigge was described as a man 'endowed with the knowledge of nature, and operation of
Herbs, Rootes, and many wonderfull secrets in Physick, and Chirurgerie'; *To The Honourable
House of Commons Assembled in Parliament* (London, 1648); see also Webster, *The Great
Instauration*, pp. 262, 289–90; Cook, *The Decline of the Old Medical Regime*, pp. 129–31.
[25] For Culpeper, see especially F.N.L. Poynter, 'Nicholas Culpeper and his Books', *J. Hist. Med.*,
XVII (1962), 152–67; Webster, *The Great Instauration*, pp. 267–71.

practice of medicine in the 1650s following his retirement from radical politics.[26]

As for Culpeper's religious sympathies, these are more easily detected. An opponent of excessive learning ('a little god-almighty') in the field of religious understanding, Culpeper seems to have adhered to a simplified form of worship based on liberal lines. Not surprisingly, he was an outspoken critic of the presbyterian system and in a manner highly reminiscent of Milton's dictum that 'new Presbyter is but old Priest writ large', he equated the elders of that church with their episcopal predecessors who were 'as like them in condition as a Pomewater is like an Apple'.[27]

A similar combination of radical religious and medical beliefs is evident in the thought of Peter Chamberlen, a Baptist and Fifth Monarchist who was perhaps one of the most eloquent spokesmen for the poor to emerge in the 1640s. A Fellow of the College of Physicians, Chamberlen's views on medicine and social reform were frequently the cause of much friction between himself and the College authorities. Among those causes which he unsuccessfully promoted both before and after 1640 were a plan to incorporate the midwives (for which Chamberlen was threatened with prosecution by the Court of High Commission in the 1630s) and an attempt to vindicate the cause of public baths, which was blocked by the College in 1648. Within a year, Chamberlen was expelled from the College, ostensibly on the grounds of non-attendance, but Chamberlen himself believed that it was his practice of administering free medical aid to the poor of London which lay at the root of the College's decision.[28]

Having been ejected from the College, Chamberlen was now free to

[26] N. Culpeper, *Culpeper's School of Physick* (London, 1659), sig. c5v; N. Culpeper, *A Directory for Midwives* (London, 1651), pp. 112–13 (my emphasis); N. Culpeper, *Catastrophe Magnatum: Or, The Fall of Monarchie* (London, 1652), pp. 11, 74. Walwyn was acquainted with Culpeper's publisher and business associate, Peter Cole; see W. Walwyn, *Walwyn's Just Defence* (London, 1649), pp. 13–14. In the preface to Walwyn's *Healths New Store-House Opened* (London, 1661), William Rand and William Rowland, who were both active in the 1650s in translating and publishing Culpeper's posthumous works, gave their approbation to Walwyn's new medical enterprise. For further discussion of Leveller links with the medical profession, see Elmer, 'Medicine and the Puritan Revolution', pp. 148–52.

[27] Culpeper, *Catastrophe Magnatum*, p. 43; N. Culpeper, *Galens Art of Physick* (London, 1652), sig. A7r; N. Culpeper, *Mr. Culpeper's Treatise of Aurum Potabile* (London, 1657), pp. 14, 161; Poynter, 'Nicholas Culpeper and his Books', p. 159. Culpeper's radical religious leanings were apparently shared at one time by his publisher Peter Cole (above, note 26); see Thomas Edwards, *Gangraena: or a Catalogue ... of the Errours, Heresies, Blasphemies and Pernicious Practices of the Sectaries* (London, 1646), pp. 111–12.

[28] For Chamberlen, see especially J.H. Aveling, *The Chamberlens and the Midwifery Forceps* (London, 1882), pp. 30–124; B.S. Capp, *The Fifth Monarchy Men: A Study in Seventeenth-Century English Millenarianism* (London, 1972).

concentrate his energies upon the grave problems posed by the wretched plight of the English poor. In 1649 he therefore proposed that the government should act immediately by introducing a scheme of public works for 200,000 men which 'if they clear but 20*l.* a head . . . The year will bring about 4,000,000*l.* to the publique Treasurie'. If the government should fail to respond, Chamberlen hinted at the dire consequences including the suggestion that the poor might 'provide for themselves' and thus dismantle all social order. It is clear from subsequent statements that Chamberlen himself was not personally averse to such an outcome. Not only was this warning to the government delivered just two days after Gerard Winstanley had initiated the Digger experiment at St George's Hill in Surrey, but it was also formulated in such a way as to leave the reader in no doubt as to the author's own utopian aspirations. It was therefore Chamberlen's view that

Meum et tuum divide the World into Factions . . . and till the World return to its first simplicitie, or . . . to a Christian Utopia, there will be repinings and Covetousnesse will be the root of all Evil.[29]

Such an opinion could just as have easily been taken from any one of the numerous works of the radical visionary Gerard Winstanley.

Medicine, as organized and controlled by the College of Physicians in London, was thus an obvious target for the radical sectaries of the revolution who bitterly resented official indifference to the plight of the poor and needy. Inevitably, many radicals, as well as defending the right of other unqualified men to practise medicine, would themselves turn to the practice of medicine, perhaps as a gesture of defiance to authority.[30] Even members of groups as extreme in their views as the Ranters and the Seekers were drawn into medical practice. The examples of the ex-Ranter leaders Abiezer Coppe and Lawrence Clarkson are well known. Clarkson eventually converted to the fanatical doctrines of Lodowick Muggleton whose views on the medical profession were to say the least highly unfavourable.[31]

---

[29] P. Chamberlen, *The Poore Mans Advocate, or Englands Samaritan* (London, 1649), sig. A4r and *passim*; P. Chamberlen, *A Voice in Rhama: Or, The Crie of Women and Children* (London, 1647), sigs. A5r–A6r; see also G.H. Sabine (ed.), *The Works of Gerrard Winstanley* (New York, 1965), p. 159. Chamberlen's religious and political ideas were in fact compared by a contemporary to those of the Ranter leader Abiezer Coppe; see Philalethes, *An Answer to Doctor Chamberlaines Scandalous and False Papers* (London, 1649), p. 6.

[30] Numerous names could be added to those listed by Hill and others: e.g. the familist and ex-army radical Roger Crab who, it was said, practised medicine at Uxbridge in Middlesex during the 1640s; see *D.N.B.*, XII, p. 1351.

[31] A. Wood, *Athenae Oxonienses*, 2 vols. (London, 1721), II, col. 367; A.L. Morton, *The World of the Ranters* (London, 1970), p. 136. Muggleton believed that the doctors were 'the greatest

Unfortunately, we possess no record of the kind of medical service provided by the ex-Ranters, Coppe and Clarkson, though it may not be too fanciful to assume that both would have inclined towards the doctrines of the iatrochemists. Clarkson, for example, did admit to studying the art of astrology and magic whilst pursuing his short-lived medical career in the 1650s. Coppe on the other hand may well have encountered similar ideas in the person of John Pordage, the Ranter sympathizer and pantheist who held the rectorship of Bradfield in Berkshire in the early 1650s. Pordage was in fact a qualified physician with a medical degree from Leyden (1639) who, like so many of his radical colleagues, served as a physician during the civil war on the side of Parliament.[32] He subsequently settled at Bradfield (the advowson was held by Elias Ashmole) where he became notorious among the local puritan clergy as a harbourer of religious fanatics (including Coppe) as well as a dabbler in natural magic and conjuration. Moreover, as an astrologer and admirer of the mystic Jacob Boehme, Pordage was unlikely to have favoured Galenic medicine and may well have inclined towards 'the mystical writings of the deep hermetic philosophers' to which he alluded in the trial for his ejection from the ministry in 1654.[33]

Further evidence of this kind of medical and philosophical thinking in Ranter and ex-Ranter circles is to be found in the work of Richard Barker, Lionel Lockyer and John Chandler. Barker, an associate of Clarkson and William Rainsborough in the days when all three shared the Ranter belief in a God who 'made all things good' so that nothing was evil 'but as men judged it', was later to become one of the leading figures in the movement to create a 'Society of Chymical Physitians' in 1665.[34] Similarly Lockyer, one of few to defend the Ranters in print during the 1650s, founded a highly profitable enterprise during the restoration which specialized in the sale of chemically prepared

cheats ... in the world ... if there were never a doctor of physic in the world, people would live longer and in better health'; L. Muggleton, *The Acts of the Witnesses of the Spirit* (London, 1699), p. 111.

[32] Pordage's medical training and subsequent career seem to have eluded his biographers; see R.W. Innes Smith, *English-Speaking Students of Medicine at the University of Leyden* (Edinburgh and London, 1932), p. 185; *Calendar of State Papers, Domestic, 1655*, p. 160. Pordage served as a physician to the regiment of John Venn at Windsor Castle.

[33] Hill, *The World Turned Upside Down*, pp. 180–1; T.B. Howell (ed.), *The Complete Collection of State Trials ... 1650–1661* (London, 1816), cols. 539–632.

[34] For Barker's friendship with Clarkson and Rainsborough, see N. Cohn, *The Pursuit of the Millennium* (London, 1970), p. 311. In December 1660, Rainsborough was charged with selling arms in his custody to civilians, but was released on the bond of £500 delivered by Richard Barker 'for the good behaviour of the former'; *Calendar of State Papers, Domestic, 1660–61*, p. 505. Barker himself led a chequered medical career. During the 1650s he was fined

arcana. According to an associate, Lockyer's experiments were even
exhibited before Charles II in 1664, though it was also reported of him
that he was 'strangely opposite to all earthly purchases' – a suggestion
which is resonant of earlier Ranter concerns for the poor and indifference to material gain.[35] Most intriguing of all, however, is the example
of John Chandler who in 1662 was responsible for the translation of
the works of the celebrated Flemish iatrochemist Jan Baptist van
Helmont. A Ranter convert to Quakerism, Chandler's adoption of
Helmontianism was, as I have argued elsewhere, fully in keeping with
the theosophical and pantheistic spirit of Ranter and early Quaker
speculation.[36]

SECTARIAN MEDICINE

The predilection of radical groups such as the Ranters and Quakers for
unorthodox scientific and medical ideas is one example among many
of the distinctly sectarian nature of the English medical reform movement in the 1650s. From an early date, in Europe as well as England,
support for the new medicine was frequently associated in the popular
mind with religious extremism, a tag which almost certainly deterred
many from open acknowledgement of its 'dangerous' tenets. Even
those who reluctantly admitted that there may be some element of
truth in Paracelsian thought were careful to warn others of the pitfalls
which might surprise those of less than pure religious faith. In 1625 the
Anglican Thomas Jackson thus wrote that only those 'might be
admitted to reade their speculations, or try the truth of their professed
mysteries' who could first prove their 'sufficiency in learning' and
'sinceritie in Religion'. Consequently, only those 'thoroughly
grounded in the orthodoxicall faith' could be trusted to study such
notions, and, not surprisingly, these included Jackson himself.[37]

by the College of Physicians for practising without a licence. After the restoration, however, he
was knighted by Charles II, became a leading member of the Society of Chymical Physitians,
and wrote a number of tracts advertising the merits of iatrochemistry. He also performed a
minor role in the Popish Plot as the patron of the chemist and nonconformist clergyman Israel
Tongue; see C. Merrett, *A Collection of Acts of Parliament* (London, 1660); Sir H. Thomas,
'The Society of Chymical Physitians', in E.A. Underwood (ed.), *Science, Medicine and
History*, 2 vols. (Oxford, 1953), II, pp. 56–7; J. Kenyon, *The Popish Plot* (London, 1972), pp.
45–51.

[35] L. Lockyer, *The Character of a Time-Serving Saint: or, the Hypocrite Anatomized, and
thorowly Dissected* (London, 1652); L. Lockyer, *An Advertisement, Concerning those ... Pills
called Pillulae Solis Extractae Being an Universal Medicine* (London?, 1664); G.S., *Aut
Helmont, Aut Asinus* (London, 1665), sig. B7r.

[36] See P. Elmer, 'Medicine, Science and the Quakers: the "Puritanism–Science" Debate Reconsidered', *J. Fr. Hist. Soc.*, LIV (1981), 270–1, 273–4.

[37] T. Jackson, *A Treatise Containing the Originall of Unbeliefe* (London, 1625), p. 183; cf. the
comment of the Galenist and presbyterian physician Robert Wittie in 1669 in his controversy

If this was an unrealistic hope before 1640, it would become a positively impossible injunction to enforce in the more liberal atmosphere of Cromwellian England. Indeed, as many conservatives feared, it was the radical sectaries and enemies of all established religion who rapidly assumed the leadership of the Paracelsian movement. Not only were the sectaries attracted to the doctrines of Paracelsus and van Helmont because of their emphasis upon non-pagan sources,[38] but numerous aspects of the new medicine were wholly conducive and easily assimilated to the religious sensibility of the sectaries. Book-learning for example, which was utterly condemned by the radicals as irrelevant to the pursuit of salvation, was equally abhorrent to many of the iatrochemists who prided themselves on their learned ignorance. John French, who served under Fairfax as a parliamentary physician in the 1640s, accordingly instructed the readers of his Paracelsian translations that the reason he published them was not to 'multiply books', but rather to advance man's knowledge of the creation. French was not opposed to books as such, but he was nonetheless convinced that 'there are too many books already; and the multitude of them is the greatest cause of our ignorance.'[39]

The full implications of this aversion to printed sources is apparent in the thought of Francis Mercury van Helmont, son of the famous Flemish iatrochemist who, on visiting England in the 1670s, was soon attracted to the Quaker circle of Lady Conway at Ragley Hall. In an earlier correspondence with Henry Oldenburg in 1658, the latter reported of van Helmont the younger that

in his discourses with us he fell constantly from philosophical or medical matters to divinity, recommending extreamly a severe scrutiny of oneselfe, as being persuaded, yt ye best and most solid knowledge comes from within a man and dissuading us from the toy (as his phrase was) of books, whereby he thought there was but another mans image and contrefait imposed upon us.[40]

with the Helmontian William Simpson: 'I have seldom seen any one so Sceptical in Reason, but the same has been Heterodox, if not Heretical in Religion'; R. Wittie, *Pyrologia Mimica* (London, 1669), sig. A6r.

[38] For references to the antichristianism of Galen and Galenic medicine in the works of English iatrochemists, see, for example, R. Fludd, *Doctor Fludd's Answer unto M. Foster* (London, 1631), p. 126; Anon., *The Method of Chemical Philosophie and Physick* (London, 1664), pp. 29–30. The Quaker Thomas Lawson, in a work highly critical of traditional university learning, likewise referred to Galen as a 'profess'd enemy to Christ'; T. Lawson, *Dagon's Fall before the Ark* (London?, 1679), pp. 45–6. There are various references in this interesting work to van Helmont and authors of the hermetic tradition; see, for example, *ibid.*, pp. 44, 52–4, 87–8.

[39] J. French, *A New Light of Alchymie* (London, 1650), sigs. A4r–v; see also E. Maynwaring, *Medicus Absolutus* (London, 1668), p. 135; Anon., *A Rational Discours Touching the Universal Medicin* (London, 1664), p. 7.

[40] A.R. and M.B. Hall (eds.), *The Correspondence of Henry Oldenburg*, 11 vols. (Madison and Milwaukee, 1965–77), I, p. 177.

The ultimate source of this kind of gnosticism was the notion implicit in both Paracelsian and Helmontian thought that the physician was created by God and not by the learned traditions of men. Biblical sanction for such a view was, as we have seen, provided by the apocryphal text in Ecclesiasticus (see above, p. 16). In the eyes of the medical reformers therefore, the practice of medicine was an occupation reserved only for those whom God had personally chosen and instructed. It was not for those educated in the traditional schools of medicine who were tainted for ever by the heathen notions of Aristotle and Galen. Often the spokesmen of the poor and illiterate, the chemical physician, like the 'mechanick preacher', denigrated university learning and applauded the learned ignorance of God's chosen *adepti*. 'Such is the ignorance of the Phyicians, and such the pertinacity of the Schools,' claimed the Helmontian James Thompson in 1657, 'that God gives Knowledge unto Clowns, and little ones; which is denied to such as are puft up with Ethnick Learning.'[41]

For many who shared this way of thinking, the new medicine was nothing less than a religious duty – an act of devotion whereby, in the words of one English Paracelsian, Henry Pinnell, 'the New Birth is first to be sought for, and then all other Naturall things will be added without much labour'.[42] Medical wisdom was therefore seen by many of the reformers as concomitant with the gift of grace, a return of the state of perfection and universal knowledge once enjoyed by Adam before the Fall. It was indeed no coincidence that the figure of Adam was widely cited by the reformers as the original precursor of Paracelsus who, it was commonly believed, possessed the key to all the secrets of nature. It was even suggested by some that the actual Eden, with the Tree of Life at its centre, had escaped the vicissitudes of time (including the Flood), and that it would soon be revealed to mankind in this last age of the world.[43] Others such as the radical physician John Webster and van Helmont the younger placed their hopes on the rediscovery of the universal language of nature, the original tongue of

[41] J. Thompson, *Helmont Disguised* (London, 1657), p. 116. Thompson was clearly opposed to orthodox scholastic methods in theological speculation. A believer in 'Apostolick sincerity', he also held that those who had been least contaminated by the pedantry of the schools were most likely to receive 'a more mild judgement' in the last days; *ibid.*, p. 5. Cf. the view of the collegiate physician Robert Sprackling who stated that van Helmont 'confined all medical knowledge to the brains of Enthusiastiques, and was so bold with the Sacred Text, as to form *Altissimus creavit Medicum* into a sence appropriate to these fantastical Tenets'; see R. Sprackling, *Medela Ignorantiae* (London, 1665), pp. 157–8.

[42] H. Pinnell, *Philosophy Reformed and Improved in Four Profound Tractates* (London, 1657), p. 132. For Pinnell, see above pp. 28–30.

[43] Culpeper, *Mr Culpepers Treatise of Aurum Potabile*, pp. 8–9; S. Hartlib, *Chymical, Medicinal, and Chyrurgical Addresses* (London, 1655), unpaginated appendix.

Adam, which the former at least believed might hold the key to a complete intellectual and medical restoration.[44]

The process of spiritual rebirth and intellectual regeneration which so many of the reformers proclaimed as the key to medical wisdom is well illustrated in the *Journal* of the young George Fox, future founder of the Quakers. Under the influence of the Silesian mystic Jacob Boehme, Fox describes how in the late 1640s,

the Creation gave another smell unto me than before . . . being renewed up into the image of God . . . to the state of Adam . . . The Creation was opened to me and it was showed me how all things had their names given them, according to their nature and virtue. I was at a stand in my mind whether I should practice physic for the good of mankind, seeing the natures and virtues of the creatures were so opened to me by the Lord . . .[45]

Though there is no direct evidence linking Fox with the Paracelsian and Helmontian reform movement, his debt to Boehme in the passage cited above certainly fits the stereotype of the radical chemical physician. Boehme himself was influenced by the mystico-alchemical thought of Paracelsus, just as the English and continental followers of Boehme frequently asserted that the iatrochemists were among the best equipped to interpret the intricacies of Behmenist thought.[46] Boehme also shared with van Helmont the elder a deep attachment to the notion that knowledge was acquired through the channels of *ecstasis*. Religious experience, according to both Boehme and van Helmont, was an inward process of self-illumination which led the initiate not only to a perfect understanding of the Creator, but also to a perfect comprehension of the objects of the creation. In the words of the Helmontian, Noah Biggs, this knowledge derived

from an inward teaching of the mindes heightning and enlightning by an invisible and yet sensible glorious emanation of light, truth, God, Intellect and Intelligible objects.[47]

For van Helmont, 'soul' and 'intellect' were interchangeable principles which, in the regenerate individual, enabled one to comprehend divine and natural mysteries as by an inner 'optic' sense. Truth, as

---

[44] J. Webster, *Academiarum Examen* (London, 1654), p. 17 and *passim*; F.M. van Helmont, *Alphabeti Vere Naturalis Hebraici Delineatio* (Sulzbach, 1657); cf. Pinnell's dictum 'Nature, grace, physick and Divinity, so returning to their unity', *Philosophy Reformed and Improved in Four Profound Tractates*, sig. A4r.

[45] G. Fox, *Journal*, bicentenary edn, 2 vols. (London, 1891), I, pp. 28–9. Quaker attitudes to the new medical ideas are examined in more detail in my 'Medicine, Science and the Quakers', 265–80.

[46] For Boehme and the English medical reform movement, see Webster, *The Great Instauration*, p. 280; Elmer, 'Medicine and the Puritan Revolution', pp. 165–8, 209n.

[47] Biggs, *Mataeotechnia*, pp. 213–14; W. Charleton, *A Ternary of Paradoxes* (London, 1649), sig. F2v.

Biggs explained, was therefore 'nothing else but the adaequation of the
Intellect to the object . . . for the Intellect knoweth objects in the reality
of their distinct Essence, and is therefore interchangeably certified of
the Nature of things, by the things, themselves'. Ecstatic communion
of this kind between man and nature was thus the key to understanding
the creation. It was also, according to the Helmontian Robert Godfrey,
a self-evident truth verified by those who claimed to have undergone
spiritual regeneration, that is the radical sectaries. Alluding to the
Helmontian idea that 'the Soul hath its prime residence in the Stomach', Godfrey explained that this must be so since those

in whom Christ's spirit inhabiteth . . . can tell you experimentally by pointing to the Pit
of their Stomachs . . . That the Spirit of Christ (which is not an imaginary thing but real
substance) appearing to refresh and consolate the distressed and thirsty soul, glanceth
forth its amiable, and thrice welcome beams in the Stomach: and that as often as he
withdraws himself . . . a load, and heavy burthen, is there felt.[48]

The predominantly sectarian character of the medical reform movement is beyond doubt. Typically, individuals like John Webster and
Henry Pinnell, who both favoured the new medicine, were equally
antagonistic to the claims of a state church, whatever form it might
take, to oversee the religious and moral welfare of the nation. Webster's well-known assault on the sterility of the university curricula was
largely prompted by his loathing for an educated and elitist clergy
which formed the basis of the state church.[49] His views were later
echoed by Pinnell, who extended Webster's earlier arguments to
incorporate the idea that true religion should complement the study of
the creation and not, as was currently the case, be divided from it in the
false dichotomy of the scholastic system. 'Every part of the creation',
wrote Pinnell, 'doth its part to publish the great mysteries of mans
salvation', a belief that was clearly out of line with orthodox thinking
on the subject (compare above, pp. 16–17). Chemistry, especially, was
envisaged as a divine science capable of revealing not only natural
truths but also the great mysteries of divinity. It was neither 'incredu-
lous or rediculous' wrote Pinnell that

[48] Biggs, *Mataeotechnia*, p. 45; R. Godfrey, *Various Injuries and Abuses in Chymical and
    Galenical Physick* (London, 1674), pp. 109–110. In this work, Godfrey stated that he was
    apprenticed at the age of twenty to a 'true-hearted Chymical Physitian', now dead, who taught
    him the rudiments of iatrochemistry.
[49] For a recent analysis of the life, career and intellectual background of Webster, see P. Elmer,
    The Library of Dr John Webster: The Making of a Seventeenth-Century Radical (*Medical
    History*, Supplement no. 6, London, 1987). Webster's vast library (nearly 1700 volumes)
    clearly absolves him from any change of obscurantism. It would also appear to contradict the
    claim of some sectaries regarding the irrelevance of books and book learning in the composi-
    tion of their ideas (cf. above p. 25).

a true Chymist . . . should find light in darknesse, darknesse in light . . . good in evill, evill in good; body in spirit, and spirits in bodies; and by a Spagyrick extraction separate each to its proper use and end, *distinctly drawing out the great Mysteries of Godlinesse and Iniquity.*[50]

In the eyes of the radical sectaries, nature was not simply a guide to faith as most orthodox theologians of both protestant and catholic persuasion held, but rather an indispensable element of their religious experience. The mystical communion of man with nature was thus one of the most attractive features of the medical philosophy of the Paracelsians and Helmontians. For orthodox puritans, and many Anglicans on the other hand, it was anathema – a potential threat to all established learning and religion. The spread of such ideas in the 1650s almost certainly widened the already large rift between the orthodox and radical branches of puritanism, and possibly helped to heal the divide between moderate Anglicans and presbyterians – a process partially realized by the restoration of 1660. Under no circumstances, however, would the sectaries accept the enforcement of religious uniformity by the state, and it is clear from the writings of the medical reformers that it was the presbyterian state church which was perceived as posing the greatest threat to the maintenance of liberty of conscience. Dogmatic presbyterianism, as Nicholas Culpeper hinted (see above, p. 21), was considered by many to be far worse than the strain of Anglicanism which it replaced, a view shared by the Paracelsian translator Henry Pinnell.

Pinnell was in fact a graduate of St Mary Hall, Oxford, who served as a parliamentary army chaplain during the civil war. He later renounced his former complicity with those who had used 'carnal violence' against their opponents in the war, possibly as a result of a mystical experience or conversion in 1646–7. His pacifism is once again evident in 1657 when he severely rebuked those who 'make the pretence of Religion or Civil Right a stalking horse to proud and imperious designes and ends'. As Christians, it was rather the duty of all men to wage 'the good fight of Faith, and earnestly contend for it, not with carnall weapons, but spirituall', including presumably the hermetic study of nature (see above pp. 26, 28). An opponent of university-educated ministers, Pinnell was especially critical of presbyterianism,

[50] Pinnell, *Philosophy Reformed*, sigs. A4r, A5r, A6v (my emphasis). Cf. F.M. van Helmont, *The Spirit of Diseases* (London, 1694), pp. 2–3 and the opinion of John Webster that 'there is not any thing in the World but it holds forth Jesus Christ; all the whol creation is a representation of Jesus Christ: all tipes, all metaphors are resemblances of him'; see J. Webster, *The Judgement Set* (London, 1654), p. 6.

which he believed differed little from 'an exhorbitant Episcopacy and a boundlesse Independency'. Pinnell was in fact an antinomian who objected to any system of church government which attempted to superimpose conformity of worship by use of laws and ordinances. Yet it was presbyterianism which incurred his gravest censures. Of the presbyterian insistence upon national days of fasting, Pinnell wrote:

Men may command the observation of dayes, they cannot command the sanctification of them; they may propose the form and time of fasting, they cannot dispose the frame and affections of the heart . . . Civil powers may command the corps, they are not captains of the Conscience.[51]

PURITAN ORTHODOXY

The anti-presbyterian, and by inference anti-puritan, bias of the medical reform movement of the 1650s was reciprocated in the position adopted by the majority of orthodox mainstream puritans to the new medicine. Richard Baxter for example described Paracelsus as a 'Drunken Conjuror, who had converse with Devils', and he rejected the natural magic which was so often associated with Paracelsism on the grounds that its exponents 'give us neither Reasons with Aristotle, nor Miracles with Christ . . . to cause us to believe any of their new Revelations'. The presbyterian Thomas Hall attacked Paracelsus for much the same reasons referring to him as 'a Libertine . . . Drunkard' and a 'man of little learning' of whom it was frequently said that he conversed 'constantly with familiars' and had 'the Devill for his Purse-Bearer'.[52] Hall much preferred the traditional authority of Aristotle and Galen ('the Father of Physitians') as did the presbyterian physician Robert Wittie. Of Paracelsus, Wittie reported that he 'never went to church . . . and seemed slightly to regard God and his Ordinances'. Galen on the other hand, whom Wittie reluctantly admitted 'was

---

[51] Pinnell, *Philosophy Reformed*, sig. A6r; H. Pinnell, *A Word of Prophesy Concerning the Parliament, Generall and the Army. With a Little of the First Adam* (London, 1648), pp. 64–5, 53–5, 68. Pinnell's dislike of presbyterianism was shared by another occult philosopher, the catholic sympathizer Robert Turner; see his *The Brittish Physician* (London, 1664), pp. 284, 362–3. For Turner's defence of catholic rituals, see his *Paracelsus of the Supreme Mysteries of Nature* (London, 1655), sig. A5v, and *The Compleat Bone-Setter* (London, 1657), p. 102.

[52] Rattansi, 'Paracelsus and the Puritan Revolution', pp. 32, 29; T. Hall, *Histrio-Mastix. A Whip for Webster* (London, 1654), p. 209. Hall was repeating, almost verbatim, the attack on Paracelsus composed by Thomas Fuller in 1642; see T. Fuller, *The Holy State and the Profane State* (London, 1840; 1st edn, Cambridge, 1642), pp. 44–7. Fuller, in turn, was refuted in Culpeper, *Galens Art of Physick*, sig. A5r and R. Turner, *Paracelsus of the Chymical Transmutation, Geneology, and Generation of Metals and Minerals . . . Translated into English by R[obert] Turner* (London, 1657), sig. A3r.

indeed no Christian,' was nonetheless considered as far more reliable a source of medical wisdom, the puritan apologist even going so far as to make the spurious claim that Galen died whilst *en route* to the Holy Land to which he was travelling in order to confirm the miraculous claims of the apostles to cure 'diseases by a word'.[53]

Typical of the educational, scientific and medical conservatism of mainstream puritanism was the work of the presbyterian Thomas Hall who in 1654 replied at length to the objections of the would-be university reformer John Webster. Despite his opposition to academic novelties, Hall was nonetheless a learned man and a keen bibliophile who helped to establish numerous libraries in the vicinity of his parish at King's Norton, Warwickshire. As a man of profoundly conservative values, however, he could not fail to be alarmed by the spread of philosophical novelties such as Paracelsism which clearly attempted to conflate the truths of the scriptures with those of natural science. Hall's view that 'every science must keep its proper bounds, for many things which are true in Philosophy, yet are not so when applied to Divinity' was thus fully in keeping with traditional maxims governing the division of natural and theological learning. Similarly, his defence of the merits of human learning in preaching the word of God was completely orthodox, and was diametrically opposed to the inspired claims of sectaries like Webster. This of course was *the* central issue which divided the radicals from both their puritan and Anglican adversaries. Hall thus repeated the highly orthodox view that God no longer operated upon his 'saints' through the process of immediate illumination (compare the observation of Wittie, (below, note 53), but acted instead through intermediaries such as 'Prayer, Reading, Study, Skill in Arts, Sciences, Languages, &c'. Although it was certainly true that in the time of the Apostles God had 'poured out an extraordinary measure of his spirit on many, who had Learning and Languages by immediate infusion', this was no longer the case for,

---

[53] Wittie, *Pyrologia Mimica*, p. 255; R. Wittie, *Scarbroughs Spagyrical Anatomizer Dissected* (London, 1672), pp. 13–14. Wittie was described by the Quaker George Fox as a 'great Presbyterian' who had 'taken ye Scotch covenant'; see N. Penney (ed.), *The Journal of George Fox*, 2 vols. (Cambridge, 1911), II, pp. 95–6. Wittie's conservatism, medical and religious, is apparent throughout his writings. On natural causation in the 'lower parts of the earth', Wittie opined that it was 'better silently to admire the power . . . of God in them, then too curiously to pry into the causes of these deep mysteries in nature' (cf. above, p. 18 and n.). He stressed the wholly conventional notion that 'the art of Physick' was of human origin rather than God-given. And in religion, he adhered to the orthodox commonplace that 'the Scriptures were given forth . . . to be a standing Rule of Faith to the end of the World, and we expect no new addition or Revelation'; see R. Wittie, *Scarborough Spaw* (London and York, 1660), p. 166; Wittie, *Pyrologia Mimica*, pp. 224, 225–6.

they had it Given, we Gotten; they by Revelation and Inspiration, we now by Industry and Study; *and yet even then we read that Paul had his books and parchments*[54]

The Calvinistic epistemology outlined by the puritan, Hall, was intended to reinforce the view that learning was, and would continue to remain, an indispensable guide to the realization of grace. The successful defence of this view in the 1650s meant that the universities continued to function as the seminaries of a learned puritan ministry, and by and large they remained untouched by curricular innovation and reform. In power, the puritans effected only minor alterations in the prescribed studies of Oxford and Cambridge students, and puritan educationalists like Hall successfully lobbied against any attempt to interfere with, or disturb, the traditional division of theology and the natural sciences (Baconianism was presumably allowed for the very reason that it too stipulated a rigid distinction in this respect).[55] Likewise, in the medical schools of Oxford and Cambridge, no fundamental alteration occurred in the traditional method or content of study as a result of the puritan takeover of the universities. Moreover, where innovation did take place, particularly in the field of physiological and anatomical research, it was more often than not the work of disaffected Anglicans and not puritans (for example, William Harvey, Thomas Willis, Walter Charleton, Ralph Bathurst). Indeed, it is possible that religious factors are once again at work here since many young Anglicans, who might under different circumstances have entered the theological faculties at Oxford and Cambridge, now opted instead for a medical career. As the devout Anglican Ralph Bathurst explained, he chose this path 'that so, in spight of the iniquities of the time, I might get a tolerable livelihood, whatever became of me in the university'. An early advocate of Helmontian physiology in England, Bathurst was in fact able to pursue a minor and clandestine role for the Anglican cause at Oxford by officiating as an archdeacon in the ordination of fellow episcopalians under the direction of the deprived Bishop of Oxford, Robert Skinner.[56]

Even men of seemingly moderate puritan persuasion such as the

---

[54] For Hall, see *D.N.B.*, xxiv, p. 975; T. Hall, *Vindiciae Literarum. The Schools Guarded* (London, 1654), p. 51, sigs. A4r–v (my emphasis). The importance of learning in puritan epistemology is fully evident in Hall's defence of the logical nature of the scriptures, which he considered was sufficient 'to stop the mouths of some, that say Christ never used logick, nor had any humane learning'; *ibid.*, p. 8.

[55] Lack of curricular reform of this kind is noted, for example, in Webster, *The Great Instauration*, pp. 178–9.

[56] *Ibid.*, pp. 130, 136–44, 498; A.H.T. Robb-Smith, 'Cambridge Medicine', in A.G. Debus (ed.), *Medicine in Seventeenth-Century England* (Berkeley, 1974), pp. 359–65; H.M. Sinclair, 'Oxford Medicine' in Debus (ed.), *Medicine in Seventeenth-Century England*, pp. 386–7; T. Warton, *The Life and Literary Remains of Ralph Bathurst* (London, 1761), p. 204 and

physician Jonathan Goddard appear to have displayed little trace of reformist intent with respect to the traditional practice or organization of medicine. A member of the Baconian group of reformers centred upon John Wilkins and John Wallis in 1645, Goddard would later attack those, such as the apothecaries, who attempted to subvert the conventional hierarchical structure of the medical profession (referring in the process to Nicholas Culpeper as a 'foul-mouth'd scribler'). When the plague struck London in 1665, Samuel Pepys reported of Goddard that he publicly defended (in front of the Royal Society) the right of his fellow Collegiate physicians to flee the city – advice that was in stark contrast to the behaviour of many Paracelsian and Helmontian physicians who continued to administer to the poor and sick.[57]

If one turns to the administration and organization of the College of Physicians during the 1640s and 1650s, it is difficult to avoid the impression that under puritan jurisdiction little, if anything, was done to reform or alter the day-to-day running of the College. During these years, the College had at least two presidents with eminently respectable puritan credentials: John Clarke (1645–9) and Edward Alston (1655–66). Clarke has recently been described as 'the staunchest presbyterian in the college and an ardent supporter of the parliamentary cause'.[58] Likewise, Alston was an active and influential presbyterian in London during the 1640s, a ruling elder in the parish of St Mary at Hill (1646), and a 'most conscientious attender of classis meetings'. Neither appear to have distinguished themselves as progressive incumbents of their office. Alston in fact was at the centre of the controversy with Peter Chamberlen over public baths (see above, p. 21). He was the chairman of the four-man committee which unequivocally rejected Chamberlen's scheme, and it may not be without significance that in the debate which ensued 'the evil influence of Paracelsus was as usual detected at work behind the proposals'.[59] At the restoration, Alston

passim. Bathurst was a close friend of the episcopalian and physician Thomas Willis. Whilst at Oxford, he attended the lectures of the 'chymist and Rosicrucian' Peter Staehl (*ibid.*, p. 44), but at the restoration he relinquished a medical career and entered the church. Cf. the career of Henry Brunsell which followed a similar path; Wood, *Fasti*, II, p. 133.

[57] Webster, *The Great Instauration*, pp. 79–80; J. Goddard, *A Discourse Setting Forth the Unhappy Condition of the Practice of Physick in London* (London, 1670), p. 26 and *passim*; W.G. Bell, *The Great Plague in London in 1665* (London, 1951), p. 292.

[58] W.J. Birken, 'The Royal College of Physicians of London and its Support of the Parliamentary Cause in the English Civil War', *J. Brit.St.*, XXIII (1983), 52; see also C. Hart, 'John Clark, M.D.', *St Bartholomew's Hospital Journal*, LV (1951), 34–40.

[59] W.J. Birken, 'The Puritan Connexions of Sir Edward Alston, President of the College of Physicians, 1655–1666', *Med. Hist.*, XVIII (1974), 370–4; V. Pearl, 'London Puritans and Scotch Fifth Columnists: a Mid Seventeenth-Century Phenomenon', in A.E.J. Hollaender and W. Kellaway (eds.), *Studies in London History* (Edinburgh, 1969), pp. 321, 324; P. Chamber-

was knighted and subsequently proceeded as President of the College
to reissue various judgements that were designed to reaffirm the
traditional privileges of the College which had been drastically undermined during the preceding years.[60] On reflection, neither Clarke nor
Alston would seem to fit the stereotype of reformist puritans which
some have attempted to draw for this period.

EIRENICISM

Elsewhere I have attempted to show that the major religious impulse to
medical reform in seventeenth-century England derived from a set of
religious beliefs and values which I have termed 'eirenic'.[61] Eirenicism,
or the desire for peace, tolerance and eventual reconciliation among
the various Christian churches had its roots in the wars of religion and
religious persecution which punctuated the history of Europe from the
middle of the sixteenth century onward. Such beliefs were always
likely to surface in times of particularly acute crisis, and the English
revolution was no exception. Moreover, as Frances Yates, R.J.W.
Evans and others have intimated, eirenic aspirations usually formed
part of a larger vision of intellectual, moral and political renewal
whose chief propagandists were often drawn from the ranks of hermetic and chemical physicians. Why this should be so is not difficult to
explain. As Peter French has observed with reference to the eirenic
motives which lay behind the work of the Elizabethan magus, John
Dee, hermeticism was itself a religious code of beliefs which 'did away
with dogmatic theology, stressed the mystical unity of all religions and
the oneness of God, and emphasized pristine Christianity and man's
innate knowledge of the Divinity'.[62] Or, to put it another way, it

len, *A Paper Delivered in to Dr Alston, Dr Hamens [sic], Dr Bates, Dr Micklethwait . . . to the
Honourable Committee for Bathes and Bath-Stoves . . . Together with an Answer thereunto*
(London, 1648); Webster, *The Great Instauration*, p. 298. Interestingly, Chamberlen alluded
to Paracelsus as one of the 'great Doctor-makers of the World'; P. Chamberlen, *A Vindication
of Publick Artificiall Baths* (London, 1648), p. 1.

[60] C. Merrett, *A Collection of Acts of Parliament, Charters, Trials at Law, and Judges' Opinions
Concerning those Grants to the Colledge of Physicians, London, taken from the Originals,
Law-Books, and Annals. Commanded by Sir Edward Alston* (London, 1660).

[61] Elmer, 'Medicine, Science and the Quakers', 280–5.

[62] For Yates, see above note 7.; R.J.W. Evans, *Rudolf II and his World: A Study in Intellectual
History, 1576–1612* (Oxford, 1973), pp. 66–7, 82, 92, 100, 142, 197; P.J. French, *John Dee: The
World of an Elizabethan Magus* (London, 1972), pp. 55–6, 118–24, 135–6. Cf. Owen
Hannaway's comment that Paracelsus and Oswald Croll belonged to a similar tradition of
religious thinking, the advocates of which 'although differing widely in their individual tenets,
shared a common belief in the essentially inner spiritual nature of Christian experience and a
common opposition to the emergent doctrinal orthodoxies of Protestantism'; see O.
Hannaway, *The Chemists and the Word* (Baltimore, 1975), p. 9. Much the same point has been
made with reference to Paracelsus in C. Webster, *From Paracelsus to Newton* (Cambridge,
1982), p. 55.

represented a pansophic vision of man, nature and God which transcended the petty distinctions of orthodox religious forms and so appealed to men from a variety of otherwise conflicting theological backgrounds.

The eirencism which can be found in the work of John Dee[63] is not easily seen in the writings of Englishmen with similar scientific interests in the period before 1640. Nonetheless, it would be wrong, I feel, to exclude such a religious intent from the work of pre-revolutionary Paracelsians and hermeticists. If, for example, van Dorsten is right in seeing the 'monad' symbol devised by Dee as an occult manifestation of the desire for religious unity and peace in Europe, the proposed translation of Dee's *Monas Hieroglyphica* by the Paracelsian clergyman Thomas Tymme may well represent an act of eirenic intent on the part of this obscure Suffolk minister.[64] Equally intriguing are the religious musings of Robert Fludd which, significantly, were reserved to the privacy of manuscript. On the surface a practising Anglican who publicly affirmed his faith in the 'reformed' doctrines of the pre-revolutionary church, Fludd nonetheless held views which seem to be at odds with conventional Calvinism. Fludd thus conceived of the world as so hopelessly depraved and 'obscured with darkness' that the best hope of personal salvation lay in the efficacious effects of pious introspection and mystical meditation. If men followed this path Fludd predicted that mankind as a whole would be 'more charitably disposed, because it makes them aware of their essentiall brotherhood in God's spirit'.[65]

Perhaps the clearest expression of the combined virtues of eirenic and hermetic speculation in the period before 1640 can be found in the work of the celebrated Anglican physician Thomas Browne. In *Religio Medici* (published in 1642, but written in the 1630s), Browne provides us with a unique insight into the mind of a man which on the surface was wholly conventional, but which in reality was highly critical of orthodox religious and intellectual precepts. As a result, Browne

---

[63] Dee was informed, for example, by one of his angelic confederates that 'whosoever wishes to be wise may look neither to the right nor the left, neither towards this man who is called a Catholic, nor towards that one who is called a heretic . . . but he may look up to the God of heaven and earth, and to his son, Jesus Christ, who has given the Spirit of his abundant and multifarious graces to those who live a natural life in purity and a life of grace in their works'; quoted in C.H. Josten, 'An Unknown Chapter in the Life of John Dee', *Journal of the Warburg and Courtauld Institutes*, XXVIII (1965), 234.

[64] J.A. van Dorsten, *The Radical Arts: First Decade of an Elizabethan Renaissance* (Leiden, 1970), pp. 23–4; Bod. Lib., Ashmole MS. 1459, fos. 472–3.

[65] Fludd, *Doctor Fludds Answer*, p. 22; C.H. Josten, 'Robert Fludd's *Philosophicall Key* and his Alchemical Experiment on Wheat', *Ambix*, XI (1963), 10–11.

maintained a life-long attachment to the Anglican church whilst at the
same time holding in private a number of opinions which were clearly
heterodox. Among these, for example, were Browne's aversion to
doctrinal controversy and religious bigotry, as well as his opposition
to any form of persecution on the grounds that it was a 'bad and
indirect way to plant religion'. In place of traditional instruments of
theological study and debate, including reason and logic, Browne thus
advocated a simplified religion of the intellect which was largely
indebted to hermetic and neo-platonic sources.[66] In this way, Browne
believed that the hermetic study of the creation might lead men to a
better understanding of true Christianity and so put an end to the bitter
conflict which currently divided Christian from Christian.

In the period before 1640, as Browne well knew, the public profession of such views was both dangerous and unwelcome. Consequently, he chose to resolve this difficult situation by taking the stance
of 'Janus in the field of knowledge', owning 'one common and
authentick Philosophy I learned in the Schools, whereby I discourse
and satisfy the reason of other men', whilst privately holding to
'another more reserved, and drawn from experience, whereby I content mine own'. After 1640 of course, the open espousal of such views
was far easier. Browne himself, whilst taking advantage of the freer
atmosphere of the 1640s, lamented the passing of the Anglican church,
yet interestingly, his published views continued to appeal to a wide
audience ranging from French catholics to English Quakers.[67] For
others, however, the experience of civil war, religious division and
general violence made many new converts to the principle of liberty of
conscience, including a significantly large proportion of the spokesmen for medical reform.

A partial explanation for this phenomenon may lie in the fact that so
many of the medical reformers had witnessed at first hand the bitter
military struggle of the 1640s. Among those already mentioned, John
Webster, John French, John Pordage, Nicholas Culpeper and Henry
Pinnell had all participated in the military events of the 1640s. The
Paracelsian Henry Pinnell, who like Webster had officiated as an army
chaplain in the parliamentary army, later expressed profound regret
for his past 'complyance with men of violence, blood-thirsty and

[66] T. Browne, *Religio Medici* (London, 1642), pp. 11, 20, 25–6, 32, 60, 96, 114, 166–7. For
Browne's interest in Helmontianism, see S. Wilkin (ed.), *Sir Thomas Browne's Works
Including his Life and Correspondence*, 4 vols. (London, 1835–6), III, p. 435; IV, p. 83;
G. Keynes (ed.), *The Letters of Sir Thomas Browne* (London, 1946), p. 35.
[67] Browne, *Religio Medici*, pp. 166–7; Elmer, 'Medicine, Medical Reform and the Puritan
Revolution', pp. 243, 274n.

deceitfull, whose feet have been swift to shed the blood of men more righteous than themselves'. Sickened by the conclusion of the wars and the defeat of the radicals, Pinnell turned instead to the popularization of a new kind of religion, one which was hermetically inspired and in which all men might come, via peaceful means, to realize the essential truths of Christianity through the study of the creation.[68] In a similar fashion, the chemist John French expressed the view that in the imminent golden age prophesied, among others, by the iatrochemist Michael Sandivogius, 'all tyranny, oppression, envie, and covetousnesse shall cease' and 'there shall be one prince and one people abounding with love and mercy, and flourishing in peace'. Two years later, French elaborated on the practical implications of such a belief when he defended the right of catholics, as well as 'those of any other heterodox judgement whatsoever' to practise their religion in peace according 'to their own light'.[69]

The popularity of eirenic aspirations amongst English Paracelsians and Helmontians might also be explained in part by the disproportionate influence continental iatrochemists exerted upon the English medical reform movement. Many of these figures had also experienced the full-scale horrors of religious wars which had devastated large parts of Europe in the first half of the seventeenth century. Many had direct experience of persecution and intolerance. The German chemist Johann Rudolph Glauber (whose *Furni Novi Philosophici* was translated by French in 1651) is certainly a case in point. An eirenicist at heart, Glauber condemned all forms of religious intolerance and proclaimed the essential oneness of mankind in the worship of Christ. Yet as Glauber sadly confessed,

every one thinketh himself better than others, and for a word's sake which one understandeth otherwise . . . (and though it be no point, wherein Salvation doth depend) one curseth and condemneth another and persecuteth one another unto death which Christ never taught us to do, but rather did earnestly command us that we should love one another, reward evil with good, and not good with evil.[70]

The solution to this desperate state of affairs lay, according to Glauber, in the conviction that the words and actions of formal religion were not necessary to salvation and so should not be enforced

---

[68] Pinnell, *Philosophy Reformed*, sigs. A1v, A6r–v.

[69] J. French, *The Art of Distillation* (London, 1650), sig. C4r; J. French, *The Yorkshire Spaw, or a Treatise of Four Famous Medicinal Wells* (London, 1652), p. 123.

[70] J.R. Glauber, *A Description of New Philosophicall Furnaces, or a New Art of Distilling, divided into five Parts . . . Set Forth in English, by J[ohn] F[rench]* (London, 1651), pp. 104–5. When Glauber's *Works* were finally published in England in 1689, the translator was advised by an 'Honourable Person' to omit 'the Author's Religious and Moral Digressions'; J.R. Glauber, *The Works* [trans. C. Packe] (London, 1689), sig. A2v.

upon those who disagreed with them. Consequently, faith in redemption through Christ was not to be sought in the dogmatic assertions of fallible men, but was rather to be acquired through the pious contemplation of the divine creation which God intended for that purpose. Although Glauber never visited England, his work and thought was very influential in iatrochemical circles after 1650. Many others, however, were attracted to England in this period, some no doubt drawn by the chiliastic expectations surrounding the country in the wake of the civil war. A hint of the kind of impact such men may have had upon the native medical reform movement is suggested by the work of two later visitors, Albert Otto Faber and Francis Mercury van Helmont.

Faber, a German iatrochemist imbued with Helmontian ideas, arrived in England shortly after the restoration and was soon attracted to the ways of the Quakers amongst whom he practised medicine. Following his arrest in 1664 for attending Quaker meetings, he undertook the defence of his co-religionists in a pamphlet which advocated, inter alia, complete freedom of conscience in religion. As Faber explained, persecution was not the correct way to implant true Christian beliefs since 'if the Principle the Quakers are possessors of, be from God, then no power of men can overthrow them'. Alternatively,

if the Principle ... be not from God, let them worship and pretend and colour and meet, and suffer Persecution, Imprisonment, Banishment, yea, Death it self, all will not keep them standing, but they must fall, without all such bustling or any man's power.[71]

Similarly, van Helmont the younger, who suffered personally at the hands of the Inquisition in the 1660s, was soon attracted to the mild and tolerant disposition of the Quakers following his arrival in England in 1670 (see above, p. 25). Despite his close association with the Quaker circle at Ragley, van Helmont nonetheless typically reserved judgement on all religions and remained throughout his life devoted to no one particular faction or sect. As he later explained, it had always been his practice to acknowledge

only but two sorts of men viz: ye good & ye bad: ye good are those who really know, love & obey God without all pretext ... & ye bad are those who are ... such as hide and cloake wickedness under some forme or profession of Religion. The sort I own, and am one wth are men of ye first sort, lett them be called by any name whatsoever & I disowne any of ye other sort lett him be amongst what sort of people soever professing Religion.[72]

---

[71] A.O. Faber, *A Remonstrance in Reference to the Act to Prevent and Suppress Seditious Conventicles* (London, 1664), p. 5. For Faber and the Quakers, see Elmer, 'Medicine, Science and the Quakers', 278–9, 280, 281.

[72] Brit. Lib., Sloane MS. 530, fo. 53v; see also Elmer, 'Medicine, Science and the Quakers', 275–8, 281.

Just as Faber and van Helmont felt an immediate attachment to the mystical and eirenic character of Quaker thought, so too did many of the English iatrochemists of the 1650s show a similar preference for those forms of religious experience which excluded learned dogmatism and the imposition of clerical authority by the magistrate (see above, pp. 21 30). John Webster and Henry Pinnell, for example, refused to acknowledge the authority of any sect in the 1650s, preferring instead to 'seek' the truth of the gospels by their own lights and that of the creation. Webster, who elevated faith above reason and denigrated the logic of the university-educated divines, was thus convinced that the scholasticism of the schools had led to the present divisions in England. The clergy trained in such schools had made 'the world of God nothing else but a Magazine of carnal Weapons, from whence they may draw instruments to fight with and wound one another'.[73]

Nicholas Culpeper echoed these sentiments when he said that few men were capable of understanding 'the mystery' of the scriptures, 'though most men understand the Letter'. As a result, religion in England was riddled with errors which Culpeper blamed for 'all that fighting both of tongues and hands, whereby so many men had lost their lives, and yet the truth more obscured'. Culpeper, who like Webster and Pinnell seemed to own no one church or sect, became increasingly antipathetic toward 'that Monster which men call Religion' which, in true eirenic fashion, he blamed for all those wars and civil disputes which had divided Europe in the previous century and a half.[74] It should be stated, however, that such conclusions, radical though they might sound, were not confined to the radical and semi-mystical sects of the 1650s. The Anglican, Walter Charleton, following his conversion to Helmontianism in the early 1650s, was also highly suspicious of the 'variable and seductive imposture of Reason', which he invoked as the cause of England's present religious divisions.[75] There may well have been many others like Charleton who, unable to comprehend God's will in the tragic events of the 1640s and 1650s, resorted to extreme views of this kind as well as seeking solace in the pious mysticism of the new medicine.

[73] Webster, *Academiarum Examen*, pp. 15–16, 17; J. Webster, *The Saints Guide* (London, 1653), sig. A3v; pp. 22, 26, 29–38. Another medical reformer to share Webster's plea for toleration was Peter Chamberlen who, in the period after 1660, actively sought to reunite the various churches of christendom; P. Chamberlen, *A Speech Visibly Spoken* (London, 1662); Capp, *The Fifth Monarchy Men*, p. 181.

[74] Culpeper, *Culpeper's Treatise of Aurum Potabile*, p. 98; N. Culpeper, *Semeiotica Uranica* (London, 1651), p. 112; Culpeper, *Catastrophe Magnatum*, p. 19.

[75] Charleton, *A Ternary of Paradoxes*, sig. F2v. For Charleton's subsequent recantation from Helmontianism, see Rattansi 'Paracelsus and the Puritan Revolution', pp. 30–1.

There can be little doubt that for many, the experience of civil war and religious and political upheaval was a traumatic one which affected men of all religious persuasions. For many, especially the sectaries, this was, however, a period of great optimism with the inauguration of the republic in 1649 heralding a new and exciting beginning. Millennial speculation at all levels of society was intense, and it extended to the medical reform movement where hopes of a return to Adamic perfection were commonplace. In particular, to those upon whom God had bestowed the gift of grace, great things were expected in this era of renewal, and many attempted to oblige. Some thus claimed to have received an infusion of the original wisdom of Adam, whereas others prophesied the enormous benefits that would accrue to mankind now that 'Nature, grace, Physick and Divinity' were restored to 'their first unity'.[76]

Another sign of this impending medical renaissance was the claim which some made (and others were only too willing to corroborate) to perform miraculous feats of healing, usually without recourse to orthodox medical methods. George Fox was renowned in Quaker circles as one adept in the performance of such cures (compare above, p. 27). Equally interesting in this respect are the careers of two of the most famous faith healers of this period, Matthew Coker and Valentine Greatrakes, particularly as both seemed to promote the cause of eirenicism. Coker, who was active in London around 1654, professed to have cured a whole range of 'difficult' diseases (including bewitchment) through a power invested in him 'by the immediate and sudden impulse of God's Spirit'. Significantly, he envisaged the bestowal of this gift as part of a general reformation in the world which God had instigated in order to reunite the various warring factions of christendom. In fact, it was Coker's opinion that in the course of time all titles such as catholic, episcopalian and presbyterian would become obsolete and that authority in the regenerate world would devolve upon a mighty and peace-loving prince (Oliver Cromwell?; compare above p. 37).[77]

---

[76] Pinnell, *Philosophy Reformed*, sig. A4r. For a more detailed account of millennial and apocalyptic themes in the writings of the English medical reformers, see Elmer, 'Medicine and the Puritan Revolution', pp. 332–67.

[77] M. Coker, *A Propheticall Revelation* (London, 1654), sig. A2v; pp. 1–2; M. Coker, *A Short and Plain Narrative* (London, 1654), p. 6; M. Coker, *A Whip of Small Cords to Scourge Antichrist* (London, 1654). For Coker, see especially M.H. Nicholson, *Conway Letters* (London, 1930), pp. 98–104. Among those who reported these cures to Lady Anne Conway was the astrologer–divine Robert Gell, who shared Coker's enthusiasm for religious tolerance and the imminence of the millennium. He was also an admirer of Paracelsus; see Nicholson, *Conway Letters*, pp. 98–9; C.E. Whiting, *Studies in English Puritanism* (London, 1968), p. 319; R. Gell, *A Sermon Touching Gods Government of the World by Angels* (London, 1650), p. 35.

Unfortunately, we know little of Coker's medical or religious background. However, in the case of the Irish 'stroker' Valentine Greatrakes, active in England in 1665, we have rather more information, much of it tantalizingly suggestive of Greatrakes's familiarity with the general aims of the iatrochemists. One of his critics, an Anglican clergyman David Lloyd, did in fact equate Greatrakes's cures with those of the Quakers, and he went on to insinuate that

he hath been in his time of most of the Factions that were largely extant; and now pretends himself a Latitude-man, that is, one that being of no Religion himself, is indifferent what Religion others should be of.[78]

Lloyd's assessment of the religious proclivities of the Irish healer is borne out to some extent by Greatrakes's own account of his early life in Ireland. A soldier in that country during the Cromwellian occupation, Greatrakes left the army in 1656 and returned to his native Affane where he took up the office of local Justice of the Peace. As part of his official duties, he attempted to convert the native population from catholicism but not, as he made clear, through the power of the sword. Instead, he applied the gentle art of persuasion 'for I bless God he has taken away a persecuting Spirit from me'. It is possible, therefore, that when Greatrakes set out for England in 1665 he was motivated by something other than a simple desire to cure the sick. Again, eirenic sentiments are certainly suggested by the archbishop of Dublin, Michael Boyle who, prior to Greatrakes's departure, reported that the 'stroker' was prepossessed by the thought of 'converting the Jew and the Turk' – a millennial notion common among those who forecast Christian reunion throughout Europe.[79]

Of Greatrakes's scientific and medical interests we can be less certain, though the fact that he was a self-confessed admirer of Jacob Boehme is suggestive. An interest in hermetic and occult thought is also intimated in the testimony of the royal chaplain John Beale, who alleged that Greatrakes had confessed to him of having once used charms, 'and tis knowne, yt he did likewise study magick'. Moreover, it would probably be a mistake to overlook the fact that Greatrakes himself admitted that his cures were effected through the superimposition of 'his own strong imagination' upon the diseased

[78] D. Lloyd, *Wonders No Miracles* (London, 1666), pp. 9, 14. There is also some evidence linking Greatrakes with the regicide and medical reformer, John Cook, who, as solicitor-general of Ireland, was well known as a protector of religious radicals; see T.C. Barnard, *Cromwellian Ireland: English Government and Reform in Ireland, 1649–1660* (Oxford, 1975), p. 273.

[79] V. Greatrakes, *A Brief Account of Mr Valentine Greatrak's* (London, 1666), pp. 18–20; *Calendar of State Papers, Ireland, 1663–65*, pp. 615–6. Among those who testified to Greatrakes's religious moderation was the iatrochemist Jeremiah Astel; see Greatrakes, *ibid.*, p. 94.

parts of his clients. This was of course a form of psychotherapy strongly recommended by Paracelsian and Helmontian physicians, and roundly condemned by their opponents.[80]

Greatrakes's mission of 1665 – described by one historian of this episode as 'a veiled sectarian protest against the Restoration' – is just one example of how men hitherto sympathetic to the republic and the cause of religious freedom might react to the return of the monarchy and religious conformity. For others, there was always the compensation of medical study and practice, especially that of the iatrochemists, to fall back upon. John Webster, for example, who seems to have despaired of the radical cause and the delayed millennium by 1657, turned his mind thereafter almost exclusively to medical practice and the study of his beloved 'mystical chemistry' in the solitude of remote Clitheroe.[81] Three years previously, Henry Pinnell, by now an acute critic of the Cromwellian establishment, announced his intention of withdrawing from radical politics when he declared his wish to 'clime further into the inward, hidden and secret world' of nature, for 'the glimpse I have of it, sets me all on fire'. Clearly the pursuit of hermetic philosophy and iatrochemistry could act as a deep source of religious consolation for those disillusioned with the course of events in England after 1649.[82]

It would be a mistake to infer from this, however, that the eirenic hopes of the chemists of the 1650s ended with the restoration of Charles II. The aspirations of the Quaker converts, Faber and van Helmont the younger, have already been noted (see above p. 38). Another to defend the principle of liberty of conscience in this period was the Helmontian Robert Godfrey in 1674. Godfrey, who seemed to have favoured some form of experiential religion, defended his mentor van Helmont from those who criticized his attachment to catholicism, and he went on to reiterate in full the case for complete freedom of worship in England. Of himself, Godfrey stated:

I am one of those who doubt whether or no the most holy God minds a name or a form so much as the Heart of a Person . . . We may also suppose that it will not be said in the last day, come hither, yee Episcopalians, that is as such an associated people, or ye Papists, or yee Presbiterians . . . Independents . . . Anabaptists, or ye Quakers (which

---

[80] Hall and Hall (eds.), The Correspondence of Henry Oldenburg, II, pp. 496–7; Thomas, Religion and the Decline of Magic, pp. 203–4. Among those who testified to the success of Greatrakes's cures were the Helmontians Thomas Williams, Astel and Faber, and the hermeticist Ezekiel Foxcroft; see Greatrakes, A Brief Account of Mr Valentine Greatrake's, pp. 43–96; H. Stubbe, The Miraculous Conformist (Oxford, 1666), p. 31.

[81] Thomas, Religion and the Decline of Magic, pp. 203–4. For Webster, see above, pp. 28 and note.

[82] H. Pinnell, Nil Novi: This Years Fruit, from the Last Years Root (London, 1655), p. 50 [postscript signed and dated Brinkworth, Wiltshire, July 1654].

are all but Nicknames) and enjoy the Kingdom prepared you . . . But rather; Come hither yee that served me with an upright Heart in Self-Denial . . . That imbrued not your hands in the Blood of the Innocent.[83]

Both during and after the English revolution, eirenicism was a common theme in the literature of the iatrochemical reform movement. This may well help to explain how men of apparently conflicting religious and political backgrounds were able to work together in ventures such as the Chemical Council in the 1650s and the Society of Chymical Physitians in the 1660s. In the case of the former, the catholic Kenelm Digby worked alongside men of such radical persuasion as John French.[84] Similarly, diversity of religious outlook seems to have posed few problems for the leadership of the Society of Chymical Physitians, *despite* the attempt of a number of College physicians to exploit this apparent weakness in the ranks of their opponents. Staunch Anglicans such as George Thomson thus worked with ex-radicals (Marchamont Nedham[85] and Richard Barker) and catholic sympathizers (Robert Turner and Kenelm Digby), whilst more general support for the Society seems to have been given freely by men of the new Anglican establishment.[86] Much of this latter support can no doubt be accounted for by factors which are other than religious or political in kind. On the other hand, the possibility cannot be discounted altogether that the proposed Society of Chymical Physitians, like the Chemical Council, attracted support because of the eirenic aims implicit in so much of the work of the iatrochemical physicians.[87]

[83] Godfrey, *A Discourse*, pp. 136–8.
[84] In the case of the Chemical Council, the influence of the moderate, Samuel Hartlib, was probably a decisive factor. As a follower of Comenius, Hartlib almost certainly imbibed eirenicist tendencies. Accordingly, Barbara Shapiro has perceived the English Comenians as quite distinct from orthodox puritans, the former being characterized by their desire 'for religious union, and a distaste for the religious warfare which was destroying both Europe and England'; B. Shapiro, 'Latitudinarianism and Science in Seventeenth-Century England', in Webster (ed.), *The Intellectual Revolution of the Seventeenth Century*, pp. 291–2.
[85] Nedham's own religious leanings yet again point to eirenicism as the common denominator among the English iatrochemists. In 1650, for example, Nedham declared that 'the great Pretenders for Nationall Uniformity in Religion . . . are the greatest disturbers of States and Kingdoms'; M. Nedham, *The Case of the Common-Wealth of England, Stated* (London, 1650), p. 91.
[86] For attempts to equate the membership of the Society of Chymical Physitians with the sectaries, see W. Johnson, *Brief Animadversions* (London, 1655), pp. 5, 18, 41–3, 68–9, 86; Sprackling, *Medela Ignorantiae*, pp 157–8, 159, 161–2; J. Twysden, *Medicina Veterum Vindicata* (London, 1666), pp. 16–17, 117; G. Castle, *The Chymical Galenist* (London, 1667), sig. A6r. For the Society itself, see especially Sir H. Thomas, 'The Society of Chymical Physitians', pp. 56–71; P.M. Rattansi, 'The Helmontian–Galenist Controversy in Restoration England', *Ambix*, XII (1964), 1–23.
[87] A key figure in this respect may be George Villiers, Second Duke of Buckingham (1628–87). Villiers combined a deep interest in chemistry and the occult with a fervent belief in the principle of religious toleration which he consistently promoted in Parliament after 1668. See *D.N.B.*, LVIII, pp. 340, 344; Thomas, *Religion and the Decline of Magic*, p. 344; Rattansi, 'The

It is undeniable, however, that the general basis of support for the new Society in 1665 emanated from the Anglican and Caroline establishment. This trend is epitomized by the career of one of the leading propagandists for the Society, George Thomson, who seems to have been instrumental in attracting many courtiers to his scheme. During the 1640s, Thomson's adherence to the royalist cause was unquestionable (he served under the king's cousin, Prince Maurice). After the civil war Thomson studied medicine at Leyden, graduating in 1648, and some time during the 1650s he was converted to Helmontianism. In 1665 he reappeared as a vocal supporter of the new regime and a stout defender of the restored Anglican church, as well as one of the leaders of the medical reformers. In his many writings which date from this period, Thomson consistently denounced sectarianism, though his explanation for its popularity in recent years was both novel and ingenious.

According to Thomson (writing in 1671), the reason why 'we are more prone to diversity of opinions in Religion then formerly' was pathological in origin, the direct legacy of the supremacy of Galenic theories and cures. Phlebotomy in particular was ripe for censure, for:

Hereupon the Organs or Instruments of the Soul being thus spoiled and deprived of their Genuine use, 'tis impossible that Regular actions should be executed: thence the mind ... becomes froward, peevish ... desparately bent to follow for divertisement, a voluptuous sensual life, or to contrive innovations, Heresies, Schisms, and factious Rebellions.[88]

This intriguing explanation for the religious condition of the nation was clearly based upon a close reading of Helmontian texts. Unlike the Galenists who tended to avoid precise discussion of these matters, the English Helmontians were only too eager to exalt the medical and intuitive properties of the soul which they envisaged as highly responsive to alterations in the physical constitution of the body. In Thomson's case consideration of these issues finally led him to conclude in 1675 that the only practicable solution to the religious div-

Helmontian–Galenist Controversy', 12 and *passim*. Nedham speculated of Villiers: 'I know not what he may effect in Philosophy and Politie, by plying his Laboratory at home, and another at court'; see E. Bolnest, *Medicina Instaurata* (London, 1665), sig. A4v. Villiers's cousin Arthur Annesley, First Earl of Anglesey (1614–86) was also a signatory of the chemists' petition in 1665, who argued in favour of toleration for nonconformists. Moreover, he was acquainted with Samuel Hartlib and was used by the latter to promote fund-raising for the troubled protestants of Bohemia, as well as being approached by Hartlib in connection with the financing of a new hospital scheme in 1661; see Elmer, 'Medicine and the Puritan Revolution', pp. 430–1.

[88] G. Thomson, *A Check Given to the Insolent Garrulity of Henry Stubbe* (London, 1671), pp. 43–4. For Thomson, see *D.N.B.*, LVI, pp. 720–1; Innes Smith, *English-Speaking Students of Medicine at the University of Leyden.* p. 232.

isions which continued to threaten the peace of restoration England was the full-scale adoption of Helmontian chemotherapy. Upon the implementation of such a medical system would depend, ultimately, the goal of Christian reunion, for,

> by virtue of our Hermetick Physick, the Head, Heart, and Hands of Hierophants, might be purified: Their Exemplary Dumb and deaf Preaching up of Vice throughout all the World, be corrected: Circumstances and Punctilios in Religion lovingly, calmly proposed, debated and Accepted. And those fierce Eager Altercations about Adiaphora laid aside . . . [in this way] Quakers, Catabaptists, Independents, Separatists, Schismaticks, and multitudes of Phanaticks, might be brought to more Integrity of mind in Religion; *be reclaimed far better than by any rigid Persecuting Course whatsoever.*[89]

This unique explanation for the cause and cure of the religious ills of the country is just another example of a variation on a theme, eirenicism, which I have endeavoured to depict as the chief religious factor in the writings of the English iatrochemical reformers. As the case for Thomson indicates, there were differences of opinion amongst the reformers as to how the goal of Christian reunification might best be brought about. It would also be foolish to suggest that everyone who dabbled in hermetic medicine was certain to befriend the cause of religious toleration. Nonetheless, it seems to me that eirenicism as an explanation for the widespread interest in new forms of medical practice and theory in seventeenth-century England does possess certain virtues lacking in previous hypotheses. In particular, it does not restrict membership of reformist medical circles to those of any one sect or religious grouping, and it avoids the confusion of meaning implicit in the use of such controversial terms as 'puritanism'. Thus, by adopting a more stringent (and I would suggest more accurate) definition and usage for puritanism, it should be possible to account for the lack of interest (and in some cases outright hostility) shown by orthodox puritans to medical reform, whilst at the same time maintaining the obviously strong links between the radical sectaries and the new medical strains of thought. Consequently, though there is undoubtedly room for a great deal more research in this area, I find it difficult at the present to avoid the conclusion that in the case of medicine at least, the 'puritanism–science' hypothesis remains largely unproven.

[89] G. Thomson, *The Direct Method of Curing Chymically* (London, 1675), pp. 186–7 (my emphasis). Thomson's hoped-for restoration of religious unity was only one aspect of a much larger plan of social and economic renewal coincident upon the adoption of Helmontianism; see *ibid.*, pp. 186–97.

2

Harvey in Holland: circulation and the Calvinists

ROGER FRENCH

INTRODUCTION

The aim of this volume is to relate medicine to the wider historical issues of the seventeenth century, particularly religion and politics. This is not simply to provide a context or background, and this chapter is written on the assumption that these wider issues – questions of men's religious beliefs and of the way in which men were to be governed – had a selective influence on what (and how) they absorbed of new medical doctrines. If this assumption is valid, it must descend from the religious and political through the external institutional arrangements of medicine to the details of medical theory. And of all medical theory, the doctrine of the circulation of the blood is one of the most difficult to see in this kind of relationship with religious and political history. Indeed, Harvey has generally been seen by historians as self-evidently right, and those who did or did not accept the circulation are placed on a scale from the hapless Primrose upwards according to their ability to recognize the truth when they saw it. But what people made of Harvey's doctrine depended partly on how they came across it, and partly on what was already in their minds – whether intellectual or not – which predisposed them to accept or reject it, or parts of it. The result was that most people's idea of what Harvey said was different, sometimes very different, from what Harvey wrote in *De Motu Cordis*. This mutation of Harvey's message I call 'misunderstanding Harvey', whether or not it was a conscious mutation. This chapter looks at the process of misunderstanding Harvey in the Low Countries in about the first quarter of a century after *De Motu Cordis*. The discussion is limited primarily to the universities and does not tap the information available, for example, in extra-university teaching and preaching.[1]

HARVEY AND DESCARTES

The doctrine of the circulation of the blood had its greatest impact on the Low Countries in conjunction with Cartesian mechanism. Descartes' reading of *De Motu Cordis* involved one of the first, and certainly the most important of the misunderstandings of the doctrine of circulation. We shall need to look first at how, and why, Descartes modified Harvey's doctrine. *De Motu Cordis* was published in 1628. Gassendi had read it before the next year was very old, and although he found circulation an attractive notion he remained convinced (on a surgeon's evidence) that the septum between the ventricles of the heart was at least as porous as Galen had said and that therefore the heart itself could not work as Harvey claimed.[2] Gassendi sent his opinions to Mersenne, who in turn discussed the idea of circulation with Descartes, and Descartes himself had read the book or at least had seen it, before the end of 1632.[3]

But by then Descartes had already been working *de cette mattière* and as a result, he told Mersenne, he 'differed a little' from Harvey. To understand the basis of this difference, this 'misunderstanding', we must look at what Descartes had been doing in the previous years, and at the circumstances in which he had been doing it. The salient point is that by 1630 Descartes believed he had developed a new philosophical method together with a complete scheme of the results of applying it to the natural world – in a word, *Le Monde*. This work was the result of Descartes' well-known dissatisfaction with his own, largely Jesuit, education and with the later renaissance naturalism of the *libertins érudits* that he had met in the Paris salons. It was a result that came after ten years of travelling through Europe, and when he had virtually settled in Holland, briefly flirting with studies at Franeker (1629) and Leiden (1630).[4]

---

[1] I am indebted to my colleague Andrew Cunningham for the phrase 'misunderstanding Harvey' and for many fruitful discussions. I am also grateful to the Dutch representatives at the conference, who pointed out more sources for a history of Cartesianism and the doctrine of the circulation in Holland. My ignorance of Dutch prevents me from entertaining greater ambitions in this direction.

[2] R. Descartes, *Œuvres*, ed. C. Adam and P. Tannery (Paris, 1896–1913; reprinted 1956) (henceforth A–T), I, p. 264. This letter to Gassendi is incompatible with Keynes's statement: G. Keynes, *The Life of William Harvey* (Oxford, 1978) p. 448.   [3] A–T, I, p. 263.

[4] G.A. Lindeboom, *Descartes and Medicine* (Amsterdam, 1978), pp. 5–8, 17.

With hindsight we can see that Descartes' doubts about current natural philosophy were fundamental and his solutions, based on a new role for God as Creator, radical, and it has often been proposed that his choice of Holland as a place to live was based on the religious toleration he hoped to find there. It might also be thought possible to find here a link between the new natural philosophy of the seventeenth century (before Descartes largely centred on the names of Bacon and Gassendi) and the protestant or puritan 'ethic' that gave dominion over nature a religious purpose. But the situation was too complex for any simple relationship of this sort and indeed the evidence points in another direction. Perhaps Descartes simply wanted, as he said, to avoid the distractions of Parisian social life; and he seems anyway to have misjudged some aspects of the religious climate of his adopted country, as we shall see. To introduce this important point, it should be said that there was no uniformity of religious feeling in the United Provinces. Although the dominant national Calvinism was undoubtedly partly shaped by the continuing struggle against Spanish – and hence catholic – dominion, yet there were were significant minorities of catholics and of 'broad church' successors of the banished Arminians. The picture is complicated by political and social divisions that had important bearings on the extent to which Descartes' natural philosophy was taken up.

PURITANS AND LATITUDINARIANS

The 'protestant ethic' argument has been used most in relation to the period of the 'scientific revolution' in England. Certainly, there were many parallels between the forms of protestantism in England and the United Provinces, and in particular between the English puritans and the Dutch Calvinists under the leadership of Voet. These were the 'strict' party, calling for a second reformation and looking to outsiders as if they wanted social change from below by revolution. But these were the people who were most resistant to the attractions of the new natural philosophy and of Cartesianism. Instead, they adopted a remodelled Aristotelianism as their educational and philosophical authority.

But Calvinism also embodied a 'latitudinarian' group, which preached religious toleration as a basis for social and national security. Naturally, the strict party saw this as dangerously lax and an encouragement to dissent and disorder. It was largely latitudinarians who found the new natural philosophy and later Cartesianism attractive. A circumstance that made this possible was that both strict Calvinists and catholics of the counter-reformation had chosen Aristotle as the philosophical authority most suitable as the basis of doctrine within the universities, which were, of course, important centres for the propagation of the true version of the faith. The latitudinarians placed less religious reliance on doctrine and needed neither a newly Thomist Aristotle nor a reborn and reformed *Aristoteles priscus*. Without this doctrinal reason for the retention of Aristotelian natural philosophy some of the latitudinarians felt free to adopt new teachings about the relationship between God and the natural world.[5]

The varieties of religious belief were inseparable from varieties of political opinion: the demotic Voetians were opposed by the aristocratic and republican Regent party, but supported by the House of Orange. Central issues of dispute were the relationship between church and state and the role of the civil magistrates in academic and church affairs. As we shall see, Descartes became involved in these issues in fighting for his new natural philosophy. But first we must return to the development of this philosophy, which determined how Descartes misunderstood Harvey.

DESCARTES' NEW NATURAL PHILOSOPHY AND THE CIRCULATION

This is not the place to repeat the story of Descartes' *dubito*, his proof of the existence of God and of the physical world. The point for us is that by 1630 Descartes had decided that the laws that God had made for the natural world – the laws of physics – had also been so impressed on the human mind as to be almost innate.[6] It was this that made his method universal in application. The earlier *Regulae* do not contain the notion: it was announced together with Descartes' dogmatic assertion about the nature of the heartbeat in the *Discourse*. Another reason for the universality of the method lay in its mathematics and Descartes, in choosing the example of the movement of the heart and blood both as the primary motion of the body[7] and as the first to be demonstrated after his announcement of God's imprinting of natural laws on our

---

[5] Further information on the politics, religion and education of the period is to be found in T.A. McGahagan, 'Cartesianism in the Netherlands, 1639–1675; the New Science and the Calvinist Counter-reformation' (University of Pennsylvania Ph.D. thesis, 1976) (University Microfilms International, Ann Arbor and London, 1980).

[6] *Ibid.*, pp. 108–32.

[7] R. Descartes, *Discourse on Method, Optics, Geometry and Meteorology*, ed. P.J. Olscamp (Indianapolis, 1975), p. 40 (section five of the *Discourse*).

souls, shows how important mathematics was for him. That is, he claims, with unusual emphasis, that it is a mathematical demonstration that shows that his account of the heartbeat is necessarily true, for the disposition of the parts of the heart, like those of a clock, make his explanation the only one possible.

When Descartes read *De Motu Cordis* in 1632 he had finished that part of *Le Monde* that dealt with man: *L'Homme*. We may suppose that Harvey's book interested Descartes because it was about a topic on which he was working (the functioning of the body) and perhaps because it was (like Descartes' own account) a clear break with the ancients. It is in *L'Homme* that Descartes deals extensively with the structure and functioning of man's body, but he modified his account after reading Harvey's book. (The whole of *Le Monde* was ready in the following year but Descartes withdrew it from publication on hearing of Galileo's condemnation.) Basically, this modification of Harvey's doctrine was that Descartes accepted that the blood circulated, but did not accept Harvey's account of the heartbeat. He was able to do this because Harvey's book is about two things, the action of the heart – forceful systole – and the motion of the blood – circulation. Harvey discovered and taught the former before discovering and teaching the latter; the title of his book refers to both, and its contents are strictly divided between them. For him the forceful systole was prior, historically and in terms of demonstration, to the circulation. In Harvey's time the two were separable, for disputed questions about the action of the heart could be quite independent of those about the motion of the blood. And in fact many of Harvey's contemporaries separated the two halves of Harvey's 'idea' at just this articulation.

Descartes 'misunderstood' Harvey in this way because of the constraints of his own system. Descartes maintained against his theological critics in the universities that his natural philosophy showed directly and clearly the hand of God in the world. The validity of his physical laws rested on their metaphysical foundation, ultimately the existence of God. These laws were concerned with the transfer of motion from particle to particle, a motion that derived from the metaphysics of creation and not from secondary causes. It seems likely then that the attraction of the doctrine of circulation for Descartes was that the single motion of the heart could be seen as a source (by particle to particle contact) for all the other motions of the body, including those of the muscles, veins, glands and spirits, none of which were related to the heart in older doctrines. There was no need for a complex of secondary causes like attraction or other faculties.

But the other half of Harvey's doctrine, the forceful systole, was unattractive to Descartes. He did not think Harvey had provided a good explanation of the source of this motion. Harvey had not made a point of separating his description of systole from older accounts of how the body worked, which were based on faculties. Faculties were traditionally functions of a physiological soul that Descartes had rigorously excluded from the animal machine. So in saying that the *propria motio* of the heart, its functional movement, was contraction, Harvey appeared to Descartes to be saying that the parts of the heart came closer to each other by a kind of attraction, a species of motion that Descartes denied. What looked like attractive motions to other people had to be for Descartes the accidental and secondary result of another, primary and particulate transmission of motion.

So it was important for Descartes that the heart was the sole source of motion in the body, but equally important that the heart did not generate its own motion. Descartes consequently derived the motion of the heart from a major principle of his natural philosophy as a whole, heat. He told Beverwyck (in explaining his problem with Plemp; see below) that this heat was purely natural (he meant not 'native' or 'innate'). It was the heat of fire (a fire without light lit by God, he said), or of hay cut and stacked too green. It was enough to vaporize the 'very large' drops of blood entering the heart through the large vessels.[8] The expanding vapour forced the heart into diastole as it escaped into the pulmonary artery and aorta, condensing in the lungs and arteries. It was with this description of the action of the heart that Harvey's doctrine of the circulation reached many people. Indeed, it is likely that it reached more people than would have been the case had it not been associated with Cartesian mechanism.

DESCARTES AS THE NEW PHILOSOPHER

For all his timidity in publishing *Le Monde*, his subsequent actions show that Descartes was not an unambitious man. In 1637 he published the *Discourse on Method* in Leiden. It was anonymous, to be sure, but Descartes took care that it should be seen by a number of well-qualified philosophers and medical men, and he sent out what we might call review copies. In some cases a single correspondent would receive a number of copies for further distribution, including Vopiscus Fortunatus Plemp of Louvain, whom Descartes had met before 1632

---

[8] Descartes, *Discourse*, ed. Olscamp, p. 40 (p. 49 in the edition of 1637).

and who received three copies. Mersenne must have received several because he forwarded a number of critiques back to the author. Almost certainly the other critics we know of, such as Sylvius and Regius, received copies, and the Frenchman Froidmont certainly did. The Jesuit, P. Vatier, received a copy and sent it on to his doctor.[9] If Descartes' friend Hogelande received a copy, he was too busy to read it. Descartes received replies from all these, from Petit[10] and from others.[11] In the *Discourse* itself Descartes requests the reader to send to the publisher criticisms for response, and he asks his friends to undertake further experiments in order to free Descartes' own time for more thought.

These are not the actions of a retiring and bookish scholar. Indeed, the circumstances of the publication of the book and his subsequent actions suggest a rather startling conclusion: that Descartes had undertaken a campaign to depose Aristotle as The Philosopher and to occupy his place, not only for the reading public, but in the universities. Just as the Calvinists and counter-reformation catholics took care to ensure that only the right philosophy was taught in the universities, so Descartes selected the universities as the target-point for the dissemination of his own creed. We shall see later in this chapter that his campaign in Utrecht was waged in a certain way and with the help of certain people, and here we need to look at the nature of the enterprise and to see how it involved the doctrines of heartbeat and circulation.

We need to remind ourselves that university education had been based on some of the works of Aristotle for about 400 years, since the invention of natural philosophy itself. His works had been arranged by the masters so that at first the student was taught the universal arts, logic and dialectic, as techniques without their own subject matter. He was subsequently taught to apply these techniques to a range of sciences, each with its own and increasingly complex subject matter. The general principles of motion were taught by Aristotle's *Physics* and applied to physical objects in the *Meteorology* and *On the Heavens*, finishing with the physical works with the most complex subject matter, the works on animals.

It was this 'Organon' of Aristotle that Bacon had wanted to replace with his own *Novum Organum*. Whether or not Descartes had Bacon's attempt in mind, it seems that his own enterprise had a similar purpose. It was an ambitious scheme. Not only was Aristotle the universal and traditional authority within the universities, but as we have seen the

---

[9] A–T, I, p. 561.   [10] A–T, II, p. 343.   [11] A–T, I, p. 377.

tradition had been revitalized in their different ways by the catholics and the Calvinists. Opposition to Aristotle in France could (in 1624) lead to exile.[12] The *Discourse* opens with Descartes' account of what was wrong with contemporary education: this was the 'house in which one lives' that had to be pulled down and rebuilt (section III). And to replace the range of Aristotle's physical works was Descartes' *Discourse on Method*, published together with the *Meteorology*, *Dioptrics* and *Geometry*, all of which Descartes called 'essays' in the application of the Method. So, the Method, applicable to each of the sciences, but not of them, was to replace Aristotle's universal arts, which had the same function; the *Geometry* is a technique or science based on the mathematical metaphysic of particulate motion; and the *Dioptrics* (in which light and mathematics are fundamental) and *Meteorology* are examples of sciences in which these techniques are to be applied. The whole recalls the way in which Aristotle's physical works had been arranged. However much the content of Descartes' natural philosophy differed from that of Aristotle, if it was to replace that of Aristotle, it had to fill the similarly-shaped space in the curriculum. One of the characteristics of this shape was that the arts course naturally led on (for those who wished to follow that path) to medicine. Not only did the arts course generally end with one of the more biological of the Aristotelian physical works, but the whole theory of medicine was based on the principles of Aristotle's natural philosophy: 'where the philosopher finishes, there begins the physician' was a common doctor's defence of his own subject. If Descartes was to be successful in replacing Aristotle, he needed a Cartesian medicine. The basis for such a medicine had been hinted at in the *Discourse*, where the motion of the heart and blood has such a prominent place, but Descartes' intention there, no doubt, had been to secure an impact at the philosophical rather than the medical level with his radically new mechanical human body. But the intention he expressed to his friend Hogelande, from whom he was borrowing some medical books, was that having finished the *Discourse* he would now take up the study of medicine. And in the *Discourse* itself Descartes writes that his future plans include establishing better rules for medicine. He hoped that his new philosophy, including the medical

---

[12] Lindeboom, *Descartes and Medicine*, p. 8. One of the few exceptions to the domination of Aristotle in the arts course was at the new, protestant university of Wittenberg, where in the early sixteenth century Millich tried to put together from Pliny a physics that excluded the objectionable features of Aristotle's (the eternity of the world and a non-divine causality). See R.K. French and F. Greenaway (eds.), *Science in the Early Roman Empire* (London, 1986): my chapter on Pliny and renaissance medicine. See also note 31, below.

improvement of the mind, would be as useful in practice as the philosophy of the schools was theoretical.[13]

So for a number of reasons, amongst which were the relationship of natural philosophy and medicine, the attention given to the heart and blood by Descartes, and the structure of university teaching, it was natural that Descartes should seek to link his new natural philosophy to medicine in the universities, or to speak more directly, seek to secure a medical man as his agent in his campaign. During the campaign he actively sought medical information,[14] such as the idiopathy and ontology of disease, the mechanism of fevers, scurvy and occult qualities, coagulation of the blood in ascites and circulation in gangrene. The survey of medicine that he told Huygens about probably included his look at botany and chemistry.[15]

THE DISPUTATION: DESCARTES' CAMPAIGN

Being outside the universities, Descartes needed an agent within. He found one in Henry (Hendrik) de Roy, Regius. Regius in his earlier years had been involved in some unorthodox Calvinism, and he was well-to-do, with Regent connections.[16] He had sought Descartes' acquaintance and adopted some of his views, with, however, considerable 'misunderstanding'. In 1638 Regius was appointed extraordinary teacher of medicine in Utrecht and wrote to Descartes to pay tribute to his physics. As a physician Regius was particularly interested in the circulation, and enquired about the reception of the doctrine.

Whatever Regius lectured on as a professor of medicine, it could not at first have been entirely Cartesian, as the evidence suggests that he and Descartes only slowly built up a Cartesian medicine. What was more effective than lectures on such a subject was the disputation. The advantages of the disputation were clear: they were public, popular, frequent and unpredictable. Members of one faculty could oppose, and insert corollaries into, the theses of another: disputations were newsworthy. Descartes told Mersenne that it was his ultimate aim to oppose 'scholastic' natural philosophy with a course in the form of theses.[17]

From April 1639 Regius, now ordinary professor, began to teach a course that included Cartesian physics. Descartes was on hand to offer advice. (It seems to have been while teaching this course that Regius, now a passionate Cartesian, took the unprecedented step of refusing to

---

[13] Descartes, *Discourse*, ed. Olscamp, p. 50. [14] A–T, III, p. 443 (Descartes to Regius).
[15] Lindeboom, *Descartes and Medicine*, p. 36: A–T, III, pp. 456, 457, 459, 462.
[16] McGahagan, 'Cartesianism in the Netherlands', p. 132. [17] *Ibid.*, p. 168.

allow victory in a disputation to a student proponent with whom he disagreed on the question of magnetism.) It was not long before Regius instituted disputations on the topic of circulation. He was not the first to do so, for Sylvius and Drake had maintained such a thesis in Leiden in Regius's first year as ordinary professor, and Wallaeus (the teacher of Bartholine, also in Leiden) was teaching the circulation in 1639 and 1640, proceeding also by disputation.

It is important to remember that disputations were not merely formal exercises to sharpen the students' powers of argument, nor simply ceremonies accompanying graduation. From the formal description of the disputation published by Heerebord of Leiden in the middle of the century[18] and thus relating to the practice in Leiden at the time when Regius was teaching in Utrecht, it is clear that discovery of truth in the outside world was among the purposes of the disputation. The disputation consisted of a number of theses centred on a theme, and a thesis was defined as a 'germ of truth' derived by the senses from the outside world, from the meaning of words, or from the statement of a teacher. Only in theological disputations was an extensive use of authority encouraged.[19] Although arguments 'from problems in nature' were not to be preferred to those arising from the opponent's presentation of his case, there was a real role for sense experience and experiment. Descartes, drawing on his eleven years of dissection[20] was careful not to allow into theses on his behalf experimental results that he had not personally seen, like the existence of the lacteals, or the experimental inflation of the heart.[21]

These theses were published in advance to allow the opponent to study the form of the propositions and to construct his reply, the antithesis. This would be syllogistic and directed in the first instance at the form of the proposition. Then (if this did not work) followed an attack on the substance of the proposition, where it was legitimate, if the proposer had relied on authority, to quote 'another man equally distinguished and learned'. It was at this point that Descartes, Harvey and experimental results would be quoted.

The published theses, then, constituted a statement of policy or a programme of teaching on behalf of the university teacher involved, and he, as senior proposer or *Praeses*, could intervene to help the junior and to bring the theses (say Heerebord's rules) always to a successful

[18] A. Heerebord, *Ermeneia Logica: seu explicatio tum per notas tum per exempla synopsis logicae Burgerdicianae . . . accedit ejusdem authoris Praxis Logica* (Leiden, 1650), book 2, ch. 23, p. 176.   [19] *Ibid.*, p. 10.   [20] Lindeboom, *Descartes and Medicine*, p. 37.
[21] A–T, III, p. 69.

conclusion. At least in Regius's case the theses were provocative, and their advance publication gave opportunity for partisan feeling to develop before the occasion. It was not unusual for the teacher, having declared his policy in the published theses, to publish the completed disputations as a textbook: in a sense the teacher had 'proved' his arguments and was free to publish and teach. The disputation was one way in which a large number of people might be exposed to, and even persuaded by, a new doctrine.

Regius sent his theses for the disputations proposed for June to Descartes in late May 1640. He took the course (at least he was doing so next year) of sending to Descartes what Descartes called *chartulae* – drafts or projects for theses, so that Descartes could see them at an even earlier stage.[22] The intention was that Descartes, in pursuance of his programme of insinuating his physics into the university, should correct Regius's interpretation of Descartes' physics, here exemplified by circulation. Descartes modified the theses freely, knowing, he wrote to Regius, that Regius's wish was to propose only what was in Descartes' mind. He was also very precise, distinguishing, for example, between effervescence and rarefaction in the heart.[23] Descartes' reply to Regius moved from the existence of God as the basis of the new physics to the motion of air particles in respiration and a correct rendering of the Cartesian theory of ebullition of blood in the heart. Descartes also insisted on the removal of Harvey's and Wallaeus's names from the theses: not only did he want to keep the action and use of the heart Cartesian, but his words reveal that he thought Wallaeus was being used by Harvey in just the same way as Descartes was using Regius, that is, as an agent within the universities to propogate his new doctrine.

The theses reveal how central was circulation to a Cartesian physiology. They begin with digestion, which is simply a mechanical production of blood, and proceed to circulation as a basis for all physiological motions. Descartes clearly saw the forthcoming disputation as an important step in his plans, and he proposed to go to Utrecht himself to hear the proceedings, but secretly, from the hidden chamber from where Anna Maria Schurmanns used to hear lectures.

The theses of 10 June were indeed important. It is worth looking at them in a little detail as they represent a critical stage in the spread of Harvey's doctrine and its relation to mechanism.[24] Advertised as 'Medico-physiological disputations for the circulation' they were due

---

[22] A–T, III, p. 455.   [23] A–T, III, p. 440.   [24] A–T, III, p. 63; XIII, p. 6.

to begin at nine in the morning with Regius as *Praeses* and John Haymann as *Defendens*. Regius began with the need for nutrition due to the loss of material from the living body. The source of the body's food (blood) was as in traditional medicine, the ingested food, but Regius, the opponent of the ancients, insisted that the change of food into blood was not a generation or corruption of substantial forms but a mechanical (and here it is Descartes speaking) adaptation of food particles to render them fit to be components of the body. This is all that is meant by the old 'concoction', Descartes says,[25] and he drops Regius's 'spiritual juice' as an agent in the process because of the ambiguity of the term in a mechanical physiology. 'Concotion' (continues Descartes) occurs generally in all vessels but especially (and in ascending order of importance) in the intestines, liver and heart, where the sequence chyme – chyle – blood is completed. Regius had included a mention of the lacteals but as Descartes had not seen them the corollary was omitted. The final stage of 'concoction', continues Descartes, is caused by the action of the 'pulsific ebullition' on the entering chyle and the returning blood. Descartes gave particular attention to this (thesis 2), modifying what Regius had said.

The account of the heartbeat that follows includes the notion that fermentation was perpetuated by a trace of blood remaining from one action to the next, an idea developed by Descartes in the argument with Plemp, but otherwise little changed from the uncomplicated inflation theory of the *Discourse*. Regius had expressed some doubt about the ebullition within the heart in the thesis as it was sent to Descartes, but the latter would hear of no doubts and asked him to omit it. Perhaps this is why Descartes quotes his experimental evidence to show that blood leaves the heart in a fermentive diastole. Probably this doubt was how the heart can contract at the end of diastole if still full of vapour: Descartes says the *impetus* of blood leaving the heart is such that it is all drawn out, except, perhaps, for the necessary fermentive 'trace' trapped by the closing valves.

It seems that 'circulators' had difficulty in explaining how the blood left the end of the arteries and entered the veins. Harvey had written about 'pores of the flesh' and had wished to avoid Galen's 'anastomoses'. Wallaeus had used *capillimenta* (and had been reviled by Primrose),[26] while other circulators talked of veins 'imbibing' the

[25] A–T, III, p. 67.
[26] J. Primrose, *Animadversiones in Johannis Wallaei Medicinae apud Leydenses Professoris Disputationem Medicam quam pro Circulatione Sanguinis Harveana proposuit: cui addita est ejusdem de usu lienis adversos medicos recentiores sententia* (Amsterdam, 1640): 'upon section 6'.

blood. Such a view seemed to the mechanists as close to 'attraction', and Regius, discussing this transfer of blood and the movement of blood to the heart, sternly warned that 'no attraction exists in nature'.

Regius argues that the need for circulation as a repeated motion of the blood is that proper nutrition of the body takes a long time, and the theses move on to the functions of respiration, its function of cooling the heart and its anatomical basis in the foetus (here again Descartes takes over from Regius's words), its absence in fish and the forceful displacement of air particles into the lungs (in place of 'attractive' *horror vacui*).

All in all, then, Descartes kept a very close eye on what Regius published as theses; whether or not he viewed the disputation from the secret *specula*,[27] he is said to have been satisfied with the proceedings.[28] If so, perhaps he saw that the disputations did not go by unnoticed. The Rector of the university, having heard of the theses and anxious to avoid trouble, had tried to persuade Regius not to defend them, or at least to defend the circulation in a corollary, where it could be presented as a mere intellectual exercise. Regius prevaricated, saying that the theses were already with the printer. The Rector, Schotanus, had the weight of the Senate behind him and relayed to Regius and his associates a formal warning not to sow dissension within the university.

At this stage Voet did not think the affair serious, and even, after the event, approved Regius's intention to reply to Primrose's criticism of the theses, as long as Regius remained impersonal. But in his 'sponge', *Spongia* he used to wipe away the critique, Regius gave way to invective. Thereafter, and perhaps as a result, Voet obtained from the Curators a decree banning the discussion of novelties.

VOET AND THE CALVINISTS

Voet had been professor of theology since 1634. 'Novelties' for him were topics that caused controversy, and Cartesianism was high on his list. What was at stake for Voet was not primarily the circulation. He was concerned with the weightier matters of religious orthodoxy and the stability of Dutch society. We must remember that the United Provinces were still in the process of freeing the Netherlands from Spanish control. Dutch Calvinism of the seventeenth century was shaped partly by the national reaction against Spanish catholicism, but

---

[27] A–T, III, p. 70.   [28] McGahagan, 'Cartesianism in the Netherlands', p. 168.

the reaction was not complete. Contemporaries saw Dutch society as largely Calvinistic with smaller minorities of catholics and of a latitudinarian group of Arminians. The Arminians preached religious toleration and emphasized points of doctrine and piety common to each extreme of the religious spectrum. They found it useful to think in terms of 'natural law' as a common basis for the behaviour of all men, a view expounded in a seminal way by Grotius. Like the related Cambridge Platonists,[29] the Arminians adopted Cartesian philosophy more readily than the Calvinists or catholics, perhaps seeing in the laws of physics impressed by God on man's mind a natural and common feature of all men.

But Arminian religious toleration proved too generous in the United Provinces, and orthodox Calvinists saw a source of conflict in the growth of dissent in an Arminian climate. It was with a feeling that the very stability of Dutch society was at stake that the Calvinists secured the suppression of Arminianism at the Synod of Dort in 1618. Even by then, the Arminians had flirted with the new philosophies of Bacon and Gassendi, while both Calvinists and catholics had reconfirmed Aristotle as the safe and orthodox philosopher for the arts course of the universities. Heerebord's 'new' Aristotle at Leiden from 1641 is an example: Aristotle's categorical logic seemed to reflect the real world and how to argue about it and make discoveries in it. And Aristotelian logic underpinned his natural philosophy and orthodox religion.

Cartesian philosophy in contrast seemed to the Calvinists to be reminiscent of the lax attitudes of the Arminians and their 'new science'. Voet in particular, as the leader of the Calvinists, and the professor of theology and later Rector of the university of Utrecht, was horrified that the whole of the Cartesian natural philosophy was founded upon a doubt about the very existence of God; a doubt moreover, that was resolved by reason, not faith. Maintaining that a knowledge of God was inherent in every man, Voet believed it was a deliberate act of atheism to suppress such instinctive knowledge for the purpose of constructing an intellectual system of the world. His theses on atheism in 1639 may have been prompted by Regius's new course of Cartesian physics.

Voet emerged as the principal antagonist of Cartesianism, and the bitter personal enemy of Descartes, whom he saw as an atheist, or what was almost as bad, a Jesuit. He saw not only Arminians but catholics as

[29] See R.L. Colie, *Light and Enlightenment. A Study of the Cambridge Platonists and Dutch Arminians* (Cambridge, 1957).

being dangerously lax in doctrinal matters, and he set his face firmly
against any kind of new natural philosophy. Voet[30] made the powerful
connection between atheism and social revolution, arguing that some
atheists wanted to overthrow both the natural order and the order of
society and the nation. This was the danger of a *rational* system of the
world, Voet held, that there was no *moral* control over where it might
lead. Much preferable to Cartesianism was the 'Mosaic' physics[31] that
could be gained from the scriptures, where faith provided a greater
guarantee than reason. For the same reason Voet held that theologians
had a right and a duty to question the use of reason in philosophy.

The circulation of the blood was offensive to Voet for these reasons
and for another, that in Cartesian dress, it denied the powers of the soul
within physiology. The same criticism had been made by Froidmont,
who had received a 'review copy' of the *Discourse* from Descartes in
1637. Descartes felt that he had been unfairly compared with the
ancient atomists by Froidmont, and this kind of reaction must have
made him aware of the dangers of being labelled as a materialistic
atheist. The personal battle between Voet and Descartes was fought
partly with an eye on the politics of religious doctrine. When Regius
was preparing more theses, including some on circulation, for disputation in April and May 1641,[32] Descartes asked for his name to be
removed from them and emphasized his own conception of the single
(not triple, as Regius had said) thinking-substance soul that was all the
church could ask for, but which played no part in the physiology. Voet,
now Rector, did not intervene when the magistrates ordered the theses
to be printed, but after the disputation (defended by Regius and his
pupil de Raey) objected to the Cartesian location of the soul in the
pineal gland and the apparent lack of distinction between the living
and dead 'animal machine'.[33] It was during 1641 in particular, when
Regius was maintaining at least five sets of theses in favour of a
Cartesian circulation that it is clear that both he and Descartes were
developing a 'Cartesian medicine', with details of physiology and
pathology. Both events – the epistolary defence of Cartesian circulation and the development of Cartesian medicine – can be seen as part of
Descartes' plan to develop his physics into the traditional extension of
physics, medicine.

[30] McGahagan, 'Cartesianism in the Netherlands', p. 162.
[31] Cf. note 12 and the attractions of a Plinian–Mosaic and anti-Aristotelian physics. See also
McGahagan, 'Cartesianism in the Netherlands', p. 164.   [32] A–T, II, p. 370.
[33] This was a persistent criticism of Cartesian mechanical physiology, which Hogelande also
faced (p. 126 of his book: see note 47). If the soul is simply reason, or thought, then its removal
from the body should render the body irrational or thoughtless, but not dead.

These disputations of 1641 show that Descartes' careful modifications to the theses before they were disputed were less respected by Regius than before. At the end of November one of Regius's students inserted a corollary about the circulation, described as 'elliptical', into a thesis to be disputed by mathematicians. The corollary was only half-heartedly opposed to circulation ('it is probable, but we prefer to stay with the old opinion'), but Regius insisted on it being changed. He argued that it was no business of mathematicians to argue medical theses, and that he felt medicine was under attack. Unknown to him, however, the respondent secretly deleted Harvey's name from the corollary, inserted Regius's and sent the theses off to be printed. This made it appear that Regius was again, and in defiance of promises already made, seeking to reject the traditional views of the university, and doing so by irregular means. Regius and the other professors were annoyed, no doubt for different reasons, and Regius attempted to defend circulation in the ensuing disputation.

Feelings were perhaps still running high from the two earlier controversial disputations on circulation (in June 1640 and May 1641) when Regius made a strategical error. We have already seen that the Cartesian position was attacked on the grounds that to explain the motion of the heart by machinery was demeaning to the substantial lower soul, and also that to attribute any physiological activity to the immortal soul was unorthodox. Regius took the Cartesian doctrine that the soul as thinking unextended substance was a category mutually exclusive to matter as extended and unthinking, and developed the thesis that man, composed of both mutually exclusive categories, was a unified being only *per accidens*.

But this time Regius published the theses (December 1641) without first showing them to Descartes. When he read them, Descartes was horrified and at once wrote to Regius that they were difficult, offensive and even criminal.[34] He urged Regius not to offend the theologians and the university; to insert a corollary saying that *per accidens* was meant 'in a certain way', not 'absolutely'; to agree that the soul is ideally suited to the body, and so the union of the two is of the very essence.

It is not clear that Regius adopted any of Descartes' advice. Probably not, for at the disputation on 8 December, there was shouting and stamping as one medical student argued for the new philosophy and another opposed it. The disturbance broke out a second time as a theology student took issue with Regius's pupil, who was defending his

[34] A–T, III, p. 459.

new medicine. In a third outbreak Regius's students and followers made such a disturbance, intimidating the opposition with aggressive displays, that the theology student was prevented from making his case. Regius succeeded in quelling the display, but did not help the situation by declaring that the disputation was purely medical and did not concern theologians. Nevertheless, the theology student pressed ahead with his syllogisms which (if we are to believe the official version of the affair, which is heavily biased against Regius) Regius found it difficult to answer. But his students made up any deficiency with a new outburst of stamping, which even Regius said was an insult to the university. The disputation came to an untimely end and as the Rector and professors left so in a new tumult the *medicus* 'seemed to explode'.

The university held a post mortem. The theology students explained that they had been offended at Regius's attack on the decent old philosophy, yet could not obtain the satisfaction of a proper disputation because of Regius's poor dialectical powers. Regius did not accept with good grace Voet's warning to avoid 'paradoxes' and returned to the topic during the course of a lecture three days later. Towards the end of December there were further disputations on circulation and Cartesian medicine.

But it was essentially the end of Descartes' attempt to introduce his physics to Utrecht. Voet began a campaign against Descartes with three days of disputations in the same December, largely on substantial forms, and Descartes and Regius collaborated on the replies. Voet's personal battle with Descartes was based on the desirability of maintaining university tradition in a situation where there was great danger of dissension. It has been suggested[35] that Voet chose this line because he could not rely on the support of the magistrates; Descartes on the other hand relied on the tolerant ethos of the Regents, which he hoped would allow Regius his course. The Regents were indeed sympathetic, but felt obliged to support the Academic Senate against a single teacher, and in the following year Voet secured from the Senate a prohibition against the new philosophy. However, this was not ratified by the magistrates. The fate of the new philosophy and its contained circulation was not, then, decided on intellectual grounds during these years, but on political, religious and pedagogic; the Senate's case was partly that the new philosophy was destructive of the usual curriculum, and prevented students from following related topics.[36] As observed above, the arts curriculum was Aristotelian, and the arts course

---

[35] By McGahagan, 'Cartesianism in the Netherlands', p. 174.   [36] *Ibid.*

was the basis of other disciplines. As the Senate and Descartes no doubt realized, there could be no piecemeal replacement of traditional teaching.

The personal battle between Voet and Descartes turned into a legal battle over a libel, and Voet was able to secure a ban on printed matter attacking theses defended at Utrecht. Descartes also conducted the battle on political lines, painting Voet as a rabble-raiser, a potential theocratic dictator who threatened civil order, and attempting to associate his own philosophy with the magisterial class. In some cases the magistrates seemed to Voet to be tainted with catholicism, and Descartes thought he could win over the magistrates by playing on their fears for their position if such a man as Voet should be allowed to continue to threaten popular disturbance by acting above his station as a university teacher. But the magistrates saw Descartes as a Jesuit and a threat to their university: they interviewed him, Regius and Voet, decided that the overriding need was stability, and returned the university to Aristotle.

LEIDEN

A similar series of events occurred in Leiden, where there was a Cartesian crisis in the mid 1640s. Harvey's doctrine was not so involved in the crisis as in Utrecht, but teaching it clearly fell into the area of the philosophical 'novelties' that were being fought over.

The 'new Aristotle' of the Calvinists was presented by Adriaan Heerebord in his inaugural lecture of 1641. The new way of looking at Aristotle, explained Heerebord, was to free him from the quibblings of the scholastics that had tied Aristotle down not only to a certain mode of philosophizing, but to the wrong kind of theology. According to Heerebord, the process of revealing the true Aristotle had begun in the renaissance and was being continued by the reformation, so that a new Aristotle now stood side by side with a pristine theology.

But, for Heerebord, so thoroughly had Aristotle been liberated that it was possible to bring his natural philosophy up to date quite radically. He read Aristotle in a very protestant way, arguing that a study of nature – of which Aristotle's physical works were a good example – leads to a knowledge of God.[37] But Descartes also claimed that his own natural philosophy showed the direct action of God in the

[37] The so-called 'natural historians' who had studied animated and vegetative nature from the early sixteenth century to Heerebord's own time were almost without exception motivated by the same feelings, and most of them were protestant.

world, and Heerebord was apparently able to interpret Cartesian and Aristotelian natural philosophy as though they were not incompatible. When Adam Stuart, a rigid Scots presbyterian and determined anti-Cartesian was promoted over his head, Heerebord became more Cartesian than ever. In 1664 he had a student defend Cartesian theses about the necessity of rejecting old knowledge to reach the new, that clear and distinct ideas are true, and that the cause of error is will running ahead of intellect. These read very much like the stages in Descartes' own progress to truth, and each is very closely paralleled in the tracts in the book by Hogelande, the Leiden physician discussed below, who may well have attended these disputations.

But trouble was not long in coming. Stuart objected to Heerebord's theses of 1644, and in the following year it was clear that the Cartesian *dubito* was worrying the theologians, that is, that a whole scheme of philosophy should be founded on a doubt about the very existence of God. Heerebord defended it in October of that year. For a number of years the philosophers and theologians kept up a war of disputations on such topics as this, whether Descartes was an atheist, Pelagian or blasphemer, and whether the two faculties could poach each other's topics (the philosophy disputations generally attracted students away from the theological).[38] In January 1647 Heerebord presented a thoroughly Cartesian oration. By now Descartes' *Principia* and *Meditations* had been published, and the theologians had all the more material to attack Descartes with. In May 1647 Trigland was disputing against Descartes as a blasphemer, and Descartes reported to Princess Elisabeth of Bohemia that he had been theologically savaged at Leiden. The Curators warned Heerebord to stick to Aristotle, and tried to suppress the circulation of pamphlets and to ensure that theses were published well in advance. There were riots on the Utrecht scale when the Scot, Stuart, disputed in Leiden in 1647 and 1648 against neoterics.

As in Utrecht, the battle was far from merely academic or intellectual. The theologians such as Revius and Trigland were concerned with the integrity of belief of the Calvinist church against the laxity of the Arminians and the wiles of the Jesuits, with order in university and society, and with people's immortal souls. Descartes' weapons were not only intellectual – the argument that philosophy should be separate from theology – but they were also special pleading and political: he argued with the Curators that his case should be judged by the magistrates, not by academics, and he successfully secured the help of

[38] McGahagan, 'Cartesianism in the Netherlands', p. 238.

the Prince of Orange and the French ambassador. But finally, in 1647, historical accidents robbed him of the support of both. His attempt to become the Philosopher had failed. On 30 August 1649 Descartes committed his papers to the care and discretion of his friend Hogelande (asking only that the correspondence between Mersenne and Voet should be preserved) and departed for Sweden.

CIRCULATORS IN LEIDEN

So while Descartes' campaign failed in Leiden as in Utrecht, yet in Leiden the doctrine of circulation was distanced from Descartes' natural philosophy. It was not taught in Leiden, as it had been in Utrecht, by a medical man as a principal example of mechanism. It was in fact taught by Sylvius (Deleboe), who had argued a series of disputations in its favour in 1639.[39] Sylvius was no mechanist, and was not, as Regius had been, an agent of Descartes. For him motion in the body was not transmitted, particle-to-particle, but arose locally, as did the effervescence of mixed chemicals, or the fermentation of plant juices. And these were different kinds of motion, not (as they were to Cartesians like Hogelande) simply different manifestations of increased intestine motion. Although the 'innate fire' of the heart was the central physiological activity, it was for Sylvius a fire maintained by the blood, without reference to wider, or Cartesian principles.

In short, Sylvius found attractions in some contemporary accounts of the workings of the body, and like everyone else was very selective in what he adopted. What he chose to adopt from Harvey and Descartes was determined by what was already in his mind. (He had probably been sent copies of the *Discourse* and he appears to have read *De Motu Cordis* because he credits Harvey by name for 'also' knowing the *ratio* and causes of the circulation.) His account of the heartbeat 'misunderstands' both Harvey and Descartes, for while the blood is said to expand by reason of the heat of the heart, yet this expansion is followed by a muscular contraction of the walls of the ventricles, expelling the blood. It is clear that, being sympathetic to 'chemical' explanations, he found Descartes' account of ebullition attractive; but not being a Cartesian, he had no need to seek a single, fire-without-light source of

---

[39] 1639 is given as the date of the defence of these theses by Keynes, *The Life of William Harvey*, p. 449. They were published in 1663. I have used the edition of 1693: *Francisci Deleboe Sylvii ... Opera Medica, hoc est, Disputationum Medicarum decas* (Geneva, 1693). Here, as was the case with other authors, having 'proved' his theses by successful disputation, the teacher published them as a text.

motion in the body. Indeed, the contraction of the ventricle walls was a
motion generated separately: it was 'animal' motion. In contrast, the
expansive diastole was 'natural'. Like other authors mentioned in this
chapter, he thought it necessary to identify the *propria motio* of the
heart, its own, proper and essential motion, directed towards the
function of the heart as a part of the body, without a knowledge of
which anatomical knowledge of the part was incomplete. Here we are
deep into academic theory of medicine, drawn from Galen and Aristotle and refined in the physicians' continuing dialogue with the
philosophers. It is the very structure of Sylvius's thought that determines what questions he will bring to bear on the topic of the action
and use of the heart, and it is a structure that as a medical man he had
no reason to abandon in favour of the radically different Cartesian
world-picture. Descartes recognized this. Having objected that there
can be no 'animal' motions in the separated pieces of an eel's heart,
distant from the soul that was considered to exercise such faculties,[40]
Descartes saw that he would not succeed with Sylvius (and urged
Regius to be gentle in further correspondence to Sylvius: Descartes
marked out the difficult passages for Regius's convenience).[41]

Also teaching the circulation in Leiden was Wallaeus. According to
his pupil, Thomas Bartholine, he was the first to do so (in 1640) from
the professorial chair.[42] Wallaeus also proposed theses for disputation.
They were attacked by James Primrose, who was almost a professional
opponent of Harvey, having written a sizeable book against *De Motu
Cordis* in 1630 and a critique of Regius's disputations in Utrecht a
decade later. Primrose was doubtless known (as Harvey's first opponent) to those disputing about circulation in the Dutch universities,
and it would have been for this reason that he was sent copies of the
publications (Regius sent him those from Utrecht). Primrose is a figure
whom historians, if they could, would equally condemn as ignore as
the man who opposed Harvey simply by reasserting the traditional
position and so being unable to see the truth when faced with it. It is
certainly true that Primrose did not like the neoterics, and he seems also
to have enjoyed controversies. But it is unlikely that he was simply
stubbornly blind to the truth. Like our other authors, his truth was
what he found worth fighting for, and part of his overall interpretation
of the world.

Primrose's world was that of the practical doctor. The purpose of

[40] A–T, III, pp. 444, 445.
[41] McGahagan, *Cartesianism in the Netherlands*, p. 13; A–T, XII, p. 25.
[42] A–T, XII, p. 25.

medicine, the reason for being a doctor was practice, and circulation and the 'circulators' added nothing to this end, and indeed distracted attention from it. Primrose was not in a university, and saw their internal squabbles with a different perspective. The ten years he spent in practice after his first rebuttal of Harvey he considers as the real source of wisdom in medicine. In contrast, he observes, academic medical men are naturally drawn to the theoretical and readily given to controversies and disputations, which he scornfully dismisses as 'these frequent games'. The insignificance of these games is also implied by Primrose's remark (made three times) that even his own rebuttal of Harvey of 1630 was the work of a mere two weeks[43] and that of the Leiden theses, though subtle, a matter of hours. In contrast, his ten years of practice have confirmed for him the true sources of medicine, Hippocrates and Galen. Disputations, subtle argument, the charm of novelty, the desire to be conspicuous – all vices of academic medicine – inevitably destroy rather than decorate medicine, warns Primrose, adding that the common opinion of the medical world was divided on the topic of circulation (so ingenious but so useless), but divided not on the basis of reason, rather of fashion.

Turning to the contents of Wallaeus's theses, Primrose was surprised to find no reference at all to the proemium and first seven chapters of Harvey's book. We have already seen than many medical men disarticulated Harvey's doctrine at this point, substituting for their own broader purposes some other explanation of the heartbeat. But Primrose had no broader purpose than to totally oppose Harvey's doctrine, which he regarded as the height of useless ingenuity. He had no novelty of his own which caused him to 'misunderstand' Harvey: indeed, to use the word in its ordinary sense, he did not misunderstand Harvey at all, but understood and disagreed to an equal and great degree. Or to put it another way, his own novelty was that he fancied his early critique of Harvey had given him a degree of fame.[44] As a defender of established medicine he had become acquainted with Harvey's doctrine thoroughly and at first hand.

In contrast, he claimed that before reading the Leiden and Utrecht theses, he had not heard of Descartes. So it is not surprising that on reading the Utrecht theses (of June 1640), which he though should have been about Harvey, he was not aware of their role in the battle for and against Descartes' natural philosophy, the battle that caused both the

---

[43] J. Primrose, *Animadversiones in Theses, quas pro Circulatione sanguinis in academia Ultrajacensi D Henricus le Roy, ibidem Medicinae Professor, Disputandas posuit* (Leyden, 1640), preface.   [44] *Ibid.*

'omission' of half of what Harvey had said, and the changes that Primrose saw in what was left.[45] Similarly, the Leiden theses reflect a local interest in chemical explanations, and Primrose, who thought he was commenting on a Harveian question, could not see the relevance of comparing circulation to the *circulatio*, (repeated distillation) of the chemists. It is a mere similarity of names, he said: Harvey's *circulatio* is imaginary, that of the chemists very real: blood is not distilled within the body because blood is actually destroyed in distillation and does not condense again into blood. So, adds Primrose, there can be no rarefaction and condensation of blood within the body, and no closed structure like the retort that compels the distilled liquid to return to the boiling mixture. But Primrose probably did not know of Descartes' ebullition theory of heartbeat, or how that would have interested those at Leiden who were sympathetic to chemical explanations. When he complains that the disputants do not understand Harvey, he does not see the purpose of the theses.

HOGELANDE

In 1637 arguably the most luminous man of the seventeenth-century 'scientific revolution', Descartes, met certainly one of the obscurest, Cornelis von Hogelande. Descartes was in Leiden, seeing the *Discourse* through the press; Hogelande was a doctor, practising at his house nearby, where, dressed in slippers and night-cap, he would dispense medicine free to the poor from eight till ten in the morning and again for a time after lunch. They became friends, and Hogeland acted as a minor post-office for Descartes, forwarding and redirecting his letters[46] (and as we have seen, finally being left with Descartes' trunk of minor correspondence).

It seems that Descartes found Hogelande's medical knowledge of interest, for as discussed earlier, it was his intention to extend his natural philosophy into medicine, and he borrowed some medical books from Hogelande. Perhaps too Descartes felt some sympathy for a fellow catholic of a genteel family. As for Hogelande, he conceived a great admiration for Descartes, and although professing never to have read a word that he had written, Hogelande composed a tract on mechanical physiology that reflected Descartes' doctrines very closely. No doubt he had talked to friends who had read Descartes'

[45] *Ibid.*, preface and *passim*.
[46] A–T, III, p. 21; Lindeboom, *Descartes and Medicine*, p. 29.

natural philosphy, perhaps as a result of Descartes sending out review copies of the *Discourse*.[47] This tract of Hogelande's was published in 1646 (and again in 1676) and is concerned very largely with the circulation of the blood as the determining fact of the new physiology. This tract did not remain entirely unread, and Bartholine's important anatomy text lists Hogelande along with Wallaeus and Descartes as those who had established the ebullition of blood in the heart. Indeed, 'Hogelandian effervescence' was used by an Irishman in attacking Harvey's English followers somewhat later.[48]

The reason for including a discussion of Hogelande here is not his 'influence', or that he is an example (of some category of person) in reacting to Descartes' version of the circulation. It is that in Hogelande we can see more clearly than in more concise or single-minded writers how existing religious beliefs determined what he had accepted from discussions about Descartes' new doctrines, or from his correspondence with Descartes. We shall also see that what he wrote was partly determined, too, by the progress of Cartesian physics in the university of Leiden.

Hogelande begins his book with a brief tract on the existence of God. This is as fundamental to his system as it had been to Descartes. God's relationship to man is that man is created as the image on earth of God's wisdom (the sun is the image of God's activity) and the substantial link is the immortal soul. The rest of the book is curiously organized: the dissertation on mechanical physiology follows directly, and is a brief account of how the blood is manufactured and circulated, together with the generation of spirits and secretions as the result of circulation.

So Hogelande's argument rests on God as Creator making man as the image of His wisdom. This means not only that man's clear and distinct ideas, in Cartesian fashion, are true, but that they are concerned with the simple and intelligible categories of extension, motion and thought. Descartes and Hogelande believed that by making clear God's direct connection with the physical world and its laws, they had strengthened orthodox religion, while the 'scholastics'' attention to secondary causes, faculties, form and privation, Hogelande believed,

---

[47] C.ab Hogelande, *Cogitationes quibus Dei Existentia; item Animae Spiritalitas, et possibilis cum corpore unio, demonstrantur: necnon brevis Historia Oeconomiae Corporis Animalis, proponitur, atque Mechanice explicitur. His accedit Tractatus de Praedestinate* (Leyden, 1676), dedication.

[48] E.de Meara, *Examen diatribae Thomae Willisii, Doctoris Medici et Professoris Oxoniensis, de Febribus* (London, 1665), p. 3; the heartbeat perhaps arises *ex Hogelandico fermento* or from Cartesian fire.

obscured the logical and causal primacy of God. Neither Hogelande nor Descartes could, then, accept the new Aristotle of either the Calvinists or the counter-reformation. But neither could Hogelande, as a catholic, agree with the latitudinarian toleration that had favoured Cartesian physics and 'new science' in general. It was suddenly clear to Hogelande why Descartes' physics reflected physical truth and the truths of catholicism: predestination. This idea occurred to him at a critical point in the history of Cartesian physics in Leiden, and he set it down on paper to be included in the second edition of his book, where the publisher, unwilling to disturb the type of the earlier edition, printed it after the general conclusion but bearing a note indicating that it should be inserted directly after the proof of the existence of God.

The doctrine of predestination was available to orthodox catholics as a development of Augustinian teaching on fore-ordination, God's previous selection of those who are to be saved. It was a doctrine also, not only available, but emphasized by the Calvinists. It was on this point alone that many latitudinarian protestants had broken with the strict Calvinists, refusing to believe that a life of good works would not influence one's salvation. So Arminians and related groups who seemed in many cases to be responsive to Cartesian physics did not believe in predestination. In contrast, it now seemed to Hogelande that he had another and a major reason to bind Cartesian physics to catholicism. God is by definition, he argued, omniscient and omnipotent. It clearly follows that He knows what every man will choose when presented with a choice: there is free will in human terms but not in God's great plan. Nothing that will happen in the world as a result of human choice will be arbitrary. It also follows that in allowing for a mathematical working out of the motion of particles that compose the world, God knows every motion that will occur. The whole world runs in a predestined way, like a great machine without random or arbitrary motion, and its laws of motion, laid down by God, are potentially, at least, intelligible by man. Mechanism in the motion of the heavenly bodies as in the effervescence of blood in the heart is the Natural Necessity of God's laws, '. . . mechanically or automatically, like the actions and motions of a clock . . . a clock from which man differs in this, that he is conscious of his actions or affections'.[49] His 'theological' treatment of the subject, a second essay, is based on biblical quotation: he is able to demonstrate that revealed knowledge agrees with rational, philosophical knowledge.

[49] '. . . mechanice vel automatice, instar actionum motuumque horologium . . . a quibus homo in eo proprie differe videtur, quod actionum passionumque suarum conscius sibi sit'. Hogelande, *Cogitationes*, p. 143.

In this way Hogelande was able to link up two areas of experience important to him, and the result, of course, was a mutual confirmation. Now, *before* he had thought of predestination his link between his physiology and his religion was little more than the rational and partly Cartesian demonstration of the existence of God and the laws of nature. Because mechanism is so important to the doctrine of the action and use of the heart in this chapter, let us look briefly at Hogelande's first image of it, before he thought about predestination. His discussion of 'what it is to think mechanically' comes (characteristically) in the middle of an enormous footnote on the action of the valves of the heart. At its simplest, to think mechanically is (he says) to accept the laws of mechanics, to 'deduce mechanically.'.[50] The striking thing about the opening and closing of the cardiac valves for Hogelande is that it is simply the mechanical behaviour of blood that operates the valves: there is no *purpose* in the closing of the aortic valve as the blood recently ejected into the aorta presses back to the heart. So 'thinking mechanically' excludes 'reasons sought from purpose'.[51] That is not to say that God or nature has not used purpose in making the structure, but the (Cartesian) 'clear and distinct' ideas that we use to investigate the part are the laws of mechanics. All bodies, all their motions, actions and affections 'are to be examined and explained' *mechanice* – not only are they machines, but our reasoning must be 'mechanical' because there is no other valid form of reason or demonstration. Hogelande says this expressly excludes the sympathies, antipathies, and *archei* used by the philosophers as explanatory principles, together with the four elementary qualities, which they used as agents of action.

Hogelande's doctrine grew more elaborate, I think, as he kept pace with what was going on in the battle for and against Descartes in Leiden. Perhaps he attended the disputations, which as Primrose reminded his readers, were public. Certainly Heerebord's theses of 1644 are on topics very similar to those of the tracts in Hogelande's book, and we would expect a friend and admirer of Descartes to interest himself in Descartes' campaign in the universities. Perhaps too, he listened to Sylvius in Leiden, for they both, referring to procedure in natural philosophy, used the same phrase, preferring to be led by the 'Duke of Reason' (*dux*, leader) and to have Count Experience (*comes*, companion) simply as a fellow traveller.[52] Nor was the theological side of the battle lost on Hogelande. He even addresses the topic of the difference between a living and dead body, raised in Utrecht against Descartes' notion of the soul (see above) by means of a

[50] *Ibid.*, p. 9.   [51] *Ibid.*, pp. 122–5.   [52] Sylvius, *Opera Medica*, p. 3.

footnote discussing what happens to flies in the winter.[53] But much more important, his commitment to Descartes was tempered by a concern for the local theological opposition. His proof of God's existence, prior to all other proofs, was not the resolution of a Cartesian *dubito* that offended the theologians of Utrecht and Leiden, but the argument from design, principally in relation to the heart, and the impossibility of an infinite regress of causes. His tract on the soul emphasized the soul's nature as the image of God's reason, rather than its (Cartesian) distinction from the body. When he postulated (see below) a possible means of union of soul and body, his speculative tone suggests that he was searching for a philosophically sound way of avoiding the difficulties of the Cartesian body–soul dualism; or more likely, of avoiding the disastrous *per accidens* thesis of Regius. When in 1653 he added to his tracts another on predestination, as an explanation of mechanism, it was surely a response to the discussions by the Leiden theologians about free will (and the freedom of philosophizing). Certainly, the relevance of his tracts in a controversy was recognized by his publisher, who brought out in Leiden an edition, including the tract on predestination, in 1676, the year in which Cartesian theses were banned in Leiden. Perhaps, indeed, Hogelande hoped that his treatment of predestination would be acceptable to the strict Calvinists, for whom this was an important dogma, and lead to a sympathetic hearing for mechanism among them.[54]

HOGELANDE AND THE HEARBEAT: A REVIEW OF THE PLEMP PROBLEM

Descartes – and Hogelande – gave such a notable place to the heartbeat and circulation that these two motions became the best example of microcosmic mechanism. It was such a good example – of great interest to men who were being told their bodies were machines – that the heartbeat and circulation provided good 'advertising' for Descartes' natural philosophy, just as in turn, mechanism, it is argued above, made the motion of the heart and blood attractive to a wider audience. Thus Beverwyck, who wrote to Harvey[55] to say that 'every-

---

[53] Hogelande, *Cogitationes*, p. 126.
[54] As Laurence Brockliss pointed out at the first hearing of this chapter, predestination was not necessarily part of strict catholic doctrine. Perhaps Hogelande's interpretation was informed by an attempt to make mechanism attractive to the Calvinists.
[55] Beverwyck's letter to Harvey: J. Beverovicius, *Exercitatio in Hippocratis Aphorismum de Calculo. Accedunt doctorum epistolae* (Leyden, 1641), pp. 190–9.

one here' accepted the circulation, also wrote to Descartes (in 1643) asking for the mechanical demonstrations by which Descartes had strengthened the theory of circulation.[56] (Descartes' reply was to give a review of the argument he had with Plemp, which is discussed below).

I have discussed in the earlier parts of this chapter the internal reason why circulation was attractive to Descartes – the derivation of all bodily motions from a single source by transmitted motion of particles – and it is the same reason that caused Descartes to 'misunderstand' Harvey and substitute his own account of the heartbeat. We have also seen that others, with Descartes' mechanical preconceptions, substituted different accounts of the action of the heart. The same is true of Hogelande and Plemp, and it will be convenient to begin with the latter.

The 'problem with Plemp' began when Descartes sent him three 'review copies' of the *Discourse* and its *Essays* in 1637. Plemp was busy writing his own textbook, and he did not believe that the blood circulated or that the body worked mechanically. It was January of the next year before he gave Descartes a considered reply. In the meantime another recipient of the *Discourse*, Froidmont, told Plemp that he thought Descartes' comparison of the heat of the heart with that of wet hay was poor, and that the heat of the heart was not great enough to rarefy blood. Froidmont thought, in fact, that the lower part of the soul performed its traditional, noble function, and to deny this ran the risk either of attributing the same function to the immortal soul, with the attendant risks of materialism and 'atheism', or using ignoble causes such as mechanism.[57] Plemp forwarded these criticisms to Descartes. Descartes' lengthy reply denies the substantiality of the soul and re-states the basis of his natural philosophy. Blood, he says in reply to Froidmont, rarefies at a lesser heat than other liquids.

When Plemp first replied to Descartes he agreed with Froidmont that the heart was not hot enough to vaporize blood. Before replying he had performed the experiment of removing a heart from a living animal and dividing it into pieces. Even in this state, it continued to beat: clearly, said Plemp, *inflation* of the heart by the entry and effervescence of blood could not be the cause of its motion.[58] Descartes appears to have found this objection uncomfortable. He told Mersenne that he thought Plemp had used every possible argument

[56] J. Beverovicius, *Epistolicae Quaestiones cum doctorum Responsis. Accedit ejusdem necnon Erasmi, Cardani, Melanchthonis medicinae Encomium* (Rotterdam, 1644), p. 118.
[57] A–T, I, p. 402.   [58] A–T, I, p. 496; Beverwyck, *Epistolicae Quaestiones*, p. 122.

against him,[59] and his reply to Plemp (15 February 1638) is long,
elaborate and difficult. He says he had repeated Plemp's experiments,
using fish rather than quadrupeds as their hearts continued to beat
longer during vivisection. The main plank of his defence is to introduce
the notion of *fermentation* in place of inflation. In the excised heart,
says Descartes, he has often seen, or judged, that blood was falling
from some higher part of the heart to the lower, where the pulsation
occurs. We can recall that in the *Discourse* he had said that the blood
enters the heart in large quantities, as indicated by the size of the
vessels. He here is at pains to insist that the quantity is very small. In the
vivisected heart, at least, the merest drop will suffice for pulsation. The
heart, he continues, has been habituated from its embryonic origin to
pulsate, and in the grown animal does so with such facility that the
smallest possible force will ensure its continuation.[60] In the vivisected
and divided heart, said Descartes, facing Plemp's most powerful
objection, these small drops of blood, falling on the pieces of the heart,
are activated by a ferment hidden in the recesses of the heart's substance. 'Fermentation' is the heat and ebullition sometimes seen in the
mixing of two liquids, and is of course entirely mechanical. (He later
supposed that traces of blood remaining in the heart from a previous
diastole would act as a ferment in the same way as a little yeast from
one brewing is used to begin another.)

This fermentation theory is very different from the account given of
the heartbeat in the *Discourse* and it seems clear that it is a major
modification of Descartes' views forced on him by Plemp's criticisms
and experiments. Experiments were important devices in the business
of promoting one's own doctrine. We can even see Descartes' experiments as part of his campaign in the universities: Plemp was the
practicus at Louvain[61] and as a teacher was in a good position to
promote Descartes' doctrine if he could only be convinced. Experiments had long been part of the armoury of practical medical men, and
Descartes was obliged to adopt their practice. Experimental vivisection of the heart and arteries had been used with great effect by Galen,
Colombo and Harvey. Plemp and Descartes knew this, and their
experiments were real, not literary devices. Plemp repeated Galen's
experiment of inserting a reed into an artery to prove that the pulsific
faculty is transmitted in the arterial tunic, but Descartes replied that

---

[59] A–T, II, p. 192.
[60] Beverwyck, *Epistolicae Quaestiones*, p. 127. V.F. Plemp, *Fundamenta Medicinae* (Louvain,
1654), pp. 128–30.
[61] He is so described on the title page of the *Fundamenta Medicinae*: see note 69 below, and
Lindeboom, *Descartes and Medicine*, p. 17.

(like Harvey) he thought the experiment too difficult to do properly and that he had not done it (and anyway that it was unnecessary as the mechanical laws proved the matter).

Descartes' experiments provided him with a range of results from which he could choose those that agreed most closely with his doctrines. As we have seen, his doctrines did not survive entirely unscathed, but he selected evidence to uphold the main contention, that diastole was forceful and during it blood left the heart. He advises his readers, in repeating the experiment, not to use dogs because their hearts have various twistings, *anfractus*, in which the expanding blood falsely makes the heart look smaller. No, the Cartesian truth is better seen in rabbits, in which the *certissimum experimentum* should be performed: expose the heart and a length of the aorta, ligate the latter at some distance from the heart, and perforate it between the ligature and the heart. Descartes claimed that blood emerged from the wound as the heart was in diastole, expansion. This was precisely the experiment that Harvey had used in preparing the anatomy lectures, with quite the opposite result. In another experiment Descartes cut the tip off the heart to see with greater ease the expansion and contraction of the heart on the inside. In a real misunderstanding of Harvey, Descartes attributes to him the belief that the heart dilates and receives blood in systole.

Plemp replied to Descartes in the following month (March 1638),[62] again defending the orthodox medical opinion. Here he makes it plain that like Froidmont and most of his fellow physicians, he held that it was the soul that was the cause of the heart's motions. But the vivisection experiments caused as much trouble for Plemp as for Descartes, because they implied that the soul was divisible along with its subject body. Plemp's conclusion was that the *anima* was not divisible and remained in the body, and that its function in the separated heart was carried out for a time by its agents, the spirits. He also attacked Descartes' new theory of fermentation within the heart. Was it not the case that all fermentive changes were slow and quite different in their nature from the rapid beating of the heart? And was it not absurd to say that the heat in the hearts even of cold fish vaporized the blood? Surely, said Plemp, our hands are hotter than the hearts of fish, but fish's blood does not boil in them. Nor did Plemp see in his vivisection any blood dropping from a higher to a lower part of the heart, as Descartes had imagined.

[62] Beverwyck, *Epistolicae Quaestiones*, p. 139; A–T, II, p. 52.

Descartes' second reply to Plemp, in answer to this, is even more involved than the first, and he again shifts his ground on the central topic of fermentation and inflation. He now argues firstly that the behaviour of the vivisected heart is unnatural, and secondly that the fermentation–inflation explanation does not apply to all parts of the heart. Thus the blood in the auricles is said to effervesce little or not at all, at least in the mutilated and dying heart. In the entire and vigorous heart the filling of the auricles is also seen, and in both cases, says Descartes, the auricles also pour out their blood (in its normal state) into the ventricles, as can be seen when the tip of the ventricles has been removed. This, in the dying heart, may happen two or three times before the ventricle itself contracts. Descartes distinguishes the motion of the whole of the upper part of the heart – the insertion of the vessels, the auricles and the substance surrounding the tricuspid valve – from the motion of the ventricles below. Only the latter is regularly inflationary-fermentive. Descartes also develops an explanation that depends on the movement of blood through the small vessels of the heart: the motion is habitual, and so occurs even in the vivisected heart. Where the heart has been cut, the blood emerges like sweat, gradually building up into discrete drops that account for the separated beats of the heart.

In preparing this second letter to Plemp, Descartes had again gone back to the dissecting table. Early in the morning of the day he was writing he excised the heart of a small eel. By the time he came to write the letter, the heart was 'clearly dead' and dry on its upper surface. But Descartes brought it back to life, warming it and injecting into it some blood he had kept for the purpose. It ejected the blood and Descartes appears to want to justify the original fire-without-light notion, combined with the new explanation based on fermentation. But it was still a forceful diastole that ejected the blood in the normal heart, he insisted; it was only when he cut off the right auricle that he found that the blood emerging from the damaged surface stimulated the remainder of the heart into a *different* kind of motion: perhaps we can guess that he saw contraction and considered it the unnatural activity of a damaged heart. He put the separated right ventricle into another bowl of blood and found that it did not beat until the drying blood began to form a skin. His explanation was that the open vessels of the excised auricle allowed a free passage for the fermentive vapours, and it was only when some obstacle prevented the free escape that pulsations began, like the alternate rising and falling of bark on a piece of green wood in the fire as the steam alternately builds up and escapes below it.

Plemp was not convinced. Like Primrose, his view was that of a practical medical man. Like Primrose too, his respect for the ancients led him to suspect novelty, and he was opposed to Descartes' natural philosophy. Thirdly, both he and Primrose were catholic.[63] Both appear to display the allegiance to Hippocrates and Galen that in many later sixteenth- and early seventeenth-century medical texts, and which is the medical manifestation of the counter reformation's return to Aristotle. We can reconstruct Plemp's attitude from his various publications. It is clear that his view of the new doctrines about the motion of the heart and blood was determined by his fundamental medical beliefs. These he drew from his training, which he saw as an autonomous and professional preserve, and from the needs of teaching, passing on that training. In presenting a translation (he claims it is his own) of parts of the *Canon* of Avicenna in 1658,[64] he reveals his antagonism to the Hellenists of the day, who had drawn up systematic and highly subdivided presentations of medicine based on Greek sources. Plemp objected that the Greeks had not written like that, but discursively, like hunters not finished with the hunt but still searching for what they had set out to find. He also objected to the Hellenists' criticism of Avicenna as barbaric and derivative. No, insisted Plemp, Avicenna was an author, not a commentator, and eloquent in his own language.

Plemp was of an age when the humanism and Hellenism of the sixteenth century had penetrated into medicine as far as the nature of the discipline would allow. Now instead we see religious differences in individuals' conceptions of medicine. In revealing and revering pre-Christian authorities the renaissance had revealed a pagan *prisca medicina* as well as a *prisca scientia*: we may recall that the 'new Aristotle' of Heerebord was an Aristotle shorn of the years of medieval (and because Christian, catholic) commentary. Both Heerebord and the counter-reformation catholics suspected that the reformation had carried on some of the work of the renaissance: to the catholics it seemed as though both events had over-emphasized the gap between ancient and modern: there was after all a continuous tradition of Christian scholarship from the first century to the present. This

[63] Lindeboom, *Descartes and Medicine*, p. 17. Primrose, son of a reformist Scot, was brought up in France: his religious convictions are not explicit, but may be gathered from passages in his writings. See for example his attack on Plemp: J. Primrose, *Destructio Fundamentorum Vopisci Fortunati Plempii in Academia Lovaniensi Medicinae Professor* (Rotterdam, 1657), pp. 128, 237. Some biographical details of both Primrose and Plemp are given in the *Dictionaire des Sciences Medicales. Biographie Medicale* (Paris, 1824).

[64] V.F. Plemp (trans.), *Avicenna. Canon Medicinae* (books 1 and 2 and 'De Febribus' from book 4) (Louvain, 1658), prologue 'To the medical reader'.

tradition had not only relied on revealed truth, which was superior to
reason, but had successfully assimilated Aristotle and the philosophers. To them, the reformers seemed to have thrown overboard
centuries of authoritative interpretation, and in philosophy the
counter-reformation came back closer to a scholastic Aristotle.

Plemp's medicine is 'counter-reformation' medicine in this way. He
thought of the Hippocratic texts as equivalent to the scriptures in
containing revealed knowledge. In making the comparison Plemp is
also playing down the pagan nature of the texts, which had been
emphasized by the earlier renaissance and by the Hellenists whom he
disliked. So the fundamentals of medicine were revealed by Hippocrates (and set down in Plemp's own *Fundamenta Medicinae*)[65] just as the
fundamenta of health and salvation are found in the scriptures. Then,
continues Plemp, Galen in a verbose and poorly organized way expounded Hippocrates, just as St Augustine had expounded in a broad
sweep the teachings of the scriptures. Augustine had been followed by
Aquinas, who set out his predecessor's discursive exposition in a
systematic way, much used in teaching. So, in Plemp's view, Avicenna
is the medical Aquinas, reducing Galen's verbosity to system and
order.[66]

Therefore, in the case of both religion and medicine the continuity of
the tradition was important to Plemp. It followed that teaching and
explaining this tradition are important for the continuity of the truth,
and Plemp's books are clearly designed with this in mind. The devices
of teaching are those that the Hellenists of the renaissance tried to do
away with: the translation of Avicenna, approved by Louvain's censor
of books, the professor of theology, has *scholia* and the apparatus of
academic teaching; the *Fundamenta Medicinae* are *ad scholae
acriboligiam aptata* and the title-page is adorned with a woodcut of the
Avicenna of religion, Aquinas, with the legend *Bene scripsisti de me
Thoma*.

Another reason for the importance of the continuity of the medical
tradition for Plemp was that medicine was co-operative and cumula-
tive. As a *scientia*, medicine is 'assent to the conclusion of a demonstrative syllogism', but its individuality and autonomy lie in the fact that it
is also an art.[67] In the art of medicine, the writ of the philosophers does

[65] V.F. Plemp, *Fundamenta Medicinae*.   [66] Plemp, (trans.), *Canon*, prologue.
[67] Plemp is here (*Fundamenta Medicinae*, ch. 2) making an academic *distinctio*: 'strictly' the
scientia of medicine is a syllogism of the form 'In those who have much innate heat, food is very
necessary: the young have much innate heat and therefore need much food'. Thus medical
aphorisms are forced into logical form, and involve natural–philosophical assumptions that
are quite opposed to those of Descartes.

not run. In the art of medicine, there are no rules for certain knowledge: as Galen says there is no sure way of telling a nephritic from a colic pain, nor how a medicine acts by its 'whole substance'. As Celsus says, in the art of medicine there are no sure precepts, as in other natural sciences and there are many possible conclusions (and, by implication, the accumulated experiential knowledge of the centuries is important). It will be readily appreciated that what was in Plemp's mind when he came to the topic of the motion of the heart and blood was very different from what was in Descartes' – the supremacy of reason, the God-given clear and distinct ideas, the divinely imprinted laws of physics, the distrust of the senses, to say nothing of the role of the soul and the machine of the body.

At first sight then, it is surprising that Plemp changed his mind. By the time the second edition of his textbook had appeared (1644) he was an advocate of circulation. But he had been won over by Harvey, not by Descartes. It was, indeed, precisely the part of Harvey's doctrine that Descartes had for his own reasons rejected – the forceful systole – that Plemp found the most attractive. In particular, Harvey's argument about the volume of blood ejected from the heart at every beat proved irresistible to Plemp.

The history of science is not full of people's own accounts of them changing their minds, and for this reason and because it is an example of how Harvey's doctrine became widespread, we should consider the question of why Plemp in fact did change his mind.

One of the reasons that made his conversion possible, I maintain, lies in the nature of the academic method he used. The medical tradition in which Plemp saw himself had, since becoming part of university teaching in the middle ages, commented upon medical texts and opinions, had raised *quaestiones* and *dubia* and had developed elaborate techniques for examining and justifying medical knowledge. In writing a textbook, Plemp's job included putting forward conflicting views, ancient and modern, in order to inform the reader about the nature of the literature on the subject, to show him the nature of resolutions of these questions and to provide 'disputed questions' and 'authorities' for use in formal disputations.

So his book was not a textbook in the modern sense, and did not have the single, proselytizing and revolutionary message of Descartes' writings. And Plemp, resistant to the attractions of Cartesian mechanism, had no need to modify Harvey's views when relaying them to the reader: he reported Harvey's views quite fairly, but said he had 'spoken and written' against them (no doubt in disputations and the letters to

Descartes).[68] What he and, he says, other medical men found offensive about the circulation was the strange conclusion that all parts would be be nourished by the same blood.[69] In attempting to judge the matter, he found it difficult to remove his old conceptions, and for a long time wrestled with himself in an attempt to defend the ancients. His first idea was to deny Harvey's quantitative argument and to say either that very little blood left the heart at pulsation, or that, as in the severed but still beating heart, no blood entered it. Or perhaps, he further argued, the blood leaving the heart was very *spirituosus* – distended by spirits and so occupying much space with little substance. As he says, that would have allowed him to maintain that the blood was, as in ancient accounts, generated in the liver, that the pulse was, as anciently, in the arterial coats, and that little blood passed into the arteries.

Secondly, Plemp found the observation that the veins swell below rather than above a ligature (as in Harvey's illustration) a difficult problem. He tried to imagine that there were bladders of some sort that were closed by the ligature: in these ways, he says, he dallied and trifled, finding such reasons good enough for teachers from the professor's chair, *e cathedra auditorio*, when nothing could be examined very carefully. But ultimately he found that these ideas, however well expressed, did not in fact succeed in defending the ancients. What appears to have happened, then, is that Plemp continued to teach the traditional account of the heart and blood in his formal lectures, where there was little opportunity for discussion. But it is probable that the later occasions on which he became 'more desperate' and 'more vehementaly denied' the circulation[70] were disputations, in which his logic and his authorities were exposed to minute analysis. This again reminds us that disputations were theatres in which new doctrines might be made attractive to large numbers of people, which is the reason they were chosen by Descartes as a means of inserting his natural philosophy into the universities. And we have seen in Heerebord's exposition of the form of the disputation that there were recognized points at which the 'authority of great men' and sensory experience were admissable weapons. In particular, in medical discussions the topic of 'anatomy' – structure and action – had been since the middle ages one where reason ultimately failed and sense alone could reveal the truth.[71] It is at this point that the results of vivisection could

---

[68] Plemp, *Fundamenta Medicinae*, p. 128.   [69] *Ibid.*, p. 131.   [70] *Ibid.*, pp. 128–30.
[71] Compare (above) Plemp's adoption from Galen and Celsus of the doctrine that the *art* of medicine went beyond certain demonstration. In the middle ages the other field beyond reason was the action of drugs.

be introduced to the discussion, and Plemp, advised by Wallaeus, resorted to experiments on dogs.

The model for vivisectional experiments was Colombo, whom Plemp called the leader of the moderns[72] and with whose vivisections Plemp was impressed. Like Colombo, Plemp opened the pulmonary vessels, and found also that they contained only blood (and not spirit or vapour, as in Galenic theory). Plemp's technique here extended Colombo's in that he ligated the vessels before opening them (and so making sure they displayed their original contents). He concluded that the pulse was the filling of the arteries with blood. To confirm this, he inserted a piece of sponge into the artery to stop the flow of blood and show that although the arterial coat was unchanged, the pulse was not transmitted by it (as in Galenic theory). Other vivisections that Plemp used were probably taken from Harvey and from his own dispute with Descartes.

To summarize, it was in opposing Descartes' point of view of the action of the heart, and the mechanism that lay behind it, that Plemp was convinced of the truth of Harvey's doctrine. By adopting this position he could preserve the bulk of the medical tradition which was so important to him: it was still the vital faculty that caused the pulse (it was also vivifying) and it still resided in the heart. This faculty was an internal *principium* of the kind that all bodily motions had. This was Plemp's *rational* demonstration of the heartbeat[73] (while vivisections provided evidence from experience) and it is clear that for Plemp Descartes' reasons simply do not fit into his category of explanation.

HOGELANDE'S CHANGE OF DIRECTION

We are now in a position to look in a little more detail at how Hogelande modified Descartes' doctrine of the heart beat. Writing in 1646,[74] Hogelande had seen the fate of Descartes' natural philosophy in the disputations in the universities, and had followed Descartes' argument with Plemp. His tracts seemed designed to further the Cartesian cause by modifying what had proved objectionable, some examples of which we have already seen.

First, it was probably the Plemp affair that turned Hogelande also to

---

[72] Plemp, *Fundamenta Medicinae*, p. 126.
[73] *Ibid.*, p. 172. As with his demonstrative syllogism (note above) Plemp is taking as self-evidently true fundamental items of belief from the medical tradition. This is much what Galen had done with the Hippocratic writings.
[74] The text of this edition appears to be identical with that of 1676, which I have used.

vivisection. The isolation and mutilation of the living heart of an animal was practised by Harvey, Descartes, Plemp and Hogelande and all came to conclusions that agreed only with the mental conceptions they brought to the experiment. The function of these experiments was not, however, solely to confirm by the senses what had been proposed or already proved by reason (this or that kind of heartbeat). They were also devices to convince, and what was at stake was ultimately the first principles that determined both a person's outlook (the metaphysics of God and creation) and the way he framed the questions the experiments were to answer. So in looking at how Hogelande set up his vivisections, we need to go back a little to where the foundations of his natural philosophy differed from those of Descartes.

Hogelande was very impressed by the dominating position given to reason in Cartesian metaphysics. His own ideal way of philosophizing, as we have seen, was to travel following the lead given by the Duke of Reason, and merely in the company of the Count of Experience, and he scorned the critics of the Rational Method 'who believe nothing without experience'.[75] This view of the role of the senses in philosophy seems somewhat Platonic, for Hogelande held that the soul, incarcerated within the body, is sometimes misled by its senses, or even deprived of its reason by its association with the material body. The business of philosophy was to overcome these difficulties by means of reason. The soul, indeed, formed the second (or third when he had thought of predestination) stage of Hogelande's demonstration of his truth about the world. Having first proved (like Descartes) the existence of God, he proceeds to the nature of the soul: immortal, immaterial, it is the image of God's reason (as the sun is the image of His power). So reason is divine, although temporarily hindered during the soul's stay in the body. Reason allows us to see the design of the world, apparent in the structure of the dissected animal. (We have met above the reasons why Hogelande preferred the argument from design to the Cartesian doubt as a proof of God's existence.) But how are incommensurables like the material body and immaterial soul to be united? Hogelande avoided the difficulties in Cartesian dualism that had led Regius into controversy and suggested, albeit rather hesitantly, that the answer lay in subtle matter.

Consider, he says, a large vessel containing liquid and being warmed in the fire. (It is the aeolipile mentioned by Descartes in the letters to Plemp.[76]) If the vessel has a hole, the vapour escapes, but if not the

---

[75] Hogelande, *Cogitationes*, p. 62.   [76] Beverwyck, *Epistolicae Quaestiones*, p. 133.

vessel will explode. But we cannot imagine that the original matter in the vessel has increased, for that would imply that there was a space around the extant particles in which the new particles appeared. That would be atomism, and the dangers of being labelled an atomist were clear from experience to Descartes and at least rationally to Hogelande. So Hogelande assumed that some subtle matter entered through the walls of the vessel and under the influence of heat somehow became bound to the matter within, and so while the vessel was hot the combined substance was compelled to adopt the shape and size of the containing vessel. In such a way, he thought, might the soul be combined with the body, for the duration of life being compelled to adopt the material limitations and distortions of the body.

The release of the subtle matter from the cooling vessel was like the escape of vapour from a barrel of fermenting beer or wine, and for Hogelande all such changes were 'fermentations', a category of fundamental importance of which the chief example was the ebullition of blood in the heart. So Hogelande considers that he has a chain of argument from first principles to physiology, and he brings to the question of the heartbeat a considerable intellectual apparatus derived from the principles of religion and natural philosopy that are not wholly Cartesian. All matter is passive; motion is passed from particle to particle; to trace it to its first cause is to demonstrate the existence of God, the first mover; and God's agent in generating motion is the subtle matter: any independent source of motion would imply that God did not have total control of, and pre-knowledge of, every local motion. In suggesting that subtle matter both binds divine reason, the soul, to the body *and* causes fermentation within the heart, he seems to give it some of the attributes of a more traditional 'spirit'.

So strong is this string of reasoning for Hogelande that he says it might seem like mere curiousity rather than necessity to consider the problem of when, in the diastole–systole cycle, blood emerges from the heart. Nevertheless, he breaks off in mid-sentence for a *Digression* on this point that gets increasingly out of hand, finally occupying twenty-six pages and requiring its own title page. The reason for the strange typography is that at a very late stage, after the manuscript had gone to press and the printer had set up the type of the early part of the book, Hogelande decided to make experiments on the living heart of an eel. The typesetter had to be content to receive and set Hogelande's new 'copy' as it came in, irrespective of length.

Hogelande handled the experiments, as we would expect, primarily as a *posteriori* confirmations of his intellectual position, and partly also as devices to convince. He recognized that the question of the heartbeat had been disputed by such figures as Harvey, Descartes and Plemp, and as Harvey had done Hogelande sets up the question in a formal way. This too is part of the desire to convince: he knew his audience, familiar with the procedures of formal argument, would expect certain kinds of evidence at certain places, and we have already seen, for example, where authority and sensory observation could be introduced into the disputation. The whole of Hogelande's *Digression* is really a *quaestio disputata* and he sets out an *ordo tractandi* in an academic way, much as commentators had been doing since the middle ages.[77] This 'order of treatment' begins with definitions, proceeds to their analysis and from there to the embryological origins of the heart's motions, the vivisectional experiments and finally to the nature of fire and heat (as a cause of fermentation). But the very definitions he employs preclude a Harveian resolution of the question. There are, he says, three stages in the heart's motion: first a natural and passive state in which the ventricles are being filled from the auricles. Second is the heart's *propria motio*, (its 'action' as an 'organ' in Galenic terms) which is dilatation; third, the 'accidental' or fortuitous contraction of the heart, which occurs merely because the expansion is complete. Hogelande recognizes that this contraction may be forceful, and his observations of the living heart may have made him less confident, even than Descartes came to be, of the first Cartesian inflation-theory of diastole. Hogelande says the convulsive nature of this contraction may be accidental, from the cold in vivisected animals, but elsewhere he gives a greater function to contraction. In a number of places[78] he says the ejection of the blood is 'possibly' helped by the contraction of fibres, resulting either from a previous over-expansion of the heart or (what is not at all Cartesian) from a fermentation within the substance of the heart that brings the walls of the ventricles forcibly *together*, stopping the previous dilatation and expelling the blood (in this case to the lungs).[79] Even though apparently regular and functional, Hogelande calls it 'secondary' and 'as it were, accidental': it is 'a sort of contraction'.[80] Any *proprio motio* would need to fit into the mechanist world-picture. Could it be that Hogelande saw his vivisected eel heart emit blood in contraction? In any case it is now outside the

---

[77] Hogelande, *Cogitationes*, p. 50. The *ordo tractandi* is the commentator's method of handling the argument of his author. It was part of the preliminary apparatus that told the reader what was going to happen in the commentary and was normally paired with an *ordo tractatus* that explained the arrangement of the text.
[78] Hogelande, *Cogitationes*, pp. 76–85.   [79] *Ibid.*, p. 110.   [80] *Ibid.*, p. 112.

bounds[81] of his formal 'disputed question' that he approaches a Harveian explanation of heartbeat. His starting point is the modified doctrine (of fermentation) that Descartes introduced to answer Plemp, and Hogelande goes a stage further and finally claims that inflationary explanations serve only for quadrupeds and that in fish (the eel) contraction is 'more natural'.[82] Even in quadrupeds it is a combination of ebullition and forceful contraction that moves the blood. Hogelande indeed, gives generous tribute to Harvey, whose doctrine of circulation had become so central to Cartesian–Hogelandean mechanism and is even able to use Harvey's quantitative arguments as *mechanical*. These are the size of the vena cava, the capacity of the auricles, and the 'dense injection' of blood into the ventricles by the stimulated auricles. Hogelande omits, of course, Harvey's estimate of the difference in size between the expanded and contracted ventricle (the forceful systole argument) and takes up the 'mechanical' explanation at Harvey's estimate that half an ounce of blood is ejected at each beat, together with the subsequent arithmetic. The great quantity of blood that passes through the heart over a period of time was as 'infallible' a reason for the circulation for Hogelande the mechanist as for Plemp the Harveian.

CONCLUSION

Harvey's doctrine on the motion of the heart and blood came to be widely accepted in his own lifetime. This was partly due to the persuasiveness of his arguments, including the quantitative, and the vivisections. We have seen that these brought about Plemp's conversion. But in other cases the doctrine became established less through the power of truth to convince than by the doctrine's compatability with the dominating interests in people's minds. The interests were dominating because they were important in the lives of these people; they concerned their private ambition, the stability of their society, the practice of their religion and their hopes of eternal reward. Descartes took up and changed half of Harvey's doctrine because it could be used as a weapon in his fight to become the new Philosopher. In this form the doctrine was unacceptable to many whose interests were best served by making Aristotle's philosophy the one that matched their society and religion. Correspondingly, the doctrine was acceptable to some who found a new natural philosophy to be a system of thought

---

[81] *Ibid.*, pp. 85, 110, 112.   [82] *Ibid.*, p. 112.

independent of the clashes of religious sects. Such a natural philosophy
had an equally firm basis in a Christian metaphysics and appeared to
gain stability in being free of sectarian dispute.

Such considerations suggest what a man may be persuaded of, but
do not suggest a mechanism for persuading him. This chapter looks, in
addition, at two such mechanisms, disputation and experiment. Disputations identified the issues within the doctrine and their relationship with the world-view of the antagonists. They also made people
very bad tempered. In such circumstances there is generally a degree of
plain speaking about what is at stake in adopting this or that view, and
the historian is not put to the necessity of inventing it. Disputation-by-
post, the exchange of letters in which repeated experiments formed a
physical rhetoric of persuasion, similarly forced attention to certain
issues within the disputed question. The result was some shifting of
ground, and a very careful use of language in showing that experimental results still tallied with the original theoretical position. It is by
looking at such mechanisms that this chapter tries to achieve what it set
out to, that is, to follow an historical argument down from the large
questions of religion and politics through institutional circumstances
to the details of theory.

3

The matter of souls: medical theory and theology in seventeenth-century England

JOHN HENRY

Heterodoxy is as old as Christianity itself but irreligion was perceived as something new in the intellectual life of early modern Europe. Atheism was widely seen as a progeny of the crisis of faith engendered by the changes of the renaissance and the reformation. New discoveries in philosophy, as John Donne said, called 'all in doubt', and religious relativism – stemming from an increased awareness of alternative religions in other parts of the world and in the multiplicity of reformed churches – made it easier to deny the absolute truth of any religious claims. Among the remedies which were prescribed for this 'very plague and pest of humane Polities' was a new emphasis on so-called 'natural theology'. It was assumed that even if the atheist remained recalcitrant before Scripture, he could not hold out against 'right reason' and the 'light of nature'. Natural theology was developed, therefore, in order to prove the existence and attributes of God and the immortality of human souls by recourse only to reason and the phenomena of the creation. Proofs of the immortality of the soul were held to be crucially important elements in this natural theology since the fear of post-mortem punishments was regarded as the only guarantee of morality and, therefore, of social and political stability.[1]

In addition to the editors and the members of the conference who offered much helpful advice and criticism, I would like to thank Drs Michael Hunter and Dorothy Watkins for their help in the preparation of this paper.
1   John Donne, *An Anatomie of the World, the First Anniversary* (London, 1611). Henry More, *An Explanation of the Grand Mystery of Godliness* (London, 1660), book, x, ch. 10., p. 516. See also Nathanael Culverwel, *An Elegant and Learned Discourse of the Light of Nature* (London, 1652). For fuller discussions of the perceived rise of atheism see the following: Paul Hazard, *La Crise de la conscience européene* (Paris, 1935); R.H. Popkin, *The History of Scepticism from Erasmus to Spinoza* (Berkeley, 1979); D. Wooton, *Paolo Sarpi: between Renaissance and Enlightenment* (Cambridge, 1983); D. Wooton, 'Unbelief in Early Modern Europe', *History Workshop*, xx (1985), 82–100; M. Hunter, 'The Problem of Atheism in Early Modern England', *Transactions of the Royal Historical Society*, 5th ser., xxxv (1985), 135–57;

The traditional pneumatology of the Roman Catholic Church and, for that matter, the major reformed churches was, of course, dualistic: body and soul were regarded as categorically distinct entities, one being material, the other immaterial. But dualism was not free from theological difficulties – the Bible being rather equivocal on the issue – and it was always fraught with philosophical difficulties. Nevertheless, it was usually invoked as an essential part of the safe way to salvation. By contrast, all monistic philosophies were generally regarded as subversive and irreligious; even if, like those of Spinoza and Berkeley, they were designed to overcome the difficulties of dualism and to set religion on a firmer foundation.

The most notorious monistic systems of philosophy in seventeenth-century England were the revived ancient philosophy of Epicurus, and the mechanistic philosophy of Thomas Hobbes, both of which were supposed to have many atheist adherents. But even the Cartesian system, which had been formulated in vigorously dualistic terms, was taken up by atheistic 'scoffers' and 'wits' who dismissed Descartes's pronouncements on *res cogitantes* and concentrated solely on a universe of *res extensae*.[2] In view of these perceived threats to sound religion, it is hardly surprising that much of the vast and varied anti-atheist literature which flowed from the presses of seventeenth-century England was directed against the new natural philosophies.

However, there was also a strong element of monistic thought in the medical tradition, and here again this was linked, at least in popular sentiments, to atheism.[3] In part, the physician's reputation for atheism was merely a function of his apparent practice. Whatever a doctor's innermost religious convictions might be, his role was to treat all

R.S. Westfall, *Science and Religion in Seventeenth-Century England* (New Haven, 1958); J. Redwood, *Reason, Ridicule and Religion: the Age of Enlightenment in England, 1660–1750* (London, 1976). On the popular awareness of the cultural relativity of religious belief see Carlo Ginzburg, *The Cheese and the Worms: the Cosmos of a Sixteenth-Century Miller* (London and Henley, 1980), pp. 41–51.

[2] S.I. Mintz, *The Hunting of Leviathan: Seventeenth-Century Reactions to the Materialism and Moral Philosophy of Thomas Hobbes* (Cambridge, 1970). On the atheistic appropriation of Descartes see the letter from Henry More to Robert Boyle, 6 December 1671, in R. Boyle, *Works*, 6 vols. (London, 1772), VI, p. 513; and Alan Gabbey, 'Philosophia Cartesiana Triumphata: Henry More (1646–1671)', in T.M. Lennon, J.M. Nicholas and J.W. Davis (eds.), *Problems of Cartesianism* (Kingston and Montreal, 1982), pp. 171–250.

[3] See the following, all by Walter Pagel: 'The Reaction to Aristotle in Seventeenth-Century Biological Thought', in E.A. Underwood (ed.), *Science, Medicine and History: Essays on the Evolution of Scientific Thought and Medical Practice Written in Honour of Charles Singer*, 2 vols. (London, 1953), I, pp. 489–509, 'Harvey and Glisson on Irritability with a Note on Van Helmont', *Bulletin of the History of Medicine*, XLI (1967), 497–514; *New Light on William Harvey* (Basel, 1976), pp. 34–6, 52–5; *Joan Baptista Van Helmont: Reformer of Science and Medicine* (Cambridge, 1982), pp. 120–3.

sickness as a purely natural phenomenon. Thus, at a time when many believed that sickness was visited upon mankind by God, the physician was seen everywhere ignoring such religious considerations and treating sickness in an entirely naturalistic way.[4] In the context of medicine, pragmatism looks like materialism. And never more so than in the case of treatment for mental illness. As Timothy Bright wrote in 1586, 'the notable fruit and successe' of medicine in curing madness and melancholy

> hath caused some to iudge more basely of the soule, then agreeth with pietie or nature, & have accompted all maner affection thereof, to be subject to the physicians hand, not considering herein any thing divine, and above the ordinarie events, and natural course of things: but have esteemed the vertues them selves, yea religion, no other thing but as the body hath ben tempered, and on the other side, vice, prophanenesse, & neglect of religion and honestie, to have bene nought else but a fault of humour.[5]

It would seem, then, that Galenic theory, which insisted upon the influence of the temperaments on the human soul, and medical practice, which was successful in treating psychic disorders by somatic means, combined to give medicine an odour of impiety. Moreover, although charges of atheism and irreligion were frequently bandied about in the early modern period as rhetorical devices in censure and polemic, there is clear evidence to suggest that some radically unorthodox thinkers did use current medical theories to bolster their heretical views.[6]

Richard Overton, for example, drew upon traditional medical accounts of the soul to establish his belief that man is 'wholly mortal'. 'Anatomize Man', he wrote, 'take a view of all his *Lineaments* & *Dimensions*, of all his *members* & *faculties*, and consider their state severally', and there will be no need to postulate the existence of a superadded soul.

> So that in veritie [he concluded] Man is but a Creature whose several parts and members are endowed with proper natures or Faculties, each subservient to other, to

---

[4] Paul H. Kocher, *Science and Religion in Elizabethan England* (New York, 1969), pp. 258–321; R.S. Porter, 'Barely Touching: Social Perspectives on the Mind/Body Problem', in G.S. Rousseau (ed.) Proceedings of the 1985–6 William Andrews Clarke Memorial Library Seminar Series on Mind and Body, (Los Angeles, forthcoming).

[5] Timothy Bright, *A Treatise of Melancholie* (London, 1586), sig. *iiir. For a survey of *religious* treatment for psychic disturbance see Michael MacDonald, 'Religion, Social Change and Psychological Healing in England 1600–1800', in W.J. Sheils (ed.), *The Church and Healing* [The Ecclesiastical History Society, *Studies in Church History*, xix.] (Oxford, 1982), pp. 101–25.

[6] Kocher, *Science and Religion in Elizabethan England*, pp. 239–57, 250–4, 284–305; Owsei Temkin, 'On Galen's Pneumatology', *Gesnerus*, viii (1951), 180–9, reprinted in Owsei Temkin, *The Double Face of Janus and Other Essays in the History of Medicine* (Baltimore, 1977), pp. 154–61.

make him a living Rational Creature whose degrees or excellences of natural Faculties make him in his kind more excellent than the Beasts.[7]

Similarly, when William Coward had *Second Thoughts concerning Human Soul*, which he published in 1702, he drew upon his medical training. Citing Harvey, Walter Charleton and Daniel Sennert, Coward suggested that 'the Operations of the Soul as it is usually call'd seem extreamly to depend *naturally* upon the Circulation of the Blood'. For Coward, blood was the organizing principle of the body, 'the instrumental cause of Life, or rather of the Operations of *Life*', and so even 'the very Understanding and Apprehension' depended upon nothing more than 'a brisk circulation'.[8]

Lady Anne Conway, author of the remarkable *Principles of the most Ancient and Modern Philosophy* (1690), insisted that the contradictions of dualism could only be avoided by recognizing that 'the Soul is of One Nature and Substance with the Body'. Like Coward, she shared William Harvey's belief that 'the blood would seem to differ nothing from the soul':

> Even thus in Man's Body, the Meat and Drink is first changed into Chyle, then into Blood, afterwards into Spirits, which are nothing else but Blood brought to perfection; and these Spirits, whether good or bad, still advance to a greater subtilty or spirituality, and by these Spirits which come from the Blood, we see, hear, smell, taste, feel, and think, yea meditate, love, hate, and do all things whatsoever we do.

The sources of Lady Anne's monistic philosophy are not known with any certainty, but her ideas clearly owe much to the thought of J.B. van Helmont whose son, Francis Mercury, became a close friend of hers in the years preceding the composition of the *Principles*.[9]

During the seventeenth century, then, the reduction of psychic phenomena to somatic states – which Timothy Bright had seen to be implicit in medical practice – became increasingly explicit in medical writings and was taken up by speculative writers with various reformist religious intentions. It is important to note that this medically inspired monism differed significantly from the more familiar monism of mechanist materialists. According to Hobbes and Descartes, matter was completely inert and all vital processes were regarded as mere epiphenomena of the interactions of particles of matter in motion. For William Harvey, Francis Glisson, Henry Power, John

---

[7] Richard Overton, *Man Wholly Mortal* (London, 1655), pp. 15–16, 8–9; see also pp. 2–3.
[8] William Coward, *Second Thoughts concerning Human Soul* (London, 1704), pp. 87, 92, 96–7, 91.
[9] Anne Conway, *The Principles of the Most Ancient and Modern Philosophy*, ed. Peter Loptson (The Hague, 1982), p. 218. First published in Latin (Amsterdam, 1690), *The Principles* must have been written between 1677 and 1679.

Mayow and others in the medical tradition, matter itself, or some forms of it, was inherently active, self-motive, and endowed with seminal or organizing powers. In this philosophy matter could be held to be not just vital but perceptive, endowed with appetites and aversions and ultimately, capable of thought.[10]

In view of the contemporary equation of monism with atheism we might expect to find such medical theories discussed in the extensive and encyclopaedic anti-atheist literature of seventeenth-century England. For the most part, however, this is not the case. The proverbial atheist, the physician, hardly appears at all in learned attacks on atheism.[11] To a large extent, this can be put down to the fact that the mechanist versions of atheism drew all the fire. For example, the 'Opinion of every Atheist and counterfeit Deist of these times', that matter has 'sensation or thought', was categorized by Richard Bentley as mechanistic: the result of 'such and such determinate Motions [of matter], by the action and reaction of one Particle upon another'. The alternative, vitalistic, view that the 'Faculties of Sensation or Perception' are 'inherent in Matter as such' was simply dismissed as untenable.[12]

Edward Stillingfleet was another who recognized only those theories of thinking matter which depended upon the principle of matter in motion:

> To imagine that the Particles of Matter, as they are in Man, should be capable of Sensation, Memory, Intellection, volition etc. merely because of a different shape, size, & motion from what they have in a piece of Wood, is a riddle that requires a new Configuration of Atoms in us to make us understand.

Similarly, a lesser thinker like Timothy Manlove showed no hesitation in labelling as Hobbist the view that the human soul is 'nothing else but the inflamed glowing Particles of the Blood, called Spirits; which are . . . the Active Principle of Life, Motion, Sense and Understanding in Man, and Beast'.[13]

---

[10] On Harvey and Glisson see the works by Pagel in note 3 above and J. Henry, 'Medicine and Pneumatology: Henry More, Richard Baxter and Francis Glisson's *Treatise on the Energetic Nature of Substance*', *Medical History*, XXXI (1987), 15–40, esp. 17–22. On Power see Charles Webster, 'Henry Power's Experimental Philosophy', *Ambix*, XIV (1967), 150–78. On Mayow, see R.G. Frank jr., *Harvey and the Oxford Physiologists: Scientific Ideas and Social Interaction* (Berkeley, 1980), pp. 224–32, 258–78.

[11] There were various proverbs about medical atheists, such as: *Ubi tres medici, duo athei*. See Thomas Browne, *Religio Medici* (London, 1643), p. 1; John Donne, 'Why are Courtiers sooner Atheists than Men of Other Conditions?', in John Donne, *Paradoxes and Problems*, ed. with introduction and commentary by H. Peters (Oxford, 1980), pp. 23–4 (first published in 3rd edn, London, 1652). See also Kocher, *Science and Religion in Elizabethan England*, p. 239.

[12] Richard Bentley, *Matter and Motion Cannot Think* (London, 1692), pp. 14, 15, 17.

[13] Edward Stillingfleet, *Origines Sacrae*, in *Works*, 6 vols. (London, 1710), II, p. 291. Timothy Manlove, *The Immortality of the Soul Asserted and Practically Improved* (London, 1697), p. 5.

The failure of these and other writers to distinguish between the mechanical philosophy and the vitalistic monism of the medical tradition is, if nothing else, clear testimony to the perceived prevalence of Hobbist ideas in late seventeenth-century England. Even so, no matter how overpowering Hobbes's ideas might have been, it remains surprising that, at a time when theologians saw atheists everywhere, there is hardly any critical discussion of medical theories. While Michel Servet's claims, that 'sanguis est ipsissima vita' and that 'the soul as a whole is in the blood, and the soul itself is blood', brought him to the stake in Calvin's Geneva (in 1553), William Harvey's conclusion, in *De Generatione Animalium*, that 'there is no need to search for any spirit distinct from blood', raised not one murmur of dissent from theologians. At a time when the nature of spirit was a crucial issue for right religion, nobody seems to have noticed Harvey's suggestion that the blood, 'furnished with the power of acting above all else' was spirit 'par excellence'. Similarly, although it is clear that orthodox theologians in the 1660s paid scant attention to Biblical statements that 'the blood is the soul', it still seems remarkable that the early experiments on blood transfusions failed to engender any theological response whatsoever.[14]

So, why were the latest medical theories excluded from the anti-atheist literature? Clearly, the answer to this question depends less upon a knowledge of contemporary medicine and more upon a full understanding of the nature of the anti-atheist literature. Michael Hunter has suggested that the focus of this literature was somewhat diffuse because its authors believed atheism to be a rather anti-intellectual movement, inspired more by a scoffing, sarcastic incredulity, and by immorality – so-called 'practical atheism' – than by philosophical critique.[15] Accordingly, if the anti-atheist was to spend any time at all in considering intellectual arguments, he would quite

[14] I quote Servet's *Christianismi Restitutio* (1533), from Walter Pagel, *William Harvey's Biological Ideas: Selected Aspects and Historical Background* (Basel and New York, 1967), pp. 137, 144 (there is further bibliography on Servet at p. 137). William Harvey, *Disputations Touching the Generation of Animals*, trans. G. Whitteridge (Oxford, 1981), pp. 283, 375, see also 240–58. John S. White, 'William Harvey and the Primacy of the Blood', *Annals of Science*, XLIII (1986), 239–55. The similarity between Harvey's views and heterodox ideas is well brought out in Christopher Hill, 'William Harvey and the Idea of Monarchy', in C. Webster (ed.), *The Intellectual Revolution of the Seventeenth Century* (London, 1974), pp. 160–81. Biblical equations between blood and soul are found at Leviticus 17:14; Genesis 9:4; and Deuteronomy 12:23.

[15] Michael Hunter, 'Science and Irreligion: an Early Modern Problem Reconsidered', in R.S. Westman and D.C. Lindberg (eds.), *Reappraisals of the Scientific Revolution* (Cambridge, forthcoming). See also G.E. Aylmer, 'Unbelief in Seventeenth-Century England', in D. Pennington and K. Thomas (eds.), *Puritans and Revolutionaries* (Oxford, 1978), pp. 22–46, and J. Redwood, *Reason, Ridicule and Religion*.

naturally concentrate on those which were most commonly alluded to by the atheists themselves. There can be little doubt, judging from the literature, that the mechanical philosophies of Hobbes and Descartes, or a simplistic version of one of them, were the runaway winners in these stakes. The hallmark of the new mechanical philosophies was their easy intelligibility, and they were all quickly available in English translations. Moreover, the traditions of renaissance scholarship ensured that even controversial works like Epicurus's letters and Lucretius's *De Rerum Natura* were published, studied and translated. The fact that Epicurus's philosophy was expounded in one of the finest examples of Latin poetry ensured that it became suitable reading for gentlemen and it evidently came to enjoy a great vogue in seventeenth-century England.[16]

Medical writings, by contrast, do not seem to have attracted a readership much beyond the ranks of those who had a professional or dilettante interest in medical practice. They were still published almost exclusively in Latin, and they usually took for granted a high level of prior knowledge of medical theory. Even when Francis Glisson stepped out of the purely medical stream in order to present the public with his new system of natural philosophy, he seems to have been constitutionally incapable of changing his habitual way of writing. His *Treatise on the Energetic Nature of Substance* was written in Latin and is incomprehensible without an advanced knowledge of the typical concerns, arguments and tropes of the learned traditions of renaissance humanism. By the time Glisson's book appeared, this kind of philosophizing was already becoming unfamiliar to the new philosophers. As Richard Baxter, who greatly admired the work, wrote:

I have talkt with divers high pretenders to Philosophy here of the new strain, and askt them their judgment of Dr Glissons Book, and I found that none of them understood it, but neglected it as too hard for them and yet contemned it.[17]

---

[16] For Epicurean influence see T.F. Mayo, *Epicurus in England (1650–1725)* (Dallas, 1934); G.D. Hadzsits, *Lucretius and his Influence* (London, 1935); W.B. Fleischmann, *Lucretius and English Literature, 1680–1740* (Paris, 1964).

[17] Francis Glisson, *Tractatus de Natura Substantiae Energetica, seu de vita naturae, eiusque tribus primis facultatibus, I. Perceptiva Naturalibus, II. Appetitiva Naturalibus, III. Motiva Naturalibus &c.* (London, 1672). Richard Baxter, *Of the Immortality of Mans Soul, and the Nature of It, and Other Spirits. Two Discourses* (London, 1682), p. 6. There are many indications that mechanical philosophers – particularly the less serious minded of them – were constitutionally unable to understand the older ways of philosophizing. See, for example, Meric Casaubon, 'On Learning' (1667), reprinted (in part) in M.R.G. Spiller, *'Concerning Natural Experimental Philosophie': Meric Casaubon and the Royal Society* (The Hague, 1980), pp. 195–214. See also J.M. Levine, 'Ancients and Moderns Reconsidered', *Eighteenth-Century Studies*, XV (1981), 72–89; and M. Hunter, 'Ancients, Moderns, Philologists and Scientists', *Annals of Science*, XXXIX (1982), 187–92.

But what of those medical writings which were based on the new mechanical philosophy? We might expect them to have had a greater impact upon popular thought. Thomas Willis's *De Anima Brutorum*, for example, looks like the sort of book that might have seemed attractive to those with a penchant for mechanistic atheism. A close look at the contents, however, soon reveals a level of technicality which would have proved very difficult for those outside professional medical circles. For example, Willis's claim that the soul is 'Bipart or Twofold' – being partly material and partly immaterial – is defended on the grounds that it has been

already, in another place, by a necessary Consequence deduced, from the Life of the Blood, as it were a flame, and from the existency of the Animal Spirits, and as it were lucid or aetherial Hypostasis, asserted and proved.

Those who were not put off by Willis's talk of a 'lucid or aetherial Hypostasis' and wished to follow up his ideas in the other place he mentions would have found themselves having to make sense of Willis's pyretology in his *De Febribus*.[18]

The same point can be made about Harvey's *De Generatione Animalium*. His statement, quoted earlier, that the blood is the supreme examplar of spirit, actually follows upon a medical definition of spirit:

for us physicians, spirit is that which Hippocrates called *impetum faciens*, namely whatsoever attempts anything by its own endeavour and arouses any motion with agility and vehemence, or initiates any action . . .

Immediately, therefore, the reader feels himself bound up in a discussion which depends upon a mastery of medical presuppositions. Harvey's subsequent elaboration of the claim that blood is spirit requires a detailed grasp of a number of abstruse Aristotelian concepts, including not just the nature of the elements but also the notion of formative powers and virtues, and the operation of teleological principles in nature. Harvey was able to speak glibly in this discussion of the 'celestial nature' of the blood – a nature 'analogous to the element of the stars' – because it was a familiar notion to the university-trained physician. It would, however, have proved a rather difficult notion for

[18] Thomas Willis, *De Anima Brutorum quae Hominis Vitalis ac Sensitiva Est* (Oxford, 1672). I have used the English translation in *Dr Willis's Practice of Physick, being the Whole Works of that Renowned and Famous Physician* (London, 1684), sig. A3v; Thomas Willis, *Diatribae Duae Medico-Philosophicae, quarum prior agit de Fermentatione . . . Altera de Febribus . . .* (London, 1659).

the unitiated, particularly if they had already become familiar with mechanistic ways of philosophizing.[19]

All in all, it seems safe to assume that the 'scoffers' and 'wits', who allegedly propagated atheism and irreligion at Court and in the Coffee House, would have taken none of their ideas from current medical opinion. There were suitable theories of life and soul to be found in Epicurus or Hobbes, which had the advantage of being much easier to grasp. Accordingly, it is easy to see why theologians too excluded the latest developments in medicine from their remit.

It must also be borne in mind that physicians and philosophers were not the only rivals to theologians on the issue of mind–body interaction. Even the most poorly educated person in the land had a common sense of his or her internal, mental life, and many people had a rich experience of the interdependence of mind and body. Indeed, there was a common perception of the link between mental faculties and specific areas of the brain. Richard Overton, for example, wrote that

experience tells us, if the former Brain-pan be hurt, the Senses are hindered, but the Cogitation remaineth sound. If only the Middle-pan be harmed, the Cogitation is maimed; but the Seat of Sense keeps all the five Senses whole . . . if the Hinder-pan be disordered only, the Memorie alone, and neither Sense nor Cogitation receive harme.

Similarly, Thomas Tryon spoke of the 'common opinion', based on experience, that the different mental faculties have 'distinct Seats, or Cells in the Brain': 'the Phantasie resides in the Formost, the Judgement in the middle, and the Memory in the hindermost Ventricle of the Brain'.[20]

If this kind of common 'experience' of mind–body interdependence created problems for theologians, so did the reformist tradition of founding all one's beliefs on the clear word of scripture. One did not have to be a heresiarch to notice that Christ and the apostles placed all their emphasis not on the immortality of the soul but on the resurrection of the body. Difficulties over this matter troubled even a pious

---

[19] William Harvey, *Disputations Touching the Generation of Animals*, pp. 374, 378–9. On the role of 'celestial' or 'astral' natures in medical thought see D.P. Walker, 'The Astral Body in Renaissance Medicine', *Journal of the Warburg and Courtauld Institutes*, XXI (1958), 119–33; and D.P. Walker, 'Medical Spirits in Philosophy and Theology from Ficino to Newton', in *Arts du spectacle et histoire des idées. Recueil offert en hommage à Jean Jacquot* (Tours, 1984), pp. 287–300.

[20] Richard Overton, *Man Wholly Mortal*, p. 8. Thomas Tryon, *A Treatise of Dreams and Visions* (London, 1689), pp. 19, 20. On the medieval antecedents of these popular notions see W. Pagel, 'Medieval and Renaissance Contributions to Knowledge of the Brain and its Functions', in F.N.L. Poynter (ed.), *The History of the Brain and its Functions* (Oxford, 1958), pp. 95–114.

Anglican like John Evelyn, as we can see from a letter which Jeremy
Taylor sent to him in 1657:

But Sir, that which you check at is the immortality of the soul; that is, its being in the
interval before the day of judgement; which you conceive is not agreeable to the
apostles' creed, or current of scriptures, assigning (as you suppose) the felicity of
Christians to the resurrection.

Taylor is immediately in difficulty because he can hardly deny or
play down the importance of the Day of Judgement: 'That the felicity
of Christians is not till the day of judgement, I doe believe next to an
article of ye creed'. However, he must refute Evelyn's conclusion: 'I
cannot allow your consequent that the soul is mortal'. Surprisingly,
Taylor seems to take refuge, in this letter, in the heresy of 'soul
sleeping' or psychopannychy:

the soul may be immortal, and not beatified till the resurrection. For to be, and to be
happy or miserable, are not immediate or necessary consequents to each other. For the
soule may be alive and not understand; so our soule, when we are fast asleep, and so
Nebuchadnezzar's soule, when he had his lychanthropy. And the Socinians, that say
that the soule sleepes, doe not suppose that she is mortal; but for want of her
instrument cannot doe any acts of life.[21]

The implication of this is that the soul is completely passive and inert
when separated from the body, but this too is an unpleasant doctrine
for Taylor to accept. Traditionally, it is the soul which is supposed to
activate the body, not the body which activates the soul. As Taylor
wrote elsewhere:

it were strange that we should be alive, and live with Christ, and yet do no act of life: the
body when it is asleep does many [acts of life]; and if the soul does none, the principle is
less active than the instrument.

Taylor's response is simply to invoke the highest faculty of the soul as
continuing to be active through this sleep: 'if it [the soul] does any act
at all in separation [from the body], it must necessarily be an act or
effect of understanding; there is nothing else it can do but this it can
do'.[22] This depends, of course, on the assumption that understanding is
'proper to the soul', but, as we have seen, there was a popular notion
that it was proper merely to the middle 'Brain-pan'. Richard Overton
was doubtless not alone in feeling that if the soul is equated with
understanding then

[21] Letter from Taylor to Evelyn, 29 August 1657, reprinted in Taylor, The Whole Works, 10 vols.
    (London, 1856), I, pp. lxxvii. On the heresy of 'soul-sleeping' see N.T. Burns, Christian
    Mortalism from Tyndale to Milton (Cambridge, Mass., 1972); and J. Henry, 'Atomism and
    Eschatology: Catholicism and Natural Philosophy in the Interregnum', British Journal for the
    History of Science, XV (1982), 211–39.
[22] Taylor, 'Funeral Sermon for Frances, Countess of Carbery', died 9 October 1650, in The
    Whole Works, VIII, p. 440.

all men are born without Souls, and some [die] before they had Souls, as Infants; and some after their Soul is gone, as Mad men that live and perish in their Madness; and some would have *Souls* but by *fits* and *jumps*, as Drunkards, persons with the Falling sickness, &c.[23]

It would be possible to pursue such arguments endlessly through the labyrinthine passages of seventeenth-century theological tomes. Like Taylor, every divine who tried to expound upon the nature of the immortal soul sank into contradiction and incoherence or glossed over the issues so quickly that too many questions remained unanswered. The history of the idea of immortality of the soul, were it ever to be written, would surely reveal the intractability of the philosophical problems it poses. Certainly, the prevalence of Socinian and other monistic philosophies among seventeenth-century sectarian groups testifies to the contemporary awareness of these difficulties, and to the widespread dissatisfaction with the standard theological attempts to defend soul–body dualism. As the Ranter Christmas Carol of 1650 asked of university-trained theologians:

Let them but tell us what a soul is, then
We shall adhere to these mad, brain-sick men.[24]

It should be clear from all this that the authors of the anti-atheist literature had more than enough to contend with in opposing the monistic tendencies of common sense together with the popular mate-rialistic versions of the mechanical philosophy. Small wonder, then, that they did not venture further by engaging with the latest medical theories. It is one thing to try to show the inadequacies of 'common sense' views, but it is altogether another to enter into dispute with physiologists and anatomists armed with a specialist knowledge of the brain and all psychosomatic phenomena.

Besides, it is perfectly clear that, in spite of – or perhaps *because* of – their reputation for impiety, medical writers themselves avoided any direct confrontation with theology. As one theologian, Simon Patrick, pointed out in 1662, it was always possible for an author to entertain 'great Paradoxes' provided he 'had the good manners to make a legg and say, *Omnia Ecclesiae authoritate submittimus*'. This formulaic submission was widely recognized by churchmen and laymen alike as a useful piece of etiquette for avoiding overt clashes of interest, such as

[23] Richard Overton, *Man Wholly Mortal*, pp. 19–20.
[24] *The Arraignement and Tryall of the Ranters* (London, 1650), quoted from Nigel Smith (ed.), *A Collection of Ranter Writings from the Seventeenth Century* (London, 1983), p. 37. For a more detailed example of the intractability of the dualist concept of soul see J. Henry, 'A Cambridge Platonist's Materialism: Henry More and the Concept of Soul', *Journal of the Warburg and Courtauld Institutes*, XLIX (1986), 172–95.

demarcation disputes about who was best qualified to pronounce upon the truth of particular matters.[25]

The pattern of medical writing, accordingly, was to begin with expressions of piety and religious devotion (in some cases reiterated once or twice in the body of the work) before embarking on an analysis of anatomical, physiological or medical notions which was entirely naturalistic and made no reference to theological considerations. We must be wary, however, of assuming that this kind of apologetic minimalism in medical works was merely lip-service. It may seem to the modern reader, for example, that Thomas Willis's careful prefatory distinction, in De Anima Brutorum, between animal souls and the rational immortal soul of humans, fails to be sustained in any meaningful way throughout the body of the book. Nevertheless, it would be unsafe to suppose that the dominance of the material, animal soul in his discussion is a sign of covert irreligious sympathies. Willis's deepest beliefs and real intentions in writing about animal souls must always remain inscrutable to the historian, and there is nothing in the evidence provided by his life or his writings which enables us to infer that he was duplicitous. Judging from what evidence there is, it seems most likely that Willis quite simply thought he had successfully excluded the immaterial, immortal soul from his considerations in De Anima Brutorum.[26]

It seems safe to conclude, therefore, that seventeenth-century English theologians deemed it unnecessary or inexpedient to include medical theories in their surveys of atheism. However, there were two notable exceptions to this rule – two leading theologians who saw in medicine dangers as real as those presented by mechanistic materialism, and who could not or would not turn a blind eye to it. The Cambridge Platonists, Ralph Cudworth (1617–85) and Henry More (1614–87) made considerable contributions to the anti-atheist literature and, unlike their colleagues, they chose to deal directly and

---

[25] S[imon] P[atrick], A Brief Account of the New Sect of Latitude-Men together with some Reflections on the New Philosophy (London, 1662), p. 23.

[26] Willis, De Anima Brutorum, sig. A2v. Paul F. Cranefield, for example, implies that Willis's distinction between animal and rational souls was dictated merely by religious expediency. See, P.F. Cranefield, 'A Seventeenth-Century View of Mental Deficiency and Schizophrenia: Thomas Willis on "Stupidity or Foolishness"', Bulletin of the History of Medicine, xxxv (1961), 291–315, esp. 306. The inspiration for Willis's pneumatology came from Pierre Gassendi and one scholar has taken a line similar to Cranefield's in his analysis of the Frenchman. See O.R. Bloch, La Philosophie de Gassendi: nominalisme, materialisme et metaphysique (The Hague, 1971). For a corrective see M.J. Osler, 'Baptizing Epicurean Atomism: Pierre Gassendi on the Immortality of the Soul', in M.J. Osler and P.L. Farber (eds.), Religion, Science and Worldview (Cambridge, 1985), pp. 163–83.

explicitly with the latest medical opinions. Nevertheless, this should not be taken to invalidate everything that has been said about the lack of theological interest in medical theory. On the contrary, More and Cudworth should rather be seen as exceptions that prove the rule.

The theology shared by the only two Cambridge Platonists who took the trouble to publish their views, was by no means as orthodox as their posthumous reputations might suggest.[27] In particular, their emphasis upon reason ran counter to the more fideistic voluntarist theology which was dominant in England at this time. Voluntarism in theology can be traced back to William of Ockham (c. 1300–49) but it received powerful support from Calvinism. The voluntarist assumed that God's most significant attribute was his omnipotent and inscrutable will. Mankind is considered to be utterly incapable of fathoming God's reasons or purposes and must, accordingly, rely upon faith in God's grace. For More and Cudworth, however, this theology had unacceptable moral implications. Cudworth summed it up as the belief

that there is nothing absolutely, intrinsically, and naturally good and evil, just and unjust, antecedently to any positive command or prohibition of God; but that the arbitrary will and pleasure of God (that is, an omnipotent Being devoid of all essential and natural justice), by its commands and prohibitions, is the first and only rule and measure thereof.

This attitude, according to Cudworth, underwrote the Calvinist doctrine 'that God can justly doom an innocent creature to eternal torment.' It was in order to avoid this theology and its abominable moral corollaries, that More and Cudworth developed their own rationalistic theology in which even God is constrained to obey the dictates of 'eternal and immutable morality'.[28]

[27] The published works of the other Cambridge Platonists, Whichcote, Smith and Culverwel, appeared posthumously. On opposition to the Cambridge Platonists' theology see P[atrick], A Brief Account of the New Sect of Latitude Men; Joseph Beaumont, Some Observations upon the Apologie of Dr Henry More for his Mystery of Godliness (Cambridge, 1665); Samuel Parker, A Free and Impartial Censure of the Platonick Philosophie (Oxford, 1666); F.J. Powicke, The Cambridge Platonists: A Study (London and Toronto, 1926); M.H. Nicolson, 'Christ's College and the Latitude-Men', Modern Philology, xxvii (1929), 35–53; J. Henry, 'Henry More versus Robert Boyle: The Spirit of Nature and the Nature of Providence', in S. Hutton and R. Crocker (eds.), Of Mysticism and Mechanism: Tercentenary Studies of Henry More (1614–1687) (The Hague, 1989).

[28] Ralph Cudworth, A Treatise Concerning Eternal and Immutable Morality (London, 1731), book I, ch. I. It is perhaps significant that this treatise appeared posthumously. I have used the edition in Ralph Cudworth, The True Intellectual System of the Universe ... with a Treatise Concerning Eternal ... Morality, to which are added the Notes and Dissertations of Dr J.L. Mosheim, trans. J. Harrison, 3 vols. (London, 1845), III, pp. 517–646, esp. 529, 530. F.J. Powicke, The Cambridge Platonists: A Study, pp. 115–16, gives as the reason for Cudworth's failure to complete his publishing ventures, his dismay at the reponse to the first part of his True Intellectual System. Cudworth's great work was evidently seen by various contempo-

Entailed in this theological enterprise was the belief that 'things are what they are, not by will but by nature': 'Every thing must by its own nature be what it is, and nothing else.' The rationalist theology of the Cambridge Platonists stood or fell with their ability to demonstrate the essential nature of things. Thus, their dualistic belief in the immaterial nature of the immortal soul could not simply be presented as a matter for faith. Both More and Cudworth felt the need to demonstrate apodictically the essential immateriality of the soul. In a very real sense, then, the writings of More and Cudworth should not simply be seen as further examples of the contemporary anti-atheist literature. In fact, they were also intended to establish, against the prevailing orthodoxy, an alternative theology.[29]

Had the leading Cambridge Platonists been concerned only to refute popular atheism, they too might have felt it permissable to ignore medical notions. Given their wider ambitions, however, it was not possible for them to overlook any theory which might jeopardize their philosophical efforts to establish the essential immaterial nature of the soul. Anything that might blur what they took to be the ontologically necessary distinction between body and spirit, or material and immaterial substance, threatened their attempt to establish the truth of their rational theology and its concomitant, 'eternal and immutable morality'. So, for them, medical theories constituted a set of obstacles which they just could not ignore.

Henry More, the 'Angel of Christ's', was the first to step in where other theologians feared to tread. In his *Antidote against Atheism* of 1653, More considered three medical suggestions for the seat of 'animadversion' and the will: the animal spirits, the brain and the 'Conarion or Pine-kernel'. Whichever we chose, he insisted, must be supposed also to be the seat of memory and reason. But the animal spirits are so 'very thin and liquid' that they could not retain a memory: 'For it is as impossible to conceive Memory competible to such a Subject, as it is how to write Characters in the water or in the wind'.[30] The brain was judged inadequate on two grounds. Firstly:

raries as Arian, Socinian, deistic, or simply infidel. On the history of the theological belief that God must obey eternal and immutable laws of morality and nature, see A.O. Lovejoy, *The Great Chain of Being: A Study of the History of an Idea* (Cambridge, Mass., 1936), and F. Oakley, *Omnipotence, Covenant & Order: An Excursion in the History of Ideas from Abelard to Leibniz* (Ithaca and London, 1984).

[29] Cudworth, *Eternal . . . Morality*, pp. 531, 522. See, Henry, 'A Cambridge Platonist's Materialism', and Henry, 'Henry More *versus* Robert Boyle'.

[30] Henry More, *An Antidote against Atheism: Or an appeal to the Natural Faculties of the Mind of Man, Whether There Be not a God* (London, 1653), cited from the second edition in Henry More, *A Collection of Several Philosophical Writings* (London, 1662), book I, ch. 11, § 3, p. 33.

Anatomists tell us, that though the Brain be the instrument of sense, yet it has no sense at all of it self; how then can that that has no sense direct thus spontaneously and arbitrariously the Animal Spirits into any part of the Body? an act that plainly requires determinate sense and perception.

Once again More has linked sense and perception to animadversion and reason, and this brought him to his second point. The substance and structure of 'this laxe pithe or marrow in man's head shows no more capacity for thought, he claimed, than 'a Cake of Sewet or a Bowl of Curds'. Moreover it would be impossible to say in which 'loop or interval' of the brain the various faculties of 'free Phansy' and 'active Reason' reside. He emphasized the unstructured nature of the brain by reference to a case reported by Fontanus 'of a boy at Amsterdam that had nothing but limpid water in his head in stead of Brains; and the Brains generally are easily dissolvable into a watery consistence'.[31]

As for the final suggestion, that the will is enacted by 'that little sprunt piece of the Brain', the conarion, More simply found this ridiculous:

If you heard but the magnificent stories that are told of this little lurking Mushroom, how it does not onely hear and see, but imagines, reasons, commands the whole Fabrick of the body more dexterously then an Indian boy does an Elephant, what an acute Logician, Subtle Geometrician, prudent Statesman, skilful Physician, and profound Philosopher he is, and then afterward by dissection you discover this worker of Miracles to be nothing but a poor silly contemptible Knob . . . would you not sooner laugh at it then go about to confute it?[32]

Six years later, in *The Immortality of the Soul*, More added to these arguments. He now dismissed J.B. van Helmont's theory that the 'Orifice of the Stomack' is the seat of common sense. The 'common sensorium', More asserted, must have the power of moving the body, but

there is no Mechanical reason imaginable to be found in the Body, whereby it will appear possible, that supposing the mouth of the Stomack were the common Percipient of all Objects, it could be able to move the rest of the members of the Body, as we find something in us does.

Van Helmont proposed the pylorus as the seat of the soul because of its extreme sensitivity and behaviour, which he took to be evidence of emotions, deliberations and decision-making. Henry More, however, gave this short shrift: 'The harsh handling of an angry Sore or the treading on a Corn on the Toe, may easily cast some into a swoon, and yet no man will ever imagine the Seat of the Common Sense to be placed in the Foot.' Van Helmont's suggestion that frenzy and madness

---

[31] *Ibid.*, I, II, 4–5, p. 34; I, II, 7, p. 35.   [32] *Ibid.*, I, II, 8–9, p. 35.

may stem from a disturbance of the pylorus is compared by More with the 'furor uterinus'; 'apoplexies and syncopes may well proceed from the wombe but nobody supposes that the wombe is the seat of common sense in women'.[33]

Similarly, More rejected the suggestion, which he attributed to Hobbes but which might equally have been ascribed to Aristotle or Harvey, that the heart is the seat of common sense. Remarkably, given what was known about the blood supply, More repeated the argument that there was no 'Mechanical connexion' between the heart and 'all parts of the body'. Perhaps more interesting, however, is his insistence that the continued motions of the heart would necessarily disturb the tenor of our mental lives:

it is very unlikely that that part which is so continually employed in that natural Motion of contracting and dilating it self, should be the seat of that Principle which commands Free and Spontaneous progressions: Perceptions also would be horribly disturbed by its squeezing of it self, and then flagging again by vicissitudes. Neither would Objects appear in the same place, or at least our sight not fixt on the same part of the Object, when the Heart is drawn up and when it is let down again.[34]

The 'Spinal Marrow', the 'concourse of all the Nerves of the Body', was also rejected on the grounds that, like the brain, it does not significantly differ from 'the pith of Elder or a mess of Curds'. But if the spinal column's 'dull pasty Matter' is inconvenient for the 'Centre of Perception', so is the 'perfectly-solid, but very small, particle of Matter in the Body', which was invoked by Henricus Regius (Henry le Roy). More objected that a filing of iron or steel may equally well be said to have sense in it before going on to deny that such a small particle could move the body. In order to move the body, it would have to move itself, he claimed, but 'it being more subtile than the point of any needle ... it must needs passe through the Body and leave it' rather than communicate its motion to the body.[35]

The theory which engaged most of his attention, however, was the Cartesian suggestion that the common sense is confined to the conarion or pineal gland. For his contemporaries this theory, as More

---

[33] More, The Immortality of the Soul (London, 1659). Again, I have used the 2nd edn in A Collection, book II, ch. 4, § 3, p. 78; and II, 7, 5, pp. 89–90. For a discussion of Helmont's view see Walter Pagel, 'The Religious and Philosophical Aspects of Van Helmont's Science and Medicine', Supplements to the Bulletin of the History of Medicine, II (1944), pp. 37–8.

[34] More, Immortality of the Soul, II, 4, 4, p. 78; II, 7, 8, pp. 90–1. Cf. Thomas Hobbes, De Corpore (London, 1655), part 4, ch. 25, § 4. Others regarded the constant motion of the heart as a sure sign that it was the seat of the soul; see Pagel, 'Medieval and Renaissance Contributions to Knowledge of the Brain and its Functions', p. 104.

[35] More, Immortality of the Soul, II, 7, 18, p. 94; II, 4, 8, p. 79. Henricus Regius, Philosophia Naturalis (Amsterdam, 1654), book 5, ch. 1.

remarked, bade 'the fairest of anything . . . for the resolution of the Passions and Properties of living Creatures into mere Corporeal motion'. Furthermore, as he knew all too well, there were a number of impious thinkers who had used Descartes' original conception in a thoroughly atheistic way:

The sum of this Abuse [he wrote] must in brief be this, That the Glandula Pinealis is the common Sentient or Percipient of all Objects; and without a Soul, by virtue of the Spirits and Organization of the Body, may doe all those feats that we ordinarily conceive to be performed by Soul and Body joyned together.

Unlike the rather facile arguments against caricatured versions of van Helmont and Regius, some of More's attacks on Cartesian psychology are detailed and trenchant. Consider, for example, his response to Descartes's account of memory, which he accurately summarized:

the transmission of Motion from . . . [an] Object, through the Nerves, into the inward concavities of the Brain, and so on to the Conarion, opens such and such Pores of the Brain, in such and such order or manner, which remain as tracts or footsteps in the presence of these Objects after they are removed. Which tracts, or signatures, consist mainly of this, that the Spirits will have an easier passage through these Pores than other parts of the Brain. And hence arises Memory, when the Spirits be determined, by the inclining of the Conarion, to that part of the Brain where these tracts are found they moving the Conarion as when the Object was present, though not so strongly.

More simply pointed out that this cannot explain our memory of colours which, according to Descartes, are produced only by the different *speeds* of motion of the particles transmitted from an object to the eye–brain system.[36]

More also attacked Descartes where he was already in retreat. Because of his fundamental principle that the amount of motion in the universe was fixed, Descartes could not allow that the soul or its instrument, the pineal gland, could initiate *new* movements of the body (a concept of change based on ceaseless chains of cause and effect entailed the idea that if motion begins somewhere in the universe, a corresponding 'amount' of motion must cease somewhere else). Consequently, he restricted the operation of the pineal gland merely to *redirecting* the constant flow of animal spirits in the body to bring about whatever movements are required. The details of this account required valves in the nerves which, as More pointed out, 'may be onely a mere fancy, these Valvulae in the Nerves not being yet discov-

---

[36] More, *Immortality of the Soul*, II, 4, 9, p. 79; II, 51, p. 80; II, 5, 7, p. 82–3. More may have had Regius in mind as an atheistic Cartesian; see II, 5, 4–5, p. 82, and II, 7, 13, p. 92. See also P.R. Sloan, 'Descartes, the Sceptics, and the Rejection of Vitalism in Seventeenth-Century Physiology', *Studies in History and Philosophy of Science*, VIII (1977), 1–28, esp. 23–8.

ered by any Anatomist to be part of the Organization of the Body of any Animal'. But More went on to argue that these valves 'would not affect what is aimed at, though they were admitted'. All the conarion can do is direct the animal spirits into one muscle rather than another, 'as Wind in a Bladder'. It follows, according to More, that 'the Tenth part of that force which we ordinarily use to open a mans hand against his will, should whether he would or no easily open it'. 'Mere Mechanical reasons' cannot explain how the spirits in the muscles can be held in place 'in despite of external force'. Instead, we must acknowledge the power of 'the mere *Imperium* of our Soul'.[37]

More conceded nothing whatsoever to any of the medical theories of psychology. He fully intended to reserve all aspects of our mental lives, and much more besides, to the exclusive purview of the immaterial soul. He held the soul responsible not only for higher level mental faculties such as understanding or reason, will, and the self-conscious perception of our 'internal sense', but also for the supposedly 'lower' mental faculties, such as the perception of the external world, the imagination and memory, which doctors had tended to regard as materialistic phenomena. Nevertheless, More still recognized the need to explain psychosomatic interactions and to determine the precise seat of the soul in the body.

His answer to these problems relied upon the animal spirits. Although the animal spirits by themselves were incapable of doing many of the things which anatomists suggested, they were the ideal vehicle for the immaterial soul. More believed that this was 'in a manner the general opinion of all Philosophers' since, for example, those who placed the common sensorium in the heart did so because they believed the left ventricle to be the fountain of these 'pure and subtile Spirits', and even those who held the soul to be corporeal chose 'the freest, subtilest & most active Matter to compound her of'. Descartes and Hermes Trismegistus were clearly in agreement with More on this matter, and even Regius spoke of 'a gale of Spirits' whose circuit in the body accounted for all movements. In view of this, More decided, the bodily site where these spirits accumulate, the 'Acropolis of the Soul', must be, 'the fourth Ventricle' of the brain (the first three being the two 'upper Ventricles' and 'the middle Ventricle').

However, the soul was not confined to this fourth ventricle of the

---

[37] More, *Immortality of the Soul*, II, 5, 4–6, p. 82. Cf. More, *Appendix to the . . . Antidote against Atheism*, in *Collection*, ch. 10, § 6, p. 171. See also Alan Gabbey, 'The Mechanical Philosophy and its Problems: Mechanical Explanations, Impenetrability, and Perpetual Motion', in J.C. Pitt (ed.), *Change and Progress in Modern Science* (Dordrecht, 1985), pp. 9–84, esp. pp. 14–28.

brain. It enacted here its duties as the common sensorium, but it also animated the whole body by spreading itself locally through the nervous system:

it is plain that the main use of the Brain and Nerves is to keep these subtile Spirits from over-speedy dissipation; and that the Brain with its Caverns is but one great round Nerve; as the Nerves with their invisible porosities are but so many smaller productions or slenderer prolongations of the Brain: And so together are but one contained Receptacle or Case of that immediate Instrument of the sensiferous motions of the Soul, the Animal Spirits, wherein also lies her hidden Vehicle of life in this mortal body.[38]

It can now be seen why More was so insistent upon the amorphous nature of that 'Cake of Sewet', the brain. His earliest pronouncements on the unsuitability of the brain for complex functions, in the *Antidote against Atheism,* predated the appearance of Willis's *De Cerebri Anatome* (1664), but even subsequently More made no attempt to take in the latest theories of brain structure. He continued this pretence even when preparing new editions of his philosophical works for the *Opera Omnia* of 1679; the extensive notes and scholia which he added to take account of recent developments offer no second thoughts on the nature of the brain and nerves. Nor did he ever acknowledge the popular view, mentioned above, that different parts of the brain dealt with sense, understanding and memory. It was crucial for More's philosophical theology that all brain functions were performed entirely by the soul. Accordingly, any suggestion that the brain had a complex structure was potentially embarrassing – this was a time when almost everyone agreed that nature did nothing in vain.

Furthermore, although More invoked animal spirits, even going so far as to admit that 'the Soul of her self, without the assistance of the Spirits' is incapable of 'Sensation & other [mental] Operations', his ideas are very different from those of current medical writers. While dualist natural philosophers like Descartes, Gassendi, Willis and Charleton tried to demarcate clearly and specifically what mental functions were carried out by the incorporeal soul and what by animal spirits, More attributed virtually everything to the immaterial soul. Indeed, it is difficult to be sure what role the spirits play in his system beyond providing a material sign that the soul is present. The spirits do not produce muscle contractions which are brought about by the 'mere *Imperium* of our Soul'; they merely assist in the act of sensation where 'the arrival of motion from the Object to the Organ . . . is received . . . by virtue of the Soul's presence there'; and neither they nor the brain play

[38] More, *Immortality of the Soul,* II, 8, 1–7, pp. 95–6; II, 8, 13, p. 98.

any part in memory which is categorically said to be 'in the Soul'. Forgetfulness, on the other hand, occurs when the spirits are 'not in a due temper', possibly because of 'overmuch coolness or Waterishness in the Head'.[39]

Perhaps the clearest indication of the philosophical and theological gulf between More and these other dualist thinkers is provided by their respective views on animal souls. One of the major assumptions of the mechanical philosophy was that matter could be organized in such a way that it could constitute a 'living' system. Life did not depend, therefore, upon an immaterial principle or soul. The immaterial soul was held to be unique to humankind, the distinguishing feature between men and beasts, and this meant that its realm of operation could not be extended very far. Anatomists were well aware that men and animals displayed, as Thomas Willis put it, 'altogether the same Conformation of the animal Organs'. Since there was nothing in the brain and 'nervous stock' of man that did not have its counterpart in other animal brains, it seemed obvious that vital and mental functions common to both men and animals could be attributed to the same organs or parts of organs in each. Hence only the higher mental faculties of ratiocination, abstract thought and understanding were attributed to the animal soul. To assign common animal faculties such as sensory perception, certain 'passions' or emotions, and memory to the immaterial soul would be tantamount to denying the significance of the anatomical structure of the brain and nervous system and would require that animals too have immaterial souls. This is precisely what More did.[40]

More's somewhat facile insistence that the brain was as amorphous as a 'Bowl of Curds' should be seen, therefore, not simply as stupidity or mere ignorance of contemporary medical developments in brain anatomy, but rather as a deliberate stratagem to promote his extreme soul–body dualism. By the same token, he felt it necessary to insist that animals, no less than men, have immaterial souls. Thus, when More declared that it was not spirits which kept muscles clenched but the 'Imperium of our Souls', he immediately confronted the anticipated Cartesian criticism head-on: 'From whence it is manifest that brute Beasts must have Souls also'. Elsewhere he stood the Cartesian argument on its head as another ploy to defeat materialist monism:

[39] Ibid., II, 11, 1, p. 106; II, 5, 6, p. 82, II, 11, 2, p. 106; II, 11, 4, p. 107. Thomas Willis, Cerebri Anatome Nervorumque Descriptio et Usus (London, 1664). Henry More, Opera Omnia, 2 vols. (London, 1679).

[40] Willis, De Anima Brutorum, p. 32. See W.F. Bynum, 'The Anatomical Method, Natural Theology and the Functions of the Brain', Isis, LXIV (1973), 445–68. See also Pagel, 'Medieval and Renaissance Contributions to Knowledge of the Brain and its Functions'.

For the wafting of one's hand near the Eye of a mans friend, is no sufficient proof that external Objects will necessarily and Mechanically determine the Spirits into the Muscles, no faculty of the Soul intermedling. For if one be fully assured, or rather can keep himself from the fear of any hurt, by the wafting of his friend's Hand before his Eye, he may easily abstain from winking: But if fear surprise him, the Soul is to be entitled to the action, and not the mere Mechanisme of the Body. Wherefore this is no proof that the Phaenomena of Passions, with their consequences may be salved in brute Beasts by pure Mechanicks; and therefore neither in Men.

Inversion of the Cartesian argument enabled More to use it against materialists: when animals blink it is a sign that they have (immaterial) souls; men blink, so they too must have souls.[41]

More's belief in animal souls was by no means a common theological opinion, but it was defended by his close friend, Ralph Cudworth. 'Life and mechanism', Cudworth suggested, were, until recently, 'two distinct ideas of the mind', which were not, 'confounded together': 'It being a thing that was hardly ever called into doubt or question by any before Cartesius, whether the souls of brutes had any sense, cogitation or consciousness in them or no.' In spite of this new intellectual fashion Cudworth, like More, insisted upon the incorporeal nature of the animal soul. The reason for this was not, as some historians have suggested, because they had a supposedly typical English sentimentality towards animals. It was an indispensable element in the rational theology of both men that souls must be *essentially* immaterial. For them, establishment of the immateriality of animal souls was as important as – and indeed inseparable from – the establishment of the incorporeality of human souls. As Cudworth wrote:

they who will attribute life, sense, cogitation, consciousness and self-enjoyment ... to blood and brains, or mere organized bodies in brutes, will never be able clearly to defend the incorporeity and immortality of humane souls, as most probably they do not intend any such thing. For either all conscious and cogitative beings are incorporeal, or else nothing can be proved to be incorporeal.[42]

This stratagem was not without its drawbacks. Neither More nor Cudworth wished to assert the *immortality* of animal souls, but this

---

[41] More, *Immortality of the Soul*, ii, 5, 6, p. 82; ii, 10, 6, p. 103; cf. ii, 5, 9–10, p. 83–4.

[42] Cudworth, *A Treatise Concerning Eternal and Immutable Morality*, i, pp. 73, 80. Historians have tended to regard More's and Cudworth's views as representative of English theology and as deriving simply from English sentimentality towards animals. See, for example, K. Thomas, *Man and the Natural World: Changing Attitudes in England 1500–1800* (Harmondsworth, 1983), pp. 104, and J. Rogers, 'Descartes and the English', in J.D. North and J.J. Roche (eds.), *The Light of Nature: Essays in the History and Philosophy of Science Presented to A.C. Crombie* (The Hague, 1985), 281–302, esp. 292. Thomas sees a dichotomy between Cartesianism and the views of More which are said to be 'more representative of English opinion', p. 35. In fact, most orthodox seventeenth-century theologians adopted the opinions of Pierre Gassendi, which held that animals were endowed with a lower, subtle material soul. As Thomas's sources show, More and Cudworth were in very radical and unorthodox company on this issue, pp. 138–9. See also L.D. Cohen, 'Descartes and Henry More on the Beast-Machine', *Annals of Science*, 1 (1936), 48–61.

meant that they had to sever the philosophical links between immateriality and immortality which other dualists had laboured to forge. It was axiomatic among mechanist dualists that all change was the result of matter in motion. It followed that a non-material entity could not change, and a fortiori could not perish. These efforts were completely undermined by More's insistence that the immaterial souls of brutes have no 'capacity of eternal life and bliss' but are only imperishable in the same sense that matter is. Similarly, while Cudworth believed that not even 'Omnipotence itself by mere will' could create a living *material* soul, there was nothing, he claimed, to prevent God from annihilating an immaterial soul 'at pleasure'. Immortality was no longer a necessary concomitant of immateriality. As one contemporary theologian, Matthew Smith, pointed out,

incorporeity does not prove immortality, if anything incorporeal be mortal: Either, therefore, the Phenomena of Sensation do not prove Incorporeity, or incorporeity does not prove Immortality; and then there's an end of all natural arguments for Immortality or all sensible Creatures are immortal.

Smith was not the only theologian to reject the Cambridge Platonist attitude. For example, Edward Stillingfleet, the later Bishop of Worcester, also preferred the mechanistic emphasis on the natural immortality of all immaterial entities. Moreover, the fact that iatromechanism was not attacked in the bulk of the anti-atheist literature suggests that most theologians agreed with him. It can hardly be a coincidence that the only theologians to attack iatromechanism were also the only ones to insist upon the immaterial nature of the animal soul.[43]

Henry More was alone, also, in his attack on another aspect of medical theory. The widely held medical belief that life processes could be equated with some kind of fire burning in the body, was regarded by More as another materialistic threat to his concept of soul. The following account of life from Willis's *De Anima Brutorum*, for example, would have struck More as dangerously materialistic in its emphasis:

there is not much more difference between an insensible and a sensible Body, than between a thing uninkindled, and a thing kindled; and yet we ordinarily see, this to be made from that; why therefore in a like manner, may we not judge a sensible thing, or Body to be made out of an insensible? Every matter, as it is not Burnt, so not animated

[43] More, *Immortality of the Soul*, II, 12, 1, p. 110; cf, *Appendix to the . . . Antidote against Atheism*, ch. 10, § 7, p. 171. Cudworth, *A Treatise Concerning Eternal and Immutable Morality*, I, p. 80, and III, p. 531. Matthew Smith, *A Philosophical Discourse of the Nature of Rational and Irrational Souls* (London, 1695), p. 3. Cf. Edward Stillingfleet, *Origines Sacrae*, I, p. 639, and II, pp. 385–6.

... But as soon as they have taken flame, from some incentive being put to it, by and by their Particles being rapidly moved, and as it were animated, produce a shining with Heat and Light ... In like manner, the Vital humour in an Egg, remains torpid and sluggish in the beginning, and like to uninkindled matter; but as soon as it is actuated, from the Soul being raised up, presently like an inkindled fire, it excites Life with Motion and Sense, and in the more perfect Creatures with Heat.

'Life', Willis emphasized on another occasion, 'is not so like to flame, but even a flame it self'.[44]

More dubbed this 'psychopyrism' and published an attack upon it in 1682 under the title 'A Letter to a Learned Psychopyrist'. The focus of his attack was the theory of generation-as-enkindling to which Willis and others subscribed.:

according to this, the production of a Soul, *ex Traduce*, would end in meer Materialism, and signifie only, that in Generation some matter only is newly modified, as the Tallow is or Wax [of a candle] when they pass out of their state of Wax or Tallow into that of a bright Flame. Which way of philosophizing, as it is most false, so it is most mischievous if men should be so fond as to believe it.

Significantly, More drew upon his knowledge of Cartesianism to refute this vitalistic view of fire:

it looks as if there were an ἀυτοκινησία, or Self-moving in Fire, it being in perpetual motion but this is a plain fallacy, for the parts of the Flame are not self-moved, but they are moved of another: As when you apply a lighted Candle to light another Candle, the parts ... are put into motion by the moved parts of the lighted Candle ...

Unfortunately for More's claims, not everyone accepted the Cartesian belief in passive matter. Willis, for example, followed Gassendi in holding matter to be active:

what is vulgarly delivered, that Matter, out of which Natural things are made, is meerly passive, and cannot be moved, unless it be moved by another thing, is not true; but rather on the contrary, Atoms, which are the matter of sublunary things, are so very active and self-moving that they never stay long, but ordinarily stray out of one subject into another[45]

Richard Baxter, the nonconformist divine, who responded directly to More's 'Letter', was utterly dismissive of More's Cartesian account

44 Willis, *De Anima Brutorum*, pp. 33, 7. Willis cited 'Hippocrates, Plato, Pythagoras, Aristotle, Galen, Democritus, Epicurus, Laertius, Fernelius, Heurnius, Cartesius, Hogelandus, Honaratus Faber, Verulam, and George Ent' as those who believed the substance of animal souls to be 'Fire it self', p. 5, but this list could easily be extended. See Douglas McKie, 'Fire and the *Flamma Vitalis*: Boyle, Hooke and Mayow', in E.A. Underwood (ed.), *Science Medicine and History*, I, pp. 469–88; Everett Mendelsohn, *Heat and Life: The Development of the Theory of Animal Heat* (Cambridge, 1964), pp. 27–66; Audrey B. Davis, *Circulation Physiology and Medical Chemistry in England 1650–1680* (Lawrence, Kansas, 1973).
45 More, 'Letter to a Learned Psychopyrist', in Joseph Glanvill, *Saducismus Triumphatus: Or Full and Plain Evidence concerning Witches and Apparitions*, 2nd edn (London, 1682), pp. 217, 241. This is discussed more fully in Henry, 'Medicine and Pneumatology: Henry More, Richard Baxter and Francis Glisson's *Treatise on the Energetic Nature of Substance*'. Willis, *De Anima Brutorum*, p. 33.

of fire. Far from being 'no more than motion', fire is, according to
Baxter, 'the active Principle by which mental and sensitive Nature
operateth on Man, and Bruits and Vegetables, and all the passive
Elements, (if it be not *ipsa forma telluris*)'. More's objection to
'psychopyrism' stemmed from his own mechanistic and materialistic
view of fire. Theologians who did not see fire in the same light were
unlikely to share More's concern. Indeed, it would seem that analogies
between fire and the soul were almost as common in theology as they
were in medical writings. Jeremy Taylor, for example, drew upon an
analogy with fire to explain how the soul when separated from the
body would no longer need to eat to survive:

fire can abide without matter to feed it: for itselfe is matter; it is substance. And so is the
soul: and as the element of fire, and the celestial globes of fire eat nothing, but live of
themselves; so can the soul when it is divested of its relative, and so would the candle's
flame, if it could get to the region of fire, as the soule does to the region of spirits.

Once again we see that More's opposition to contemporary medical
theories reveals more about the differences between his theology and
that of his colleagues than it does about general perceptions of
medicine.[46]

Similarly, More and Cudworth were the only theologians to recognize a threat to their religion in the work of Francis Glisson. The
monistic vitalism of his *Treatise on the Energetic Nature of Substance*
was in many respects a greater danger to their dualist endeavours than
the mechanical philosophy of Cartesians and Hobbists. More and
Cudworth made great play with the claim that no organization of dead
matter could possibly produce life. More spoke for them both when he
ridiculed the suggestion 'that *Organization* may do strange feats', as if,
'a Watch may be a living creature, though the several parts have neither
Life nor Sense'. Such arguments, however, had no force against the
new theories of the Regius Professor of Physick at their own University. Glisson agreed that life could not be a mere epiphenomenon of
particular organizations of matter. Instead, he argued that all matter
was endowed with a primitive form of life which could be seen to be
manifested not only in the ability of matter to move itself but also in its
apparent perceptivity and appetites.[47]

[46] Richard Baxter, *Of the Immortality of Mans Soul*, pp. 57–9. Jeremy Taylor, *The Whole
Works*, I, p. lxviii.
[47] More, *Immortality of the Soul*, II, 4, 1, p. 77. On Glisson's theory of matter see: O. Temkin,
'The Classical Roots of Glisson's Doctrine of Irritation', *Bulletin of the History of Medicine*,
XXXVIII (1964), 297–328; reprinted in *The Double Face of Janus*, pp. 290–316; O. Temkin,
'Francis Glisson', in C.C. Gillispie (ed.), *Dictionary of Scientific Biography*, 14 vols. (New
York, 1970–80), V, pp. 425–7; Pagel, 'Harvey and Glisson'; Henry, 'Medicine and
Pneumatology'.

These three powers or faculties of matter enabled Glisson to explain how parts of matter could organize and 'improve themselves' to produce sentient animals and man. For Cudworth the atheistic implications of this 'hylozoism', as he called it, were all too plain. The mechanistic proposition that matter was passive demanded some kind of external principle to account for movement and so it could be said that 'atomism . . . hath in it self a natural cognation and conjunction with *incorporealism*'. But 'hylozoism, seems to have altogether as close and intimate a correspondence with *corporealism*'. Indeed, 'there is no necessity at all left,' Cudworth went on, 'either of any incorporeal soul in men to make them rational, or of any Deity in the whole universe to solve the regularity thereof'.[48]

Originating as it did from Glisson's anatomical and physiological researches, the *Tractatus de Natura Substantiae Energetica* is a difficult work and there is little in More's and Cudworth's critiques that suggests they really understood it. Their response was one of ridicule rather than reason, frequently misrepresenting Glisson's ideas to suit their rhetoric. Here, for example, Cudworth's argument depends on the false assertion that Glisson attributed understanding to bare matter:

If matter as such, had life, perception and understanding belonging to it, then of necessity must every atom or smallest particle therefore, be a distinct percipient by itself; from whence it will follow, that there could not possibly be, any such men and animals as now are, compounded out of them, but every man and animal, would be a heap of innumerable percipients, and have innumerable perceptions and intellections; whereas it is plain, that there is but one life and understanding, one soul or mind, one perceiver or thinker in every one.

The idea of every man being a 'commonwealth of percipients', Cudworth averred, was 'absurd and ridiculous'.[49]

The True Intellectual System of the Universe, Cudworth's massive survey of different kinds of atheism, informs us that 'hylozoick' atheism had found so few subscribers sinces its origins in Hellenistic philosophy that it had looked 'like a forlorn and deserted thing'. Since being 'urged by the writer of "The Life of Nature"', however, Cudworth believed that it 'began already to be looked upon, as the rising sun of atheism'. If Cudworth's judgement of the contemporary scene is to be relied upon, it would seem that Francis Glisson's *De Vita Naturae* had a far greater impact than historians of medicine have previously thought. Certainly, by the end of the seventeenth century

[48] Cudworth, *A Treatise Concerning Eternal and Immutable Morality*, I, p. 145; I, p. 144.
[49] *Ibid.*, III, p. 406.

and throughout the eighteenth, matter's putative ability to think was a major focus of theological polemic. Unfortunately, it is not easy to assess Glisson's role in this development. The concept of thinking matter was suggested as a possibility by John Locke in 1690, and his subsequent debate with Edward Stillingfleet made the whole issue a notorious aspect of contemporary philosophy.[50]

As a physician Locke knew Glisson's work and owned a copy of the *Tractatus*. He may even have discussed it with Lady Masham, Cudworth's learned daughter, but so far this must remain speculative. Anyway, it seems true to say that once Locke made the notion of thinking matter well known, Glisson's work, based on a recondite knowledge of anatomy and physiology, was no longer invoked. More and Cudworth, the only theologians to pay serious attention to medical theories in their anti-atheist writings, had been alone in pointing to the dangers of Glisson's 'hyloziosm'. Other theologians continued to ignore medical ideas. Hylozoism only became a focus for their attention when it had been brought out of medicine and into the realms of mainstream philosophy by John Locke.

In this chapter I have tried to offer suggestions as to why the new ideas in seventeenth-century medicine were disregarded in the otherwise comprehensive anti-atheistic literature of that time. Moreover, I have argued that the unusual interest shown in current medical theorizing by Henry More and Ralph Cudworth should alert us to the fact that their concerns were somewhat different from those of their fellow theologians. The Cambridge Platonists were concerned not only to refute atheism but also to reject the dominant Calvinistic emphasis on voluntarist theology. Repelled by the principle that 'things are good and just, because God Wills them so to be', More and Cudworth wanted to establish the claim that even God's activities are constrained by 'mutual Respects and Relations eternal and immutable, and in order of Nature antecedent to any Understanding either created or uncreated'.[51] The rationalist theology which they built up from these

---

[50] Ibid., I, pp. 215–16; III, p. 405. John Locke, *An Essay Concerning Human Understanding* (London, 1960), book IV, ch. 3, § 6. For a full discussion of the subsequent response to Locke's suggestion from Stillingfleet and others see John W. Yolton, *Thinking Matter: Materialism in Eighteenth-Century Britain* (Oxford, 1983).

[51] [Joseph Glanvill and George Rust], *Two Choice and Useful Treatises: The One Lux Orientalis or An Enquiry into the Opinion of the Ancient Sages concerning the Praeexistence of Souls. Being a Key to unlock the Grand Mysteries of Providence, in Relation to Mans Sins and Misery. The Other a Discourse of Truth ... With Annotations on them Both* (London, 1682), sig. N6v, and p. 45 of More's 'Annotations upon *Lux Orientalis*' (separately paginated). This edition, including More's copious annotations, was seen through the press by Henry More. The authors, by this time deceased, had both been devoted disciples of his.

beginnings depended on a strict ontological dichotomy between matter and immaterial spirit – to blur this categorical distinction was to deprive God of one of the immutable 'Respects and Relations' which was supposed to have guided His hand in creation.

One of the ways by which More and Cudworth sought to maintain this strict dichotomy was by denying any activity whatsoever to matter. For them, matter could not even fall to the ground without the intervention of the incorporeal 'Spirit of Nature'. So, although the dualism of the mechanical philosophy was perfectly acceptable to most contemporary English theologians, More and Cudworth regarded it as a threat to their rational theology – the mechanical philosophy granted too much activity to matter itself.[52] It was important for the Cambridge Platonists, therefore, to deny that any mental or vital events could be accounted for solely in material terms and it was this which led them, uniquely, to engage with medical theories. As we have seen, this, in turn, set them equally against those theologians who denied the scriptural validity of immaterial souls and the more orthodox but less severely dualistic theologians who only invoked the immaterial soul to account for the 'highest' mental faculties, such as abstract reasoning.

Although More and Cudworth were alone in taking issue with medical speculations, we should not conclude that the medical tradition was without influence. Eighteenth-century developments in theological controversy tend to suggest that the vitalistic monism which had always been present in the medical tradition came to be perceived as the major threat to the dualism of religious orthodoxy. It would seem, therefore, that More and Cudworth were right to regard medical theory as heralding 'the rising sun of atheism'.

[52] On the role of activity in mechanistic matter theory see: J. Henry, 'Occult Qualities and the Experimental Philosophy: Active Principles in pre-Newtonian Matter Theory', *History of Science*, xxiv (1986), 335–81.

4

Mental illness, magical medicine and the Devil in northern England, 1650–1700

DAVID HARLEY

Modern concepts of mental illness have usually been depicted as first forming in reaction to witch hunts and demonic possession, so that scientific beliefs triumphed over superstition.[1] Such a view dismisses as irrational belief in the Devil's activity in the world and it overlooks the extent to which medical naturalism was produced out of political struggle in France and England, which combined with a social process of distancing elite from popular culture throughout Western Europe. It was not the triumph of self-evident ideas that led first Anglicans and then dissenters to abandon their belief in supernatural causation and therapy when they had only the first inkling of an alternative explanation.

Historians have turned to anthropology in the search for conceptual tools to help explain belief in the supernatural and its decline. Unfortunately, the static models of society produced by the older schools of anthropological thought, viewing beliefs in terms of their function in maintaining the status quo, were unable to explain change unless imposed from without by a process of modernization or accultura-tion.[2] More recent work has attempted to apply techniques of linguis-

I would like to thank Jonathan Barry, Stuart Clark, Michael Hunter, Michael MacDonald, Keith Thomas and Charles Webster, both for their published work on this subject and for discussion and encouragement. I am also grateful to the Women's History seminar at the Institute of Historical Research for helpful comments on an earlier version of this paper. Although Stephen Greenblatt's essay, 'Shakespeare and the Exorcists', was first published in 1984, I did not read it until 1988, when it appeared in his book, *Shakespearean Negotiations*. I regret being unable to incorporate his approach in the present study.

[1] Irving Kirsch, 'Demonology and the Rise of Science: An Example of the Misperception of Historical data', *Journal of the History of the Behavioural Sciences*, XIV (1978), 149–57; Nicholas P. Spanos, 'Witchcraft in Histories of Psychiatry: A Critical Analysis and an Alternative Conceptualization', *Psychological Bulletin*, LXXXV (1978), 417–39.

[2] Vinigi L. Grottanelli, 'Witchcraft: An Allegory?', in F.X. Grollig and H.B. Haley (eds.), *Medical Anthropology* (The Hague, 1976), pp. 321–9; Malcolm Crick, *Explorations in Language and Meaning: towards a Semantic Anthropology* (London, 1976), pp. 109–27.

tics and semiotics and to set magical healing rituals in the context of a culture's other beliefs and practices.[3] When these developments have been fully absorbed, they may provide a more sophisticated understanding of demonology.[4] Nevertheless, given the relative lack of interest shown by English villagers in absolute, transcendent evil, the beliefs of ordinary English men and women may remain inaccessible.[5] The afflicted and their friends are usually seen through the eyes of those who were convinced of the ubiquity of the Devil and historians lack the raw material necessary for a thorough anthropological analysis. With the revival of interest in popular culture, historians have perhaps been too ready to assume that accounts of dispossession written by interested parties can provide access to the beliefs of this mute group.

An interactionist view of illness and the supernatural is probably more useful for tackling the thorny problems of how far definitions are shaped by the various participants.[6] Such a perspective would help to give due weight to the viewpoint of the afflicted and to disentangle different roles and beliefs in the borderland between mental illness and supernatural affliction. Historians have not always borne in mind the possibility that religious healers and the afflicted viewed matters very differently.[7]

Northern England was an area where the conflict between educated beliefs and those of the ordinary people was particularly sharp since throughout the seventeenth century the inhabitants were widely regarded as ignorant of any religion but the most superstitious remnants of catholicism, their prayers being 'more like spels and charmes than devotions'.[8] Protestants were concerned to undermine traditional cus-

[3] Anthony D. Buckley, *Yoruba Medicine* (Oxford, 1985); Bruce Kapferer, *A Celebration of Demons: Exorcism and the Aesthetics of Healing in Sri Lanka* (Bloomington, 1983); Emiko Ohnuki-Tierney, *Illness and Healing among the Sakhalin Ainu* (Cambridge, 1981); Janice Reid, *Sorcerers and Healing Spirits: Continuity and Change in an Aboriginal Medical System* (Canberra, 1983).

[4] Michael MacDonald, 'Anthropological Perspectives on the History of Science and Medicine', in P. Corsi and P. Weindling (eds.), *Information Sources in the History of Science and Medicine* (London, 1983), pp. 61–80. Stuart Clark, 'Inversion, Misrule and the Meaning of Witchcraft', *Past and Present*, no. 87 (1980), 98–127.

[5] Alan Macfarlane, 'The Root of all Evil', in David Parkin (ed.), *The Anthropology of Evil* (Oxford, 1985), pp. 57–76.

[6] Kai Erikson, *Wayward Puritans: A Study in the Sociology of Deviance* (New York, 1966); Eliot Freidson, *Profession of Medicine: A Study of the Sociology of Applied Knowledge* (New York, 1970), pp. 205–331; Christina Larner, *Enemies of God; The Witch-hunt in Scotland* (Oxford, 1981); Richard Weisman, *Witchcraft, Magic, and Religion in 17th-Century Massachusetts* (Amherst, 1984). I am grateful to Clive Holmes for drawing this last work to my attention.

[7] Kaja Finkler, *Spiritualist Healers in Mexico* (South Hadley, Mass., 1985), pp. 51, 59.

[8] *Memoirs of Sir Benjamin Rudyerd, Knt.*, ed. James A. Manning (London, 1841), p. 136; Dr Williams's Library: MS. 59.1/30, letter from John Rawlet.

toms and beliefs such as the cult of holy wells, seeking to replace it with a secular interpretation of the medicinal use of waters bestowed by God's general providence. Pilgrimage to Holywell was denounced as a pagan custom, and the catholic priests as 'brazen fac't Empiricks'. When holy wells were turned into profitable spas, protestants deplored the attitude of the populace, 'as if the Water were a Spell, not a Medicine', but traditional customs continued unchecked, especially among 'the vulgar neighbouring people of the Red Letter'.[9]

The belief in charms and amulets, although explained in corpuscularian terms by Robert Boyle, was generally attacked by protestants in the North as 'ye Knavery of ye Romish Priests yt gull their superstitious and credulous Votarys with such fopperys'. John Webster was exceptional in his pragmatic approach, regarding charms as essential to calm the imagination of ordinary Northerners who, 'if they chance to have any sort of the Epilepsie, Palsie, Convulsions or the like, do presently perswade themselves that they are bewitched, forespaken, blasted, fairy-taken, or haunted with some evil spirit'.[10] Webster was less tolerant in his attitude towards charms to staunch bleeding, having lost a patient through being called too late to prevent his death, but belief in their efficacy was widespread even among nonconformists such as Roger Lowe and Anglicans such as the deputy registrar of the Chester ecclesiastical court.[11]

Orthodox theologians of the Church of England had no time for supernatural phenomena, since they held that the age of miracles was long past, but nonconformists and Anglicans influenced by the Cambridge Platonists, who were alarmed by the perceived threat posed by materialism, differentiated sharply between papist miracles and God's special providence. They believed that God and the Devil were active in the world and collaborated in collecting tales of the supernatural from dissenting ministers and elderly gentlewomen, in the North as

[9] M. Sutcliffe, *An Abridgement or Survey of Poperie* (London, 1606), p. 163; Michael Stanhope, *Newes out of York-Shire* (London, 1627), p. 28; E. Borlase, 'A further Account of Latham-Spaw', p. 3, in *Latham Spaw in Lancashire*, 2nd edn (London, 1672); Henry Taylor, *The Ancient Crosses and Holy Wells of Lancashire* (Manchester, 1906), p. 17.

[10] [Robert Boyle] *Some Considerations touching the Usefulness of Experimental Natural Philosophy* (Oxford, 1663), part 2, pp. 214–15, 239–40; Manchester Central Library: MS. 922.3, N. 21, p. 41: Henry Newcome the younger, Memorandum book (publication forthcoming from Chetham Society); J. Webster, *The Discovery of Supposed Witchcraft* (London, 1677) pp. 323–4.

[11] Webster, *The Discovery of Supposed Witchcraft*, p. 330; *The Diary of Roger Lowe*, ed. W.L. Sachse (London, 1938), pp. 76–7; Henry Prescott, Diary, 4 Feb. 1704/5. I am grateful to Dr Addy for allowing me access to this manuscript, to be published by the Lancashire and Cheshire Record Society.

elsewhere.[12] Leading presbyterians such as Philip Henry and Oliver Heywood noted in their diaries the apt deaths that God inflicted on persecuting clergy and magistrates, on catholics and the ungodly.[13] Nonconformists saw the direct hand of providence in their delivery from disease, although arrogance could lead to God striking down even a godly minister like Timothy Manlove of Leeds, who sought to succeed to the lucrative pastoral and medical practice of Richard Gilpin in Newcastle, despite contrary advice.[14] There was caution, however, when it came to interpreting the will of God when the godly suffered, as when a young woman was driven by melancholy fantasies to suicide and Heywood commented, 'its not good to judge a persons final state by outward providences about him'.[15] In time, such doubts led to nonconformists interpreting only the meaning of providences about themselves, perhaps as a result of the bitter attacks of Anglicans such as Dr Hook of Halifax on any attempt to explain misfortune by saying that 'god had a special hand for punishing of some sin'.[16]

During the late seventeenth century, however, northern presbyterians continued to explain many phenomena as deriving from the activity of God or the Devil where their Anglican contemporaries insisted that only natural causes were involved. They were especially inclined to attribute the wild behaviour and prophetic utterances of enthusiasts to some form of Satanic activity, despite being aware that 'Doctor Merick Causabone, indeavours to shew how this may be done by natural causes'. The account by John Gilpin of Kendal of his demonic enthusiasm and the behaviour of feverish Quakers were widely cited as evidence.[17] Although Quakers did not publicize George Fox's healing miracles, performed in Quaker strongholds like north

[12] Charles Webster, *From Paracelsus to Newton: Magic and the Making of Modern Science* (Cambridge, 1982), pp. 88–100; *Yorkshire Genealogist*, II (1890), p. 110; W. Turner, *A Complete History of the Most Remarkable Providences* (London, 1697), [cited below as *Providences*] part I, p. 52; Bodleian Library: MS. Eng. letters, e. 29, fo. 180; B.L.: Add. MS. 22, 548, fo. 99; Egerton MS. 2618, fo. 159; Add. MS. 4460, fos. 54–6; *The Diary of Ralph Thoresby, F.R.S.*, ed. J. Hunter, II (1894), pp. 103, 124.

[13] B.L.: Add. MS. 4460, fo. 19v.; P. Henry, *Diaries and Letters*, ed. M.H. Lee (London, 1882), pp. 159, 171; O. Heywood, *Autobiography and Diaries*, ed. J.H. Turner, 4 vols. (Brighouse, 1882–5), II, p. 191; II, pp. 262, 266; III, pp. 93–5, 99, 195, 211.

[14] John Bickerton Williams, *Memoirs of the Life, Character, and Writings of the Rev. Matthew Henry* (London, 1865), pp. 18–19; W. Tong, *An Account of the Life and Death of Mr. Matthew Henry* (London, 1716), p. 107; B.L.: Add. MS. 4460, fo. 24v.

[15] O. Heywood, *Autobiography*, III, p. 191.

[16] B.L.: Add. MS. 4460, fo. 21v; O. Heywood, *Autobiography*, II, p. 278.

[17] Richard Hollinworth, *The Holy Ghost on the Bench, other Spirits at the Bar* (London, 1656), p. 71; J. Gilpin, *The Quakers Shaken* (London, 1653) Richard Gilpin, *Daemonologia Sacra* (London, 1677); part 3, p. 114; William Turner, *Providences*, p. 65; [H. Newcome] *A Faithful Narrative of the Life and Death of . . . Mr. John Machin* (London, 1671), p. 21.

Lancashire, it was easier for presbyterians to make the accusation of diabolism than for Quakers to refute it, despite their vociferous opposition to all illicit magic.[18]

The deployment of medical naturalism against enthusiasm, by restoration Anglicans, coexisted awkwardly with their stress on the supernatural in their struggle against atheism. This tension, implicit in the works of More, Baxter and Casaubon, was partly responsible for the abandoning of most forms of supernatural explanation, especially among whigs. Although Charles Owen of Warrington and some of the Anglican critics of the French Prophets used demonic explanations, most eighteenth-century criticism of enthusiasm was couched in the secular terminology of mental illness.[19] Since the end of the sixteenth century, the mainstream theologians of the Church of England had used concepts like 'suffocation of the mother' to combat puritan diagnoses of witchcraft and possession, as in the criticism of Darrel and the Mary Glover case. Although mental and physiological explanations did not immediately supercede all belief in the supernatural, the reading of sceptics like Weyer, by a Lancashire magistrate investigating witchcraft, for example, promoted much greater care in the taking of evidence.[20] During the course of the seventeenth century, an increasing range of supposedly supernatural afflictions were dismissed as merely examples of 'People handled by strange Diseases', a tendency perceived by Henry More as highly subversive.[21]

Secular concepts of mental illness were widely familiar in the North of England, used comfortably by all classes of society, from the poor woman whose husband had 'fallen into a Lunary and Violent distraction' to the archdeacon who tried to use the opinions of catholic and nonconformist physicians to prove his wife 'subject to maniack pas-

---

[18] George Fox's 'Book of Miracles', ed. H.J. Cadbury (Cambridge, 1948), pp. 115, 123–5, 130–1, 135, 138; Francis Higginson, A Brief Relation of the Irreligion of the Northern Quakers (London, 1653), p. 18; Jonathan Clapham, A Full Discovery and Confutation of the Wicked and Damnable Doctrines of the Quakers (London, 1656), pp. 44–8; James Naylor, A Publicke Discovery of the Open Blindness of Babels Builders (London, 1656), pp. 41–2; R[ichard] F[arnworth], Witchcraft Cast Out from the Religious Seed and Israel of God (London, 1655), p. 7.

[19] Michael Heyd, 'The Reaction to Enthusiasm in the Seventeenth Century: towards an Integrative Approach', Journal of Modern History, LIII (1981), 258–80; C. Owen, The Scene of Delusions Open'd (London, 1712), pp. 24–39, 69–79; Hillel Schwartz, Knaves, Fools, Madmen, and that Subtile Effluvium: A Study of the Opposition to the French Prophets in England, 1706–1710 (Gainesville, 1978), p. 41–56.

[20] C. Webster, From Paracelsus to Newton, p. 87; The Diary of John Dee (Camden Soc., XIX, 1842), p. 57, 59.

[21] T. Ady, A Candle in the Dark (London, 1655), p. 169; H. More, An Antidote against Atheisme (London, 1653), pp. 119, 121, 125.

sion'.[22] Natural explanations were not alien to the thinking of nonconformist ministers and they believed in the use of medical means to cure mental disorders, but their commitment to the doctrine of special providence and the minute examination of their own experiences led to their detecting the purposes of God in such afflictions.[23] God's providence invested all events with meaning for devout nonconformists, who sought God's mercy through prayer and solemn fasting, a frequent spiritual resource among them which was not confined to cases of sickness.

Historians interested in dispossession sometimes give the impression that prayer and fasting was predominantly a therapeutic resource used to combat supernatural affliction and mental distress. Oliver Heywood often employed prayer, preaching and fasting to help melancholy and distracted persons, but he would also assist such sufferers as a young woman dying of consumption or a woman about to give birth. Moreover, his healing fasts should be seen in the context of the far larger number of private fasts which Heywood attended for purely spiritual purposes. He was present at about three every month, on the evidence of his diary, becoming a connoisseur of prayer.[24]

Anglican clergymen were often outspokenly hostile towards the inspirational power of extempore prayer, associating it with the Devil, as did the abusive neighbours of isolated nonconformists. Healing fasts were even more provoking, since large numbers of ordinary parishioners were attracted to what was, in effect, an illegal conventicle. The vicar of Kirkburton preached furiously after Heywood had prayed by the bedside of a girl who was 'wofully frantick': 'I believe if one discoursed with them they would not pretend to casting out devils, if they can work miracles why doe you not bring your sick, lame and blind to them to be cured?'[25]

It was in such cases of mental illness that the reputation of nonconformist ministers spread far beyond their co-religionists. Richard Baxter was much consulted in cases of religious melancholy but, although he advocated prayer and a moderate, Bible-based religion as essential remedies, he was most emphatic that this was a physical disorder and no more a sign of gracelessness than any other disease, a position markedly different from that of his Northern friends. He

[22] Lancs. R.O.: QSP 51/1; *The Correspondence of John Cosin, D.D.*, part 2 (Surtees Soc. LX, 1872), pp. 244–5.
[23] Timothy Rogers, *A Discourse concerning Trouble of Mind and the Disease of Melancholy* (London, 1691); O. Heywood, *Autobiography*, IV, pp. 109, 170–1, 268, 273., II, p. 211.
[24] *Ibid.*, pp. 251, 255, 279, 282, 287, 292, III, pp. 125, 147.
[25] *Ibid.*, II, pp. 269, 280; vol. III, p. 147.

cautioned against excessive piety and feared that enthusiasm could open the door to demonic powers, whereas melancholy was dangerous only because it offered an opportunity for Satan to tempt the faithful. Baxter advocated physic as a last resort: 'If it were as some of them fancy, a possession of the Devil, it's possible Physick might cast him out.'[26]

Many nonconformists in the north ran far closer to enthusiasm than Baxter, to the embarrassment of some of their fellow ministers. Oliver Heywood's father-in-law was so powerfully moved when praying that he was known as 'Weeping Angier'. A specialist in healing fasts, 'so great was the esteem of him generally, that he was frequently sent for to pray with some Melancholy persons, and some possessed, as was supposed and sometimes they brought such persons to him from afar, and God was pleased in some cases to hear prayers'. Heywood candidly admitted that he did not care to recount the stories of Angier's healing activities, since he lacked corroboration.[27]

Conscious of the criticisms made by Anglicans, Heywood was meticulous in describing 'the occasions of a fast', basing his practice firmly on a scriptural foundation. One of them was 'casting out the devil, in his obsession or possession of a person which hath been a frequent case in the primitive times, and hath fallen out in our own dayes . . . An obstinate devil needs extraordinary means to eject him: and . . . to convince us of the difficulty, god calls for more extraordinary means and methods for attending it: and this fasting and prayer is better then all the popish charms and Exorcisms, yet nothing must be ascribed to the instruments, but to efficient causes: god doth it, but he will be sought unto in his own way'. This response to demonic affliction was widely believed to have been encouraged by John Dee, when warden of Manchester during the Darrel affair, and licensed on another occasion by Richard Vaughan, the bishop of Chester, a story propagated by John Bruen's biography.[28]

Under Jacobean canon law, Anglicans were forbidden to use not only the catholic ritual of exorcism but also the puritan dispossession technique of prayer and fasting, unless equipped with an unobtainable

---

[26] R. Baxter, *Reliquiae Baxterianae* (London, 1696), part 3, pp. 85–6; R. Baxter, letter to Lady Holles, Dr Williams's Library MS. 59.4/58; R. Baxter, *The Certainty of the World of Spirits*, (London, 1691), pp. 171–85; R. Baxter, *Preservatives against Melancholy and Overmuch Sorrow* (London, 1713), p. 81.

[27] J. Fawcett, *The Life of the Rev. Oliver Heywood* (Halifax, 1797), p. 108; O. Heywood, *The Life of John Angier of Denton*, ed. E. Axon (Chetham Soc., new ser. XCVII, 1937), p. 74.

[28] O. Heywood, *Autobiography*, II, pp. 325–6; G. More, *True Discourse* (London, 1600), pp. 14–15, 49; William Hinde, *A Faithfull Remonstrance of the Holy Life and Happy Death of John Bruen* (London, 1641), pp. 150–1.

episcopal licence. It was easy for them to denounce exorcism as 'a heap of folly, madness, superstition, blasphemy, and ridiculous guises and playings with the Devil', but they were left with no accepted method of countering demonic forces. They were obliged to avoid defining afflictions as supernatural, although Anglican clergymen might pray with persons thought possessed without accepting the demonic diagnosis, as Henry Newcome the younger did in 1682.[29]

The naturalist position adopted by most Anglican clergymen was supported by medical writers, many of whom shifted their stance during the 1650s to expand the definitions of mental diseases. Most important among them was Thomas Willis, who had formerly believed in the utility of exorcism, but increasingly excluded the Devil from physical interference with the brain. Although he conceded the possibility of demonic activity, he demanded truly monstrous contortions and voidings in such cases since he defined most supposed examples as merely natural. The work of Willis was immediately recognized by Anglicans as offering an explanation of diseases which 'have usually by ignorant People, been ascribed to Witch-craft and possessions of the Devil' purely in terms of 'an Anatomical consideration of the Brain and Nerves', as George Castle triumphantly announced in *The Chymical Galenist*, a famous book much quoted by Edward Wilson of Durham, a catholic physician.[30] Medical practitioners in the North occasionally met with cases of alleged possession, like the crafty-looking young man seen by John Webster, who was accompanied by a deceitful cunning woman, and much promoted by catholic interests. Webster was very short with such claims. As a conforming ex-radical, he could blithely refer to 'Darrell and his Accomplices' as 'divers Non-Conformists, to gain credit and repute to their way, that did by publick writing labour to prove the continuation of real possession by Devils, and that they had power by fasting and Prayer to cast them out'. Like many more orthodox Anglican physicians, Webster did not accept demonic possession in modern times, and he argued that it was the disciples' lack of faith that Christ intended to be remedied by fasting and prayer, dispossession being a separate power given to them alone.[31]

[29] D.P. Walker, *Unclean Spirits: Possession and Exorcism in France and England in the Late Sixteenth and Early Seventeenth Centuries* (London, 1981), pp. 77–83; J. Taylor, *A Dissuasive from Popery to the People of Ireland* (Dublin, 1664), pp. 135–43; H. Newcome, memorandum book, fo. 54.
[30] T. Willis, *Pathologiae Cerebri* (Oxford, 1667), pp. 70, 90–1; G. Castle, *The Chymical Galenist* (London, 1667), p. 8; E. W[ilson], *Spadacrene Dunelmensis* (London, 1675).
[31] J. Webster, *The Discovery of Supposed Witchcraft*, pp. 124–5, 273, 335.

Since catholics were in no position to publish accounts of their dispossessions in England, descriptions of demonic afflictions in the later seventeenth century are mostly provided by dissenting ministers or protestant relatives of the afflicted. Such accounts are coloured by hindsight and it is not easy to see the process of definition at work, but on occasion an incomplete diagnosis is revealed, as when Heywood attended a private fast in Wakefield, organized by some fellow ministers, 'on the behalfe of Nathan Dodgson a young man whom they judged to be possessed or bewitched'. The ministers in this case are likely to have been moving from the diagnosis of witchcraft offered by the young man's family towards their own diagnosis of demonic possession.[32]

A fully-articulated diagnosis of demonic possession does not appear to have arisen outside a religious context. A young woman in Worcestershire 'who formerly was little taken notice of for her Religion, untill about 4 years since, who after the hearing of a Sermon, seemed to be much wrought upon and dejected, who afterward fell into some passion, and (as was conceived by her friends) Convulsion fits'. Despite her fits coinciding with times of prayer, like those of the famous Throckmorton children, there appears to have been no suggestion of supernatural causation until the religious young man who was acting as her keeper prayed 'without uttering of words, that if she were possessed, the Lord would be pleased to make it manifest'. Instant demonic convulsions led to a visit from a minister, who conversed with the Devil.[33]

Outside godly circles, the laity were more inclined to suspect witchcraft than the direct intervention of God or the Devil, since they might suffer the malign attentions of a witch without their affliction casting any doubt on their moral status. Such popular accusations were apt to be criticized by theologians for underestimating the power of the Devil. As George Gifford wrote in 1587, 'It is the common opinion among the blind ignorant people, that the cause and the procuring of harme by witchcraft, proceedeth from the Witch, that either the Devill could or would do nothing unlesse he were sent by her.' Such delusions played into the hands of the Devil. 'Hee seeketh therefore to bring many such unto their death for witchcraft as are no witches.'[34] The power of Satan

[32] O. Heywood, *Autobiography*, I, p. 199.
[33] James Dalton, *A Strange and True Relation of Young Woman possest with the Devil* (London, 1647), pp. 1–2; *The Most Strange and Admirable Discovery of the Three Witches of Warboys* (London, 1597), sig. B3.
[34] G. Gifford, *A Discourse of the Subtill Practises of Devilles* (London, 1587), sig. F4, G4.

and the extent to which his activities were permitted by God was a recurrent subject of debate. Those who believed the Devil had relatively untrammelled powers found a diagnosis of possession more congenial than accusing someone of witchcraft, of causing demonic obsession, which would lead to an investigation by the civil authorities.

Nathaniel Homes, preaching before the lord mayor of London in 1652 after an eclipse, set the Devil's activities in the apocalyptic context of Revelation 12:12. He saw the Devil as acting, with God's permission, in three main ways against individuals. Possession, 'when he is permitted to enter into a man and is there powerfully predominant over his soule and body', was reserved for those wholly given over to wickedness. Obsession involved power over the body and afflicted those not completely departed from God. Even Christ was transported through the air to be tempted in the desert. Finally, through suggestion or temptation the Devil 'doth trouble the senses, and puzle the phantasie'. The leading demonologist of northern England, Richard Gilpin, made similar distinctions and he was even able to cite a local example of obsession by the unusual 'Power of conveying Persons in the Air'.[35]

Gilpin was the pre-eminent dissenting minister of the north-east after the restoration, when he moved from Cumberland. With the protection of Alderman Ambrose Barnes and the medical tuition of George Tonstal, he was able to establish a highly lucrative ministry and medical practice, based on the reputation of his book, the *Daemonologia Sacra* of 1677. Although this was published after his Leyden M.D. thesis on hysteria, it appears to have been condensed from a series of sermons preached in Newcastle several years previously.[36] In his *magnum opus*, Gilpin expresses respect for 'the accurate searches into the Secrets of Nature which this Age hath produced', but does not expect them to reveal 'the true causes of things'. The struggle between God and Satan for the souls of the godly is his subject and, although his perspective is not explicitly apocalyptic, he cites Revelation 12:12 when stressing Satan's anger and malice. Gilpin engages with sceptical views of witchcraft, expounded by Scot

[35] N. Homes, *Plain Dealing, or the Cause and Cure of the Present Evils of the Times* (London, 1652), pp. 2, 78–81; Gilpin, *Daemonologia Sacra*, part 1, pp. 39–40; part 3, p. 92.
[36] *Memoirs of the Life of Mr. Ambrose Barnes* (Surtees Soc., L, 1866), pp. 142, 145, 153–4; R. Gilpin, *Disputatio Medica Inauguralis: de Hysterica Passione* (Leyden, 1676); R. Gilpin, manuscript of parts 1 and 2 of *Daemonologia Sacra*: Bodleian Library, MS. Eng. misc. e. 523, fols. 1–3.

and Hobbes, arguing from the evidence of continental demonologists in support of the defence against irreligion being constructed by Baxter, Glanvill and Teneson. By contrast, the reality of demonic possession is asserted on a biblical basis, although Gilpin is clearly aware of the sceptical position.[37]

In the work of Gilpin, as in the practice of many nonconformists, the middle ground of obsession is neglected as problematic, despite his defence of belief in all the extraordinary powers attributed to witches. On the one hand, nonconformists occasionally identified the extreme case of demonic possessions and, on the other hand, there was the mundane problem of melancholy which might be divine, demonic or medical in its origin. Melancholy offered a prime opportunity for Satan to take advantage of the soul's weakness, but it might have its origin in God's desire to punish the conscience of a sinner. Since 'we are not of God's Counsel', it is impossible to say that medicine should not be used in any given case, but God 'can suspend the power of Physick, so that it shall not do its work till God hath performed all his Purpose. And the unsuccessfulness of Remedies in this Distemper, (while seems to be wonderfully stubborn, in resisting all that can be done for Cure) is more to be ascribed (in some cases) to God's Design, than every Physician doth imagine.' Equally, a demonic involvement might obstruct a purely medical cure, since 'there are many Diseases wherein Satan hath a greater hand, than is commonly imagined'.[38]

Nonconformist ministers offered to their congregations an effective practice of psychological medicine since they alone in restoration England could offer a suitable blend of religion and medical advice. The price that had to be paid was a detachment from the beliefs of the uncommitted, who were less concerned to engage in the rigorous self-examination and consideration of God's providence that characterized the old dissent. The godly were well known for morbid mournfulness, as Ralph Thoresby recognized when he heard with approval a sermon, 'Spiritus Calvinisticus est spiritus melancholicus', long before he conformed to the Church of England.[39]

The ordinary recourse of many poorer people, in the north as elsewhere, was to take any puzzling ailment to the cunning folk, whose services were cheaper and more available than those of physicians, and less intrusive than those of nonconformist ministers. After the restora-

[37] R. Gilpin, Daemonologia Sacra, sig. BI; part I, pp. 8, 29–33, 39–40, 53–62.
[38] Ibid., part 2, pp. 345–7, 380–4; part 3, p. 92.
[39] R. Thoresby, Diary, I, p. 76; Michael MacDonald, 'Religion, Social Change, and Psychological Healing in England, 1600–1800', in W.J. Sheils (ed.) The Church and Healing, Studies in Church History, XIX (Oxford, 1982), pp. 101–25.

tion, Anglicans generally regarded cunning folk as simply fraudulent, and John Webster blamed demonologists such as Perkins for perpetuating belief in their powers. He sneered at the 'strange lustrations, suffumigations and other vain superstitious Rites and Ceremonies' that were used to cure diseases or drive away evil spirits.[40] The church courts of restoration England ceased to regard cunning folk as a matter of concern, despite occasional interest around Kendal or in the Isle of Man.[41] Unless they became entangled in a witchcraft accusation, cunning folk were usually investigated by the civil courts only when their activities led to discord, as in the case of William Dean of Congleton, an affluent surgeon–physician arrested for his use of a scrying-glass.[42] Minor medical counter-magic, such as providing horseshoes to cure a sick child, only rarely came before the courts.[43]

Nonconformists continued to regard cunning folk in a sinister light, finding even their locating of missing cows horrific, and collecting biblical texts that appeared to threaten them and their clients. After persuading a woman to refrain from counter-magic suggested to help her sick child, where he saw only a natural disease, Heywood commented, 'oh how subtile and insinuating is this tempter! What panders and wicked or ignorant agents doth he employ! Oh wretched Empericks!' In seeing cunning folk as the Devil's agents, Heywood followed a long tradition. Even the relatively sceptical Ady held that the real witches were 'such as silly people call Cunning men, who will undertake to tell them who hath bewitched them'.[44]

For all the scorn of Webster and the loathing of Heywood, cunning men were not necessarily ill-educated. The Rev. Charles Atkinson, who had a poor living near York, offered 'Resolutions on Nativities, things lost, stole, and all temporary and horary Questions resolved by the Author, also Physic intended by him, for any that will make use of him' in his almanac for 1670, adding to his list of services in 1671 the teaching of English, Latin, Greek, Hebrew and writing. Whereas nonconformists often practised medicine among their congregations,

---

[40] J. Webster, *The Discovery of Supposed Witchcraft*, pp. 75, 330.

[41] Philip Tyler, 'The Church Courts at York and Witchcraft Prosecutions, 1567–1640', *Northern History*, IV (1969), 84–110; Lancs. R.O.: ARR 15/17a, fo. 13v.; ARR 15/40, fo. 11; ARR 15/43, fo. 6v.; Neil Matheson 'Ecclesiastical Courts on the Isle of Man', *Proceedings of the Isle of Man Natural History and Antiquarian Society*, vol. V/III (1952), 261–70.

[42] Ches. R.O.: QJF 109/3/75, 78, 114; QJF 110/3/58; EDV 1/47, fo.19v.; WS 1686, will and inventory of William Dean. For similar cases, see Ches. R.O.: QJF 110/2/141; Manchester City Library: MS. L1/48/10/3; P.R.O.: PL 26/21 (Lancaster gaol delivery of March 1669/70), CHES 21/4, p. 333.

[43] Manchester City Library: MS. F347/96/M2, p. 191.

[44] B.L.: Add. MS. 4460, fo. 19r.; Add. MS. 45973, fo. 94v.; O. Heywood, *Autobiography*, IV, pp. 53–4; T. Ady, *A Candle in the Dark*, p. 169.

the poorly paid clergyman in a rural area might well supplement his
income and enhance his local prestige and usefulness by using esoteric
knowledge to take on some of the attributes of a cunning man, as
happens today in the mountain parishes of Portugal.[45]

The lack of any obvious distinction between village wise men,
clerical almanac writers and gentlemen astrologers was found distinctly threatening by some of the latter, like George Wharton of
Kendel, but it was inevitable given the profound disagreements that
divided restoration astrological writers. Whereas the sophisticated
John Gadbury denied the existence of supernatural afflictions, Joseph
Blagrave believed that witchcraft caused the worst sort of madness and
that, 'since the Apostles time', the only way to cure those bewitched or
possessed was by 'the Astrological way of Phisick'. In style as well as
content, Blagrave's work was better calculated to appeal to village
cunning men, among whom it appears still to have been current in the
early nineteenth century.[46]

For presbyterians, astrology was not only highly suspect on theological grounds but also tainted by its association with interregnum
radicalism, as when John Wilkins had used John Webster's interest in
judicial astrology to show 'what kind of credulous fanatick Reformer
he is likely to prove'. So it was that in restoration England the
connection between astrological medicine and religion survived long-
est among Anglicans, many of whom continued to consider astrology a
useful tool while their presbyterian contemporaries were turning to
Sydenham as a medical guide. Robert Maudsley, 'student in phisick
and astrology', dedicated his 'Flora's Cabinett Unlocked' to the celebrated educator of clergymen, Richard Sherlock, rector of Winwick.
Among the hundreds of herbal remedies he listed was 'a pomander to
be hunge a bout on's neck to keep a bearer thereof free from Witchcraft
& Divils'.[47]

Before the civil war, some of the remoter northern districts, such as
Pendle Hill, had been nationally notorious for witchcraft, but after the
restoration, concern about witchcraft apparently waned even more
quickly than in the south, with fewer prosecutions reaching the courts

[45] C. Atkinson, *Panterpe: Or, a Pleasant Almanacke* (London, 1670), sig. A1v.; *ibid.* (London,
1671), sig. A1v.; João de Pina-Cabral, *Sons of Adam, Daughters of Eve: The Peasant
Worldview of the Alto Minho* (Oxford, 1986), pp. 201–2, 206–7.
[46] G. Wharton, *Merlini Anglici Errata* (1647) in *Works*, ed. J. Gadbury (London, 1683),
pp. 275–6; J. Gadbury, *Thesaurus Astrologiae: Or, an Astrological Treasury* (London, 1674),
sig. A8; J. Blagrave, *Blagrave's Astrological Practice of Physick* (London, 1671), pp. 124, 186;
James Heaton, *Farther Observations on Demoniac Possession and Animadversions on Some
of the Curious Arts of Superstition* (Frome, 1822), pp. 34–88.
[47] J. Wilkins in [Seth Ward] *Vindiciae Academiarum* (Oxford, 1654) p. 5; B.L.: Sloane MS. 1051,
fos. 2, 104v.

and a low conviction rate. Anglican clergy in the north were less concerned than their southern colleagues to warn their flocks against witchcraft. Richard Sherlock, for example, mentions it only in passing, among 'the sinful Lusts of the Flesh', in a list taken from St Paul, rather than under 'the Devil and all his works'. Northern magistrates such as Sir Roger Bradshaigh of Wigan openly doubted sworn testimony and confessions. Witchcraft beliefs were increasingly seen as incredible by members of the gentry and aristocracy, such as the young Elizabeth Delaval who questioned the supposedly Satanic source of a cunning woman's powers on both naturalistic and theological grounds.[48]

One of the local factors encouraging a division between elite opinion and popular belief was the outbreak of witch-hunting sponsored by the corporations of Berwick and Newcastle in 1649–50, when they paid the expenses of a Scottish witchfinder. In Newcastle, the town bellman was sent out, crying 'All people that would bring in any woman for a Witch, they should be sent for and tryed by the person appointed.' The magistrates of Northumberland sought to bring the witchfinder before the courts, 'but he got away for Scotland, and it was conceived if he had staid he would have made most of the women in the North Witches, for mony'.[49]

The contrast between the hesitant Northumberland justices and the heightened apprehensions of Berwick puritans is well documented in the dramatic narrative of the Muschamp children, told by their mother. A girl of eleven was visited by angels, to the satisfaction of the minister, but she then lost the use of her limbs. She rejected the drugs prescribed by physicians because 'God had layd it on her, and God would take it off her'. She recovered after a miraculous fast and gave thanks in a puritan lecture. A few months later, her eldest brother began to waste away. He died after his mother, 'not doubting or suspecting any unnatural Disease', had consulted physicians at Durham, Newcastle and Edinburgh.[50] The girl's affliction resumed, now taking a more recognizably demonic form, with the addition of monstrous visions, and during her convulsions she would scribble hints which enabled her friends to identify a cunning man and a neighbouring woman as responsible for her affliction. He died in gaol, after being

[48] R. Sherlock, *Mercurius Christianus: the Practical Christian, A Treatise Explaining the Duty of Self-examination* (London, 1673), p. 15; *Calendar of State Papers Domestic 1664–5*, p. 225; *The Meditations of Lady Elizabeth Delaval*, ed. D.G. Greene (Surtees Soc., CXC, 1975), pp. 77–9.
[49] John Fuller, *The History of Berwick on Tweed* (Edinburgh, 1799), pp. 155–6; Ralph Gardiner *England's Grievance Discovered, In Relation to the Coal Trade* (London, 1655), pp. 107–9.
[50] Mary Moore, *Wonderfull News from the North* (London, 1650), pp. 3, 5.

successfully scratched for blood, but she was released. The girl claimed that judges and justices had been swayed and that her step-father was being turned against her mother. An informal meeting with a judge was arranged and she promptly had a fit, during which she lectured him on his duty to do justice 'with many more significant expressions, that the Judge thought she feigned'. Worn out by fasting and convulsions, the girl died and justices were persuaded to act at last, inducing two accomplice witches to confess and issuing warrants for the arrest of the prime suspect.[51]

The definition of the affliction as produced by witchcraft, rather than by direct supernatural intervention, developed gradually in the Muschamp case and so the mother's account provides unusually detailed information about the way in which the behaviour of the afflicted girl changed over time. At the outset, angelic voices and miraculous fasting were the main features but, after her brother's death, a witchcraft accusation emerged which was confirmed by scratching. Nevertheless, the authorities were reluctant to move against a respectable suspect until the accusation was corroborated by the confessions of accomplices, some months after the death of the afflicted girl.

The signs offered by the afflicted constituted a traditional semiotics well understood by friends and relatives, who would put an accusation procedure, whether formal or informal, into motion. During the seventeenth century, the gentry magistrates and grand jurors became increasingly sceptical about this familiar system and sent fewer cases to trial. When trials did take place, the householders on trial juries were likely to disagree with the judges about the validity of such evidence as scratching the accused or the prodigious vomiting of 'wool, and crooked pins and the hafts of knives'. A pamphleteer expressed alarm about the spread of irreligion in high places when judges, at York Assizes in 1658, 'thought it requisite to give some respite of time for more deliberate determination, being uncertain whether this wonderfull Vomite proceeded from the Divel, or whether it were some artificial combination of the two women to impose on the Judges, and the Court'. Popular beliefs had become ludicrous in the eyes of many lawyers, gentlement and physicians, for whom witchcraft was no longer part of the everyday world, and they interpreted the accustomed signs as proof of fraud.[52]

[51] *Ibid.*, pp. 5–8, 10, 13, 15–16, 24–8.
[52] [Anon.] *The Most True and Wonderfull Relation of two Women Bewitched* (London, 1658), pp. 1–4; John Webster, *The Discovery of Supposed Witchcraft*, p. 252.

Popular beliefs about the diagnosis of supernatural afflictions are central to any understanding of the interaction between different groups of participants, since they shaped the behaviour of the afflicted and provided the context within which spectators understood that behaviour. Such beliefs, which are glimpsed only in pamphlets and the criticism of educated writers such as John Webster, are best recovered through an examination of pre-trial depositions. Northern witchcraft cases in this period have the same domestic character as other English accusations, with only a single example of full-blown Devil-worship alleged.[53] As might be expected, animals die, rye bread goes sour, butter fails to churn, but such events did not generally form the substance of formal accusations, rather corroborating suspicions concerning lingering death or mysterious illness.[54] Afflicted adults often named their tormentors and sought to employ the traditional remedy of drawing blood from the accused, which led in some cases to full or partial recovery, thus substantiating the charges.[55] Although a full recovery might lead to a peaceful settlement, the accused were not always willing to incriminate themselves through the ordeal and one man lamented on his deathbed that 'hee intended to have drawne blood of her, if hee could but have gotten her'.[56]

Reports of such deathbed accusations were occasionally produced as evidence, even years after the event,[57] but a more frequent form of accusation was the description of a tormenting visitation, in human and animal form, which was experienced almost only by the afflicted, usually a child or young woman.[58] Some of the younger afflicted supported their accusations with prodigious vomiting of pins, nails and pieces of horn comb, in the manner familiar from Elizabethan and Jacobean pamphlets.[59] In one case, a young gentlewoman near Ripon vomited blotting paper full of pins, as well as feathers, wool and stick, accusing an unduly grateful beggar and her husband. He attempted to counter her charge with a suggestion that the girl was possessed, but

---

[53] P.R.O.: ASSI 45/10/3/34–55. The transcriptions of northern circuit material in *Depositions from York Castle* (Surtees Soc., XL, 1861) are incomplete, inaccurate, and generally exclude statements by the accused. They are cited here, whenever possible, only for ease of reference. This case will be found in D.191–201.

[54] ASSI 45/3/1/242; 5/2/30–1 (D.67); 7/1/107–10; 9/3/94–7 (D.76–7); 10/2/80–4; 14/1/151; 16/3/54–6 (D.58, wrongly dated).

[55] ASSI 45/3/2/81 (D.38n); 4/2/13 (D.51–2); 5/1/34 (D.64–5, but not this statement); 5/7/95 (D.82); 6/1/69; 7/1/7 (D.124–5, but not this passage); 7/1/187A (D.112–14); 10/2/82, 84.

[56] ASSI 45/3/1/242.

[57] ASSI 45/7/1/188 (D.112–14); 9/3/96 (D.76–7); 9/3/124; 16/3/56 (D.58).

[58] ASSI 45/3/2/129–35 (D.28–30); 5/1/36 (D.64–5, but not this statement); 6/1/88–90 (D.88–9); 6/1/165 (D.92–3, but not this statement); 7/1/59–61 (D.124–5n); 7/1/69 (D.124–5); 7/1/185–7 (D.112–4).   [59] ASSI 45/5/5/1–3; 9/3/97 (D.176–7).

'after she was assured Certaynely that they were both in holde she was ffreede from her ffits'.[60]

Although the crucial symptoms were exhibited by the afflicted alone, in most of the witchcraft cases all the parties involved appear reasonably familiar with the symptoms appropriate to obsession inflicted by a witch's conspiracy, but in some instances the borderline with possession is approached, the symptoms being more psychological than physical. The wife of a Newcastle tradesman was 'most strangely and wonderfully handled: in soe yt phisicions could not fynd out or Know her Malady'. She suffered 'most sad and Lamentable: ffits to ye admiration and astonishment of all spectators'. Her condition varied, being at different times 'rayving madd . . . Laughing & singing . . . dispareing & disconsolat . . . solitary: & mute'. A diagnosis of possession was forestalled by the woman's vision of her two tormentors, one of whom was allegedly seen by her husband. When he confronted the women, he was told that it was really the Devil that he had seen but the afflicted woman 'had a desire to have blood of them: telling them that they had wronged her and she would be revenged of them'. Her total and instant recovery was immediately followed by criminal charges laid before the mayor.[61]

If the afflicted identified the witch, her blood could be drawn, either forcibly or with her acquiescence. If the nature of the problem was only suspected or the identity of the witch was unconfirmed, the afflicted might have recourse to cunning folk, most of whom dealt mainly with physical ailments but some of whom had a reputation as specialists in the supernatural. Nicholas Johnson of Newcastle supplied ointment for legs and arms after examining a patient's urine but, when the man suggested witchcraft as the cause, he identified a Seaton Delaval widow and urged the victim 'to rate hir and defye hir, and bid him not to doubt but in a short time he should recover'.[62] Such diagnosis of witchcraft did not put cunning folk at risk, but more active intervention with magical theory could lead to them being suspected as cause rather than cure.

The over-confident Ann Greene of Gargreave was accused by three men whom she had treated or sought to treat as bewitched. She employed crossed garters, a charm, and the hair and urine of the afflicted. They suspected her of causing their distress and one claimed to have been tormented by her in a night vision.[63] A Newcastle case of

---

[60] ASSI 45/5/3/132–5 (D.75–8).   [61] ASSI 45/7/1/7 (D.124–5 is a partial transcript).
[62] ASSI 45/6/1/134.   [63] ASSI 45/5/1/30–9 (D.64–5 omits several depositions).

such measures arousing suspicion is often cited by historians because it involved a midwife. According to his wife, a pitman 'being not well: haveing a paine in his his [*sic*] head & a faintnes at his stomach: he had a desire to sent his water to ye doctor: to Know his disease: and being advised to send the same to Mrs Pepp[er] a midwife: and one that uses to cast water; she sent his water: p[er] one Thomisine Young: to her; to cast ye same & take her advice'. Mrs Pepper's methods were decidedly suspect, involving unweaned children, holy water and a silver crucifix. She was reported as saying both that he was possessed and that he was bewitched. She fell under suspicion because he had been grievously afflicted ever since 'to the astonishment and Admiration of all spectators'.[64]

Most of the activities of cunning folk did not involve witchcraft or other supernatural phenomena and they were generally able to ply their trade without hindrance. They were an essential resource of their localities and, in the circumstances of otherwise inexplicable diseases, they provided ordinary people, in towns and villages throughout the country, with an interpretative framework for coping with misfortune as well as power and protection against evil forces. The most important characteristics of popular explanations of mysterious ailments were that they were personalistic and that they assigned responsibility to a third party. Anglican authorities and intellectuals adopted naturalistic explanations which assigned responsibility to the afflicted, diagnosing either fraud, which was to be severely punished, or exotic mental and physical diseases, which were to be combated with painful and expensive therapy that was of doubtful efficacy. The nonconformists achieved a prominence out of proportion to their numerical strength by offering a distinct but intermediate system of explanation. It was personalistic, putting the afflicted at the centre of the stage, but it placed a considerable degree of responsibility on the individual by regarding an examination of the state of the afflicted's soul as a precondition of any medical or religious therapy.

The most extensively documented and debated instance of these three perspectives coming into conflict was the case of the 'Surey Demoniack'. Several dissenting ministers from east Lancashire and the West Riding of Yorkshire were closely involved in combating the possession of Richard Dugdale of the Surey, near Whalley, from April 1689. A wide range of clerics, medical practitioners, and lay observers

---

[64] ASSI 45/7/2/62, 103 (D.127 omits passages). This is the only confirmed instance of a woman described as a midwife being persecuted for witchcraft in England. Result unknown.

had interested themselves in the affair and, after it had petered out, nonconformists circulated manuscript accounts to demonstrate the truly supernatural character of the affliction, to counter suggestions of fraud or natural disease. Richard Baxter suggested that a narrative should be attached to his book, *The World of Spirits*, and it was also thought in London that it might form an appendix to a book by Increase Mather on the Salem trials. After many delays, and some prompting by a spectral voice, a pamphlet was published in 1697 with a preface signed by six ministers, led by Thomas Jolly.[65]

The text of *The Surey Demoniack*, although edited by Jolly, appears to derive from an account by a young minister, John Carrington, who was not yet ordained when he was singled out by the possessing demon for special attention. Although Jolly was the minister first consulted and most nearly affected by the affair's repercussions, Carrington appears to have taken over the fasts from the older man, imposing a theatrical character on them and debating with the Devil to an extent that disquieted some visiting ministers. He became the interpreter of the Devil's comments, many of which were made to him alone, or withheld until he was present, and all of which are presented in the pamphlet as focusing mainly on him since the Devil saw him as the main antagonist, even attempting to destroy him by magical poisoning and mysterious doings on the moors.[66]

Events prior to the arrival of Carrington had been considerably less spectacular. According to the ministers' account of their original examination of the family, after they had first applied to Jolly for help, the afflictions of the young gardener had started after a drinking bout and a scuffle at the Whalley rushburying in April 1688. Dugdale had experienced visions and temptations, eventually giving himself to the Devil in exchange for dancing skill, as it seemed to the ministers. This mention of a demonic pact may have been imposed by Carrington's hindsight, since it does not appear in Jolly's notes on the events. Before turning to Jolly, the family had consulted a physician, who had given the case up, and 'then they sought unto a reputed Wise Man for help, viz. Dr. Crabtres, who said, he was amazed at several thing which befell him whilst under his charge, as particularly at his precise fore-telling various sorts of Weather, he at last confessing, as some told us,

---

[65] [John Carrington and Thomas Jolly] *The Surey Demoniack* (London, 1697), sig. A2r., A3r., A4v.; Full titles of the pamphlets in this dispute are provided by Wallace Notestein, *A History of Witchcraft from 1558 to 1718* (Washington, 1911), pp. 371–2. Notestein is confused about the order of publication.   [66] *Ibid.*, pp. 6–20, 23–4, 26–46.

that there was no help for him, except from the Ministers'. The ministers engaged in prayer and fasting on behalf of the afflicted Dugdale, and until mid-July his recorded symptoms were mainly physical, although extreme. As soon as Carrington had arrived, a complex verbal battle developed between him and a demonic voice. His recollection of events attributes to him a prolix rhetorical style when fearlessly mocking his opponent, peppering him with biblical citations of dubious relevance. He reports the Devil as quoting Latin, Greek and the Bible, but he himself nobly abstained from answering in abstruse tongues lest his unlearned listeners should imagine he was using 'Charms and Spells, and Enchanting Words, and Magical Expressions'.[67]

The Anglican attack on *The Surey Demoniack* was mounted by a career clergyman seeking advancement. During the reign of Charles II Zachary Taylor had written against sticklers in religion. During the reign of James II, he had co-operated with pro-catholic Bishop Cartwright. After the Glorious Revolution, he had written against the non-jurors, reconciling the oath of allegiance with the doctrine of passive obedience, but his pamphlet was lost under the deluge of words it provoked from Sherlock and Wagstaff. He was rewarded with the post of bishop's chaplain and curate at Wigan, a parish held *in commendam* by the bishop of Chester. The bishop prevented him from obtaining a lucrative post at Whitehaven, but royal patronage supplemented his income as King's Preacher for Lancashire with the rectory of Croston, vacant through simony.[68] In seeking to enhance his reputation by attacking both catholic and protestant dispossession methods, he fulfilled his responsibilities as King's Preacher and emulated an Elizabethan bishop's chaplain, Samuel Harsnet. His first publication on the topic was an attack on catholic exorcisms in which he reviewed some cases in the area over the previous twenty years, concentrating on the case of a weaver near Wigan. He was convinced it was a conscious fraud, designed for propaganda, 'the occasion for which is as foolish as it is unchristian; for they pored abroad a rumour as if he was bewitched by a neighbouring old Man'. Taylor put an end

[67] *Surey Demoniack*, pp. 2–5, 13–16; Thomas Jolly, *A Vindication of the Surey Demoniack as no Imposter* (London, 1697), p. 72.
[68] Z. Taylor, *A Disswasive from Contention* (London, 1683); *The Diary of Dr. Thomas Cartwright* (Camden Soc., XXII, 1843), p. 3; Z. Taylor, *Obedience and Submission to Present Government Demonstrated from Bishop Overall's Convocation Book* (London, 1690); *The Correspondence of Sir John Lowther of Whitehaven, 1693–1698*, ed. D.R. Hainsworth (London, 1983) pp. 68, 75–80, 83–90, 98–107; Bodleian Library: MS. Rawl. A. 241, fo. 100.

to the demonic dialogues by securing arrest warrants from the Quarter Sessions, whereupon both catholic priest and alleged demoniac fled.[69]

When the Surey narrative was published, Taylor was fully prepared, having already collected statements and transcripts of manuscript accounts. In his first assault, he treats the whole affair as originating in a popish imposture, which had fooled the credulous Jolly and the fanciful Carrington. This was a distinctly plausible explanation for Anglican readers accustomed to thinking of the regicides as tools of the papists, in view of the proximity of catholic gentry households such as Stonyhurst and Towneley Hall. He also flirts with a physiological explanation, to which end he attacks the medical comments of the ministers. Taylor accused the nonconformist physicians who endorsed the demonic diagnosis of being 'Mr. Jolly's own Son, that must needs be his Tool' and a former 'petty School-master' who 'ventured to set up for a Doctor'. He produces the recollection of the rector of Sladeburn to suggest that the latter, Robert Whitaker, was guilty of bad faith in his assertion of a supernatural element in the affliction. Taylor insists that it was Edward Chew, the first physician consulted, whose medicine eventually cured the young man, not any fasting and prayer. Chew was a respectable Anglican who belonged to an ancient freeholding family near Blackburn, members of which increasingly moved into medicine and were well established as asylum-keepers by the middle of the eighteenth century. Jolly, in his reply to Taylor, accuses Chew of being an 'unlearned Empirick' compared with the two nonconformists, who were extra-licentiates of the Royal College of Physicians.[70]

Taylor's anger is especially aroused by the suggestion that Krabtree, no longer living, had been a cunning man: 'Now this is a Devilish insinuation of some Bodies, to abuse a Minister of the Church of England . . . no great Scholar, a blunt, but an honest Man' who supplemented his meagre income by rural medicine. 'But this would not do Mr. Carrington's turn, you must be made to believe that he was a Conjuror, (and Mr. Carrington in one of his Letters expressly calls him so, tho' his Corrector in the Narrative mollifies it, into a reputed Wiseman) and made use of unlawful Means'. Taylor cites the statements of the Dugdale family to show that Krabtree had used only 'Physicking and Blooding' and they only stopped consulting him for

[69] Z. Taylor, The Devil Turned Casuist (London, 1696), sig. A4v–B3v, pp. 2, 12.
[70] Z. Taylor, The Surey Imposter (London, 1697), pp. 7–8, 57–8, 73–4; W.A. Abram, A History of Blackburn (Blackburn, 1877), p. 443; Lancs. R.O.: QSP 1488/14, 16; Edward Hughes, North Country Life in the Eighteenth Century 2 vols. (Oxford, 1965) II, p. 100; Jolly, A Vindication, pp. 27, 40; Munk's Roll, I, pp. 359, 405, 426.

lack of money. The bishop's chaplain was not acquainted with a clergyman 'as mean as poor Crabtree was', so he was probably unaware of the reasons why nonconformists distrusted the means employed by the curate of Todmorden. Henry Krabtree was one of the last of the clerical almanac-writers, an astrological physician who offered medical advice in his *Merlinus Rusticus* of 1685 and who even noted, in the chapelry register of that year, the state of the stars at the time of a child's birth as 'a sure token of short life'. Krabtree was likely to have used precisely the sort of popular magical methods that would have aroused the dissenters' hostility.[71]

Taylor regards the physical symptoms exhibited by Dugdale as trickery and produces the testimony of school-fellows as to his capacity in that direction. He also cites the opinion of a physician, Dr Buckley, that fraud was involved in the prodigious vomiting and the exaggeration of symptoms. Like his medical informant, Taylor did not entirely exclude the possibility of physical disease and quotes Willis on the pathology of the brain. He adds a letter from John Radcliffe M.B., who belonged to a Leigh family of Anglican gentry. Although he lived in style among the aldermen of Wigan, Radcliffe left little to his widow, presumably because he experienced difficulty breaking into the medical monopoly of the catholic Worthington family. Unsurprisingly, he suspects an alliance between papists and dissenters, but he suggests epilepsy with convulsions as the cause of the affliction, without having seen Dugdale, and cites Willis, Galen and several continental physicians.[72]

Despite the force of his argument suggesting that the position of the dissenters was ridiculous, Taylor does not deny the possibility of demonic pacts, dialogue with the Devil, or possession. An anonymous defender of the dissenters accuses Taylor and his physician friends of weak theology in refusing to consider the possibility that the Devil might be involved over and above the presence of disease. Taylor insists that he never said or believed that such a thing was impossible, to which his critic replies that such was the implication of his medical

[71] Z. Taylor, *Surey Imposter*, pp. 19–20; Jolly, *A Vindication*, p. 72; *The History of the Town and Parish of Halifax* (Halifax, 1789), pp. 320–1; Joshua Holden, 'Todmorden Antiquities', *Halifax Antiquarian Society* (1907), pp. 207–9; *Todmorden Chapel Register, 1666–1780*, Lancashire Parish Register Society 117 (1978), p. 6.
[72] Z. Taylor, *Surey Imposter*, pp. 27–31, 59, 70; Evelyn M. Darlington, *The Radcliffes of Leigh* (privately, 1918), p. 19; David Sinclair, *The History of Wigan* 2 vols. (Wigan, 1882), II, p. 175; Lancs. R.O.: WCW 1700 supra, administration of John Radcliffe.

arguments and to admit the possibility was to abandon the contest, a point that Taylor does not deign to answer.[73]

When Jolly published his pamphlet in defence of his actions, having been delayed by waiting for a contribution from Carrington that never materialized, he pointed to the inconsistency of Taylor explaining the phenomena by fraud and his medical informants explaining them by disease. 'Some Persons are so taken up with visible Powers, that they regard not the invisible; are so taken up with second causes, that they neglect, if they don't deny the first cause.' Jolly argues that the predominant cause was supernatural and this was why the nonconformist physicians 'honestly declined intermedling as Physicians (tho they might have made considerable advantage by it, apprehending that his affliction was not mainly a bodily Distemper'. The Dugdales had already spent a considerable sum on Chew and Krabtree without any advantage and Jolly insists that 'the Spiritual Means were the only Means of his Cure'. Jolly is able to turn Willis against Taylor, since 'the Doctor doth not deny Possession' in some cases and he points to the biography of John Bruen as showing that the Church of England had formerly granted licences for dispossession. What Dugdale experienced was 'not to be denominated a Mania, or Distraction, a Spasma, or Epilepsy, Convulsion, or any such bodily Diseases; tho there might seem sometimes to be something Symptomatical thereof'. It was 'evident that it was a Diabolical Possession, and that it was a righteous Judgment of God upon him for his Profane and Debauched Life: But we cannot say, whether it was by the immediate Hand of God, or by Witchcraft'.[74]

For the nonconformists, the ascription of guilt by diagnosis of possession was not incompatible with imputing guilt to a witch, but Taylor was incensed by the suggestion of witchcraft, even though he thought the family guilty of conspiracy with papists for the sake of lucre. He seizes on the ministers' statement that 'offers were made to procure or bestow more Moneys, either for the legal prosecution of such as might justly be suspected, as Wizards, or Witches concerned in this Affair, or else for engaging Doctors of Physick to join their assistances herein'. The ministers saw such measures as prudent in case the possession was mixed with witchcraft or disease, but Taylor saw

---

[73] Z. Taylor, *Surey Imposter*, pp. 2, 4–6, 32; *The Lancashire Levite Rebuk'd or, a Vindication of the Dissenters* (London, 1698), pp. 7–8; Z. Taylor, *Popery, Superstition, Ignorance and Knavery very unjustly by a letter in the general pretended* (London, 1698), p. 5; *The Lancashire Levite Rebuk'd: Or, a Farther Vindication of the Dissenters* (London, 1698), pp. 4–5; Z. Taylor, *Popery, Superstition, Ignorance and Knavery, Confess'd, and fully Proved* (London, 1699), p. 12.   [74] Jolly, *A Vindication*, pp. 15, 20, 26–8, 44–5, 80.

an intention to persecute the Dugdales, especially when some of the ministers saw fit to test for witchcraft, using the Lord's Prayer. This procedure, contentious even among the ministers, gave a positive result, 'after which the said Ministers threatned further Tryals, yea Law severities against all in those parts, who on good grounds were suspected of Witch-craft'. Taylor did his own field-work on this issue and questioned 'the Old Woman (whom they would have the World to think a Witch)' and found she could say the Lord's Prayer perfectly, but he questions the relevance of the test, suggesting it was taken from Darrel. Taylor also produces witnesses to allege that Dugdale made witchcraft accusations when young and reveals that one of his keepers was known as 'Boggard Fletcher' from the pretended haunting of his house. The only benefit Taylor grants to the threat of witchcraft persecutions is that they obliged Dugdale to take Chew's medicine. If the Anglican was hostile to witchcraft beliefs, the nonconformist was far from sympathetic to specific accusations. Jolly makes it clear that, unlike Carrington, he was not one of those who suspected Dugdale's mother, thinking her 'the most sensible Person of the Family', and he did not oppose enquiry only 'that all might be satisfied and the innocent cleared'.[75]

Both Carrington and Taylor, from their different perspectives, were concerned to attack popular beliefs and condemn Dugdale. As a result, they could not hear the messages Dugdale was trying to send. Half-way through the events at the Surey, a minister reported that Dugdale had written down the cause of his problems after coming out of a fit, 'Obsession in and with Combination', and a Harwood saddler deposed in 1695 that Dugdale had made a similar remark during his last fit. Taylor seizes on this phrase as indicting the hidden hand of catholic conspirators, 'Obsession, being a Popish Word; and by them distinguished from Possession, directs us where to inquire for the Contrivers of it'. In this, he makes explicit the suspicions of an unnamed correspondent, probably Dr Buckley, who read the same words in a semi-legible letter from Dugdale to his landlord and employer, Sir Edmund Ashton, and enquired how that youth could remember words communicated by the demon.[76]

Subsequent debate on this point turned on the acceptability of the term. Taylor's anonymous critic admits that he is not clear as to the difference between possession and obsession, 'tho' I know what is said

[75] *Surey Demoniack*, pp. 48–9; Taylor, *Surey Imposter*, pp. 21–2, 27, 53, 70; Jolly, *A Vindication*, pp. 20, 27.
[76] *Surey Demoniack*, pp. 22, 53; Taylor, *Surey Imposter*, pp. 58, 62–3.

of the distinction', and points to the presence of the word 'obsession' in Canon 72 of the Church of England. Jolly asserts by citation from the Church Fathers that 'obsession' had formerly been simply another name for possession, quotes Psellus on the cure of it, and suggests that the combination mentioned was a contract with the Devil. Taylor treats both these positions with contempt, pointing out the Canon's condemnation of the use of fasting and prayer upon pretence of possession or obsession, a rule designed to prevent a repetition of the Darrel affair. He continues in his insistence that such a distinction is intrinsically Romish.[77]

None of the disputants considered the significance to Dugdale himself of the use of this term, Carrington because he accepted it as a demonic communication, Taylor because he assumed it came from catholic conspirators, and the others because they were on the defensive. Carrington clearly believed that it pointed to witches or Jesuits, but his questioning of the Devil indicates confusion about the distinction between possession and obsession. Their understanding of orthodox demonology may well have been muddied by the reliance of Jolly and Carrington on such neo-Platonist authorities as Agrippa, Trithemius and Ficino's translation of Psellus, an intellectual heritage that vastly amused Taylor, who also points to the failure of Jolly to distinguish between possession and witchcraft.[78]

Although Dugdale variously exhibited the symptoms of both possession and obsession, and the demonic voice indicated that 'A wish, and a Vow' was the origin of the affliction, it seems likely that he picked up the distinction from overhearing the conversation of some of the more sophisticated visitors to the Surey, since it was assumed throughout that he was deaf and blind during fits. Although conflicting interests and confused questioning led Dugdale to adopt differing responses, it would appear that he was eager to absolve himself from the guilt which the ministers sought to impute.

Both the nonconformists and the Anglicans were unsympathetic towards popular beliefs and were unable to hear the messages that Dugdale was attempting to convey, since his viewpoint was not of interest to them. The dispossessing ministers held to the belief that Dugdale's speech during fits was not his own but that of the Devil,

[77] Jolly, A Vindication, pp. iv, 12, 14; A Vindication of the Dissenters, p. 5; A Farther Vindication of the Dissenters, p. 20; Taylor, Popery, Superstition, pp. 9–10, 13; Taylor, Popery, Supersition ... Confess'd, p. 31; Taylor, A Refutation of Mr. T. Jolly's Vindication of the Devil in Dugdale (London, 1699), p. 14.
[78] Surey Demoniack, p. 29; Taylor, Surey Imposter, pp. 12–13, 15–16, 18; Jolly, A Vindication, pp. 14, 47; Taylor, Refutation, pp. 6, 16.

despite some awkward inconsistencies concerning Dugdale's recall of remarks made during fits. Taylor and his informants were mainly interested in detecting fraud and the involvement of catholic priests, although they used medical explanations as a backstop. Neither group entertained any serious consideration of a folk aetiology for unusual diseases, whether real or invented, since the popular understanding of supernatural affliction belonged to the realm of the excluded middle. Demonic obsession through the agency of a witch did not fit into any of the categories acceptable to protestant theologians in the later seventeenth century. Dugdale's explanation of his own condition could not be heard.

The attention of the participants in the debate was elsewhere. During the events at the Surey, Carrington played to his large audiences but Jolly was more concerned with the ministers' relationship with God. In December 1689, he wrote that 'the main work and speciall temptation was the case of Surey which is soe great an exercise to our faith and patience'.[79] When the pamphlet war began, attention switched to the readership. Heywood started to write up a sermon he had preached at the Surey on the text 'He that committeth sin is of the devil', but decided to stay out of the fray after reading *The Surey Demoniack*.[80] Although he approved of its publication, as helping in the campaign against atheism, he was worried that the demonic interrogations would arouse criticism and he thought they should have been left out. He warned Jolly of Taylor's intention to reply. When Jolly responded to Taylor's attack, Heywood applauded and felt the Anglican would be silenced 'except he find something further to say from Mr. Carrington', whose behaviour at the Surey was the weakest point in the nonconformist case. Jolly was repeatedly attacked in print, but Heywood preferred to wait on providence rather than joining the campaign against 'the devil and his agents', despite Jolly's entreaties.[81]

Committed Anglican opponents of demonic beliefs, such as Abraham de la Pryme of Hull, were 'very glad' to read Taylor's attack on 'ye papist priests, and their bretheren in iniquity, about ye existence of corporial possession in these latter days, not doubting at all but that it may easily be proved that they are all seasd long ago'. Nevertheless, there was no published support for Taylor's uncharitable invective and

---

[79] *The Notebook of the Rev. Thomas Jolly, AD 1671–1693*, ed. H. Fishwick (Chetham Soc., new ser., XXXIII, 1894), pp. 96–7.
[80] *Yorkshire County Magazine*, III (1893), pp. 18–19; *Surey Demoniack*, p. 26; Jolly, *A Vindication*, p. 75.
[81] Dr. Williams's Library: MS. 12.78, p. 131; O. Heywood, *Works*, ed. W. Vint, 4 vols. (London, 1827), I, p. 431; B.L.: Add. MS. 4276, fo. 5.

he complained of a lack of co-operation from his colleagues, perhaps caused by a fear of offending their parishioners or prominent presbyterian aristocrats in their area. Neither his theoretical analysis, which was to circulate in manuscript, nor his complete history of the Surey affair, promised for 1699, ever saw the light of day.[82]

Although it was difficult to use Taylor's criticisms to determine what had actually happened, his became the accepted version. After Richard Boulton had used the dissenters' account, he was comprehensively savaged by Francis Hutchinson, who ignored Taylor's suggestions of fraud by the Dugdale family and employed his work to accuse the dissenters of incompetence and slandering the family.[83] Conyers Middleton used the case as an exceptionally well-documented example of credulity and his opponents were obliged to concede that there were 'no well attested instances of demoniacks, sorcery, or witchcraft in the present age'.[84] The dissenting ministers have been portrayed as credulous dupes, and Zachary Taylor as an enlightened sceptic, even by historians sympathetic to presbyterianism, although two recent authors have made more favourable comments about the Surey fasts.[85]

The seeds for this incomprehension of dissenting dispossession were sown during the seventeenth century. Apart from the Cambridge Platonists and their followers, most Anglican intellectuals abandoned belief in the supernatural. As early as 1599, Bishop Bancroft was smiling at the testimony in a witch trial and, by the restoration, coffee house society was openly sceptical. Although John Webster's materialism led to the York ecclesiastical authorities refusing him a licence to publish, he had no difficulty in obtaining permission from the Royal

---

[82] Taylor, *Refutation*, p. 3; *The Diary of Abraham de la Pryme*, (Surtees Soc., LIV, 1870), pp. 190–2, 199.

[83] R. Boulton, *A Compleat History of Magick, Sorcery and Witchcraft* 2 vols. (London, 1716), II, pp. 166–235; F. Hutchinson, *An Historical Essay Concerning Witchcraft* (London, 1718), pp. 124–8; R. Boulton, *The Possibility & Reality of Magick, Sorcery, and Witchcraft, demonstrated* (London, 1722), pp. 110–19.

[84] C. Middleton, *A Free Inquiry into the Miraculous Powers* (London, 1749), p. 232; William Parker, *The Expediency of Some Divine Interpositions* (London, 1749), p. 46; William Dodwell, *A Free Answer to Dr. Middleton's Free Inquiry* (London, 1749), pp. 131–3.

[85] J. Hunter, *The Rise of the Old Dissent, exemplified in the Life of Oliver Heywood* (London, 1842), pp. 167, 220n, 365n, 368; John Harland and J.T. Wilkinson, *Lancashire Folk-Lore* (London, 1867), pp. 98–102; Francis Nicolson and Ernest Axon, *The Older Nonconformity in Kendal* (Kendal, 1915), pp. 175–9; C.G. Bolam et al., *The English Presbyterians: from Elizabethan Puritanism to Modern Unitarianism* (London, 1968), pp. 138–9; K.V. Thomas, *Religion and the Decline of Magic* (London, 1971), p. 585. More sympathetic treatment is given by M. MacDonald 'Religion, Social Change and Psychological Healing in England, 1600–1800', pp. 108–9, 114 and Henry D. Rack, 'Doctors, Demons and Early Methodist Healing', in W.J. Sheils (ed.), *The Church and Healing*, pp. 148–9, 151–2.

Society, even though his Helmontian philosophy was 'different from the common opinions of the age'.[86]

Since the catholics were unable to publish freely, the only opposition to Anglican rationalism came from the nonconformists and the Cambridge Platonists. They too espoused reason as their weapon against Calvinist excesses and Richard Baxter, despite his commitment to the world of spirits, did much to encourage rationalism and Arminianism among dissenters, to the horror of more evangelical veterans in the north. Although Richard Frankland and Timothy Jolly held to Calvinist orthodoxy, the dissenting academies did much to undermine traditional beliefs among their pupils. James Clegg of Rochdale abandoned Calvinism while studying at Manchester in 1699 and the supernatural is notably absent from the record of his ministry and medical practice in the Peak District.[87] Although events at the Surey were dominated by traditionalists, even there the new tendency could be detected. Henry Pendlebury of Rochdale, for example, could discuss hell and the last judgement with barely a reference to the demonic, although he did not entirely reject such phenomena as the Devil of Mascon. After his death, it was suggested by Taylor that he had not been convinced by the Dugdale possession.[88] Northern ministers such as Samuel Acton of Nantwich and Jonathan Harle of Morpeth published works in which they described even the evil spirits of the New Testament in purely medical terms, making little allowance for any religious intervention.[89]

The Old Dissent abandoned healing fasts and adopted naturalistic systems of explanation in the eighteenth century, just as the Anglicans had done before them, thus distancing themselves even further from popular healing. Not only were the methods illegitimate and the metaphysics suspect, now the very phenomena were deprived of supernatural significance. Only among pietist circles, mainly in south west England, were witchcraft and possession still taken seriously, on a theoretical level by high churchmen and more practically by method-

[86] D.P. Walker, *Unclean Spirits*, p. 72; Bodleian Library: MS. Lister 34, fo. 148; B.L.: Add. MS. 4255, fo. 40.

[87] C.G. Bolam et al., *The English Presbyterians*, pp. 103–12, 191–6; R. Frankland, *Reflections on a Letter* (London, 1697); *The Diary of James Clegg of Chapel en le Frith, 1708–55*, ed. V.S. Doe, part 3, Derbyshire R.S. (1981) v, p. 913.

[88] H. Pendlebury, *Invisible Realities the Real Christian's Concernment* (London, 1696), pp. 88–9; H. Pendlebury, *The Books Opened* (London, 1696), pp. 15–16; Taylor, *Surey Imposter*, p. 73; Taylor, *Refutation*, pp. 18–19.

[89] S. Acton, *Fruit from Canaan: Or, Fore-Tasts of Glory: in Several Discourses on Assurance* (London, 1709), pp. 131–3; J. Harle, *An Historical Essay on the State of Physick in the Old and New Testament and Apocryphal Interval* (London, 1729), pp. 22–3, 37–40, 124–5.

ists.[90] The gap which opened between different social classes could be recognized and exploited by early methodists but, for most ordinary people, desertion by religious leaders who would no longer provide or condone traditional counter-magic led to an increased demand for the explanations and remedies provided by cunning folk, a phenomenon to be seen in modern France and Portugal.[91] A blend of renaissance magic and popular practices survived well into the nineteenth century, practised by fairly respectable people such as the parish clerks of Skipton, who impressed John Wesley. Among their services, they included the exorcism of 'elfe or elfes, spirits or Fevers, devils or witches', for which the overseers of the poor at Bramley, near Leeds, appear to have paid 12s in 1784.[92] The customers for such expertise probably continued to be mainly women and the young, with men using cunning folk for more physical problems. Adult males had never featured prominently in possession cases or in the more psychological witchcraft accusations, perhaps because they were able to take more active counter-measures than merely consulting ministers or cunning folk. Violent retribution against witches continued long after prosecutions had come to an end.[93]

It is clear that 'the decline of magic' was largely confined to the more educated groups within English society, especially those influenced by whiggish rationalism. What is less clear is the extent to which beliefs were already divided long before that decline. Historians have begun to understand the ways in which educated attitudes towards witches differed from popular attitudes, but this perception needs to be extended into the more nebulous realm of other supernatural phenomena. The comments of seventeenth-century writers cannot be taken as fully authoritative on the subject of popular beliefs and historians who rely on them are likely to miss important distinctions,

[90] M. MacDonald, 'Mystical Bedlam' (Cambridge, 1981), pp. 167–72; H.D. Rack 'Doctors, Demons and Early Methodist Healing', pp. 137–52; Jonathan Barry, 'Piety and the Patient: Medicine and Religion in Eighteenth-century Bristol', in R. Porter (ed.), Patients and Practitioners (Cambridge, 1985), pp. 143–75; Christina Hole, Witchcraft at Toner's Puddle, Dorset R.S., vol. II (1964).

[91] E.P. Thompson, 'Anthropology and the Discipline of Historical Context', Midland History, I (1972), pp. 41–55; Jeanne Favret-Saada, Deadly Words: Witchcraft in the Bocage (Cambridge, 1980), pp. 97, 143; de Pina-Cabral, Sons of Adam, Daughters of Eve, pp. 207–8.

[92] James Obelkevich, Religion and Rural Society: South Lindsey, 1825–1875 (Oxford, 1976), pp. 259–312; Kathryn C. Smith, 'The Wise Man and his Community', Folk Life, XV (1977), 24–35. W. Harbutt Dawson, 'An old Yorkshire Astrologer and Magician, 1694–1760', The Reliquary, XXIII (1882–3), 197–202; John Wesley, Journal, 4 vols. (London, 1827), II, p. 66–7.

[93] P.R.O.: PL 27/2, coroner's inquest of 17 June 1695 (death of Margaret, wife of John Hollinhurst of Tarleton); PL 27/2, depositions of 17 May 1694 (death of Ann, wife of James Crook of Over Hilton); A Gentleman of Middle Temple, A Northern Circuit: Described in a Letter to a Friend (London, 1751), p. 42n; Northampton Mercury, 28 May 1808; Worcester Herald, 12 May 1845.

just as early students of spirit possession among shamans did.[94]

The distinction between personalistic types of explanation, used by restoration dissenting ministers as well as cunning folk and witchcraft victims, and naturalistic explanations, used by Anglican clergymen and physicians, has dominated most discussions of seventeenth-century beliefs about the supernatural. Other distinctions tend to separate the dissenters more sharply from popular beliefs. The ascription of guilt is one such distinction that arises from the present study. Having diagnosed the nature of the ailment, popular practice attempted to locate an agent that might be attacked by counter-magic, often violently. Even though the ultimate source of evil was still external for the dissenters, their doctrines of special providence and demonic possession laid stress on the guilt of the afflicted person. They gave no credence to popular notions of intermediate beings, such as elves and fairies, and increasingly avoided the official process of witchcraft accusations.

Another distinction, which has been hardly mentioned here, is that between public and private affliction. The victims of supernatural agents were generally women and young people, relatively powerless individuals within their families and communities, who became the focus of attention, able to wreak vengeance on even more marginal individuals if they wished. Yet few witchcraft accusations came to court since most were settled informally, without employing official procedures. Only the local community was involved. Cunning folk, even if they accused a witch or suggested some supernatural origin for an affliction, preferred to employ relatively private counter-measures. Partly because their status depended on success and they had no desire to attract official attention, cunning folk may be seen as defining 'small afflictions'. The petty maleficences of local witch or minor spirit could be dealt with privately.

Although some Anglican intellectuals continued to be interested in fairies, nonconformists could never countenance Henry Krabtree's reported statement that 'if the Spirit in Richard Dugdale was a Water Spirit, there was no Cure for it'. If the symptoms of an afflicted person were defined as demonic, perhaps as a result of them being influenced by the intervention of godly observers, then nonconformists had no doubt that this was a 'great affliction', calling for heroic prayer.[95] The

[94] Jane M. Murphy, 'Psychotherapeutic Aspects of Shamanism on St. Lawrence Island, Alaska', in Ari Kiev (ed.), *Magic, Faith, and Healing: Studies in Primitive Psychiatry Today* (New York, 1964), pp. 68–9.
[95] Jolly, *Surey Demoniack*, p. 62; for an anthropological example of such a distinction, see Robin Horton, 'Types of Spirit Possession in Kalabari Religion', in J. Beattie and J. Middleton (eds.), *Spirit Mediumship and Society in Africa* (London, 1969), pp. 45–7.

nonconformists beseeched God to expel the Devil as publicly as judges condemned the Devil's minions. Their thaumaturgical drama was played upon the largest of stages, the apocalyptic struggle between God and the Devil for the souls of mankind. To display this for the edification of the faithful and the conversion of the ungodly was their sacred duty, although it began to embarrass the more sophisticated graduates of Leyden and the dissenting academies.

The younger generation of nonconformist ministers had not experienced the full rigours of persecution and were unsympathetic to explicitly eschatological interpretations of current events. When they abandoned the supernatural explanation of affliction that their fathers had readily employed, they were not creating a new gulf between themselves and popular belief. They merely widened an existing gap to such an extent that they were isolated from ordinary villagers outside their own congregations. Popular beliefs about the origins of unusual disorders continued to flourish, as the methodists were quick to realize.

5

Passions and the ghost in the machine: or what not to ask about science in seventeenth- and eighteenth-century Germany

JOHANNA GEYER-KORDESCH

INTRODUCTION

What not to ask about science as it lies in the cradle of the 'scientific revolution' and in its early childhood, the age of enlightenment, is what ideas it supressed. To concentrate on this question would be to risk simplification in the complexity of the philosophy and natural science that was emerging in the seventeenth century. Ideas construct reality and their successful support by the important men of a period exercises pressure on other methods of perceiving the truth. Although little of what was believed to be scientific in the past would be reconcilable to our own construction of scientific reality, the claim of 'science' to 'truth' became firmly established by the eighteenth century. That science became equivalent to truth in a world which was primarily religiously oriented was a major shift in the *Weltanschauung* of an age and much more important than the 'decline of magic'. In this sense, and indeed more so where science began to define human nature, it is justifiable first to ask who paid the price in political and cultural terms, and secondly to enquire whether science did in fact help to dislocate fundamental perceptions in its seemingly victorious advance.

Science in the seventeenth century has received much attention. Its opposite, 'superstition', has, like the 'decline of magic', more than equally found its historians.[1] This convenient dichotomy, however, supports a two-class system in which only science is linked with the advancement of learning. In this chapter I wish to examine various opposing views within the discussion of seventeenth- and early eighteenth-century science. The central theme is that of truth: whether science or religion can make a better claim to explain nature. What must be understood is that this precludes the discussion of a dichotomy

---

[1] Keith Thomas, *Religion and Decline of Magic* (Harmondsworth, 1973), (first published 1971).

of 'science' and 'magic' or 'superstition'. The opposition between the new science and a religiously oriented interpretation of nature, at least in early eighteenth-century Germany, was discussed on a very high intellectual level. It was not a matter of enlightening those caught in superstitious beliefs, nor was it a debate about purely scientific discrepancies. The core problem centres upon what science *meant*. In medicine, where the debate comes closest to the thorny questions of the interpretation of the nature of man, no one of consequence was unaware of the new scientific discoveries or explanations. However, the new science was considered dangerous where it related to such primary considerations as the soul. It is this focus on the soul and its relation to the body that determines much of the debate about what the new science meant. Because of the uncertainties concerning the defini- tion of the soul, the issue of the passions and the imagination also came to be of major importance.[2] This was also significant for the social context because the more radical religious groups based their concep- tions of truth on subjective realities such as visions and emotive perceptions while the new scientific men did not. Therefore the debate on the soul and its truth in relation to the new scientific view of reality had a very solid base in the social and political tensions of the period. I will try and show how the sides taken in the intellectual debate concurred with the aims of different groups and the social changes effected in the period.

Dualism (the body–mind problem) and the emergence of the me- chanical philosophy were essentially foreign to the still predominant perception of the world as governed by spiritual forces. The outcry over the 'mechanization of the universe' in the printed evidence of the age makes this clear enough.[3] At the end of this paper I discuss 'mechanism versus organism' as part of a significant debate on the soul, much neglected, between Gottfried Wilhelm von Leibniz and Georg Ernst Stahl.

The second and related dilemma involved with the establishment of natural science concerns the definition of what is 'natural'. Here we

---

[2] Oskar Diethelm, *Medical Dissertations of Psychiatric Interest Printed Before 1750* (Munich, 1971). Diethelm comments that after Stahl's medical theory appeared, the dissertations on soul-related topics in medicine, such as diseases related to the imagination, increased in number.

[3] This is especially true for Germany where popular writers, such as the theologian and doctor Johann Conrad Dippel, published scathing rebuttals to Descartes and mechanism: *Anderer Theil des Wegweisers zum Licht und Recht in der äusseren Natur*. . . (n.p., 1705); *Fatum Fatuum, das ist thörichte Notwendigkeit* . . . (Amsterdam, 1710); *Analysis Cramatis Harmonici Hyper-Metaphysico-Logico-Mathematica* . . . (n.p., 1729); *Vitae Animalis Morbus et Medicina* . . . (Leiden, 1711).

encounter the construction of a scientific 'reality' in which nature becomes equivalent to the laws of physics, mathematics and chemistry and the disciplines of anatomy and physiology. The 'natural' has little room for unexpected events, and in the seventeenth century, 'chaotic' political developments justified themselves outside the 'natural'. The beheading of Charles I by religious radicals was just such an 'unnatural' event. In the restoration the order of nature, the 'natural', became a key factor in re-establishing a truth to be set against the truth of the inspirational movements, a cultural and political act embodied in the 'revolt against enthusiasm'.[4] I shall touch only briefly on this English 'revolt' to show how international was its scope, as the same issues were taken up somewhat later in Germany among the radically minded pietists, excluding, of course, a political culmination in regicide.

The debate on nature takes issue with the idea of the book of nature, a heritage of religious thought which declared that nature could be 'read', much as any text is readable if its alphabet be understood, and therefore interpretable.[5] Interpretation, however much objectified, ultimately rests – in such a case – on a quality science scarcely admits: the subjective. Subjectivity in religious radicalism comes to the fore in two areas, one being a claim that inspiration contains as much truth as science, the second being that science cannot master those most subjective of experiential and creative elements, the passions and the imagination. Within the scope of my chapter I discuss some aspects of the debate on the passions and on the imagination. In particular, the difficulty of their 'placement' as natural science embraces the question of reason as a method and the measure of all things. In the important debate between Leibniz and Stahl this is again a point at issue.

The 'book of nature' approach to the interpretation of the natural world continues into the enlightenment, and this, too, needs to be recognized. As a representative of religious opposition to post-Cartesian dualism I have selected the medical doctor and follower of Stahl, Johann Samuel Carl, to show the viability of a 'spiritual' interpretation of nature. This variant of the 'spiritual' view of nature was holistic,

---

⁴ See Georg. Rosen, '"Enthusiasm" a Dark Lanthorn of the Spirit', in *Bulletin of the History of Medicine*, XLII/5 (1968), 393–421; John F. Sena, 'Melancholic Madness and the Puritans', in *Harvard Theological Review*, LVI/3 (1973), 293–309; George Williamson, 'The Restoration Revolt against Enthusiasm', in *Studies in Philology*, XXX (1933), 571–603; Truman Guy Steffan, 'The Social Argument against Enthusiasm', in *Studies in English*, XXI (1941), 39–63.
⁵ The tradition was still alive in the eighteenth century. Here two examples from very popular poets of the time: Barthold Hinrich Brockes, 'Das schöne Weltbuchsblatt, so hier vor Augen lieget / Liest der zu Gottes Ruhm, der sich daran vergnüget'; and Anna Luisa Karsch, 'Ich lese, großer Schöpfer! dich / Des Nachts in Büchern, aufgeschlagen / Von deiner Hand. O lehre mich / Nach deinem Lichte fragen'.

linking 'outer' nature to an 'inner' intelligence or spirit. It is this view which is hardest for us to accept, as it is the most remote from our own conceptualizations, and the most difficult to describe – we have, significantly, no vocabulary for it. However, I would argue that it is precisely this area of holism, the soul incarnate, the embodiment of spirits, or 'mystical nature' that was the undeclared enemy of natural science. The social and political antagonisms of the period would support this assessment. In contrast to this, the area of so-called superstition, either in the religious context or in its secularized version, is relatively negligible because the main opposition generated by the new science set the credo of naturalism against the belief that the organizing principle in nature is the soul. Dualism has since become so pervasive that today we find a formulation such as the *immaterial soul* comprehensible.

ENTHUSIASM AND ENLIGHTENMENT

Although the case can be made for the ambivalence of many of the men advocating the new science, since most of them still had a sustaining interest in occult writings,[6] the momentum of the scientific *Weltanschauung* was gathering force. Socio-cultural as well as intellectual reasons began to set a pattern for the preferred acceptance of those ideas acclaimed as the scientific revolution. A number of factors seem to converge, which I will try to describe very generally. No exhaustive study has yet been made of the intellectual geography involved, but all indications point towards an intensive interchange between England, Holland, and Germany in establishing the 'new' science as well as harbouring its most outspoken opposition.

One major factor to be reckoned with in the political and cultural changes in England and on the continent was certainly the 'revolt against enthusiasm'. This well-documented intellectual attack of English restoration writers and divines sought to disparage the English revolution. Its main aim was to devalue what had legitimized the social reform led by the religiously enthusiastic.[7] The revolt against enthusiasm is generally associated with particular works by Henry More, Joseph Glanvill, Meric Casaubon, Jeremy Taylor, Samuel Parker and Thomas Hobbes. Their writings have one thing in common, even if they defend orthodox religious beliefs: they attack inspired and subjec-

---

[6] Charles Webster, *From Paracelsus to Newton, Magic and the Making of Modern Science* (Cambridge, 1982).
[7] See especially Steffan, 'The Social Argument against Enthusiasm'.

tive guidance. Both had been the mainstay of sectarian radical protestantism since the reformation. Dreams, prophecies, signs and wonders and speaking in tongues graced the often unintellectual, but biblically well-informed world of religious radicalism, and these sources instigated a flood of books and political actions which were not all in accord with hierarchical authority. Paracelsianism in its original form had this flavour, as did the reception of – to name only one of the striking foreign imports into the seventeenth-century world of English thought – the writings of Jacob Boehme.[8] His works were translated between 1645 and 1663 and their mystical–spiritual–theosophist content 'travelled' via two routes, that of the English *Behmenists* (John Pordage, Jane Leade) and via the Dutch, back to German pietism. Boehme's influence alone substantiates how lively were the interchanges which fed into renewed religious radicalism in the eighteenth century. Even though Newton, Henry More and Leibniz dipped into Boehme, the essential difference becomes apparent if one tries to imagine any of these settled scholars becoming inspired enthusiasts. Boehme's own life and works and his reception among religious radicals are of a piece, and they weave well into the renewed fabric of an inspired, impassioned vision of *Naturmystik* and religious communities whose concern is an immediate, personal relation with a *living* God. Not particularly fond of universities,[9] these enclaves of the inspired had established in themselves a verification of their beliefs which necessarily repudiated dogmatism.

The legitimization for being the 'true' church rested on manifest signs of inspiration, that very field in which one could tangibly assess the workings of the Holy Spirit. Dreams, prophecies, signs and wonders, speaking in tongues and fervent pietism were much more than experiences, they were the truth of enthusiasm, the seal of veracity for an inspired community.[10]

Thus it becomes much more than a purely intellectual argument when the prominent men of society begin to write against the inspired guidance of radical religion. The aim of the new science after 1660 can be seen as an attempt to undermine the cohesion of these communities

---

[8] A good summary of Boehme's ideas and the history of his publications and translations can be found in Eberhard H. Pältz, 'Jacob Böhme', *Theologische Realenzylopädie*, VI, (Berlin, 1980), pp. 748–54.

[9] The well-known separatist and pietist Gottfried Arnold (1966–1707) resigned his professorship in Gießen because it prevented him from becoming truly pious. He justified this in his book *Offenherzige Bekäntniß von Ablegung seiner Profession* (Frankfurt, 1698), which was reprinted several times.

[10] See, in particular, Martin Schulz, 'Johann Heinrich Sprögel und die pietistische Bewegung Quedlinburgs', (University of Halle, theological dissertation, 1974).

and to relegate the signs of their truth to categories that discredit deeper claims. The revolt against enthusiasm contains the meat and drink of disparagement. The dividing line between the new science and radical religion is none other than the definition of truth and authority. Anti-enthusiast writing is very focused indeed: all the sources of inspirational truth are redefined as insubstantial fictions. What the inspired believed to be the indwelling guidance of the Holy Spirit became recategorized as a subjective spleen. Visions, dreams and prophecy, instead of being sources of wisdom, became mere products of the imagination. Truth sought by means of personal insight into the divine will, and so often recorded in radical writings, was relegated to the category of disease, as writers explained a cause and effect relationship between somatic conditions, such as fasting and isolation, and prophetic or utopian vision or the imagination which carried men and women to unorthodox or subjective interpretations of the world or their condition.[11] The definition 'disease' not only ameliorated, as an 'enlightened' view, the idea of witchcraft,[12] it also disempowered the idea of divine inspiration. The concept of 'natural' events drew boundaries: within the gates the objectively recognizable and its symptoms, outside the gates the inexplicable relations of 'possession', the divine will and its relation to the believer, the nature of evil, the invisible peripatetic nature of love or inspiration. 'Disease' became an omniverous 'new science': an 'ill' mind as part of an 'ill' body is obviously not an objectively truthful one.

In order to validate themselves and distance themselves from the claim to truth of inspirational guidance, the opposition to radical religion chose the invention, or discovery, of an order of nature independent of any human feeling or anagogic reading. The word 'invention' is a gleaning from Georg Ernst Stahl's epistemological criticism of mechanical philosophy.[13] The desire of the 'moderns' to base truth on experiment is to his mind an *inventio* because it produces artificial conditions. *Experientia*, meaning, in Stahl's sense, the observational knowledge that nature puts before one, and which one can 'read' (my term), seemed a better source of truth. The revolt against enthusiasm which merged with the new science did not support the idea of nature *discovered* through experience; rather it wished nature

[11] The above is a summary of the ideas to be found in the articles of Rosen, Sena, Williamson and Steffan.
[12] In Germany medical reasons were used to disqualify the legal persecution of witches. Johann Jacob Reich includes a medical dissertation in his collection of writings criticizing the practice of persecuting witches: *Kurtze Lehr-Sätze von dem Laster der Zauberey* (Halle, 1704).
[13] Georg Ernst Stahl, *Theoria Medica Vera*. (Halle, 1708), p. 5.

to conform to discovered laws. The epistemology of *relation* (not of *causal* necessity) turns on the problem of soul and body, or, putting it another way, the problem of the inner nature of an entity and its material embodiment. This is not precisely definable in the mechanical philosophy, where exact cause and effect relations are sought in physical substances alone. Any introduction of spirit or soul inevitably reverts to 'inspiration' or to the admittance of an 'immediate' or personally interventionist God (the indwelling of the Holy Spirit, not only on a personal level, but as an ever present historical event, a thought ever dear to radical religion).[14] A deist God, one who only pulls the first lever in the ordered machinery of the universe, is the only conceptualization consistent with *laws* of mechanical order.

Ridding itself of the uncertainties of unexpected visions, of inexplicable speaking in tongues, of the passions in general (by relegating them to the positon of 'corruptive' influences), or of feelings as significant indicators, the new science turned its floodlights on physics, mathematics, chemistry and a physiology of fibres, fluids and a mechanical model of motion. The epistemological aim was to reinstate order of a kind which was predictable for what was to become eighteenth-century 'nature'. The physicotheology of the eighteenth century then sought 'God' in 'nature', an objectified relation, not a subjectified one.

The aim of the new science was to reinstate order and find, above all, the order in nature which could, beyond doubt, establish authority. The authority of nature was, in essence, a discovery of laws.[15] Once thinking was established in this direction, the sceptics' vision discovered an ultimate authority to which man could also be subjected: the laws of nature itself. Those who sought nature as the *via regia* to truth and objectivity, extolled science. The new experimental science explained the edifice of nature in terms of identifiable and verifiable laws. The touchstones of these laws were first, reason and second, empirical observation. Both produced facts, and the reconstruction of nature through facts, undeniable as proven truth, elevated nature to the level of an ultimate authority, one whose objectivity cannot be further questioned (*Sachautorität*).[16] This factual authority of nature as the ultimate basis of truth was widely advertised by the revolt against enthusiasm. Samuel Taylor, the Anglican clergyman, quite revealingly put it thus:

[14] Still very readable: Heinrich Bornkamm, *Mystik, Spiritualismus und die Anfänge des Pietismus im Luthertum* (Gießen, 1926).
[15] See Richard Toellner, 'Zum Begriff Authorität in der Medizin der Renaissance', in G. Keil and R. Schmitz (eds.), *Humanismus und Medizin* (Weinheim, 1984), pp. 159–79.   [16] *Ibid.*

Experimental knowledge is of all others the most safe and unquestionable . . . At least when our knowledge proceeds in an empirical way, 'tis solid and palpable, and made so undoubtedly certain from the plain and most undoubted testimony of sense and experience.[17]

Experimental knowledge is safe and unquestionable: its appeal lies in the authority which it is made to represent. Casaubon puts this unequivocally when he writes: 'it is safer to err with authority than through singularity'.[18] Thus, increasingly, ideas were linked which supported one another. The discoveries made by way of the experimental methods acquired the character of the unquestionable, they were palpable. Authority was depersonified in nature and nature redefined in law. Singularity had no room to move. The combination of authority and nature extended then to the idea of 'the natural', the verbal and conceptual opposite of the singular, the eccentric, the irregular, the overly passionate, the baroque imagination. Hand in hand with the natural goes common sense and reason.

Not to err on the side of singularity became a postulate of enlightened science, and the ways and means of its apotheosis are to be found in the resounding names of the age: Newton, Descartes and their planets. Newtonian physics, Cartesian philosophy, mechanical medicine, the pre-established harmony, Leibniz's mathematics: these established the texture of science, and in whatever variation they were debated, modified, 'misunderstood', they none the less introduced axiomatically the factual authority of the experiment, the division of spirit from matter (however tortuous were the conceptual bridges that still accounted for 'soul') and of mechanism, the idea that nothing intervenes in a process that does not conform to matter acting on matter and to the laws of physics and mathematics. This fundamental set of ideas was the matrix of the new science. The construction of nature in this form is an eighteenth-century event. As Fritz Wagner has written, seeking to define the essence of the new science:

What could be counted and measured, mechanically constructed and analysed, that which could be logically combined by explaining cause and effect became so powerful that it entered the very lives of people and dominated it in various forms.[19]

Wagner does not mean this critically. He chronicles admiringly the socially ascribed 'greatness' of men of science and their ability to 'discover' in nature a powerful order.[20] But Wagner does not realize

---

[17] Quoted from Steffan, 'The Social Argument against Enthusiasm', 61.
[18] Quoted from Steffan, 'The Social Argument against Enthusiasm', 56.
[19] Fritz, Wagner, 'Der Wissenschaftsbegriff im Zeitalter der Aufklärung', in Karl Hammer and Jürgen Voss (eds.), *Historische Forschung im 18. Jht., Organisation, Zielsetzung, Ergebnisse* (Bonn, 1976), p. 16. I have translated from the German.   [20] *Ibid.*, p. 22ff.

that nature *becomes* or is transformed into orderliness by the scientific discoveries made about it. Because this order is discovered in nature it also applies to life, very pervasively, giving new authority to the agent which enables science to complete this transformation: reason. Reason is the macroscopic microscope by which to view the stars of the firmaments and the things to which the eye has been blind.

Reason, Nature, Authority, Science: in sum the full weight of the modern ideology of the enlightenment, ideas and interconnections which historiography has gladly handed down to us and to which we are accustomed. Richard Toellner has examined the changes in the claims of authority from the early renaissance to the enlightenment and has shown that the authority of the ancients, undermined through various shades of scepticism was squarely replaced in the eighteenth century by the *Sachautorität* of nature. *Sachautorität* means subordinating the question of who defines what is real to the knowledge that scientific facts are evidence. Nature – for the eighteenth century – possessed the right qualities by which to ascertain truth, to wit: 'an authority not mediated by prophets or apostles or any chain of tradition, and therefore not subject to falsification as it is received and passed on, it being representative always of an immediate contact to its (Divine) source'.[21] The conflation of God and nature, although the great men of science who were orthodox believers might not have condoned it, results from this 'immediate' contact with the source, excluding, as it does, the possibilities of inspiration. The prophets and the apostles are to bow before the laws of nature, whereas the New Testament and significant parts of the Old testify to the dominion over nature: the raising of the dead, the healing of the sick, the calming of the storm, the passage through the Red Sea, the plagues of Egypt, the Manna in the desert. The unsettling conflict between religious radicalism and the *Sachautorität* of nature only briefly reached a cease-fire as science rose to its high noon. The enthusiastic revolt against science took up arms again in early eighteenth-century Germany.

SOUL AND REASON

The new science had decisive effects on medicine. It is necessary to evoke a sense of these influences before examining the controversy between Leibniz and Stahl, a controversy which once more focuses the main issues. The most far-reaching consequence for medicine lay in the

[21] Toellner, 'Zum Begriff der Authorität in der Medizin der Renaissance', p. 170. I have translated from the German.

Cartesian introduction of dualism. The *res extensa* was defined as qualitatively different from the *res cogitans*. Mind was separated from matter and mind and was equated with rational thinking. This 'freed' the body for somatic investigation, for the processes of dissection. The consequences were far-reaching.

I am going to draw on a German language translation of Hermann Boerhaave's *Physiologie*[22] by the professor of medicine in Halle, Johann Peter Eberhard, published in 1754, first, because it shows the continuity of late seventeenth-century scientific ideas, and, secondly, because it clarifies the medical dissociation of body from mind. Boerhaave maintains that there is no causal relation between the soul, in this case the will, and the movement of the muscles, either in its voluntary aspect or in the processes 'necessary to life'.[23] 'Both movements occur according to a primarily ordained law without voluntary influence.'[24] The soul possesses only a voluntary power over the instruments necessary to life. 'The boundaries of its activity are so narrow that no mortal and no animal could change anything by way of the will affecting the heart, the stomach, or other internal organs, or replace, add or subtract anything from life.'[25] Mainly, and most importantly, however, the soul can only – according to Boerhaave – conceive clearly one idea at a time, and it is therefore impossible that it could consciously influence the many physiological processes in the body.[26]

This dispossessing of the soul of any influence on physiology is a central issue to which, for example, both Leibniz and Albrecht von Haller refer when they defend the purely corporeal (*res extensa*) investigation of bodily functions. Both these men of science use the – to their mind – irrefutable example of the heart which continues to beat after it is separated from the body and which is therefore beyond any influence on the soul and still 'moves'.[27]

Leibniz embraced dualism because for him there was no logical basis for any other alternative.[28] Cause and effect in material things had to

---

[22] Hermann Boerhaave, *Physiologie* ... *übersetzt und mit Zusätzen vermehrt von Johann Peter Eberhard* (Halle, 1754).   [23] *Ibid.*, p. 954.   [24] *Ibid.*   [25] *Ibid.*, p. 955.   [26] *Ibid.*, pp. 956–7.
[27] Leibniz discuss this in the *Negotium Otiosum*, the controversy between him and Stahl (see note 28) and Albrecht von Haller uses this argument frequently. See Richard Toellner, '*Anima et Irritabilis*, Hallers Abwehr von Animismus und Materialismus', in *Sudhoffs Archiv*, LI, (1967), 140.
[28] The following elucidation of the ideas of Leibniz is taken from the translation of a part of the *Negotium Otiosum*, the debate between Leibniz and Stahl on mechanism, the laws of nature, and on the soul which was originally published in Latin (Halle, 1720). L. J. Rather has provided a translation of the introductory *Dubia* of Leibniz and a part of Stahl's counterarguments. See L. J. Rather and J.B. Frerichs, 'The Leibniz-Stahl Controversy–I, Leibniz Opening Objections to the *Theoria Medica Vera*', *Clio Medica*, III, (1968), 21–40; and 'The Leibniz–Stahl Controversy–II. Stahl's Survey of the Principal Points of Doubt', *Clio Medica*, V (1970), 53–67.

conform to natural laws. Mechanism in the widest sense was, in its conception of matter as subject to order, a rational axiom. If the soul, defined as the opposite of matter and of an entirely different quality, were able to influence the body, the fundamental order of natural laws would be called into question. Neither grace nor miracles were really admissible. Leibniz did not dismiss the soul as such, but set it in intimate relation to matter in his construct, the monad. The soul is the perceptual element and to it Leibniz ascribes teleological goals. This philosophical solution through the monad leaves reality much as it is, but that is not the point. The more crucial aspect of the pre-established harmony is that matter remains separated from 'soul' and can be scientifically abstracted in laws of physics and mathematics. Nothing in the universe, states Leibniz, is illogical or irrational. He firmly anchors the *Sachauthorität* of the eighteenth-century view of nature in objectifiable laws.[29] Dualism is also crucial for the suggestion that reason is (almost) perfectly independent of the senses in its logical and deductive capacities. Leibniz differentiates reason from sensual perception.[30] Sensual perception is part of the mechanism of the body because impressions are received by the sense organs and are instrumental for 'motion' (processes) in the body. Only voluntary motion and reason are conscious efforts of the soul.

This, of course, is where Leibniz, Descartes and the above-mentioned medical empiricism of Boerhaave join forces. Christian Wolff, professor in Halle and popularizer of Leibniz and Descartes, underlined this hierarchical conception of the faculties of the soul by differentiating reason as the capacity to shape ideas into clearly conscious entities.[31] Reason becomes a reflective faculty. The ability to compare and discern the elements of what is perceived is the very essence of rational thinking. Against this all other perceptual possibilities, in particular those of the senses or the emotions, are defined by Wolff to be *verworren*, unclear and mitigating reason.[32] In a memorable statement Wolff describes the passions in their opposition to reason. The passions, as sensual desires, 'move' a person, but they are bereft of all reason:

Through the passions human beings are swept into doing this or that, or into refraining from something; they heighten desire or aversion, alterning normal states. Because man does not reflect on what he does when inflamed by passion, and because he is no longer in control of his actions, he is moved to carry out or leave undone what by use of his reason he would have conceived to do differently. Because the passions arise from sensual images and from the imagination, it follows that the reign ('Herrschaft') of the

[29] *Dubia* III., Rather, 'Leibniz–Stahl I.', 25ff.   [30] Rather, 'Leibniz–Stahl I.', 25ff
[31] Christian Wolff, *Vernünftige Gedanken von Gott, der Welt und der Seele des Menschen* (Frankfurt and Leipzig, 1720), pp. 457ff and 527ff.   [32] *Ibid.*, p. 482, 504ff.

senses, the passions, and the imagination make men slaves. And one calls those slaves who let themselves be ruled by the passions and who do not elevate their knowledge above the confused impulses of the senses and the passions.[33]

This is the *non plus ultra* statement of the enlightenment on the place of reason and the corruptive influence of the passions and the imagination. As a psychological pronouncement it creates a hierarchy crowned by 'pure reason' and equates logical thought with man's most perfect self-realization. At the same time a scale of values is set forth, the reasonable man being the measure of all things, the passionate and imaginative human a prey to 'forces' beyond his or her control. The term 'soul' in the eighteenth century is then very easily used as a synonym for reason. Boerhaave and Albrecht von Haller do just this when they exempt all physiological processes and muscular activity from consciousness.

Wolff also split the imagination. In accordance with the hierarchical position of 'pure reason' Wolff formulated the law of association in which information already stored in the mind is recalled, made fully conscious, compared, and combined with new ideas, a product of reasonable reflection. This association of ideas localizes the imagination as part of the creative process of thinking.[34] The imagination connected with the passions, an emotive imagination, remains a 'dark' force, and its disassociative (in the sense of logical cohesion) production is the very source of chaos and fantasies.[35]

STAHL AND LEIBNIZ

Enthusiasts did not disappear with the restoration of monarchy in England since religious revival was by no means national. Even the scholars of the restoration made telling remarks about 'Amsterdam' and 'Germany'.[36] By 1670 the pietist revival, not yet institutionalized in Halle, was gaining a significant following. Once more speaking in tongues, the interpretation of dreams, prophecy, inspiration and an intensive and personal scrutinizing of the Bible recalled that the Spirit goeth where it will. Between 1670 and 1694, the founding date of the University of Halle, the pietist revival consolidated itself not only as a

[33] *Ibid.*, p. 298–9. The translation from the German is my own. The German vernacular of the eighteenth century is very cumbersome and I have tried for accuracy rather than fluency.
[34] *Ibid.*, pp. 502ff., 513ff.   [35] *Ibid.*, pp. 266ff., 509ff.
[36] See Steffan, 'The Social Argument against Enthusiasm', 41: 'Amsterdamian Sects and Sectaries' (Richard Burton); Williamson, 'The Restoration Revolt against Enthusiasm', 582: 'in several remote parts of Germany, Sweden and some other countries' (William Temple); the same statement from William Temple, made *c.* 1690, i.e. when pietism in Germany was coming into its own, quoted in Rosen, 'Enthusiasm', 394.

movement, but also ideologically.[37] This does not imply uniformity in its ideas. But certain patterns emerge that re-inaugurate enthusiast and nonconformist living and thinking. The sense of immediacy is present, a millennial perception that this is an 'endtime', one of visitation in which, to use the phrase of the pietists, the anger of God (*der Zorn Gottes*) is manifest in war, disease and the complacency of the church. Gottfried Arnold, radical pietist in Quedlinburg, sees all the established churches as Babylon.[38] Arnold writes that history documents the backslidden decadence of all who have betrayed the ideals of early Christendom, excepting only the sectarians and 'heretics' (*Ketzer*).[39] Against this enormous weight of an unreformed and unredeemed Protestantism the 'tiny number' (*kleine Hauffen*/'small heap') must guarantee the following of Christ.[40] These are the persecuted, and a sign of their truth is their unacceptability to the world at large. Their 'unworldliness' they demonstrated by behaviour disruptive of social norms (marriage across class lines, preaching against court immorality, associating freely with the unlearned and the poor, disregarding leisure, games, theatre, clothes and other pleasures, and by emphasizing prayer and work). This disregard of the world and its social demarcations was, of course, immensely worldly in its effects: turning the world 'upside down', as has been noted for English radical protestantism.[41] But apart from these marked tendencies to a specific lifestyle, the ideological interaction among the pietists – and they were an intensely communicative group – produced a method of apprehending and interpreting nature of necessity opposed to the new objective appeal of science. This is one of the major differences between the earlier radicalism in England and its German mutation: monarchical absolutism was on the rise as was the establishment of the new science. Politically, Prussia was never revolutionized, but the enthusiasts did fight an ideological battle against the main precepts of the new science: rationalism and dualism.

[37] I discuss the connections between the 'revolt against enthusiasm' and German pietism in my forthcoming book, *Georg Ernst Stahl: Pietismus, Medizin und Aufklärung in Preußen im 18. Jahrhundert* (1989). The following summary is extensively documented there.

[38] For an extensive study of Gottfried Arnold and his views, see Erich Seeberg, *Gottfried Arnold, die Wissenschaft und die Mystik seiner Zeit* (Meerane, 1923).

[39] Gottfried Arnold, *Unparteiische Kirchen- und Ketzer-Historie* (Frankfurt, 1699–1700). For a short biography and good bibliography, see Martin Schmidt, 'Gottfried Arnold', in *Theologiche Realenzyklopädie*, IV (Berlin, 1979), pp. 136–43.

[40] This self-description is emphasized in, for example, Christian Weißbach, *Wahrhaffte und gründliche Cur aller dem menschlichen Leibe zustossenden Kranckheiten* (Straßburg, 1725), p. 3.

[41] Christopher Hill, *The World Turned Upside Down, Radical Ideas During the English Revolution* (Harmondsworth, 1982, first published 1972).

A very different psychology, physiology and pathology developed with the theory and teaching of Georg Ernst Stahl (1659–1734) in Halle. Stahl's theory takes up main tenets of enthusiast thought, but also claims to be in accord with the latest scientific knowledge. In the symbiosis of pietist thinking and Stahl's *Theoria Medica Vera* (Halle, 1708) his work was envisioned as an 'advancement of learning', an instauration of knowledge adequate to the new age.[42] The prime difference between the enlightenment ideal of pure reason and Stahl's ideas is contained in his holistic theory of the union of body and mind.

The most important of Stahl's medical writings were printed by the Waisenhaus Verlag, a publishing house owned and operated by the pietists in Halle. His medical theory was fully accessible by 1708 in the *Theoria Medica Vera*. When Leibniz read this work he formulated a series of objections to Stahl's theory and these, together with Stahl's reply were published in 1720, also by the Waisenhaus Verlag. This book, the *Negotium Otiosum*, represents the last full discussion by Stahl of his medical ideas. He clarifies and substantiates once more the principles upon which he bases his medical insights and in his answers to Leibniz we find a cogent reply to the premises upon which the new science was based. It is from the *Negotium Otiosum* that I take the following description of the opposing points of view between Leibniz, as a representative of the new science, and Stahl as – perhaps – the only thinker of the early eighteenth century who developed an alternative medical theory, that of the organism.

A fundamental disagreement such as that between Leibniz and Stahl, of course, also implies a very different approach to nature. First of all, Stahl does not agree with the definition of reason as bound to full consciousness. He differentiates between reasoning and reason,[43] the former being equivalent to Wolff's conception of logical thinking, the latter drawing on the idea of *intellectus*, intelligence in the broadest sense receptive of perceptual information.

Intelligence is integral to the powers of the soul and not inherent in matter.[44] The second integral power of the soul is the will, and this for Stahl means direction, the initiation of process to achieve an end. Again, and here Stahl does not negate the Cartesian principle of *res extensa*, direction (desire and aversion) is not inherent in matter. Thus the soul encompasses for Stahl all perceptual powers without which no

---

[42] I substantiate and develop this view in my forthcoming book, *Georg Ernst Stahl*, (see n. 37).

[43] Georg Ernst Stahl, *Propempticon Inauguralis de Differentia Rationis et Ratiocinationis* (Halle, 1701).

[44] This and the following summary is taken from the *Theoria Medica Vera* and the *Negotium Otiosum*.

living thing can exist. These, he states, must be coextensive with matter (in living things) because, as he argues against Leibniz, one does not have to predicate the absolute opposition of spirit and matter.[45] On the contrary, Stahl writes, experience shows us that spirit and matter, although different in kind, can never be separated. The soul is coextensive with the body in *intellectus* and *voluntas* because only in their unity (as a whole) is life present. Without life matter falls apart into its various chemical substances. Stahl stringently separates not the soul from the body, but the organization (organism) of life from the inorganic. Thus the abstraction of laws of cause and effect when applied solely to matter, as in eighteenth-century physics and mathematics, cannot solve the problems of organic change.

Thus Stahl's answer to dualism and the mechanical philosophy in medicine, in which the body is investigated as *res extensa*, is essentially a simple one: the organizational principle of the soul works with the body as with an instrument because the soul is incarnate. The soul incarnate is not reducible to reason alone and does not represent a hierarchy of faculties, but encompasses an interplay of teleological possibilities, including sense perception, will, emotion and imagination. All of these are realized in the body. Stahl does not subscribe to the view of the 'best of all possible worlds', therefore neither *intellectus* nor *voluntas* are infallible, and the teleology of process can lead to illness and death.

In thus defining the living organism as an intelligent and self-directing unit, Stahl opposes the mechanist view. Even if the heart continues to beat when separated from the body, it will not be able to beat any the faster for love. Stahl's theory presupposes that medicine deals with living individuals and is not subsumed to chemistry or anatomy, physics or mathematics. The passions and the imagination are much more vital in assessing the condition of a man or woman than any purely somatic approach. Moreover, the passions and imagination make havoc of any conceptions of cause and effect on mechanical (somatic) lines and their influence is much more powerful than reason. Stahl justifies his emphasis on the emotional life thus:

It seemed to me useful and necessary to direct attention to the fact that man's nature has a special propensity toward error and excesses, brought about by his impatience, hastiness, irresolution, fearfulness, feelings of terror, melancholy depression or ill-judged euphoria, as well as his tendency to oscillate between willful impulse and despondency, between carefree negligence and overbearing pride in his accomplishments. All of these emotions culminate in imprudent actions not regulated by rational

[45] Rather, 'The Leibniz–Stahl Controversy – II, 58.

consciousness because they are part of subliminal awareness and are not completely accessible to memory. Nor can they be entirely subsumed to the conscious actions of the will or reason.[46]

This interplay of actions where all perceptions are conscious because the body reacts to them, undermines the idea of an exclusive relation between reason and consciousness. The 'objective' approach of the scientific observer, one who penetrates the body in order to dissect its functions, and seeks to lay bare its mechanisms, is replaced by an observer mindful of symptoms. Stahl observes the instability of the dynamics of feeling, thinking and acting, and this fitfulness makes him utterly sceptical of the mechanical model. Instead of the *Sachautorität* of nature, that binds body and soul to its objective laws, as the endproduct of the axioms of science, Stahl insists on an *a posteriori* method, using signs and symptoms to comprehend the subjective expression of states of illness or health as they appear and disappear. The *Theoria Medica Vera* is subtitled 'from experience' and carries the warning 'uncontaminated through rationalisations'.[47]

Such a decisive defence of psychosomatic realities, together with a refusal to accept as a methodology an *a priori* view of nature, certainly flew in the face of the *Weltanschauung* the enlightenment sought to create. In turning once more to the enthusiasts' view of nature, we can now assess more precisely what it was they wished to defend. To work *a posteriori*, from experience, as opposed to *a priori*, from objectified laws of nature (first principles), means to pose and keep posing the problem of individuation and mutability in nature. One of the favourite words of the pietists is *lebendig*, 'living', and this implies *dynamis*, the interplay of movement and change. There are many relations of this kind in pietistic perceptions of self and nature: the dynamics of spiritual rebirth, the dynamics of community, the dynamics of soul in body, the dynamic of creation (nature). The last two named are so intimate that they define life itself. The dynamics of the subjective, as they are not reproduced in the immutability of

---

[46] Stahl, *De Scriptis Suis ad Hunc Diem Schediasmatibus, Vindicae Quaedam, et Indicia* (Halle, 1707); my translation is taken from Karl Wilhelm Ideler, *Georg Ernst Stahls Theorie der Heilkunde* (Berlin, 1831), p. lx. My translation takes some liberties by using modern terms. But I have preferred to render as precisely as possible the thoughts that Stahl pursued in attempting to define 'intelligent' processes in the body which are not a function of reason. The passions may not be wholesome, but they are certainly a very important part of the 'action'. Ideler's German translation of Stahl's *Theoria* uses the language and concepts of the middle of the nineteenth century. His translation of Stahl's book is unreliable because he omits passsages without designating the lacunae.

[47] The full title of the Theoria: *Theoria Medica Vera, Physiologiam et Pathologiam tanquam Doctrinae Medicae Partes vere Contemplativas, e Naturae et Artis veris Fundamentis, intaminata ratione, et inconcussa Experientia sistens.*

nature's law, imply a different epistemology, that of seeking in the 'signs' of nature, in the 'outer shell' so to speak, the inward order. This order of nature does not necessarily correspond to that analysis which enlightenment science seeks, the discovery of the reliable, reproducible effects of nature. In trying to penetrate the order of nature, all traditions in search of the spiritual, which are always holistic, seek to establish the relation of essence and substance. Essence and substance are soul incarnate, or as Stahl put it, *intellectus* and *voluntas* 'quod est organicum' (which *is* organic).[48]

A student of Stahlian medicine, Johann Samuel Carl (1667–1757), whose pietiest convictions tended toward the radical side of enthusiasm, shows in his medical writings how closely Stahl can fit in with theosophist traditions, the heritage, among others, of Jacob Boehme. I will use just one quotation to illustrate a more widely held opinion that nature acts on intrinsic spiritual principles. The way to learn about nature and through nature about God is to observe and contemplate. If one seeks only the mechanical laws of nature, one is presented with a puppet-show, a favourite metaphor of the critics of the new mechanical philosophy.[49] A puppet-show presents seemingly live movements. One knows exactly the physics and mathematics involved. But the difference between puppets and living beings is the same as the difference between repetition and creation. All creation changes because the 'body', as the theosophically influenced pietist doctors of the eighteenth century describe it, is a husk or shell (*Hülse*), a skin or wrapper (*Schale*), or a hut (*Hütte*) or instrument (*Werckzeug*) in which the soul completes itself.[50] This idea does not mean that the body is only an outer container. The metaphors used seek to express an organic idea: the soul *and* the body grow with one another (or decline and sicken with one another) just as fruit ripens or a house is built or an instrument is used. The comprehension of nature has to be synergetic if it is to discover growth and change. Spiritual rebirth, the process most dear to enthusiastic pietism, fits in with the idea of nature incorporating a meaningful growth whose vast variations depend on inner and outer perception, the last being always an element of soul or spirit. Let us return to the quotation I mentioned from the medical writings of Carl, who expresses this view succinctly:

---

[48] Stahl, *Theoria Medica Vera*, p. 5ff.
[49] See Michael Alberti, *Medizinische Betrachtungen von den Kräften der Seelen nach dem Unterschied des Leibes* (Halle, 1740), p. 9; Johann Conrad Dippel, *Die Kranckheit und Arzney des thierisch-sinnlichen Lebens* (Leipzig, 1713), p. 89.
[50] See especially Christian Friedrich Richter, *Die Höchst-Nöchige Erkenntnis des Menschen* (Halle, 1709).

Instead of seeking to touch ('betasten') the Creator/Mover as the source and purpose [of all things] by means of the large and visible alphabet created by His kindness or His anger as visible nature, those who are appointed to teach only propagate a natural history of all things and remove God [from creation] so that in the end neither they themselves nor their innocent pupils can taste or see the covering [outer skin] and the core of all creation's being, nor can they then be taught how to pass from visible apprehension to the invisible ('aus dem Sichtbaren ins Unsichtbare übergeleitet zu werden').[51]

The criticism of 'naturalizing all things' and removing, in this secularization, the soul from all things shows where the deeply felt antagonism toward the mechanical philosophy lies: it denudes nature of its common spiritual ground. What is left in the 'new' science is necessarily exclusive of passions, ghosts, imagination and the fellowship of living things. It was a brave new world of nature.

'To be guided from the visible to the unseen' has a direct bearing on the emotions and the imagination, if we acknowledge Stahl's opposition to mechanism and dualism, and accept the dynamics of the soul incarnate. Both the emotions and the imagination can be induced, through an 'object' seen or envisioned. Their effect is palpable. Perception *always* has a bodily component. In this process the soul 'constructs' or 'forms' the body. In this system one cannot 'objectify' the mechanics, of, say, love, hate, envy, sadness, fear, because to taste and see the outer skin *and* core' (body and soul) predicates the subjective. Perception has no other agent than the soul. And the soul is organic, that is, it is bound to individuation, setting thereby a boundary not between spirit and matter, but between perception (in living beings) and inorganic matter.

Taking this a step further, one could say that imagination is the introjection of the world into the self, however it is perceived, and upon it depends the quality of the body's well-being and self-organization. Reason is then only a small part of this whole.

This would reverse the claim of the enlightenment to have found a way to objectify nature. And this is exactly what the opposition to the enlightenment wished to express: that prophecy, dream, inspiration, passions and the imagination represented a subjective and sensual truth. The comedy of the puppets, whereby the great puppeteer pulls the strings of nature, and science discovers its 'true' laws, is not nearly complicated enough to account for the soul. If mechanism accomplished the reduction of the soul to the 'ghost in the machine', making it ineffectual because it had no place, say, in physiology, then it had to

---

[51] Johann Samuel Carl, *Zeugnisse von Medicina Morali* (Büdingen, 1726) *De Paedogogia Cordis*, p. 19. The translation from the German is my own.

dislocate the passions and the imagination as well. The synergetic principles of Stahl's theory were unmanageable for 'progressive' science's hierarchies and dissections. In the enthusiast vision and Stahl's medical proof of the soul incarnate (in the physiology and pathology of the *Theoria Medica Vera*) no one is afraid of a subjective truth, and the often painful reality of the passions merges into the specifics of medical healing. Transposed to an understanding of nature this means that the palpable signs of the seen are an accurate indication of otherwise unidentifiable processes in the soul. The view that the seen and unseen are inseparable but visible through symptoms ('signs') led to an observational healing method (the 'natural' or 'Stahlian' method) and forms the basis of a psychosomatic approach to disease. Had the political appeal of the mechanical philosophy not been so strong and the proponents of Stahl's medicine not been religious enthusiasts, who seemed so disquieting to a hierarchical order, medicine to-day might have a different theoretical foundation.

6

Thomas Sydenham: epidemics, experiment and the 'Good Old Cause'

ANDREW CUNNINGHAM

QUESTIONS

My central question here will be: *why, with respect to medicine, did Thomas Sydenham see what he saw and do what he did?* Answering this will of course entail answering the question *what it was* that Sydenham did with respect to medicine in the London of the three and a half decades 1656 to 1689.

Thomas Sydenham has posthumously acquired one of the greatest of all names in the history of western medicine. He is celebrated amongst historians of medicine as the inaugurator or reviver of *clinical* or (to express it in English rather than Greek) *bedside* medicine – which we treat as a highly positive achievement – and has been awarded the title of the 'English Hippocrates'. Such was his fame in early nineteenth-century Britain that two successive societies dedicated to the publishing of modern and ancient 'classic texts' in medicine were named after him. The works of Sydenham, in Latin and then in English, were amongst the earliest works issued, and I like to think they were planned to be the first.[1] Naturally enough, therefore, Sydenham has attracted his share of medical historians to celebrate his work and achievement. I trust that nevertheless it does not appear too arrogant of me to claim that all this effort has not yet given us a satisfactory account of either the activity or the achievement of Thomas Sydenham.[2] At all events, it is to this most fundamental of issues that I address myself here.

---

[1] See G.G. Meynell, *The Two Sydenham Societies* (Acrise, Kent, 1985). He numbers the Latin edition as the third of the works published by the first Society.

[2] The main biographers are J.F. Payne, *Thomas Sydenham*, (London, 1900), still very valuable; Payne wrote the article in the *Dictionary of National Biography* too; R.G. Latham, who presented a 'life' in volume 1 of his *The Works of Thomas Sydenham, M.D., translated from the Latin Edition of Dr Greenhill* 2 vols. (London, Sydenham Society, 1848–50); Kenneth Dewhurst, *Dr Thomas Sydenham (1624–1686): his Life and Original Writings* (Berkeley,

To answer my question, what we need to discover and establish is an account which is *about Thomas Sydenham and his world*. An account which locates Sydenham's experience of, and his thinking and decisions about, medicine and its practice in the same place where all his other experiences of the world were registered, and where all his other thinking and decisions took place. In other words, in his mind: one mind, undivided. The mind of a particular Englishman alive, active in and affected by, the specific events of his own time. I am going to look at Sydenham's activity to reform medicine (and that means every last thing about that medicine) as a product of the life he led in the world in which he led it. Approaching the matter this way will necessitate us putting aside from our minds the reputation that we (I speak as a historian of medicine) normally ascribe to Sydenham: what Sydenham intended and achieved in his own world and his own terms may well have been quite different from what we, centuries later and with different interests, usually credit him with having achieved (and hence persuade ourselves that he must have intended!). How and why Sydenham was given his later reputation is a different question, and one to which we shall return. So I want here to argue that Sydenham's medicine was the produce of a person highly *politicized*, and in a particular way; that his attempt to reform medicine was a continuation of politics by other means. And I want further to suggest that this was evident to his contemporaries: the *adoption* of Sydenhamian medicine by other people was thus also a political act. If we do not understand the politics we will not understand the medicine.

First, however, a note on texts. A number of English manuscripts in the handwriting of Sydenham or Locke (and sometimes even of both of them on the same page) have been brought to light. But Sydenham's works were all published in Latin: whether or not (as rumour had it) they were translated into Latin by other hands,[3] these Latin editions must for the present be treated as the 'original' texts. Sydenham's major work (and the focus of our present concern) appeared in two forms. First in 1666 as *Methodus Curandi Febres, Propriis Observationibus Superstructa* (Method of curing fevers, built on my own observations). This was given a second, slightly modified edition

---

1966); Donald Bates, 'Thomas Sydenham: the Development of his Thought, 1666–1676' (Johns Hopkins University Ph.D. thesis, 1975); Bates also wrote the article in the *Dictionary of Scientific Biography*. But all of the writers on Sydenham seem (to my mind) to leave out the medicine: or rather, they deal with the life of Sydenham and, quite separately, with the medicine – as if the medicine owes little or nothing to the life.
3 On the rumours about other people translating Sydenham's works, see Payne *Thomas Sydenham*, ch. 13: 'In what language did he write?'

in 1668; neither of these were ever published in English. Then in 1676 Sydenham published the *Observationes Medicae circa Morborum Acutorum Historiam et Curationem* (Medical observations on the history and cure of acute diseases), announcing it as the 'third edition' of the *Methodus*. However, it is significantly different in structure, size, presentation, title and content from the *Methodus*. It is this 'third' edition which has been the basis of all English translations.[4]

MEDICAL PRACTICE: WHY?

Let us start right in the middle of the story, at the moment when Thomas Sydenham is taking up the practice of medicine. The date is about 1656 or a little later; the place is London. Sydenham is in his early thirties. Let us ask: why does he take up medical practice at all? This is a most important question since, on his own account, the only good medicine is practical medicine; and what he advocated was a particular form of practical medicine. Let us begin our exploration by inspecting the accounts of this event that Sydenham himself published. First, let us take the account of 1676 (the dedication to Mapletoft):

It is now the thirtieth year since, being on the way to London in order to go from thence a second time to Oxford (from which the calamity of the first war had kept me away for some years), I had the good fortune to fall in with the most learned and highly honourable man, Dr Thomas Coxe (who even throughout those years, and right up to today, practised Medicine with great renown), then attending my ill Brother. He, with his well-known kindness and courtesy, enquired of me to what art I was preparing to devote myself, now that I was resuming my interrupted studies, and had reached man's estate [i.e. age 21]. Hitherto undecided, and not even dreaming of the Medical Art, I [now] readied myself seriously for it – greatly stimulated by the urging and counsel of so great a man, and in some way I suppose by my own fate. And certainly, if these my efforts [i.e. the book] turn out to be in the smallest way for the common good (*in publica commoda*), the credit must be thankfully referred to him, with whom as promoter and inspirer I first began those studies. After a few years spent in the academic arena, having returned to London I came to Medical Practice . . .[5]

Thus does Sydenham account for the years and events: they are largely ignored. There is nothing here about the fact that Sydenham comes from a gentry family (the fifth son of nine); nothing about the fact that, like all the other adult male members of his family, he fought in the parliamentary army (1643–5 in Dorset in 'the first war', six months of so of 1651 in the midlands and north in the 'second' war). In

---

4 It was first translated by John Pechey in 1696, and again by John Swan in 1742. Greenhill's nineteenth-century Latin edition, and Latham's English translation from it, are of the 'fourth edition' of 1685, itself a revised version of the third.

5 This is my translation from the Latin as printed by William A. Greenhill, *Thomae Sydenham, M.D., Opera Omnia* (London, Sydenham Society, 1844), pp. 3–6.

the above account the civil war simply plays the role of a mysterious calamity which kept him away from Oxford for some years. There is no mention either of the fact that Thomas Coxe, at the time that Sydenham met him, was a physician to the parliamentary army. And then, the period at Oxford, some ten years (*c.* 1647–*c.* 56), is simply time 'spent in the academic arena'. There is nothing here about the medical degree (the M.B.) that he was awarded in April 1648 – a mere year or so after arriving – nor of the medical fellowship at All Souls that he was thrust into (October 1648) by the Visitors set up in the university by the victorious parliamentary authorities. Most important of all, there is no mention of the Commonwealth and Protectorate, nor of the political career that Sydenham had been promoting for himself: he twice stood for parliament, for one of the Weymouth seats (in 1658 the election was abandoned on Oliver Cromwell's death, and in 1659 Sydenham was defeated); he also held the Exchequer post of 'Comptroller of the Pipe' from 1659.

So what, one might say: why should he have mentioned such things? He was, after all, writing to his contemporaries and not for the benefit of the historians, and writing about how he took up medical practice, not how he was detained from doing so. To which the answer must be this: that Sydenham is here offering a fragment of autobiography to explain to his contemporaries the source and nature of the book which follows. Hence what he mentions and what he omits in this account are the result of active choice on his part. But for him to omit mention of the things I listed above, and especially of his political commitment (as exemplified by his service in the parliamentary army), was for him to omit his *raison d'être* for these years. It is Hamlet without the Prince. And it is to leave unexplained why ten years passed between him being 'greatly stimulated by the urging and counsel' of Thomas Coxe to take up medical practice, and him actually doing so – time which was not being spent on a conventional eleven-year university training in medicine. In this context we should note that in this account of how he came to take up medical practice there is actually no direct mention of the circumstances which led him to do so! From this account we are none the wiser: and, more important, nor would his contemporaries have been. Could it perhaps be that Sydenham had good reasons for not mentioning what he did not mention?

We return to our question: why did he take up medical practice at this period? It would seem to have been connected with him giving up some other things. For Sydenham took up medical practice when he (i) left his fellowship at Oxford, and when he (ii) abandoned active politics. His leaving Oxford in 1655 was the price he paid for getting married (to a Dorset girl): resignation from the celibacy of his Oxford fellowship was obligatory. He was now short of an income.[6] Even though he was now the eldest surviving Sydenham brother, there was no chance that Thomas would inherit the family estate; when his father eventually died the estate went to Thomas's eldest nephew. The necessity of seeking stable employment was pressing. He had been holding a 'physic place' at All Souls for some eight years. Medicine it had to be. But, although he now in 1656 did engage in medical practice in London, he did not yet abandon his ambitions in the political arena, for he was to stand (unsuccessfully) for election as an M.P. in both 1658 and 1659. He did not abandon such ambitions until 1660 – until the restoration of Charles II. Could this be what drove Thomas Sydenham to become a full-time medical practioner: the failure of the Commonwealth?

Already we have had a taste of the awful silence in Sydenham's published writings about politics or life outside medicine: Sydenham would, on this evidence, seem to live in a world where the political was as seemingly distinct from the medical as it is in our world today. But there are reasons why our medicine and science are performed and presented as if they are free from social or political content. Sydenham, in his turn, may have had reasons to present his medicine in a similar light. If so, his political concerns can nevertheless be recovered by us from the extant thing that would contain them: the medicine that Sydenham was now to practise, and on whose remarkable properties he was to report in the two versions of his book in 1666 and 1676.

Sydenham's political position and commitment is partly visible in the preface he wrote to the first edition of the book (in 1665). This is how it begins:

Whoever takes up medicine ought to weigh these matters seriously. First, that he will one day have to give to the supreme Judge an account of the life, committed to his care, of his patients. Second, that whatever skill or knowledge he has acquired by Divine favour, is to be devoted above all to the glory of the Highest Numen and to the health of the human race, for it would be unworthy that those heavenly gifts should be in the service of either avarice or ambition. Third, that he has taken on the care not of some ignoble or contemptible creature; for, so that we should acknowledge the value of the human race, the Only-Begotten Son of God was made man, and thereby ennobled by his own dignity the nature he had assumed. Finally he should remember that he is not exempt from the common fate, but that he is subject and liable to those same laws of

[6] It may be his shortage of money which led to him making a petition (printed in Payne, *Thomas Sydenham*, pp. 72–4, and elsewhere) in 1653/4 for the arrears of salary due to his dead brothers; it is certainly curious that Sydenham claimed that these arrears were due to him as a *brother*, rather than to his father, who was still living.

mortality, the same accidents and tribulations as everyone else; how much more diligently should he try to bring help to the suffering, and with a more refined compassion (being himself in the same situation).

. . . it behoves all Physicians who want to be and to be considered honorable and prudent, to behave thus; so that, first acknowledging the Divine goodness and then also calling upon it, they may await from it wisdom and a favourable outcome of their cases; and also so that with every effort and application, they should thereto so apply themselves that they procure not only health for the sick but also some greater certitude for the Medical Art which they profess: steering their *experimenta* in this direction so that the procedure [*ratio*] of healing may daily become fuller and more reliable, and ultimately so that the human race might more securely and universally enjoy the benefit of improved medical practice even after they themselves have passed on.

Therefore, aware of my duty [*officii mei conscius*] I offer to the world this *Method of Curing Fevers, Built on my own Observations* . . .[7]

It is clear that Sydenham felt that as a practitioner of medicine he had a moral obligation to take active steps to improve medicine. He refers thus this obligation to a religious (perhaps a Christian) motive. It is also clear, from the fact that he mentions it at all (let alone at such length) that he did not think most of his fellow physicians shared this attitude. It was an unusual attitude, and Sydenham is here preaching it: the sacred obligation on physicians to do 'research' (as I shall call it) to improve medicine.

To see how this expresses a political position we need to consider the interests and concerns of the group of which Sydenham was a member and product. Sydenham and folk like him had by this date been to war with and executed their king, and then set up a form of government alternative to monarchy. For what cause had the Sydenhams and their like been fighting? We have an account of that cause from someone very close to Thomas Sydenham, his eldest brother William, who rose to be a colonel. In a letter of 1645 to a Royalist commander who was threatening an eternal vendetta on him for killing innocent people, William wrote that he had looked upon his own heart

and find written there, in the fairest characters, a true desire of advancing God's honour, maintaining the King's just power, and contending for the privileges of the Parliament at Westminster, and the liberty of the subject; which when I find you so maliciously opposing and despitefully styling treason and rebellion, I am induced to think this age hath produced unparalleled monsters.[8]

God's honour, a monarchy with limited powers, the privileges of parliament, the liberty of the subject: it would be difficult to give a

---

[7] My translation from the Latin as printed by Greenhill, *Sydenham . . . Opera Omnia*, pp. 22–4; this passage is also translated in part by Payne, *Thomas Sydenham*, p. 118, and Latham, *The Works of Thomas Sydenham*, I, pp. 25–7.

[8] Printed in A.R. Bayley, *The Great Civil War in Dorset, 1642–1660* (Taunton, 1910), p. 245, and elsewhere.

better short account of the cause as seen from the parliamentary side. The 'subjects' whose liberty was to be protected were of course primarily the people whose representatives sat in the house of commons: the English gentlemen (gentry, lesser nobility, burgesses, the 'middling sort'), predominantly rural, exclusively male.

The Sydenhams and their like had, thus, been fighting primarily for the rights of the *free-holder*, the independent land owner who could 'live off his own'; they were not democrats. Seeing themselves as natural leaders of their society, they had been fighting for a greater share of political power for people like themselves. And this is what we should expect. But the predominant political formulation they used – the way that they conceived and experienced it – was that they were fighting to *recover* their historic rights, which had been usurped by 'tyranny', usurped that is by an unlimited, an unjust, monarchy. They came to believe that there had been an 'Ancient Constitution' before the Norman conquest, when all was peace and harmony, royal power was limited and the English gentleman's house was his castle.[9]

But most of them conceived and experienced their current plight also in *religious* terms. In the decades previous to the civil war more and more such people had come to find the attraction of extreme protestantism irresistible. Whether it was the stress on individual responsibility inherent in such protestantism; whether the strict moral and spiritual practices typical of it gave them a means of regulating the details of their own and other people's lives in their own material interest, or whether it was some other feature of it which served this function for them, must for now remain a matter of conjecture. At all events they had taken to it in their thousands. Their enemies called them 'the godly people' and they have come to be especially associated with the description 'puritan'. And because (in the words of no less than their chief enemy, the 'tyrant' Charles I) 'the people are governed by the pulpit more than the sword in time of peace', so 'no concessions will content them [i.e. the rebels, the puritans] without the change of church government, by which that necessary and ancient relation which the church hath had to the crown is taken away'.[10] Hence much of the struggle took place over religious issues and in religious terms. But every religious position was also a political one, with implications, direct and immediate, for the kingdom of this world. Thus we can see

[9] See for instance Zera S. Fink, *The Classical Republicans* (Evanston, 1945); J.G.A. Pocock, *The Ancient Constitution and the Feudal Law* (Cambridge, 1957).
[10] Charles I, in 1646; as quoted in Christopher Hill and Edmund Dell (eds.), *The Good Old Cause: The English Revolution of 1640–60, its Causes, Course and Consequences* (London, 1949), p. 173.

why the principled core of the parliamentary army was constituted by those who were at the same time both 'godly pretious men' and also freeholders and freeholders' sons who 'upon matter of conscience engaged in this quarrel'; such men were the ones that Cromwell chose to have in his own regiment.[11] They were fighting to recover a holy commonwealth; they were 'good commonwealth men'. Such were the Sydenham brothers. And their personal attitudes closely resembled those of Cromwell himself: like him they were 'Independents' in both politics and religion.[12]

This locates Sydenham with fair precision on a clear and familiar political–religious spectrum. But we are still some way from understanding why Sydenham as a member of this group who by chance was obliged to be a practising physician in the 1660s, should have thought his urgent duty lay in improving medical practice by new (and radical) investigations. Fortunately the work of Charles Webster can help us here. Webster, in an astonishing piece of reconstruction,[13] has uncovered the existence, the membership and the activities of an extensive network of such puritans in mid-seventeenth-century England. Around Samuel Hartlib, who offered himself as a general co-ordinator, there appears to have been, in the period *c*. 1626–*c*. 60, a movement to bring about the 'Great Instauration' which Francis Bacon had called for. It was carried out, according to Webster, under the prompting, and to achieve the goals of, millenarian puritanism. Such puritans felt it was their duty – urgently – to follow a text in the Book of Daniel and thus to 'run to and fro, and knowledge shall be increased'. That running, as Webster has shown, was aimed at changing the material (and spiritual) circumstances of the whole of life, and in a highly directed manner. The improvement of education, trade, husbandry, surveying and medicine were among their concerns, and Webster has documented their projects and plans for these areas fully. Webster judges this movement to have been successful in parts, and robbed of final success only by the collapse of the Commonwealth. He also claims that this pre-restoration movement was the source of many of the enterprises that we have customarily put to the credit of the restoration (in particular, the origins of the Royal Society).

The millenarianism embraced by these puritans was of quite recent vintage. To be a millenarian at all one has to believe in and welcome the

---

[11] Bulstrode Whitlock, as quoted by Brian Manning (ed.), *Politics, Religion and the English Civil War* (London, 1973), p. 99.
[12] On whom see George Yule, *The Independents in the English Civil War* (Cambridge, 1958).
[13] Charles Webster, *The Great Instauration: Science, Medicine and Reform, 1626–1660* (London, 1975).

inevitability of the thousand-year reign of Christ with his Saints. But whether one believes this lies in the distant future, or in the immediate future, or is already taking place, depends on circumstances. The puritans whose activities Webster studies believed that the millenium was imminent and – most important – that they had to work urgently to prepare the earth to be a new Garden of Eden. Why should they have felt this need to work – to run to and fro – why with this urgency, and why promoting these particular things? We can, I think, expect that the form of any future earthly paradise would coincide nicely with the interests (in every meaning of the word) of those proclaiming it: it would reflect their present interests, and its implementation would represent a furthering of their interests too. No one promotes a millenium which has no place for people like themselves, nor one which would be an expression of all the values they despise. Thus the social position, power and aspirations of any group of millenarians should be detectable from their characterization of the millennium.

The millennial vision of the puritans that Charles Webster studies seemed to call on them to be active and urgent in improving the material conditions of the world. In other words (and these are now my words) they created and held up to themselves this particular characterization of the millennium in order to encourage themselves, and everyone else, to work in the interests – the material and power interests – of people just like themselves. The rewards would not have to wait for the hereafter; indeed, if everyone buckled down to it, the rewards were just around the corner. Hence (I suggest) the urgency, the call to be making improvements in whatever one's sphere of activity might be. This is a millennium fit for those who in *this* world are nearly in power. We need (they claimed) to recreate the Garden of Eden, where Nature obviously was for man's benefit. It should take little imagination on our part to guess who were to be the saints ruling at Christ's side when the millennium came: the saints would be the gentry come into their own. *That* is how the millennial puritan movement charted by Webster is a political position: its realization would have changed the world in the interests of those advocating it, changed it into a fulfilment and expression of those interests. Thus it can be little surprise that the people who were millenarian puritans in their religion at this time were so often 'commonwealth men' in their politics. This is why Sydenham's authentically religious call (in the preface of 1665) to other physicians to treat their calling as a sacred duty, a duty to seek out new ways of improving medicine, was also a political call.

Such people, the advocates and entrepreneurs of the millennium, are the very people Thomas Sydenham had been in contact with: it was one of them who had introduced him to and inspired him to take up medicine – Thomas Coxe. Coxe was a friend of Samuel Hartlib. The class that these people represented and came from was the same class that Sydenham himself came from.

But all that happened in the 1640s and 1650s. In 1660 that world suddenly came to an end, as the old order and its symbol (monarchy) were restored.[14] But Sydenham never gave up his political ideals. Instead, once resigned to the full-time practice of medicine, he set out to exemplify the principles of the now-defunct Commonwealth in his medical practice. His medicine was now to be the focus and expression of his politics. And hence the fact of the restoration accounts for Sydenham's silence about his engagement in the war on the side of parliament and about his other political activities since. It was political circumstances (not personal choice nor, as we might assume, some self-evident separateness between the enterprises of medicine and politics) which led Sydenham to write about his medicine as though it had no political content.

In the period of Sydenham's practice of medicine, (c.1656–88), his political position (and hence his medicine) was to be that of the 'Good Old Cause'. This term expresses (and was coined to express) all the things that people like Sydenham had been fighting for – but in defeat. The term came into use in the late 1650s as Cromwell, with his growing ambitions to set up a family dynasty, seemed to be abandoning the last principles for which the pious gentry of the parliamentary army had fought. The cause was 'good' because it was the defence of freedom against tyranny, it was 'old' both because it was (supposedly) pre-Norman and because it had inspired the parliamentarians in the civil war, it was a 'cause' because it still needed to be fought for. The 'Good Old Cause' was the cause of those who had not compromised and who refused to compromise with 'tyranny'. From the 1690s it was to be the rallying cry of those who wanted to keep the 'whig' interest and party true to its roots. To speak of the Good Old Cause was to try and keep alive a particular political position and ambition. Other terms were sometimes used of adherents of this position, such as 'commonwealth men' and (later) 'radical whigs'. The position was indeed radical; but it was also backward looking, and adherents of it could look like living fossils who were unaware of the realities of the new age of restored

---

[14] For a good account of the changes that the restoration brought about, and their effect on the world of learning, see Steven Shapin and Simon Schaffer, *Leviathan and the Air-Pump: Hobbes, Boyle and the Experimental Life* (Princeton, 1985), ch. 7.

monarchy. Sydenham was an adherent of this position. If (as I claim) he now turned his energies from overt public politics to a politically-informed kind of medicine, then that medicine too would represent a view which was both radical and out of date: it would be the medicine, in the 1660s, 70s and 80s, of someone who still lived mentally in and with the aspirations of the 1640s and early 1650s.

MEDICAL PRACTICE: WHAT?

Let us now turn to that medicine and try and trace the way in which Thomas Sydenham conceived and built his new approach to curing diseases. Our question here is: *what* precisely was he studying, and why?

First let us inspect Sydenham's own accounts of these important events. Here he is writing in 1676:

After a few years spent in the academic arena [Oxford], having returned to London I came to Medical Practice; which when I inspected it with a very intent eye and carefully using all diligence, I soon came to that opinion (which has grown with me right up to this very day) that this Art is to be in no way more properly learnt than by the exercise and use of the Art itself; and that it is definitely the case that he who has turned his eyes and mind most accurately and diligently to the natural phenomena of diseases, will be best at eliciting true and genuine curative indications. Therefore I gave myself over wholly to this method, confident enough that if I followed Nature as my leader, even

Wandering through desert places of the earth, trod before
By no man's foot

I would never depart a finger's breadth from the correct path. Guiding myself by this thread, I first applied my mind to a closer observation of fevers, and after much weariness and the most troublesome agitations of mind by which I let myself for some years be fatigued, I at last fell on the method by which fevers could be cured; and this, under pressure from my friends, I long ago [i.e. in 1666] allowed to be published.

He had described that process in print in 1666 slightly differently. He had claimed then (as we will recall) that the physician had a duty to get greater certainty for the medical art,

steering their *experimenta* in this direction so that the procedure [*ratio*] of healing may daily become fuller and more reliable . . . Therefore, aware of my duty, I offer to the world this *Method of Curing Fevers, Built on my own Observations* . . .

Though this earlier account is much thinner (and more pious in presentation), it has additional information for our story; if we put the two together we can produce the following account of the sequence of events:

[1676:] 1. He comes to London and sets up in medical practice (in about 1656).

[1666:] 1a. He believes that the physician has a (religious) duty to do 're-search' to improve the art.

[1677:] 2. From the experience of practice itself (but not before) he now
realises that only (i) accurate *observation of the natural phenomena
of diseases*, giving the (ii) *true and genuine curative indications*, will
enable one to do this.

[1666:] 2a. The route is by performing *experimenta*.

[1666:] 2b. The work should be built on *one's own* observations.

[1676:] 3. He turns to the study of *fevers*, and after a number of years of very
hard work he strikes on the *method* by which fevers can be cured.

We have already dealt with 1 and 1a, and located them in his life and
experiences as a young man. But why did Sydenham believe that
accurate observation and consideration of the true and genuine curative indications was the necessary route to improving the practice of
medicine? What does he mean by *experimenta*? Why should one's
work be based on *one's own* observations? And, first of all, why in
particular does he turn to the study of *fevers*?

He studied *epidemic fevers* because of the nature of the early medical
practice open to him. In the years between about 1656 and 1665 when
he wrote the first version of the book about the new method of cure,
Sydenham lived in Westminster and then in Pall Mall in London. He
was one of the first residents of Pall Mall; his neighbours were to
include members of the aristocracy such as Katherine Lady Ranelagh,
and fashionable people like Mary Beale the painter and Nell Gwyn the
actress. Sydenham was in full-time medical practice now, and some of
his practice was amongst the reasonably wealthy. He was for instance
sometimes called to offer a second medical opinion for certain aristocratic families. But there were really only two such families in his life,
and both of them were (at least sometimes) of similar political leanings
as himself. One was that of Anthony Ashley Cooper (from 1672 the
Earl of Shaftesbury) who had been a republican and was still if
necessary prepared to oppose the royal prerogative; and the other was
that of the Percys who supported the 'Good Old Cause' and whose
famous scion was Algernon Sidney (who had also been a friend and
colleague of Sydenham's elder brother on the Cromwellian Council of
State). And even to these Sydenham had access to only through his own
friends: Cooper's physician from 1668 was Sydenham's close friend
John Locke; the physician of the Percy family was John Mapletoft,
another close friend.

Such work thus does not seem to have made up even a significant
fraction of Sydenham's medical practice.[15] Even as late as 1687 he was
aware that the – presumably political – 'scandal of my person' was still

---

[15] Dewhurst, *Dr Thomas Sydenham*, pp. 49–50, has a different opinion of the extent of
Sydenham's practice amongst the well-to-do.

a problem for many people. The consequence of this seems to have been that Sydenham had to find most of his medical practice amongst the *poor*, those the conventional physician did not usually treat (except as an occasional favour). In a letter in 1677, for instance, advising his fellow physician Mapletoft about the treatment of the Countess of Northumberland (Algernon Sidney's mother), he writes: 'were she one of *those poor people whom my lot engages me to attend* (for I cure not the rich till my being in the grave makes me an Authority) I would take the following course . . .'[16]

Thus Sydenham based his practice amongst the poor, and it may well be that it was force of political circumstance which obliged him to do so. It takes the fees of many poor people to match the fees obtainable from the rich. Thus in order to gain a reasonable living, Sydenham would have seen probably far more patients than most of his fellow physicians. He already believed that it was the duty of physicians to work to improve medicine, in whatever sphere of practice they found themselves. The poor *en masse* was the particular realm of practice in which Sydenham perforce chose his first topic of 'research'. This topic was highly unusual, to say the least, and probably unique to Sydenham. For his first and primary object of investigation – the 'what' of our question – was *epidemic fevers*: 'epidemic' means '(a disease falling) on the people'. Without an extensive practice amongst the poor such a topic would have been impossible and indeed unthinkable. His experience of practice (see item no. 2 on p. 175 above) was thus the experience of seeing *many* patients and, at times of epidemics, of seeing many patients suffering from the *same* disease.

It is important that we appreciate the radical novelty of this position. It is not just that Sydenham was studying the diseases of greatest virulence, the diseases with the highest mortality, the diseases which are apparently the least curable; it is also that he was studying them as affecting the people that the physician did not conventionally treat – people in the mass. Now, although many conventional physicians were of course concerned with fevers and their cure, yet their approach to fever was locked in the one-patient-one-doctor pattern. They certainly treated a whole range of fevers if their (rich) patients showed the symptoms of them: but always they treated them *as the fevers of individual patients*. It was not the nature of the *fever* which was their starting-point, but the predisposition of their *patient* to suffer from it, and the particular capacity of their *patient* to withstand and overcome

---

[16] My emphasis. Cited from Dewhurst, *Dr Thomas Sydenham*, p. 170.

it. For the university-educated physician (whether by allegiance a 'Galenist', a Cartesian mechanist or anything else), the curability of a fever depended on the physician understanding *how the human body works*, and how *drugs work* in the human body; and to treat any case of fever (or anything else) successfully, the physician needed to know the constitution of the *individual* patient affected by the fever. For the conventional physician, called to his patient, the fever was what the patient *complained of* – it was the disease itself, or more properly, it was the consequences of the disease itself. And even if, in the course of an epidemic, a physician should see several cases of the same fever, they were to him *different* instances because they were in different, individual, patients. Within this way of seeing patients and conceptualizing fever, there was no room for a long-term programme of 'research', for every case urgently demanded cure, and every case was by definition different from any other case. There was neither room nor occasion for *experimenta*; nor was there any particular need for *new* observations; and given the large numbers of practical medical books with authoritative guidance in them that one could consult, there was specially no need for *one's own* observations! The *theory* one had been brought up on told one all one needed to know. Finally, because it was assumed that the fever was the consequence of the disease itself, so the adherents of each medical approach had come up with explanations of what prior events in the human body constituted *the cause* of the fever, whose rectification was necessary for a successful cure (let it be an imbalance of the humours, or a blockage of the tiny pores in the glands).

If we now visualize Thomas Sydenham engaged in earning a living as a physician amongst the poor, we can see that he would have had much more freedom of action than he would have had as a rich man's physician. For, if his cure failed on the poor, then his reputation would not be at such risk as if it failed on the rich. Thus some at least of the *urgency* of treatment would be gone – and hence the need to stick to conventional formulas of treatment. If we add to this what we know of Sydenham's resolve to *improve* medical practice – encapsulated in his reported statement that when he started to practise he resolved 'to act directly contrary in all cases to the common method then in fashion among the most eminent physicians' – then we know that he was also *giving himself* a certain freedom of action and vision. We can thus appreciate that Sydenham was making it possible for himself to see something different from what his fellow physicians were seeing.

Now, the first such thing which Sydenham could see from his

unusual position was that most of the poor who fell ill were not treated by physicians; yet most of them survived their illnesses, they even survived epidemic fevers. Hence with smallpox, for instance, a disease conventional physicians thought of as one of the most dangerous, he came to believe 'that if no mischief be done either by physician or nurse, it is the most slight and safe of all ... diseases'.[17] The body left to itself cures itself: 'Nature by herself determines diseases, and is of herself sufficient in all things against all of them',[18] as he put it, quoting Hippocrates. The second thing he was able to see was that in the course of an epidemic, everyone who suffers is suffering from the *same* disease. In his own words: 'the order of Nature in producing diseases is so equable and everywhere so self-consistent, that in different (human) bodies, the same symptoms of a given disease may be usually found; and the very symptoms which were observed in the ill Socrates can generally be applied to any person whatever suffering from the same disease'.[19] Hence he could appreciate that each epidemic fever has its own set of manifestations, its own course, it own period, its own form of crisis. Because of his unique position, Sydenham's attention was on the fever, not on the body-of-the-suffering-patient and its workings: his attention was not on how the body 'fights' the disease – he was not seeing diseases 'as only the confused and disordered effects of Nature ill defending herself and thrown down from her customary state'[20] (as he characterized the common view). Finally, putting two and two together, he could see that since most people recover without the doctor's intervention, then the fever must itself be the *process of cure* – rather than being (the consequences of) the disease itself. 'A disease ... is nothing else than the effort of Nature endeavouring with might and main the expulsion of the morbific matter for the health of the sick person.' [*Morbum . . . nihil esse aliud quam Naturae conamen, materiae morbificae exterminationem in aegri salutem omni ope molientis'.*][21]

These are the grand novelties of Sydenham's view: he looks at

[17] Letter Sydenham to Boyle, 1668, as printed in *ibid.*, p. 163. In a draft essay on smallpox (1669) he also wrote, 'Here by the way, from what hath been now said, it will appear how easy it is to solve that common doubt how it comes to pass that in the smallpox so few die amongst the common people, in comparison of the rich, which cannot be thought referable to any other cause, than that they are deprived through the narrowness of their fortunes and their rude way of living of the opportunities of hurting themselves with a more precise and tender keeping' (*Ibid.*, p. 116).

[18] Latham's translation, (*The Works of Thomas Sydenham*, p. 17) from the Greek of Hippocrates, as cited by Sydenham.

[19] My translation from the Latin in Greenhill, *Sydenham . . . Opera Omnia*, p. 13.

[20] My translation from the Latin *ibid.*, p. 13.

[21] My translation from the Latin *ibid.*, p. 26.

epidemic fevers while they fall on the demos; he sees that the
unattended patient usually recovers; he sees the fever as the process of
cure – as the solution, not the problem. He now set himself the task of
improving nature's success rate, and of finding a new role for the
physician – not interfering, but constructively helping nature, 'joining
hands with Nature'.[22]

To return for a moment to Sydenham's choice of epidemic fever as a
topic to investigate. Rather than locating it as a chance consequence of
his enforced way of earning a living, should we instead be crediting the
Honourable and ubiquitous Robert Boyle with first suggesting it to
Sydenham? For Sydenham not only dedicated the first and second
edition of his book to Boyle (and appears to have had Boyle's blessing
for doing so),[23] reprinting this dedication again in the third edition, but
in this dedication he also credited Boyle with having steered his
attentions to this *provincia*.

> I confess that I have thus offered this Treatise to Your patronage, most especially
> because in the same way I took up this subject [*hanc provinciam suscepi*] by Your
> persuasion and instigation, so also You Yourself, the most sufficient witness, by [Your
> own] experience on several occasions have seen proven the truth and efficacy of the
> matters which are here related, when You several times so kindly condescended (a
> mark of Your outstanding goodness to others) to Yourself join me as a companion in
> visiting my patients.
> . . . Besides Fever (here to be considered), there are very many other diseases about
> which – since the core of their practice appears less satisfactory, and to be supported on
> a method contrary to reason (at least to mine) – I ought to have written as well, to have
> fulfilled the trust given by You to me.

But what does *provincia* refer to here? Given that Sydenham says that
'to have fulfilled the trust' given to him by Boyle he should have
worked on many other diseases too, it would seem that it refers not to
'fevers' but more generally to the search for new cures for diseases.

Boyle's persistent concern with the improvement of medicine is well
known. Not only was he always experimenting in dosing himself, but
as early as 1649 he wrote a piece (to be published under Hartlib's
auspices) on the need for people to make their secret remedies public.
Again, in 1650 he is reported to have said that 'physicians hitherto had
achieved better skill to know and discern diseases than to cure them',
and that he wanted to improve this situation.[24] Equally well known is
Boyle's life-long concern with the pursuit of 'useful knowledge' and its
pertinence to the welfare of all mankind. Yet Boyle's own hopes for the

---

[22] My translation from the Latin *ibid.*, p. 18.
[23] Letter Sydenham to Boyle, 1668; printed in Dewhurst, *Dr Thomas Sydenham*, pp. 162–4.
[24] Marie Boas, *Robert Boyle and Seventeenth-Century Chemistry* (Cambridge, 1958), p. 18.

improvement of medicine lay down the chemical path; and this Sydenham most certainly was not interested in. So the debt Sydenham owed Boyle was an inspiration not from Boyle's own work, but from his general approach to natural philosophy. As we shall now see, the inspiration of Boyle is indeed the key to just how Sydenham went about his mission to improve medicine.

MEDICAL PRACTICE: HOW?

If we are right in assuming that Boyle was intellectually the senior, then Sydenham's debt to Boyle is everywhere apparent in his work. We have seen that epidemic fevers was Sydenham's primary choice of a topic for 'research'. In the pursuit of this he had of course to settle on some more precise objects of study – that is, certain particular things he was looking at and for. He also had to adopt certain ways of looking. It is for the specification of his initial set of these that he was indebted to Boyle. They constitute the core of the 'how' of Sydenham's clinical medicine. They are items 2, 2a and 2b as we numbered them above:

2. ... that only (i) accurate *observation of natural phenomena of diseases* ... will enable one to improve medicine.

2a. The route is by performing *experimenta*.

2b. The work should be built on *one's own* observations.

These matters are of such consequence for our understanding of Sydenham's medical work, that it is important to establish that Sydenham knew and could have met Boyle often, that their relationship was (at least for a period) more than that just of an author seeking a non-controversial dedicatee. In fact, their paths could hardly have been closer. First, the man who introduced Sydenham to medicine, Thomas Coxe, was Boyle's physician; like Boyle himself, Coxe was part of Hartlib's retinue. Second, the house in which Boyle lived, experimented and wrote in Oxford (1654–)was opposite All Souls College, where Sydenham lived until 1656. Third, in London Sydenham lived next door to Boyle's sister, the one Boyle often visited and with whom he was eventually to live. And, if these did not provide enough opportunities for them to meet, there was always Dorset, where Sydenham's family lived, and where Boyle had his estate. Finally, their brothers (Lord Broghill and William Sydenham) not only knew each other and had similar political outlooks, but they also worked together for a while in the Protectorate government. Even their enemies knew that Boyle and Sydenham shared an approach in common. As Henry Stubbe wrote, in attacking Boyle:

I know what any physician may, as the mode is, tell you to your face, but except it be such as Dr Sydenham and young Coxe, I believe not one lives that doth not condemn your experimental philosophy.[25]

It has recently been shown that from his earliest investigations Boyle was concerned with (i) the doing of experiments, and with arguing for their crucial and indispensable role in natural philosophy; and (ii) with establishing certain things as 'matters of fact' – things on which one could gain general assent – and with arguing that discussion in natural philosophy ought properly to be limited to such 'matters of fact', and that there should be close restrictions on giving physical explanations to 'matters of fact'. The authors of this view of Boyle are Steve Shapin and Simon Schaffer, and rather than trying to summarize their recent book,[26] let me just make a little patchwork for my own purposes from some of their salient sentences about the practices of Robert Boyle. They are talking about work and writing Boyle was carrying out in his Oxford lodgings in the late 1650s, concerned with the air-pump:

Boyle proposed that matters of fact be established by the aggregation of individuals' *beliefs* . . . Matters of fact were the outcome of the process of having an empirical experience, warranting it to oneself, and assuring others that grounds for their belief were adequate. (p. 25)

His [Boyle's] overarching concern was to protect the matter of fact by separating it from various items of causal knowledge, and he repeatedly urged caution in moving from experimental matters of fact to their physical explanation. (p. 49)

There was a strong boundary placed between speech about the spring [of the air] as an explanation about matters of fact and speech about explanations of spring. Thus, in the first of the *New Experiments* Boyle claimed that his 'business [was] not . . . to assign the adequate cause of the spring of the air, but only to manifest that the air hath a spring, and to relate to some of its effects'. (p. 51)

Boyle's desire to revamp the defining criteria of natural philosophy may have derived from his eirenical inclinations, which have been pointed out recently by Jim Jacob.[27] For both in religion and in natural philosophy Boyle was looking constantly for the common ground of opinion that men shared, so that agreement could be built upon it in the interests of social stability and peace. In his life-long pursuit of this goal, the civil war gave Boyle early doubt about the possibility of reaching such common ground through the traditional route, the use of reason. Experiment is what Boyle found to stand in place of it. Quite why experiment was an alternative candidate (and why it became such a popular route to certainty among some people at this time) is still an

---

[25] 1670; as quoted by Dewhurst, *Dr Thomas Sydenham*, p. 63. I assume that 'young Coxe' is the son of Thomas Coxe.   [26] See note 14 above.

[27] J.R. Jacob, *Robert Boyle and the English Revolution* (New York, 1977).

open question. But experiment is what Boyle chose. Shapin and
Schaffer have shown how he tried to claim that only 'matters of fact'
brought into existence and visibility by the artifice of experiment, were
to count: thus for Boyle it was primarily experiment which *created*
'matters of fact'. And such 'matters of fact' of course, consisted of
'natural phenomena' (to use a phrase of Sydenham's); and they had to
be objects of perceptual experience.[28] Establishing what the natural
phenomena produced by experiment are, is a matter of (i) seeing for
oneself (personal experience); and (ii) having confirmation of what one
sees by the complementary experience of witnesses. As Boyle himself
warned, people should not believe even (chemical) experiments 'unless
he, that delivers that, mentions his doing it upon his own particular
knowledge, or upon the relation of some credible person, avowing it
upon his own experience'.[29]

We can see here Sydenham's indebtedness to Boyle for vocabulary
and concepts. Indeed Sydenham's dedication of his book to Boyle is
itself couched in just this 'boyleian' language: experience, tested,
sufficient witness. He even claims Boyle himself as his primary witness
for the truth of what he is saying: of, that is, the accuracy of his own
observation of the natural phenomena. And 'matter of fact' keeps
appearing in Sydenham's published writings and in his letters; it is a
phrase he constantly uses. As he wrote, for instance, to his friend
Mapletoft in 1687, looking back over his life's work:

I can only say this, that as I have been very careful to write nothing but what was the
product of faithful observation, so when the scandal of my person shall be laid aside
and I in my grave, it will appear that I neither suffered myself to be deceived by
indulging to idle speculations, nor have deceived others by obtruding anything upon
them but downright matter of fact.[30]

Experiment was (as Boyle was to find) suspect amongst the natural
philosophers. Amongst the physicians, however, it had an even lower
reputation. For experiment was exactly what *empirics* did and relied
on. Authentic (university-educated) physicians rely on reason–sense–
experience, a quite different handful. As Gideon Harvey put it in an
attack on Sydenham and others: 'it's necessary we should make a
Transit to the reason of the thing, without resting satisfied, like
Empiricks, in experiment only'.[31] When Sydenham took up and advocated experiment in medical practice, he was thus letting himself be

[28] Shapin and Schaffer, *Leviathan and the Air-Pump*, p. 36.
[29] *Sceptical Chymist*, quoted by Shapin and Schaffer *Leviathan and the Air-Pump*, p. 58.
[30] Printed in Dewhurst, *Dr Thomas Sydenham*, p. 174.
[31] Gideon Harvey, *The Conclave of Physicians, detecting their Intrigues, Frauds, and Plots against their Patients* (London, 1683), p. 149.

allied with the empirics, the enemies to good learning and good medicine. It would seem that it was Boyle who first convinced Sydenham of the proper role of experiment. And after the restoration, Sydenham may well have been pleased to continue to look like an empiric in contrast to those members of the College of Physicians who had (in his eyes) sold out politically.

The final area in which we may here point out the debt Sydenham owed to Boyle lies in the *air*. In all the experiments with his pump Boyle's object of study was the air (the very thing he was trying to exclude from his engine) and its properties. The air – rather than the human body – is where Sydenham was to locate the source of fevers; in changes in the air he was to find the origin of changes in the nature and kind of prevailing fever.

It was such beliefs about knowledge and experimental practice, absorbed from Boyle, that prompted Sydenham to resort to the clinic. Or, as he put it to the young Hans Sloane, 'You must go the bedside, it is there alone you can learn disease.' Only at the bedside can you make 'accurate observation of the natural phenomena of diseases' – one's own observations, confirmed (if possible) by reliable witnesses such as Boyle or Locke. We can now see why Sydenham would have described his method, on the title-page of his book, as being 'built on my own observations', and we can also now recognize the force of the title he chose for the revised edition: 'Medical Observations'. In a moment we shall turn to the nature of the *experiments* Sydenham performed at the bedside. Thus shall we see how he acquired the 'true and genuine curative indications' that he needed for the proper improvement of medicine.

For his first set of intellectual tools Sydenham was thus indebted to Boyle. But Sydenham parted company intellectually with Boyle after the restoration, for now their political aims were at odds. Boyle personally led the campaign to make experimental natural philosophy serve the new political arrangements. As Shapin and Schaffer put it:

producers of knowledge could find a place in Restoration society if they could supply weapons for the weakened churchmen. Boyle reckoned that experimental philosophy did provide such weapons. During the 1660s he instructed others on the way these weapons could be made and the right means of using them.[32]

Sydenham, however, was made of sterner political stuff. So much so that he was to be open to an account which dispensed altogether with 'physiological' explanations. He was to find it in the companionship of

---

[32] Shapin and Schaffer, *Leviathan and the Air-Pump*, p. 298.

discussion, thought and writing with John Locke as Locke moved politically nearer and nearer to supporting the Good Old Cause over the years.[33] It is through Locke's intellectual collaboration (and political sympathizing) that by 1676 Sydenham had come to the view that in medicine there can be no useful discussion at all about cause – and hence about the inner working of the human body. Cause was simply not the physician's concern. This is the most radical difference between Sydenham's books of 1666 and 1676 (the first and 'third' editions): the first is a product of his relationship with the politically moderate Boyle, the other of his encounter with the politically more radical Locke.

<h3 style="text-align:center">HISTORY AND METHOD</h3>

How did Thomas Sydenham actually perform his *experimenta* at the bedside – what did they look like? – and thus reach the *true and genuine curative indications* that he so earnestly sought? What was Sydenham's *method* (as he himself termed it) of discovering cures for diseases?

We will recall that Sydenham's practice was, perforce, primarily amongst the poor. In this circumstance he was able uninterruptedly to build what he regarded as the first requirement: *a history* of the disease. This is an account of the course of the disease (without intervention), of the symptoms it shows in the body, of the day and nature of its crisis, of its natural mortality (or recovery rate). None drawn up by Sydenham himself appear to survive, but here is one drawn up by his close friend John Locke in his role as physician and, curiously enough, concerning an illness of Sydenham's own son:

Measles. March 7th. 1670.
W. Sydenham, a boy of 11 years old, with only a delicate constitution by nature, rather weak lungs and very prone to cough, was seized by a shivering and rigor, followed by a slight praeternatural heat. Defluxion of the nose, drowsiness, cough, anorexia.
4th day. The rigor and shivering and all these symptoms increased daily to the fourth day, the tongue on the fourth day also white and dry, bowels natural but the fever increased, and breathing difficult around the first two days, more frequent than usual, and vomiting.
5th day. In the evening there appeared on the forehead and cheeks some small red spots like flea bites, and all the other symptoms increased, especially the drowsiness; the defluxion ceased . . .[34]

[33] On Locke's political opinions see, for instance, John Dunn, *Locke* (Past Masters Series) (Oxford, 1984); on Locke's relations with Sydenham see Patrick Romanell, *John Locke and Medicine: A New Key to Locke* (New York, 1984).
[34] My translation from the Latin as given by E.T. Withington, 'John Locke's "Observationes Medicae"', *Janus* IV, (1899), 579–81. For other individual case histories à la Sydenham (and again by a follower of Sydenham), see those printed by Andrew Brown at the end of his *De Febribus Continuis Tentamen Theoretico-Practicum seu nova febrium hypothesis mechanica audacta ex principiis Bellini constructa* (Edinburgh, 1695).

And so on, day by day, to the fourteenth day, when everything was much better. Such things are what you list. They are all *observable* phenomena, and (supposedly) *only* observable phenomena. Locke's journal has many such cases in it. They remind us, of course, of Hippocrates, of the so-called 'case-histories' of the books of *Epidemics*. That Sydenham (and thus Locke) took such histories may well be due to a desire to follow a direction for the improvement of medicine pointed out by the promoter of the Great Instauration himself, Francis Bacon:

> The first [deficiency of current medicine] is the discontinuance of the ancient and serious diligence of Hippocrates, which used to set down a narrative of the special cases of his patients, and how they proceeded, and how they were judged by recovery or death . . . This continuance of medicinal history I find deficient.[35]

To go back to Hippocrates and to emulate his diligence was of course, for both Bacon and Sydenham, to go back beyond Galen and the medicine of the Schools.

But taking such histories of *individual* cases is not all you do, if you are Thomas Sydenham. For these are simply the raw material for making an *induction*, and thus reaching an account (a history) of that disease shorn of any of the restrictions, limitations, or special conditions that it shows in its occurrence in each individual it affects. You end up, that is, with a *general account* of the disease: that is Sydenham's own usage of the term 'history', and the 'histories' of diseases he published in his books are like this. After giving such a history of smallpox, for instance, he writes:

> This is the natural history of the smallpox as comprehending the true and genuine phenomena belonging to them [i.e. the pocks] as they are in their own nature; but other anomalous accidents there are which attend the disease when unduly managed.[36]

The history deals with the disease as it is in its own nature, not in its particular manifestations. You do not explore any supposed 'causes' of the disease (there is no room for such speculation in a 'history'); you do not assume you know what has gone wrong in the body itself. You might perhaps (as Sydenham came to do) chart the seasons and weather onto your history, but that is about all. This, then is how you reach a proper account of a particular disease; and the history is itself your evidence that there exist *constant* diseases. It is also your way of distinguishing between diseases, as they are distinguished *in nature itself*.

Now, what about the cure? Just as the 'history' of the disease that

---

[35] Francis Bacon, *The Advancement of Learning* (1605), book 2, section X. 4.
[36] Dewhurst, *Dr Thomas Sydenham*, pp. 111–12.

Sydenham sought was a general history of that disease, so the cure too had to be a *general* cure. As he wrote in a 1669 (manuscript) revision of his book:

About the following observations I desire to premise these things – First, that these observations are not, as others commonly published, the history of particular cases, but (together with the nature and phenomena of several species of diseases) established practices and methods of curing, collected from a careful observation of a great number of instances in each disease.[37]

Here, in the finding of cures, we reach Sydenham's deployment of his *experimenta*. The 'history' of a disease has laid bare the 'true and genuine phenomena belonging to them as they are in their own nature'; the 'experiment' will make visible 'the true and genuine curative indications'. To Sydenham an experiment at the bedside consisted of nothing more sophisticated than *trial and error* in the administration of drugs and of medical techniques such as bleeding or purging. If a treatment seemed to be working, it was continued with, if not it was dropped. *Experimentum* thus meant making up, or working out, a sequence of cure as one went along! We can conveniently follow Sydenham's working in his own words, taken from a defensive account he gave (in English) of how he found the cure for smallpox:

it was not a forward affectation of novelty and opposition that made me run headlong upon this condemned course . . . but finding that notwithstanding the most diligent attendance and careful use of the choisest cordials many, of not only mine, but other physicians' patients miscarried in the smallpox . . . I first therefore bethought myself whether the sweats usually prescribed and prosecuted in the beginning might not be prejudicial in a disease the discharge whereof Nature had designed in another way, by pustules and little imposthumes. The first thing, therefore, that I decided on towards the curing of this disease was the cutting off and preventing those sweats, which attempts had no ill success but yet was not enough wholly to secure my patient. The next step therefore was to abate in great measure the plenty of cordials that used to be given in the smallpox, which I did but by slow degrees . . . my daily experience as I forebore their use gave me new encouragement the more to forebear them and that I found that those people always underwent this disease with least sickness and danger who took the least of them, and were most removed from hot-keeping either by clothes on their body or fire in their room. But finding that in the heat of summer in people of high and sanguine constitutions and a flox pox, bare abstaining from heat and hot medicines was not enough to preserve my patient . . . I had at last ventured to make them rise [out of bed] . . . But to perfect the cure there was one thing more yet required . . . actually to cool them not only by rising and wearing very thin clothes, but by giving them whey, which for several days together was the only physic or food they took. And by these slow steps has it been that after long and pensive thoughts about the smallpox I have in many years been able to perfect the cure of this disease . . .

If it were necessary to raise theories, and from thence draw probable arguments to prove that to be likely, which is already verified in matter of fact, and experience has justified to be true, the method I make use of in curing this disease is as capable of a fair

37 As printed in Latham, *The Works Dr Thomas Sydenham*, I, lii.

defence and may be made out from as rational grounds as the cure of any disease whatsoever.[38]

Nothing could be more home-made than Sydenham's experiments; nothing could owe less to a millenium and a half of the authoritative and learned (Galenic) medical tradition, than Sydenham's method of improving medical practice. Here is how in the 1680s an enemy – quite accurately – described Sydenham's way of finding a cure. Amongst the London doctors Gideon Harvey is critizing there is

particularly the *Doctor of Contraries*, who with *Opium* and *Jesuits-Powder* shall make more various sorts of passes at Diseases, than even any *Roman* Gladiator with his *Weapon*; and these shall be hits, and do execution. As for instance, if the doctor is applyed unto, for his assistance against a continual *Feaver*, according to his last good or ill success in the like case, gives his direction for bleeding, or omits it; then with an unparallel'd assurance makes at the Distemper with an ample Dose of the *Jesuits-Powder*, pursuing this fierce on-set with a fresh supply of the same Bark every fourth hour; And finding the fiery adversary provoked, produces his other Champion (*Opium*) to encounter him, so between these two *Bravo's* frail Nature doth too oft lie down, and yield, and the Patient is brought to his *ultimum vale*.

The *Small Pox*, (a Distemper so unaccountable to most Physicians, and therefore Empirically treated, whence Nurses do equally vie with their Worships [i.e. with members of the College of Physicians of London] in the Cure) is by this *Generalissimo* (contrary to all sence and experience) countermined with Spirit of *Vitriol* and *Opium*, by which beyond all others he is infallible in procuring an *Euthanasia*. Good God, how the Universities do rob the Plough![39]

It was this way – 'according to his last good or ill success in the like case' – that Sydenham arrived at his unique treatments, such as 'the Bark and *Opium* in continual *Feavers*, and . . . *Spirit of Vitriol* and *Laudanum liquidum* in the *Small Pox*', as Harvey recorded with disgust.

What most outraged Gideon Harvey (and, we may assume, other of Sydenham's contemporaries) was the fact that Sydenham thought that this 'experimental' procedure qualified for the title of a 'method of healing' (*methodus medendi*): it was no accident that Galen's greatest book and Sydenham's book of 1666 both had the title of 'Method'. In Gideon Harvey's eyes, the last thing a proper method of healing was, was experimental! This is how he described a proper 'method of healing', for the edification of people like Sydenham. Harvey's usage of the term here is perfectly conventional, and perfectly Galenic:

[38] As printed in Dewhurst, *Dr Thomas Sydenham*, pp. 105–6.
[39] Harvey, *The Conclave of Physicians*, pp. 81–2. Harvey had a grudge against all the physicians of the London College of Physicians, and is here attacking Sydenham as just another member of the College. The language of this passage is sarcastic and full of political allusions; in calling Sydenham a 'Generalissmo', for instance, Harvey is probably making reference to the rule of the Major-Generals in the 1650s. (I am indebted to Julian Martin for pointing this out to me.)

188   ANDREW CUNNINGHAM

*Concerning the Description of the true Method of Physick, whereby a Physician is
distinguish'd from a Quack:*
... The Method of Physick is a rational order of Remedies to be applyed to the body of
man, to cure Internal and External Diseases; which consists, first in the knowledge of
the Distemper, and cause thereof, the Election or Choice of proper sufficient Remedies,
and then reasoning within himself, which Remedy ought to be applyed first, when, and
how, which Second, and Third, &c. How long each is to be continued, and when the
First, Second, or Third is to be changed. So that here you see the *Method of Physick*
implyes naturally two particulars; First, the knowing of the Distemper and cause;
Secondly, adequate Remedies, that shall remove those Distempers, and their causes . . .
3dly, There is necessary (according to what my description of *Methodus* doth express)
a Ratiocination in the Physician within himself, the result whereof makes a practical
Indication, or conclusion: Thus, This Distemper is hot, therefore the Remedy must be
cooling; it is caused by a Plethory, therefore Bleeding is the Remedy; or a Cacochymy,
therefore purging is to be advised. So that the reasoning part is nothing else, but the
apprehending rightly the nature of the Disease, and collecting thence, what Remedy it
naturally doth point at, shew, or Indicate . . . 4ly, As then the *Methodus Medendi* doth
imply the knowledge of all Diseases, Causes, Symptoms, and what parts they are
inherent in, and likewise the knowledge and experience of all Remedies, so it doth
consequently comprehend the sum, and substance, or total of the whole Art of Physick,
and is the end and the ultimate point, whereto all the parts of Physick do tend, and
therein concenter; so that only he, that is Master and Doctor in the Method of Physick,
doth alone deserve the Name and Title of a Real Physician; all others that pretend to
Physick, being Empiricks, Quacks, or Mountebancks.[40]

Sydenham's *methodus medendi* failed this test in every particular. He
intended it to. For he was seeking to redefine what a medical method
ought to be: it ought to be 'built on one's own observations', it ought to
be a way of discovering *new* cures. Its 'history' revealed to the physician how a given disease is *in its nature*; given this, 'experiment' will
show him its 'true and genuine curative indications'. This is to walk
hand in hand with nature.

'AFTER MY DEATH, WHEN I AM BECOME AN AUTHORITY'

Little if any of the above is part of our familiar story about Sydenham.
Our view of Sydenham is of an *empirical* practitioner (rather than an
'empiric'), sensibly rejecting Galenic theory while embracing anew the
Hippocratic approach. 'Experiment' (like politics) seems to have been
lost from our accounts of Sydenham. To us Sydenham is the restorer of
clinical, bedside-medicine. For this we hold him to be a hero. Yet he
was obviously not a hero to his contemporaries. Except of course to a
handful, a handful of politically-motivated men, such as John Locke
and Andrew Brown of Edinburgh.[41] When and how did Sydenham get

[40] *Ibid.*, pp. 96–100.
[41] See my 'Sydenham versus Newton: the Edinburgh fever dispute of the 1690s between Andrew
Brown and Archibald Pitcairne', in W.F. Bynum and V. Nutton, (eds.), *Theories of Fever from
Antiquity to the Enlightenment* (Supplement to *Medical History*, London, 1981), pp. 71–98.

sanitized and sanctified? Whence came that title of 'the English Hippocrates'? And whence indeed came the privileging of the matching reading of Hippocrates (the one we hold today) – of Hippocrates the bedside physician, the empiricist, working with nature, abjuring high-flown theory, practising expectant medicine?

It was in Leyden that Sydenham's reputation seems to have been laundered. While at home in England any defender of Sydenham was still virtually identifying himself as a supporter of the Good Old Cause (an unpopular position, especially after 1689) and the advocacy of Sydenhamian medicine was a politically loaded act, at the same time on the continent Sydenham was being presented as bland, safe, unpolitical, empirical, sensible. The transformation was performed above all by Hermann Boerhaave, who made Sydenham into one of the great masters of the history of medicine. In the early decades of the eighteenth century Boerhaave created a history whose peaks were Hippocrates, Bacon, Sydenham and Newton.[42] Hippocrates first practised proper medicine, Bacon pointed out the means for its restoration, Sydenham effected its restoration into practice, and Newton provided the (supposedly complementary) means to understand properly the workings of the body. Boerhaave also created a medical system which was (he claimed) constructed out of the eternal truths which had been brought to light primarily by the efforts of these four. And this medical system became the most widespread of any of the century, its influence being particularly felt in England and Scotland. Thus, some twenty years or so after Sydenham's death, a new image of Sydenham began to be re-imported into Britain by English-speaking students of Professor Boerhaave.

What is most remarkable about Boerhaave's list of heroes is how short it is: there is no-one significant between the fourth century B.C. and A.D. 1600. To put it another way, three of his four heroes come from the century immediately before his own (and all three of them from England, it may be noted). This is not the place to explore how and why Boerhaave created this particular pantheon. It will suffice for the moment to point out who, above all else, is missing from Boerhaave's list. It is of course Galen. Galen's domination of learned medicine for fifteen hundred years, Galen's interpretation of what Hippocrates was saying – they now count for nothing. It is indeed with and through the influence of Boerhaave's teaching that Galen's rule came to an end. What Boerhaave put into the vast space that Galen had occupied, was Thomas Sydenham. This Sydenham was restoring the

---

[42] For Boerhaave praising his heroes in his orations, see E. Kegel-Brinkgreve and A.M. Luyendijk-Elshout, *Boerhaave's Orations* (Leiden, 1983).

practice of Hippocrates. That Hippocrates, naturally enough, looked remarkably like Sydenham himself: making case histories and histories of disease, refraining from speculating about cause, working hand in hand with Nature.[43] And when Boerhaave had finished with them that Hippocrates and the Sydenham on whom he was modelled also sounded free of any interest but the impartial pursuit of truth in medicine for the good of mankind, inspired by a disinterested love of mankind. In other words, they began to sound like Boerhaave himself.

Finally we come back to the first Sydenham Society in the 1830s and 40s. In the lives of the people who ran and patronized this, clinical medicine was all the rage. That clinical medicine was, however, Parisian in origin, and hospital-based. In a roundabout way *an* image of Sydenham had indeed helped inspire this clinical medicine, but the way was very roundabout. *En route* the image of the true Thomas Sydenham, experimental physician of the Good Old Cause, had unfortunately been lost.

[43] Sydenham himself did quite a good job of characterizing Hippocrates as an early-day Sydenham:

> by these means and helps, the excellent Hippocrates arrived at the top of Physic, who laid this solid foundation for building the Art of Physic upon, viz. *Nature cures Diseases*. And he delivered plainly the *Phaenomena* of every disease, without pressing any Hypothesis for his service, as may be seen in his books of Diseases, Affections, and the like. He also delivered some Rules gathered from the Observation of the Method that Nature uses in promoting and removing Diseases; such are his *Praenotiones*, his *Aphorisms*, and the like. And of these things consisted the Theory of the Divine Old Man, which was not drawn from a vain and lascivious Fancy, like the Dreams of sick men, but it exhibited a legitimate History of those Operations of Nature, which she produces in the diseases of men. And now seeing this Theory was nothing else but an exquisite Description of Nature, it was very reasonable that in practice, his only aim should be to relieve her when she was oppressed, by the best means he could; and therefore he allowed no other Province for [medical] Art, than the succouring of Nature when she was weak, the restraining her when she was outrageous, and the reducing her to order, and to do all this in that way and manner whereby Nature endeavours to expel Diseases; for the sagacious Man [Hippocrates] perceives that Nature judges Diseases, and does in all, being helped by a few simple forms of remedies, and sometimes without any.

(Pechey's 1696 translation of part of the Preface to the *Medical Observations*). Though the fact may seem very strange to us now, this reading of Hippocrates was not a common one at Sydenham's time – even among men who were actually trying to model their own medical practice on that of Hippocrates; see Iain M. Lonie, 'Hippocrates the Iatromechanist', *Medical History*, XXV (1981), 113–50.

7

The medico-religious universe of an early eighteenth-century Parisian doctor: the case of Philippe Hecquet

L.W.B. BROCKLISS

INTRODUCTION: THE MAN

The eponymous hero of this chapter is unlikely to be a familiar figure to many historians of medicine of the post-Cartesian era. This is scarcely surprising for from the vantage point of the nineteenth and twentieth centuries, Philippe Hecquet (1661–1737) was just another Paris physician, indistinguishable from the large majority of the three hundred or so medical men who legally or illegally practised their craft in the French capital at the turn of the eighteenth century. Certainly, there were a number of Paris doctors at this time whose shades have been duly honoured in the medical pantheon, such as the botanist J.P. de Tournefort (1656–1708). Hecquet, however, was decidedly not of their stamp. Unlike his more prestigious colleagues, Hecquet's primary concern was with healing the sick. He was totally uninterested in helping push back the frontiers of medical knowledge by personally torturing nature to reveal her secrets. Significantly, he never presented an account of any experimental work to a learned society which he himself had performed; indeed, there is no evidence that he ever did any research.[1]

Nevertheless, in the early eighteenth century the mention of Hecquet's name to a fellow physician, not just in Paris but in virtually any European city, would have elicited an immediate electric response.

---

[1] Shortly after his death Hecquet was the subject of two important obituary notices: see J.P. Nicéron, *Mémoires pour servir à l'histoire des hommes illustres dans la république des lettres, avec un catalogue raisonné de leurs ouvrages*, 43 vols. (Paris, 1729–45), XLI, pp. 83–111 [1740]; Le Fèvre de Saint-Marc, 'La Vie de M. Hecquet', in Ph. Hecquet, *La Médecine des pauvres*, 3 vols. (Paris, 1740), III, end. These formed the basis for later biographical notices, such as the one that appeared in L. Moréri, *Le Grand Dictionnaire historique*, ed. Drouet, 10 vols. (Paris, 1759), V, pp. 552–5. The notice by Saint-Marc is by far the longer and more informative and is the primary biographical source relied on in this account. Saint-Marc's account is reproduced almost verbatim in Jules Roger, *Hecquet, docteur régent et ancien doyen de la faculté de médecine de Paris* (Paris, 1889), the most recent evaluation.

To some, like the Scot Thomas Bower, professor of mathematics at the university of Aberdeen, Hecquet was the principal physician of the French capital.[2] To others, he was a figure of fun, the supposed original of Dr Sangrado in Lesage's *Gil Blas*.[3] The reason for Hecquet's contemporary notoriety was twofold. In the first place, he owed his European renown to the fact he was an ardent polemicist in favour of medical mechanism. Hecquet may have added nothing of permanent substance to the science of medicine, but he was a great pedlar of other men's opinions, between 1712 and his death publishing, often in the vernacular, a number of dogmatic and vituperative pamphlets and books in support of his mechanist prejudice. Thereby, he became the darling of the mechanist school and the avowed enemy of its iatrochemical opponents.[4] In the second place, Hecquet owed his peculiar celebrity in Paris, not just to his colourful propaganda, but also to his highly visible lifestyle. In an age when most physicians rushed after wealthy, aristocratic clients and lived in luxury, Hecquet was a medical saint. He lived frugally, scarcely ever touching wine, was noted for his charity, and was particularly interested in treating the poor:

A quelque heure qu'ils vinssent, quelque occupé qu'il pût être, ils étoient sûrs d'être bien reçus. Il leur accordoit tout le tems qu'ils pouvoient souhaiter; il leur parloit avec une bonté, qui les consoloit; il accompagnoit les conseils, qu'il leur donnoit pour la guérison de leurs maux corporels, d'exhortations à remplir leurs devoirs chretiens.[5]

---

[2] T. Boerus, 'Epistola ad Archibaldum Pitcarnium . . . qua respondetur libello Astrucii Franci', in A. Pitcairne, *Dissertationes Medicae*, 4th edn (The Hague, 1722), p. 283; the letter was written probably in 1713. Boerus's dates are not known.

[3] A.-R. Lesage, *Histoire de Gil Blas de Santillane*, ed. R. Laufer (Paris, 1977), book II, chs. 2–5. This part of the work was published in 1715. The account of Dr Sangrado's prophylactic and therapeutic preferences make it impossible to doubt that Le Sage is intent on parodying Hecquet. In book IV, ch. 3, Hecquet again appears, this time thinly disguised as Dr Oquetus. The latter is described as a pupil of Dr Sangrado, so logically Hecquet and Dr Sangrado cannot be one and the same. *Gil Blas*, however, is a picaresque novel and logical consistency was not expected by its readers.

[4] A list of Hecquet's works are given in the biographical notices mentioned in note 1. Saint-Marc, pp. 93–4, provides a check-list of Hecquet's international contacts, surnames only: (Italy) G. Baglivi (1668–1707), Fr. Torti (1658–1741), Bianchi (?G.B. Bianchi, 1681–1767), A. Valisneri (1661–1730), P.A. Michelotti (dates unknown), J.B. Morgagni (1682–1771), Ricla (?); (United Provinces) H. Boerhaave (1668–1738), F. Ruysch (1638–1731); (Scotland) A. Pitcairne (1652–1719); (Germany) N.P. Garelli (d. 1732), Lexhner (?); (Austrian Netherlands) A.C.J. Van Rossum (1706–89), H.J. Réga (1690–1754); (Spain) Marianus Seguer (dates unknown). Letters from a number of these figures were apparently found in his *cabinet* when he died; most are professors of medicine; Garelli and Lexhner were imperial physicians.

[5] Saint-Marc, p. 66. (In this and future quotations the orthography follows the original text.) It was this aspect of Hecquet's life which was exclusively noted in the epitaph on his tomb and in the biographical notices which appeared in Nicéron and later Moréri. Saint-Marc, a physician himself, gave equal weight to both reasons for his subject's notoriety. Interestingly a later biographical notice which appeared in the official faculty hagiography made no mention of his piety and abstemiousness: see J.-A. Hazon, *Notice des hommes les plus célèbres de la faculté de médecine 1110–1750* (Paris, 1773), pp. 187–91.

The date when Hecquet became a medical mechanist cannot be known exactly. His adherence to the doctrine can only be traced to the years 1695–7 when he applied to become a doctor of medicine of the Paris faculty, so that he might regularize his position as a practioner in the capital. In the dissertations he submitted in order to graduate, his mechanist allegiance was unequivocal, especially in the thesis he sustained on 27 January 1695, where he launched a bitter attack on the iatrochemists, whom he condemned as modern idolators.[6] Whether he had been a mechanist for a long time before this, however, is impossible to say. Certainly, he may have been, for he had taken his first medical doctorate at Reims as early as 1684, after initially studying in the Paris medical faculty in 1682–3. In 1695–7, therefore, he was no medical tyro. Nor was he new to the capital, for after an initial interlude in his home town of Abbeville, he had practised in the city on and off since his graduation.[7] What can be said definitely is that Hecquet was a convert to mechanism. In the years he passed through the Paris medical school he would have encountered either a Galenist or a iatrochemical account of the human body.[8]

Hecquet's commitment to a life of Christian asceticism, on the other hand, undoubtedly began in 1688. In that year he became physician attached to the convent of Port-Royal-des-Champs. As this was a religious house situated some leagues south of Paris, Hecquet was forced to abandon his practice in the capital and retreat to the countryside. In his new surroundings, he seems to have begun a new life. The convent was notorious as a centre of fasting and mortification, and the example of the nuns was understandably infectious. Moreover, Hecquet was replacing as physician in residence another medical saint, the venerable Hamon, who used to shock even his friends with the shabbiness of his apparel.[9] Hecquet threw himself into a life of service

---

[6] Ph. Hecquet, 'An functiones a fermentis?', *Quaestio Medica Quodlibetaria* 27 Jan. 1695 (printed), p. 4. Hecquet sustained two other theses, on 13 Oct. 1695 and 12 Jan. 1696. All three can be consulted in the British Library under the classification 1182 e 2 (nos. 83, 103, 113). In this period all candidates for a licence in medicine from the Paris faculty had to sustain three theses in the course of the two years after they had been awarded their baccalaureate. Hecquet was licensed on 3 Sept. 1696 and became a doctor of medicine of the Paris faculty on 15 Jan. 1697.

[7] Saint-Marc, pp. 3–4. I have been unable to find a copy of Hecquet's Reims thesis which would indicate his medical opinions in 1684. The collection of Reims theses in Bibliothèque Municipale, Reims, *collection des imprimés*, no. 725 (5 vols.) begins only in 1720. References to late seventeenth-century theses in this collection are given in O. Guelliot, 'Les Thèses de *janséniste*, 2 vols. (Paris, 1922). The most recent studies are L. Cognet, *Le Jansénisme* (Paris,

[8] L.W.B. Brockliss, 'Medical Teaching at the University of Paris 1600–1720', *Annals of Science*, xxv (1978), 231–2. The judgement is based on information from student theses. Hecquet was taught physiology, pathology and anatomy by a professor called Douté (dates unknown) but the latter's course does not survive.

[9] Saint-Marc, pp. 4–6; other details in C.A. Sainte-Beuve, *Port-Royal*, 5 vols. (Paris, 1840–59), IV, p. 507n. Hecquet seems to have been enticed to Port-Royal by the appropriately named Mlle

and deprivation with gusto, so much so that he had to resign his post in
1693 on the grounds of ill health. Nevertheless, he remained an
enthusiastic ascetic and stalwart supporter of the monastic ideal (when
properly lived) for the rest of his days. Eventually, he himself went into
retreat. Suffering from paralysis of both legs and an arm, he entered a
Carmelite convent in 1726 and spent the last ten years of life active in
consultation but a virtual prisoner in his cell.[10]

The fact that Hecquet was closely attached to Port-Royal means
that he was not just a Christian ascetic. Port-Royal was the spiritual
centre of French Jansenism, the convent that in the middle of the
seventeenth century had sheltered alongside the nuns the founding-
fathers of the movement, who had formed a separate lay community.
For Hecquet to have been appointed physician there in 1688, he must
have been already a prominent figure in the sect for a number of years.
The nature of Jansenism need not detain us. Suffice it to say that it was
a theological movement whose members found God so awesome and
powerful and man so corrupt that they completely played down the
role of human free will in performing meritorious acts. Their theological position was outlined in the *Augustinus* of Jansen, bishop of Ypres,
a work published posthumously in 1640. In the eyes of the church,
Jansenist theology was determinist and contrary to the fundamentals
of post-Tridentine catholicism, which stressed that man's will was
'radically' free. Jansenists, then, were neo-heretics. They were saved
from total persecution only because they acknowledged the heterodoxy of a number of determinist propositions outlawed by the papacy
in the Bull *Ex Occasione* of 1653, while denying that these were to be
found, as the church maintained, in the *Augustinus*. By identifying
himself with Jansenism, therefore, the young Hecquet was nailing his
colours to a wobbling mast. It was a mast, however, that managed to
stay upright at least until Hecquet's death, thanks to the support it
received from the lower clergy and important sections of the laity,
especially the *robe*. Jansenism's attraction lay in the fact it was not, as
it might seem, a theology of despair which encouraged retreat from the
world. On the contrary, it promoted a life of devotion – prayer,
mortification and Bible study – not simply as a means of grasping
man's nothingness, but as the starting-point for a life of active Christian charity. Certainly not all ascetics and saints were Jansenists in late

de Vertus, one of the aristocratic ladies who were in perpetual retreat in the convent. On the
saintly Jean Hamon (1613–87), see N. Fontaine, *Mémoires pour servir à l'histoire de Port-
Royal*, 4 vols. (Cologne, 1753) IV, pp. 393–400; Sainte-Beuve, IV, chs. 4–5.
[10] Saint-Marc, pp. 64–6, 90. He had been *médecin* to the convent from 1695; it was there that he
died and was buried.

seventeenth- and early eighteenth-century France, but the Jansenists as
a group were the undoubted leaders of a great moral crusade to rescue
the country from the clutches of Venus and Mammon.[11]

Hecquet's Jansenist proclivities unfortunately remain shrouded in
mystery. Wisely, his contemporary biographer, Saint-Marc, to whom
we are chiefly indebted for our detailed knowledge of Hecquet the
Christian ascetic, ignores completely his religious heterodoxy. Probably, Hecquet's attachment to the sect stems from the later 1670s.
Originally he had been intended for the priesthood, and after studying
philosophy at the Paris Collège des Grassins spent the years 1679–81 on
the benches of the Paris faculty of theology. Interestingly, one of his
professors was the Jansenist sympathizer, Edmond Pirot (1635–
1713).[12] There can be no doubt that Hecquet remained a Jansenist until
he died. In the last years of Louis XIV's reign an attempt was made to
eradicate the sect and in 1713 as part of the campaign a popular
devotional manual composed by the exiled Jansenist Oratorian,
Pasquier Quesnel (1634–1719), was subject to a scathing papal censure
on royal orders (the Bull *Unigenitus*). On Louis's death the Jansenists
fought back, and an attempt was made to get the censure rescinded by
appealing over the head of the pope to a general council of the church.
Hecquet was definitely among the *appelants*. One of the leading
institutions to appeal against *Unigenitus* was the university of Paris
where Jansenism had powerful supporters among the doctors of
theology. When the move was debated in the faculty of medicine on 1
October 1718, Hecquet was one of the forty-six physicians present
who gave the appeal their blessing.[13]

Hecquet remained a Jansenist and an *appelant*, too, in the 1720s and
1730s when the movement was once more on the defensive. In an
anonymous pamphlet of 1726, almost certainly an attempt to ward off
a move in the faculty to revoke its appeal, he was totally unrepentant.

[11] The standard authority on Jansenism is still A. Gazier, *L'Histoire générale du mouvement
janséniste*, 2 vols. (Paris, 1922). The most recent studies are L. Cognet, *Le Jansénisme* (Paris,
1961); A. Adam, *Du Mysticisme à la révolte. Les Jansénistes du XVIIe siècle* (Paris, 1968);
A. Sedgwick, *Jansenism in Seventeenth-Century France. Voices from the Wilderness* (Charlot-
tesville, Va., 1977). On Jansenism in eighteenth-century France, see E. Préclin, *Les Jansénistes
du XVIIIe siècle et la Constitution civile du clergé. Le développement du richérisme. Sa
propagation dans le bas-clergé 1713–91*, (Paris, 1929).
[12] Saint-Marc, p. 2. For Pirot's putative heterodoxy, see J. O'Leary, 'The Irish and Jansenism in
the Seventeenth Century', in Liam Swords (ed.), *The Irish–French Connection* (Paris, 1978),
p. 41.
[13] Bibliothèque de la Faculté de Médecine de Paris, MS. 18, fo. 189r, faculty minutes. For the
history of the Bull *Unigenitus* in the university generally, see Ch. M.G. Brechillet Jourdain,
Histoire de l'Université de Paris aux XVIIe et XVIIIe siècles, 2 pts in 1 vol. (Paris, 1862–6), part
1, pp. 300–72, *passim*.

'La saine Théologie nous répond que la Doctrine de la Constitution [*Unigenitus*] n'est point celle de la Foy de nos Peres.' The appeal, then, was a sacred duty. It was 'Un engagement contracté avec l'université envers Dieu pour la défence de l'Eglise et le maintien de la Foy. C'est un engagement solemnel qui interesse la Religion, la réputation, la raison et l'honneur.'[14] Appropriately, the Jansenist movement honoured Hecquet on his death. The epitaph on his tomb was composed by the Jansenist educationalist and historian, Charles Rollin, himself a victim of state-led persecution.[15]

Philippe Hecquet, therefore, for most of his adult life was in the grip of two distinctive but equally powerful and controversial *idées fixes*, if he sensibly limited his role as a propagandist to the promotion of only one: medical mechanism. A man driven by twin gods, however, especially in the early-modern era, is unlikely to have inhabited a dual universe where his theological and medical interests were completely separate.[16] It is the aim of the present chapter to examine to what extent Hecquet's mechanism was informed with or perhaps even moulded by (in the light of his putative earlier attraction to the creed) his Jansenist sympathies. But before this can be done, Hecquet's medical philosophy must be examined in greater detail. Hecquet's passionate advocacy of mechanism led him to take violent issue with not only the medical theories of his iatrochemical opponents, but also a wide variety of, in his eyes, pernicious contemporary customs and medical practices that iatrochemists too often seemed to support.

IATROMECHANISM

Hecquet's mechanist identity progressed through three distinct stages.[17] In the mid-1690s his adherence to the philosophy was still incomplete. Although stressing in his graduand theses that in a state of health every aspect of human physiology could be explained mechanically, he was not exclusively a mechanist in his understanding of the

[14] Anon. [Ph. Hecquet], *Reponse à la question: si les medecins peuvent ou doivent prendre part dans les affaires de l'Eglise* [dated 1 August 1726] (n.p., n.d.), p. 7. This and other anonymous pamphlets referred to below were included in the list of Hecquet's works published in the first obituary notices. Their authorship has never been questioned.

[15] The epitaph is printed in full in the biographical notices referred to in note 1 above. Charles Rollin (1661–1741) was principal of the Paris Collège de Beauvais until removed for Jansenism in 1712.

[16] B. Vickers has recently argued in his introduction to his *Occult and Scientific Mentalities in the Renaissance* (Cambridge, 1984), that early modern man did indeed compartmentalize his different intellectual activities (esp. p. 13 ff.); but his to date is a lone voice.

[17] This is something that neither his contemporary biographers nor Roger realized, even if Saint-Marc (p. 83) understands that Hecquet did alter his views towards the end of his life.

formation of the bodily fluids. At this date, he believed that the chyle created in the stomach under the impact of muscular pressure was composed of particles of different shape and size. It was then metamorphozed into homogeneous globules of blood or lymph not by the pummelling effect of vascular dilation, but by passing through perfectly constructed vascular pores which permitted the entrance of particles only of the optimum diameter.[18] Moreover, Hecquet's mechanism extended only as far as the body in its natural condition. His pathological doctrine drew heavily on iatrochemical theories, for he identified the internal cause of disease as a pernicious poison entering and attacking the bloodstream. The resultant reaction, he claimed, produced a malignant serum, which in turn had a deleterious effect on the body and engendered the symptoms of illness.[19]

In the next few years, however, Hecquet converted to a thoroughgoing mechanism through coming into contact with the works of Baglivi, L. Bellini (1643–1741) and Pitcairne.[20] In 1704, the same year in which he edited the Lyons edition of Baglivi's *Opera Omnia*, he almost certainly composed the thesis which was presented under his presidency to the Paris faculty by one Antoine Pepin. The graduand's stance was totally mechanist.[21] The solids were considered to be a congeries of fibres (*villi*) whose elasticity under stimulus completely explained the formation of the fluids and their circulation, the latter phenomenon was attributed originally by Hecquet to the elasticity of the air in the vessels. At the same time, Pepin stressed the inadequacy of iatrochemical pathology. The internal cause of the disease was now to be sought in the hypertension or laxity of the solids which changed the natural velocity of the fluids, not in some chemical reaction.[22]

Baglivian mechanism remained the fundamental influence on Hecquet's medical philosophy until at least the middle of the 1720s, if by 1714 he was also drawing on the medical *Institutes* of Hermann

---

[18] Hecquet, 'An Functiones a Fermentis?', p. 3.

[19] *Ibid.*, pp. 6–7. In constructing his pathology Hecquet acknowledged the influence of the English physician Richard Morton (1637–90), author of a posthumous work on fevers, and of the Leipzig professor Michael Etmüller (1644–83).

[20] In the mid-1690s Hecquet's chief physiological influences seem to have been the Italian G.A. Borelli (1608–79) and the Englishman W. Charleton (1619–1707), notably the latter's *Oeconomia Animalis* (first published in 1659).

[21] Antoine Pepin, 'An impeditae Transpirationis sanguinis missio?', *Quaestio Medica Cardinalita* 7 Feb. 1704, p. 3. A reference in the margin sends the reader to Baglivi, *De Fibrorum Motu* (Rome). This is probably the *De Fibra Motrice et Morbosa* (Rome, 1700). The thesis can be found in British Library, 1182 e 3 (no. 38).

[22] *Ibid.*, p. 4. In the same thesis Hecquet also rejects the idea that vascular porosity plays a role in fluid creation. This thesis was almost certainly written by Hecquet, for it was customary practice for members of the faculty to advance their ideas under the cover of graduand debates.

Boerhaave (1668–1738).[23] Faculty dissertations and full-scale works which he later composed and published, merely elaborated his 1704 position by offering a detailed mechanist explanation of particular physiological functions or specific diseases. As Hecquet's views were generally extremely derivative his output during these years need not detain us. Of greater interest are the works he composed in the last decade of his life when his philosophical principles changed once again.

None of Hecquet's works in the period 1710–24 displayed much interest in the function of the nervous system. Significantly, his *magnum opus*, the *Novus Medicinae Conspectus* of 1722, whch otherwise dealt comprehensively with physiology, pathology and therapeutics ignored the animal spirits altogether.[24] It comes as a shock to find, then, that from the mid-1720s Hecquet abandoned his Baglivian mechanism in favour of a physiology and pathology founded on the nervous system. Unravelling the medical philosophy he finally embraced is difficult, but his evident starting-point was that fibre elasticity alone could not explain the mechanism of the human body. Rather, the contractability of the solids was dependent on the presence of nerves filled with incredibly subtle 'fluide spiritualisé'. It was the nerves' superfine elasticity under stimulus which determined physiological movement, not any inherent property of fibrous matter. Similarly, it was the damage to the nerves which caused disease, not a lesion of the solids *per se*. Hecquet seems to have considered the 'fluide spiritualisé' of the nerves analogous to the air we breath. While never explicitly stating that they were one and the same, he seemed to imply that the animal spirits comprised attenuated air which had been introduced into the bloodstream by eating and breathing and then separated from the blood in the brain. When the air was pure and infused in the right proportion, then the nerves functioned properly. If the air was poisoned, however, or ingested in too great a quantity, the elasticity of the nerves would be impaired and disease would inevitably follow. The atmosphere thus became the key to a healthy existence.[25]

In casting off the shackles of Baglivian mechanism, Hecquet believed that he had created a unique medical philosophy. In this he was certainly mistaken, since a similar system was developed contempora-

---

[23] The earliest reference to Boerhaave's *Institutes* is to be found in Ph. Hecquet, *De Purganda Medicina a Curarum Sordibus* (Paris, 1714), 'Proloquium', p. xl.

[24] Ph. Hecquet, *Novus Medicinae Conspectus* (Paris, 1722).

[25] Hecquet's final philosophical position was developed in particular in two works: *La Medecine théologique (ou la medecine crée, telle qu'elle se fait voir ici, sortie des mains de Dieu)* (Paris, 1733), and the posthumous *La Medecine naturelle*, 2 vols. (Paris, 1738).

neously by a number of physicians. As Hecquet's biographer, Saint-Marc, quite rightly remarked, the Paris physician's position was broadly shared by the Italian Felice Rosetti for one.[26] In addition, Hecquet acknowledged no philosophical influence behind his creation, maintaining that his system was entirely his own. Here again he was surely deluding himself. Anglo-Scottish proponents of a medical system based on the controlling role of a superfine nervous fluid were Newtonians, convinced of the impossibility of the conservation of motion in any mechanical system and anxious to locate an active principle which would maintain the body in equilibrium. Moreover as Anita Guerrini points out in her chapter, their commitment to some sort of ether theory was clearly encouraged by Newton's own speculations about the role of an invisible fluid in explaining inter-planetary attraction. In consequence, it is difficult not to believe that Hecquet himself had not also come under the English philosopher's spell. As we will see, Hecquet in the 1730s was definitely cognizant of the *Opticks* and the work of a number of English Newtonians in the field of botany. Arguably, Hecquet at the end of his life had merely exchanged a Baglivian for a Newtonian mechanism.[27]

Whatever the truth of the matter, there can be little doubt that Hecquet's final philosophical position was an appropriate resting-place. Hecquet's medical philosophy moved in an increasingly one-dimensional direction. Beginning as a mechanist with iatrochemical tendencies, he passed through mechanism *tout court* and ended by promoting a physiology founded on a single part. At the same time, his understanding of the external cause of disease became steadily more exclusive, eventually focusing on the primacy of the air above the other non-naturals.[28] But this development was scarcely surprising in the light of the epistemology that underlay his medical philosophy as early as 1695. Like many other mechanists, Hecquet insisted that the human body was a simple machine: one and the same law must control every physiological function. It was the complexity of iatrochemistry that

---

[26]   Saint-Marc, p. 83. Rosetti (dates unknown) published a booklet in 1728 entitled *Sistema nuovo intorno al'anima pensante, e alla circolazione degli spiriti animali . . . discusso in tre lettere . . . fra il signor Rosetti e signor Vallisneri.*

[27]   For eighteenth-century medical philosophies based on the nervous system, see R. French, 'Ether and Physiology', in G.N. Cantor and M.S. Hodge (eds.), *Conceptions of Ether. Studies in the History of Ether Theories 1740–1900* (Cambridge, 1981), pp. 110–34. French makes no mention of Hecquet.

[28]   As early as 1714 Hecquet had reduced the non-naturals to two; food and air. These were the primary causes of disease together with the soul whose changes in state could adversely effect the nerves and ultimately alter the behaviour of the solids; see *De Purganda Medicina a Curarum Sordibus*, ch. 6.

damned it from the beginning. Throughout Hecquet ardently sought
to identify the fundamental physiological principle which could explain the corporeal mechanism. That in his search for simplicity he
became simplistic merely emphasizes how powerful was the grip of the
Cartesian aesthetic.[29]

Hecquet, naturally, was seeking not just a simple but a watertight
and unimpeachable medical theory. Unlike earlier systemizers –
Galenists and iatrochemists especially – the mechanists, he insisted,
were not building castles in the air but uncovering the truth. The earlier
systematizers were in fact not the inventors of systems at all but the
fabricators of woolly hypotheses. Where they had erred was to assume
that they could identify the essence of things and erect a medical theory
from a knowledge of primary causes. This, however, was an improper
method of proceeding, for such causes were hidden from the physicians' gaze.[30]

A true system, Hecquet believed, was built on facts: it was the
distillation of experience, especially the study of anatomy.

Ainsi le systéme en Médicine ne doit estre qu'un arrangement de réflexions,
d'observations, et de conséquences tirées de la nature, qui n'est bien expliquées que
quand on l'explique par elle-même. Ce n'est pas que la véritable Médicine n'ait ses
suppositions, mais elles sont de faits avouez, de véritez constantes; ce sont les
observations qui en font le fondement et les principes. Or ces principes ne se prouvent
pas, parce qu'ils ont esté mill fois vérifiez; il est donc permis de les supposer vrais, parce
que personne ne les soupçonne de faux.[31]

Medical mechanism was just such an experientially orientated system.
It was not based, like iatrochemistry, on dubious analogies between
what happened in vitreo and in vivo, but firmly founded on the
observation of the body. It was thus a natural and not an imaginative,
quixotic system.[32]

Hecquet, therefore, was an empiricist as well as a systematizer. It
was for this reason that he professed particular admiration for Hippocrates. While accepting that the Hippocratic corpus did not contain a
developed medical philosophy, Hecquet praised it nevertheless for the
completeness and perspicacity of its observations. He felt very angry in

29 Its grip, be it said, left an indelible trace on all French medical mechanists; e.g. the Caennais,
J. Fr. Callard de la Ducquérie (d. 1754); cf. his defence of Baglivian mechanism in 'Oratio
contra Rationem qua probatur Experientiae Necessitas' n.d. (early eighteenth century), in
Bibliothèque Municipale Caen, MS. 114, fos. 15–20.
30 Hecquet, 'An Functiones a Fermentis?' [1695], p. 1.
31 Ph. Hecquet, De la Digestion et des maladies d l'estomac, suivant le systeme de la trituration et
du Broyement (Paris, 1712), preface, p. xii.
32 The chemists, said Hecquet, were guilty of playing God and remaking nature according to
their will; see De Purganda Medicina, 'proloquium', pp. xiii–xiv. He compares the
iatrochemists to Don Quixote on p. xlviii.

consequence that Hippocrates had fallen out of favour along with the other ancients and he did his best in promoting medical mechanism to rehabilitate the physician of Cos.[33] Hippocrates' observations and warnings, he maintained, were a powerful support to the mechanical case. The old and new medicine should march hand in hand: 'What the ancients have taught us to describe, the moderns have taught us to explain; the former provide the matter of medical discourse, the latter our grounds of understanding.'[34]

This is not to say that Hecquet believed that Hippocrates, or indeed the ancients' works generally contained every pathological or therapeutic detail that the physician would need to know. Far from it, for Hecquet in a publication toward the end of his life, presented a grandiose scheme for updating and adding to medical knowledge.[35] It does emphasize, however, that the Parisian doctor did not believe that the science of medicine only began with the iatromechanists. Rather, medicine had a long history and the ancients were still a store-house of wisdom.

PROPHYLAXIS AND PROFESSIONALISM

The importance of the truth of mechanism for Hecquet lay in the benefits that the dissemination of the doctrine would bring mankind. Before his own paralysis finally laid him low in the 1730s, Hecquet was always a medical optimist. Once mechanism was adopted, diseases would be correctly understood and successfully fought.[36] Indeed, mechanists could even ensure that disease was kept at arm's length to a

[33] In so doing, he claimed that he was following in the footsteps of a number of Parisian doctors from the middle of the sixteenth century, such as Guillaume Baillou (1538–1616), who had replaced the dogmatism of the Arabs by a return to Hippocratic 'simplicity': *De Purganda Medicina*, p. ix. For a recent study of the work of Baillou and his colleagues, see I.M. Lonie, 'The "Paris Hippocratics": Teaching and Research in Paris in the Second Half of the Sixteenth Century', in A. Wear, R.K. French and I.M. Lonie (eds.), *The Medical Renaissance of the Sixteenth Century* (Cambridge, 1985), pp. 155–74.

[34] 'Quod enim exequi vetus, eloqui docet medicina recens, illinc veniunt operum medicina documenta, hinc momenta rationum.' Ph. Hecquet, *Hippocratis Aphorismi, ad mentem ipsius, artis usum, et corporis Mechanismi rationem expositi*, (Paris, 1724), 'proloquium', pp. xiii–iv.

[35] In a publication of 1733 Hecquet proposed the foundation of a medical academy which would digest and rationalize the observational knowledge of the ancients and moderns so far committed to print. It would next identify the gaps and entrust the task of filling them to honoured contemporary practitioners. The *mémoires* of the academy would become a medical 'law' code. See [Ph. Hecquet], *Le Brigandage de la Medecine dans la manière de traiter les petites veroles et les plus grandes maladies par l'Emetique, la saignée du pied et le Kermes mineral*, part 2 (Utrecht, 1733), pp. 206–30.

[36] E.g. *Novus Medicinae Conspectus* [1722], part 1, 'Physiologia', prologue, no pagination.

certain extent through their proper understanding of prophylaxis. However, the new Jerusalem would take time to build for certain aspects of contemporary culture and medical practice seemed guaranteed to destroy the human machine rather than keep it properly oiled. Most of Hecquet's *œuvre*, therefore, was devoted to educating both public and physicians into the dangers of not following the logic of mechanist principles in their everyday lives.

Above all, Hecquet took exception to the dietary habits of the well-to-do, from whose midst, of course, most physicians (if not Hecquet himself) drew their clientele. The rich, he maintained, ate lots of meat, laced with spicy sauces and washed down with strong wine. Nothing could be more deleterious to their health. Such a diet was difficult for the body to digest, led to an imperfect coction and ultimately impaired the elasticity of the fluid-bearing organs. Given the construction of the human machine, the person who wanted to preserve his health would be a water-swilling vegetarian:

Rien n'a tant de pente à se fondre dans un suc laiteux que les semences et les grains, qui sont aussi les choses du monde qui se broyent le mieux sous le meule.[37]

If flesh was to be eaten, then it should only be fish, but not salt fish for salt was the worst enemy of the human organism, destroying the fibres.[38]

The prophylactic potential of diet, Hecquet believed, was totally ignored by contemporary physicians.[39] This was particularly true in the case of suckling infants where doctors were quite happy to permit the contemporary upper-class custom of putting out children to nurse. A more pernicious dietary habit could not be imagined. To begin with, it threatened the well-being of the new born child. Breast milk was simply a nutritive lymph of 'une tenuité inconcevable' created by trituration and pressure. As no two women had vessels of the same size and oscillatory force, the quality of their nutritive juice inevitably differed from person to person. Thus, to deprive the infant of its mother's milk, to which it had become accustomed, would have untold physiological consequences. Moreover, the nurse was usually already in full lactation and would provide the new baby with an over-rich diet:

Un lait donc trop succulent troublera tout dans l'oeconomie de ce petit corps: s'il est trop épais, il embrassera les parties au lieu de les démêler; s'il est trop vif, il les

---

[37] Ph. Hecquet, *Traité des Dispenses du Careme* (Paris, 1709), p. 16.
[38] *Ibid.*, p. 123. Ch. 18 is on fish *tout court*, and ch. 21 on salt fish.
[39] Only Sydenham (one of Hecquet's medical heroes) had understood its importance. Hecquet even in his later works, showed no awareness of the vegetarian prophylaxis of the English early eighteenth-century doctor, George Cheyne (1671–1743). Cheyne's *Essay of Health and Long Life* first appeared in 1724.

enflammera; d'où viennent tant de tranchées, de coliques, de cours de ventre, et de convulsions, qui enlevent si brusquement du monde ces tendres victimes de l'ignorance ou du préjugé.[40]

Moreover, Hecquet insisted, were mothers to start suckling their children, then their own health would subsequently benefit. The number of post-partum deaths among nursing mothers was far fewer than among those who abandoned their children. Even the prevalence of breast cancer might be linked to putting out children to nurse:

Car enfin qui empêchera de croire, que les glandes des mamelles faites comme elles sont pour dépurer le sang et filtrer une liqueur, puissent s'imbiber d'une serosité maligne au lieu du suc laiteux auquel elles étoient destinées.[41]

Clearly man's own stupidity lay at the root of much of his ill-health. What angered Hecquet in addition was that when disease inevitably struck the physicians themselves compounded the evil with the way they abused the therapeutic weapons they had at their disposal.

In particular Hecquet objected to the contemporary adulation of purgatives, a reflection, he believed, of the pernicious influence of his iatrochemical opponents who avidly championed their use. Hecquet was not against the prescription of purgatives altogether, as he was always careful to emphasize. He did feel, however, that they should be deployed very carefully. This was because they worked, not by causing a reaction in the fluids as the chemists believed, but by stimulating the solids. As the latter could very easily be over-stimulated, administering a purgative might make the disease even worse. A careful physician, therefore, would avoid using violent purgatives and never purge at the onset of a disease, when the body was most out of equilibrium. Moreover, the careful physician would never purge indiscriminately. Carthartics were to be used only to evacuate a humour which had become lodged in the wrong place. Because of their dire effect on vascular elasticity they were not to be applied in a non-humoral disease or simply for giving the system a shake-up.[42]

Unfortunately, contemporary physicians paid no heed to the potential dangers of purgation. Rather they gave their patients cathartics at the moment the disease appeared.[43] At the same time, misunderstanding the internal causes of many diseases, they tended to use purgatives as a cure-all. Purgatives, for instance, were constantly and ineffectively

[40] Ph. Hecquet, *De l'obligation aux femmes de nourir leurs enfans*, (Trevoux, 1708), p. 72. The dangers to the child are related in ch. 4. Hecquet was still emphasizing the need for the mother to feed her own child at the end of his life; see Ph. Hecquet, *Le Brigandage de la Chirurgie ou la Medecine opprimée par le brigandage de la Chirurgie* (Utrecht, 1738), pp. 129–30.
[41] Hecquet, *De l'obligation*, p. 82.
[42] See esp. *De Purganda Medicina*, chs. 13, 18, 19, 21 and 22.
[43] Hecquet, *Brigandage de la Medecine*, p. 3.

used to counter the plague, although there was no sign that this was a humoral disease.[44] Worst of all, Hecquet's colleagues favoured the strongest purgatives on the market, not mild cathartics such as the *anodin minéral* of the Halle professor Friedrich Hoffmann (1660–1742), a drug that Hecquet supposedly introduced into France through his friendship with the imperial physician, Garelli.[45]

As Hecquet's life drew to a close, his suspicion of all chemically prepared drugs, even anodyne ones, seems to have grown. Eventually he favoured a pharmacoepia of none but natural substances, on the grounds that composite preparations, even if their effect was purportedly mild, could be too easily constructed from adulterated ingredients. Why, then, should the physician risk the well-being of his patient by prescribing these concoctions, when there were natural alternatives more readily available? If a physician needed a purgative, he could have recourse to a mild mineral water.

[Hot springs] conservent depuis la Création du Monde une chaleur toujours égale, sulphureuse, souvent sans aucune apparence sensible de souffre; de sorte que comme des basins toujours prêts, elles conservent depuis tant de siècles une égalité de chaleur qui a toute la puissance du feu sans en avoir le brûlant ou le caustic.[46]

Hecquet's advocacy of natural remedies led him at the end of his life to promote the value of numerous folk medicines whose efficacy and preparation he had learnt from conversations with friends and from his wide reading of medical literature and contemporary journals. It was his contention that the homespun remedies of peasants and wise women often cured much more quickly and successfully than the exotic drugs of medical practitioners. Their knowledge, therefore, was not something to deride but rather collect and popularize for the benefit of the poor, especially in the countryside, who had no chance of availing themselves of professional help. It was for this reason that Hecquet was preparing on his death a self-help medical manual for the poor, which finally appeared in 1740.[47]

---

[44] As there was no great vomiting or diarrhoea, see Hecquet's *Traité sur la peste* (Paris, 1722), pp. 115–25. If any drug was administered to a plague victim, it should be opium to calm the solids, whose elasticity had been impaired by inhaling air infected by plague particles (p. 37).

[45] Saint-Marc, p. 105; Hecquet also apparently used the 'gouttes anodines' of Sydenham.

[46] Ph. Hecquet, *Le Brigandage de la Pharmacie*, pp. 54–5. Separately paginated in Ph. Hecquet, *Le Brigandage de la Chirurgie*, [1738]. It had to be a mild mineral water. In *Le Brigandage de la Medecine* he complained that contemporary physicians were no longer recommending the gentle waters of Bourbon or Vichy, but promoting instead more vitriolic springs, especially 'les eaux de Vahls'; these, moreover, they made totally insupportable by getting their patients to drink them mixed with Glauber or Epsom salts (part 2, pp. 149–52).

[47] Ph. Hecquet, *La Médecine et la chirurgie des pauvres* (Paris, 1758). Hecquet's belief in the value of homespun remedies is stressed in the 'Avertissement'. A number of similar publications had appeared in France in the course of the seventeenth and early eighteenth centuries, so

Hecquet's growing alienation from the use of composite drugs was a reflection of his deep-seated belief in the 1720s and 1730s that the medical profession was in crisis. A therapeutics which emphasized above all the indiscriminate application of violent, chemical purgatives, turned the practice of medicine into an empirical art. No longer closely tied to physiology and pathology, the profession lost its scientific status and could be exercised by the unqualified quack as easily as the licensed physician. (This was a view also held in England as Harold Cook and Andrew Wear point out in their chapters.) It was for this reason, Hecquet believed, that medicine had now fallen prey to so many amateur interlopers:

Une femme donc entreprenante, un Barbier présomptueux, un Droguiste téméraire, un Moyne ennuyé, et tout ce qu'il y aura de gens desoeuvrez, oisifs, ou malheureux, entreprendront d'exercer la medecine, parce qu'on a leur aura rendüe aisée à entendre, plus aisée encore à pratiquer.[48]

Of all the different *gens desoeuvrez* who raised Hecquet's hackles in the evening of his life because they had breached the physicians' legal monopoly, the most bitterly attacked for their audacity were those who belonged to the Paris Company of Surgeons. Instead of acting as the physician's manual assistant, many of the Company's members had set themselves up as independent practitioners. The surgeons, however, were completely ill-equipped to play such an unaccustomed role. They might know how to set bones and dress wounds but they were absolutely ignorant of the internal cause of disease. It made no difference either that from the middle of the 1720s the Surgeons of Saint-Côme were providing apprentices for the first time with lectures on physiology, anatomy and other medical subjects. Contemporary candidates for the *maîtrise* were just as unable to practise medicine as their predecessors, for these freshly appointed *demonstrateurs* provided totally unsuitable tuition. Generally there was no attempt to explain the human machine but merely to describe it, while what physiology was actually taught was based on hackneyed iatrochemical principles.[49]

Hecquet's dislike for this new breed of surgeon was intensified by

Hecquet's venture was not original. These are discussed in A. Wear, 'Popularized Ideas of Health and Illness in Seventeenth-Century France', *Seventeenth-Century French Studies*, VIII (1986), pp. 229–42. Earlier works differed from Hecquet's in that they attempted to instruct the poor in the causes of disease; Hecquet merely supplied a list of remedies. For eighteenth-century popular pharmacopoeias, see Mireille Laget and Claudine Lou, *Médecine et chirurgie des pauvres aux XVIIIe siècle* (Paris, 1984).

[48] Ph. Hecquet, *Observations sur la saignée du pied et sur la purgation (au commencement de la Petite Vérole, des Fievres malignes et des grandes maladies)* (Paris, 1724), pp. 344–5.

[49] Hecquet, *Le Brigandage de la Chirurgie*, 'lettre introductoire', 25 Oct. 1736, esp. p. 8.

the fact that these modern descendants of Ambroise Paré were threatening the livelihoods of pharmacists and midwives, not just those of fellow physicians. The surgeon, in his conceit, was playing the role of general practitioner. Hecquet's denunciation of the male midwife at the end of his life was nothing new, for he had inveighed against the practice as early as 1708. It was only in the 1730s, however, that he specifically identified the fashionable *accoucheur* as a renegade surgeon.[50] Hecquet regarded the male midwife as a superfluous and dangerous species. Ninety-nine births out of a hundred were unproblematic and could easily be dealt with by a *sage-femme*. Where there were complications, then a physician, not an ignorant surgeon needed to be called. The danger in using a male midwife was that the latter, confident in his own powers, would fail to seek professional advice when it was required, whereas the dutiful *sage-femme* always knew when she was out of her depth. Male midwives, moreover, had a habit of ingratiating themselves into a family and becoming permanent consultants of female and infantile disorders, for which again they were totally unqualified. The result could be an unnecessary and fatal resort to the knife. 'Car par un jugement précipité qui fait traiter de cancer ou de scrophules, par exemple, toutes glandes endurcies dans les mamelles, [il] conclut trop volontiers à abattre une mamelle ou à extirper des glandes.'[51]

A MEDICO–RELIGIOUS UNIVERSE

Like most contemporary mechanical philosophers, Hecquet assumed in his medical works the existence of a Supreme Being, by whose divine fiat the universe had been created and organized to run according to a series of simple, identifiable rules. Hecquet's God, however, was not some distant enlightenment deity, who made heaven and earth and then stood aside. Rather, he was the Christian, if not especially Jansenist, Jehovah, with whom man had a particular relationship and whose person was always immanent.

On the one hand, Hecquet's God was the stern judge of the Old Testament. In the beginning the world had been made for man. There had been no disease for God had ensured an ecological balance whereby the elasticity of the air was perfectly suited to the physiologi-

---

[50] Ph. Hecquet, *De l'indécence aux hommes d'accoucher les femmes* (Trevoux, 1708); *Le Brigandage de la Chirurgie*, pp. 79–146. On the surgeon's role as the male midwife in early eighteenth-century Paris, see *Johannes Gesners Pariser Tagebuch 1727*, ed. U. Boschung (Bern, 1985), pp. 149–57.   [51] Hecquet, *Le Brigandage de la Chirurgie*, p. 131.

cal well-being of all forms of life. Man's disobedience, however, had brought with it a destruction of nature's equilibrium. Nature was no longer submissive to man and 'chaque être soulevé est devenu ennemi'.[52] Man thus became naturally prey to not only death but also disease, a flail that could be supernaturally intensified whenever God wished. The plague, for instance could be attributed to a subterranean inferno which existed in a particularly hot part of the world. Released on God's whim through an earthquake, its great heat periodically corrupted the air and engendered a fresh epidemic.[53]

On the other hand, Hecquet's God was the loving father of the new Covenant. It might be impossible to cheat death. Hecquet was a preformationist who believed in his Baglivian phase that God had primed the human machine to run for an alloted seventy- to eighty-year span after which the solids irreparably lost their elasticity.[54] It was impossible, too, for man to prevent himself falling foul of disease periodically. The tension of the solids could be so easily disturbed that the body's equilibrium was always finely balanced. God, however, was *adorable* not simply *puissant*. He wanted man to live out his natural span and had provided the means to counter the ills of the body, just as he had the ills of the soul.

The knowledge of how to keep fit and healthy was not something God had revealed directly. Admittedly, Genesis provided support for Hecquet's prophylactic vegetarianism in that for sixteen centuries before the Flood God had forbidden man to eat meat. As neither man nor nature changed as a result of the Deluge, it could only be concluded that human beings could survive perfectly well on a vegetarian diet and had indeed been originally constructed to do so.[55] But beyond this, divine revelation was silent. The Bible was no medical textbook. It offered instruction for the life to come, not the present life. Nor had the Christian Church through the centuries been singularly privy to the mysteries of health and disease. All that could be gleaned from the history of Christian witness was that the sober and frugal life demanded by the Gospels was no impediment to self-preservation. Longevity and sanctity seemed to go hand in hand: 'Remarque-t-on plus de santé en ceux qu'une vie licentieuse fait tous les jours vieillir avant l'âge, que parmi les personnes religieuses, qui au contraire à force de se retrancher sur tout, cedent enfin moins aux attaques de la mort.'[56]

---

[52] Hecquet, *Traité de la peste*, p. 80.   [53] *Ibid.*, pp. 61–2.
[54] See *Traité des Dispenses du Careme* [1709], p. 48. He quoted in support of this position Thomas Burnet (1635?–1715, *Telluris Theoria Sacra*), Baglivi and Pitcairne.
[55] Hecquet, *Traité des Dispenses du Careme*, esp. ch. 8.   [56] *Ibid.*, p. 3.

A knowledge of how to survive in this world came instead from being able to read the book of nature. God expected man to learn for himself the way to counter the perils which surrounded him. Evidently, from Hecquet's interest in popular medicine, this knowledge could be acquired by anybody. All the same, it is evident, too, that Hecquet believed purely empirically acquired knowledge lacked solidity; it was gained haphazardly and always imperfectly. Only the professionally trained physician, who understood the proper cause of health and disease could constantly and successfully ensure man his natural span. Such professional power made the physician extremely important. In Hecquet's eyes he was a quasi-priest administering to the body as the clergyman administered to the soul. This analogy was sanctioned, moreover, by the activity of Christ and his Apostles as healers. The profession was thereby hallowed and its members set apart from other laymen. Furthermore, at Paris at any rate, the quasi-religious function of the physician was peculiarly emphasized by the manner in which graduands received their licence to practise, which took the form of a second baptism. The degree was bestowed by the chancellor of the cathedral of Notre-Dame, who admitted the new physician in the name of the Trinity and made the sign of the cross over his head. At the same time, the licentiate swore to uphold the truth to the last drop of his blood. This, insisted Hecquet, was not just the truth of Hippocrates but the truth of the Christian faith.[57]

If the physician was a quasi-priest he necessarily had to behave in a manner that would accord with his dignity and calling. He must set an example to the outside world by his commitment and sobriety. Hecquet believed, too, that the libertine would be an unsuccessful practitioner, however learned. Although never specifically stating his metaphysical opinions (indeed, as we saw, suggesting that the study of the essence of things was not the duty of the physician), there can be little doubt that he was an occasionalist, attributing the movement of matter, not to matter itself, but to the will of God. Jehovah might work through nature but the efficacy of a cure depended on the co-operation of the Holy Spirit, elicited through the piety of the physician:

C'est aux prieres des Medecins, c'est à la pureté de leurs moeurs, à la sagesse, et à leur piété... que le Saint Esprit attache les succès des Remedes; et ces succès deviennent par consequent des benedictions, quand les Remedes sont administrez dans les vûes et suivant l'institution du Créateur.[58]

[57] Anon, [Ph. Hecquet], *Reponse à la question: si les Medecins peuvent ou doivent prendre part dans les affaires de l'Eglise*, (m.p., 1726) pp. 2–4.

[58] *Ibid.*, pp. 1–2. According to Nicéron, p. 101, Hecquet, when faced with a difficult case, would always preface his treatment with a prayer for divine aid.

Medicine was in crisis in the early eighteenth century not simply because the influence of the iatrochemists promoted dangerous therapies and encouraged unqualified interlopers. It was also in crisis because of a breakdown of medical mores. The younger generation of physicians especially, maintained Hecquet, were venal, immodest and expensively dressed. 'C'est le velours, l'or et l'hermine qui font aujourd'hui la parure de jeunes medecins.' Whereas the true physician travelled on foot, the contemporary *médecin* always travelled by coach, eager to see as many patients as he could in a day. Such physicians, all too prevalent in the Paris faculty of the 1730s, were turning the practice of medicine into a commercial art:

Ces guerisseurs... attirés à Paris pour la plus part, par l'odeur ou le fumet de la fortune, ils n'y viennent que pour gagner de l'argent, en se fourant dans les pratiques (comme ils parlent) par l'intelligence, ou par brigue, et dans les postes ou places vacantes, par presents ou par argent. Ce sont des esclaves de l'argent, qui y asservissent ainsi leurs personnes et leur travail . . ., en faisant d'un art libre et desinteressé, un metier, un gagne-pain ou une profession assujettie à l'interêt.[59]

Needless to say, the iatrochemist and the venal physician were one and the same, just as the impudent interloper could not possibly be a well-meaning quack but must necessarily be a mercenary scoundrel. Indeed, Hecquet was at pains to paint the surgeon-turned-general practitioner as godless as well as greedy. It was the accepted medical custom that the physician handed over his incurable patients in good time to the church, so that they might receive the appropriate spiritual consolation. Surgeons, however, ignored this convention and let the wretched inhabitants of their venereal clinics expire without the comfort of the priest.[60] Male midwifes, too, were criminally blasé about miscarriages. An aborted foetus was a potential human being, not a 'faux germe', and in consequence destined for eternal damnation like all unbaptized infants. The *accoucheur*, instead of encouraging society women to lead their normal lives during pregnancy, should warn his clients of the terrible results of miscarrying. Pregnant women should always be vigilant 'pour ne pas peupler l'enfer de réprouvés'.[61]

[59] Hecquet, *Le Brigandage de la Medecine* part 1 [1732], pp. 18–20. Hecquet himself abandoned visiting patients on foot in 1698 and took to horseback. Later in life he even travelled by coach. However, he used the coach, we are told, not for display, but as a mobile library in order not to waste precious time. All Hecquet's biographers agree that he deliberately had few patients and tried to spend an equal amount of time with each, rich or poor. It was for this reason that he turned down the prestigious position as *médecin* at the Hôtel-Dieu; there were far too many patients there for him to treat them properly: see Nicéron, *Mémoires*, pp. 90–1.
[60] Hecquet, *Le Brigandage de la Chirurgie* [1738], pp. 148–9. Not surprisingly, Hecquet himself was exceptionally scrupulous. On one occasion he even refused to begin the treatment of a dangerously ill libertine until she had called a priest and confessed: Roger, *Hecquet*, pp. 24–5.
[61] Hecquet, *Le Brigandage de la Chirurgie*, pp. 105–6.

The Hecquet who attacked the mores of contemporary medical practitioners clearly spoke from the standpoint of the Jansenist, not just the Christian physician. It was the voice of the man who viewed all human beings as depraved and automatically equated opposition, be it to the blinding truth of medical mechanism or to the legally sanctioned medical hierarchy, with self-seeking wilfulness. To a man for whom the Fall was a living and pervasive event, the therapeutic anarchy engendered by the activities of the iatrochemists must have seemed analogous to the breakdown of the natural order that was the consequence of the disobedience of Adam and Eve. Similarly, the young physicians who flaunted the advice of their wiser elders and the surgeons who broke their oath of fealty to the faculty were the true successors of our first parents, trying to raise themselves above their appointed station: 'C'est la vanité, le faste, l'esprit de revolte contre leurs maîtres, ou la présomption qui enivre la plupart des Chirurgiens contre la Medecine.'[62]

Hecquet's Jansenism also fuelled his hostility towards male midwifery in particular. Like the good Augustinian he was, he considered mankind not only greedy and ambitious but also lascivious. Thus, to allow a man to examine a woman intimately over several months and be present at the birth of her child was not just embarrassing to the female sensibility; it was morally dangerous. The *accoucheur* himself would always be a prey to lustful thoughts as a result of such an association, however much he brought a professional detachment to the task, and sin lay in the thought as much as the deed.[63] But the subject of his attentions was placed in a much more perilous position. The daughters of Eve were notorious for their libidinous instincts. Once roused by the clinical caress of the male midwife, their sexual desires would become uncontrollable. Thereby male midwifery threatened the social, not just the medical, order:

Car à force de se laisser toucher par des hommes, ne pourroit-on pas se familiariser à des attouchemens étrangers et dangereux? Et en ce cas la fidelité dans les mariages seroit-elle bien en sûreté?[64]

The drift of the argument is clear: Hecquet's Jansenist Christianity coloured his hostility towards his medical opponents by encouraging

---

[62] *Ibid.*, 'avertissement', p. iv.

[63] Hecquet, *De l'indécence aux hommes d'accoucher les femmes*, [1708] esp. pp.4–5 and ch. 4, *passim*. Hecquet's fears had been raised on many previous occasions in the works of opponents of male midwifery; Louise Bourgeois (c. 1563–1636), the *accoucheuse* of Marie de Medicis, had warned of the effect on private morals if men were introduced into the delivery chamber as early as 1609: see F. Damour, *Louise Bourgeois* (Paris, 1900), pp. 30–1.

[64] Hecquet, *De l'indécence*, p. 39. Note the use of the impersonal "on". Is this indicative of Hecquet's fear or contempt of the female sex?

him to equate iatrochemists and interlopers with libertines. It is possible, however, to go further and suggest that Hecquet's mechanist convictions themselves were stimulated by his Jansenist leanings. Admittedly, there is no evidence for this in the Parisian doctor's writings. The plausibility of the hypothesis lies in the fact that the mechanical philosophy seemed to have had a particular attraction for the Jansenist community *tout court*. This is not to say that every Jansenist was a mechanist, for this is patently untrue. A number of important members of the movement in the middle of the seventeenth century dismissed all natural philosophies as vain and idle speculation. Man's intelligence was too grossly impaired by the Fall to understand the divine handiwork.[65] Nor can it be seriously maintained that every supporter of mechanism in the France of Louis XIV was a Jansenist. This is an equally absurd assertion when the foremost French exponent of Cartesianism in this period, Nicolas Malebranche (1638–1715), developed a view of the relationship between God and man which won the applause of the Jansenists' bitterest opponents, the Jesuits.[66] Nevertheless, that there was a definite connection between the two movements was recognized by contemporaries and has been commented on by a number of historians of philosophy. It was not just that Port-Royal was the spiritual Alma Mater of several famous mechanical philosophers, especially the redoubtable Antoine Arnauld (1612–94). More importantly, mechanism was taken up by the wider Jansenist movement. Thus the two regular orders most successfully penetrated by the ideas of the *Augustinus*, the Benedictines and the Oratorians, were also hotbeds of philosophical radicalism. Furthermore, it was Jansenists or crypto-Jansenists who first introduced the mechanical philosophy into the university and college classroom, figures such as Pierre Cally at Caen in the 1670s.[67]

[65] E.g. Monsieur de Sasi; his views are discussed in Fontaine, II, pp. 50–74.

[66] Fr. Bouillier, *Histoire de la philosophie cartésienne*, 2 vols. (Paris, 1868), II, ch. 5. Malebranche is remembered in particular as the author of the *Recherches de la vérité* which first appeared in 1674 and was then revised on several occasions until the definitive edition was published in 1712. For a recent study of his thought, see D. Radnor, *Malebranche. A Study of a Cartesian System* (Assen, 1978).

[67] Unfortunately, there is no detailed study to date of the linkage. For information about the spread of Cartesian ideas in French universities and colleges, see L.W.B. Brockliss, *Higher Education in Seventeenth and Eighteenth Century France: A Cultural History* (Oxford, 1987), chs. 4 and 7, *passim*. Telling evidence of the close relationship between Cartesianism and Jansenism in the academic world lies in the fact that the authorities often moved to outlaw both sets of opinions together; for example, at the university of Paris in 1704: see Jourdain, 'pièces justicatives', pp. 134–8. Pierre Cally (1630–1709) was never openly accused of Jansenism but he had a very Augustinian view of man's freewill; see the theses sustained before him in 1670 where freedom is defined simply as liberty from constraint and no attempt is made to discuss the Tridentine doctrine that the will is 'radically' free (Bibliothèque Nationale, *Départment des Imprimés*, RZ 104), pp. 35–6.

The reasons for this Jansenist penchant for the mechanical philosophy were arguably twofold. To begin with, the supporters of mechanism, like the Jansenists themselves, were only tolerated under sufferance in the second half of the seventeenth century. Although mechanists were not persecuted in the same way as many Jansenists, who were often forced into exile (for example Arnauld and Quesnel), the crown and the church made no secret of their hostility towards dogmatic upholders of the philosophy, especially if they were in a position to influence the young. Thus, before 1700 an attempt was definitely made to keep full-blooded Cartesian mechanists out of the new *Académie des Sciences*, and on numerous occasions in the period 1670–1705 regular and secular professors of philosophy and physics were ordered not to teach the fundamental tenets of Cartesianism.[68] Primarily, the authorities seem to have felt that the Cartesians in particular were crypto-protestants in that an equation of matter with extension made a philosophical defence of transubstantiation impossible. Like the Jansenists, the Cartesians loudly protested their innocence, Descartes himself suggesting two defences of the orthodox position, but the accusation was never dropped.[69] It seems quite likely, then, that some Jansenists were attracted to the mechanical philosophy simply out of an understandable sympathy for another movement which had unjustly incurred the wrath of the establishment.

However, there was also a more solid intellectual affinity drawing Jansenists towards the mechanist camp. In the first place, there was the fact that Descartes had underpinned his philosophy with an omnipotent, nominalist God, only partially knowable by man and certainly not restricted in His creation of the world to the rationally feasible. Such a deity could not but be attractive to rigid Augustinians antagonized by the attempt of Jesuit theologians to define and limit God's grandeur by the canons of human logic.[70] In the second place, the dualism implicit in all mechanist thinking struck an immediate chord in the Augustinian mind. Jansenists, too, interpreted the world

[68] R. Hahn, *The Anatomy of a Scientific Institution: the Paris Academy of Sciences 1666–1803* (London, 1971), pp. 30–4; J. Duhamel, 'Quaedam Recentiorum Philosophorum ac Praesertim Cartesii Propositiones Damnatae ac Prohibitae', in J. Duhamel *Philosophia Universalis, sive Commentarius in Universam Aristotelis Philosophiam ad usum Scholarum Comparatam*, 5 vols. (Paris, 1705), v, appendix; the latter provides a list of institutional pronouncements against the new philosophy.

[69] Bouillier, *Histoire de la philosophie cartésienne* I, pp. 207–9, 431–50. Many later Cartesians, too, attempted to develop a mechanist explanation of transubstantiation but the establishment was always hostile. Cally, for instance, author of one such attempt, was made to retract his views from the pulpit in 1701; see G. Vattier, 'La Doctrine cartésienne de l'Eucharistie dans Pierre Cally' *Annales de la philosophie chrétienne* (1911–12), 274–96, 380–409.

[70] This is not to say that Descartes himself was an Augustinian. A detailed study of his view of the relationship between knowledge and faith suggests that he is more correctly described as a Thomist; see H. Gouhier, *La Pensée religieuse de Descartes* (Paris, 1924), esp. pp. 266–313.

through a series of polar opposites: God and the Devil, the saved and the reprobate, sin and grace, flesh and spirit. The idea of the man machine, an automaton responding in a predictable, unstoppable way to external stimuli, gelled neatly with their view of post-lapsarian man, the slave of his passions and deservedly damned unless a merciful God guided his actions through divine grace. Finally, the whole mechanist enterprise suggested that its supporters and the Jansenists were engaged in a common struggle. Both were fighting a common enemy in medieval scholasticism. Mechanists wanted to wipe the slate clean and construct a new natural philosophy based on the study of things rather than words. Jansenists, on the other hand, wanted to simplify and refurbish theology by going back to its original roots. They may not have been in the business of creating a science of God *de novo*, but in elevating Augustine above the scholastics, they were imitating the mechanists in attempting to place theology on a sure foundation. For the mechanist, this was the book of nature; for Jansenists, the Bible and the works of the church fathers.

Both Jansenists and mechanists, moreover, were involved in a great utilitarian crusade. Just as the mechanists looked to the material benefits (especially in medicine) which would accrue from a better understanding of nature, so the Jansenists, paradoxically given their pessimistic view of mankind, hoped to promote the true Christian life. The mechanical philosophy and Jansenism, therefore, if independently developed, were definitely analogous, secular and spiritual manifestations of a common conceptual approach to the world. If it is right to assume that Hecquet's Jansenism predated his adherence to iatromechanism, it is surely plausible that his religious commitment aided his scientific conversion. Even if he failed to grasp the analogy between the two movements, the very fact that he worked as physician to Port-Royal must surely have encouraged him to explore the mechanical philosophy.

Admittedly, Hecquet did not embrace the dogmatic Cartesianism associated with Antoine Arnauld and the mid-seventeenth-century *Port-Royalistes*. His was a more empirically orientated mechanism with an impatience of metaphysics and a stress on experimentation which was a long way removed from Descartes' aprioristic natural philosophy.[71] But this was understandable. Hecquet's more

---

[71] It is now accepted that Descartes was not a rationalist *tout court*. He insisted that his causal physics was experientially based and that mechanical explanations of natural phenomena must be experientially validated. Nevertheless, he rejected the idea of torturing and measuring nature to test the success of his hypotheses and promoted the sufficiency of commonsense observation; see D.M. Clarke, *Descartes' Philosophy of Science* (London, 1982), esp. chs. 2 and 7.

probabilist mechanism was a commonplace among French experimental philosophers in the early eighteenth century. To the extent it came to dominate the *Académie des Sciences* it could be called the scientific orthodoxy. It would have been well-nigh impossible, therefore, for him to have been a rigid Cartesian.[72] As it was, in adopting a more flexible mechanism Hecquet was scarcely reneging on his Jansenist roots. There was more to Jansenist mechanism than *arnauldisme*. Hecquet's empiricist mechanism had been anticipated in the middle of the seventeenth century by the one serious Jansenist experimental philosopher, on the fringe of the Port-Royal community but not of it, Blaise Pascal (1623–62). Indeed, if there is one predominant influence underlying Hecquet's medico-religious universe it is undoubtedly the author of the *Pensées* and the *Lettres Provinciales*. To describe Hecquet as a Jansenist and a medical mechanist is to distinguish quite inappropriately his religious and scientific interests. He should be called much more accurately a *Pascalien*. The only aspect of Hecquet's philosophy (before his final years) with which Pascal would have disagreed was the Parisian doctor's reverence for Hippocrates. Pascal could not accept 'authorities' in natural philosophy. But Pascal was not a practising *médecin*, forced by the limitations of personal experience to rely on the observations of others willy-nilly. Had he been one, then he might have been more sympathetic to the scientific inheritance of classical antiquity.[73]

MIRACLES AND CONVULSIONS

Hecquet did not only strengthen his medical prejudices through his religious opinions, but also used his science to confirm his theology. Like most mechanists before Kant, he saw in the simplicity and elegance of the human machine unimpeachable evidence for the existence of a wise and powerful creator. Less conventionally, in his old age at any rate, he believed that the actual practice of medicine had a positive moral value as it taught the physician the vanity of human wishes. In contrast to his earlier therapeutic optimism, the dying Hecquet saw the medical art as always uncertain. Even if the patient was saved, the physician only delayed the hour of death:

[72] The fullest, if rather indigestible, study is C. Salomon-Bayet, *L'Institution de la science et l'expérience du vivant: méthode et expérience à l'Académie Royale des Sciences 1666–1793* (Paris, 1978).

[73] Pascal's conception of the correct method of investigating nature is forcefully stated in his preface to the posthumous *Traité du vide*; see B. Pascal. *Œuvres complètes*, ed. L. Lafuma (Paris, 1963), pp. 230–2. Pascal's view of science is most recently discussed in H.M. Davidson, *Blaise Pascal* (Boston, Mass., 1983), ch. 2.

Si la contemplation des merveilles du Créateur dans l'ordonnance des parties du corps humain, est si propre à élever la Foi d'un Médecin, à l'exercer et à l'exciter, quoi de plus capable de la nourrir par la piété, que cette considération continuelle de la mort, et la présence non interrompuë de la derniere fin de l'homme.[74]

This readiness to use science in support of religion was most amply demonstrated in the pamphlets which Hecquet wrote against the *convulsionnaires* of Saint-Médard in the years 1733–6. The history of this celebrated group of religious enthusiasts needs to briefly sketched. The Jansenists, like many persecuted religious minorities, had always been strengthened in their conviction of the godliness of their movement by the number of apparently miraculous cures which had occurred when believers touched relics belonging to the Port-Royal community or sympathetic bishops. It was only after 1725, however, in response perhaps to the obvious failure of the appeal to a General Council against the Bull *Unigenitus*, that the trickles of Jansenist miracles became a flood. In particular, a thaumaturgical cult quickly developed in the late 1720s around the tomb of the saintly Jansenist deacon, François de Pâris, who had died in May 1727 and been buried in the Paris cemetery of Saint-Médard. By 1731 the cult was so extensive and so many people claimed to have been cured by the intercession of the pious deacon, that the civil and ecclesiastical authorities became disturbed. Moreover, their hostility grew even greater after July 1731 when first of all patients actually placed on the tomb and then many observers began to experience uncontrollable convulsions. As a result, the cemetery was closed by royal decree in January 1732. But this was not the end of the affair. A number of women, who had been supposedly cured at Saint-Médard, continued to have convulsive fits in the privacy of their own or others' homes. More importantly, while in the grip of their frenzy, many claimed the ability themselves to cure diseases, notably one Charlotte de la Porte, known from her therapeutic technique as 'La Suceuse'.[75]

Even in the second half of the seventeenth century a number of important Jansenists, such as the moral philospher Pierre Nicole, were highly sceptical of the miraculous cures attributed to Jansenist relics. Such extravagant claims, they felt, only gave ammunition to the Jansenists' enemies. The unseemly cult of the deacon Pâris and the contemporaneous sponsorship of provincial Jansenist thaumaturges convinced many of the educated supporters of the movement (both

---

[74] Hecquet, *La Medecine théologique* [1733], preface, pp. xlix–xli.
[75] The two most recent studies of the movement are: J. Kreiser, *Miracles, Convulsions and Ecclesiastical Politics in Early Eighteenth Century Paris* (Princeton, N.J., 1978); C.L. Maire, *Les Convulsionnaires de Saint-Médard* (Paris, 1985).

laity and clerics) that the earlier suspicions had been well founded. In the dawning age of the enlightenment the irreverent antics in the cemetery of Saint-Médard made Jansenism a laughing-stock. The movement in consequence abruptly divided into two and a flurry of pamphlets appeared from Jansenists pens either supporting or condemning the *convulsionnaires*.[76]

Hecquet's position in the controversy appears to have been midway between the two sides. Initially, he seems to have accepted the genuineness of the spate of Jansenist miracles that began in the mid-1720s. Certainly, he supported the authenticity of the first reported miracle in the series, the cure of the semi-paralyzed Mme La Fosse in May 1725, divinely purged in the course of a religious procession by the sight of the holy sacrament, which had been consecrated by the appellant doctor of theology, J.B. Goy (dates unknown).[77] Even as late as 1733 he insisted that he had no quarrel with the miracles originally worked 'par l'intercession de Monsieur de Pâris'.[78] On the other hand, Hecquet broke totally with the enthusiastic wing of the Jansenist party over the godliness of the *convulsionnaires*. The latter, he insisted, were neither cured by the thaumaturgical powers of the Jansenist saint, nor divinely inspired to heal the sick in their turn. The convulsions that they experienced were not a gift of God but a punishment. While the true believer visited the deacon's tomb in the hope that God in his mercy *might* relieve their ills, the first *convulsionnaire* had attended Saint-Médard *expecting* a cure. God, therefore, had given her convulsions for her temerity.[79]

Hecquet's alienation from the *convulsionnaires* had two roots. In the first place, he was convinced that their ecstasy was erotic, not religious. What other explanation could there be for the women's readiness to display their underclothes and their constant demands, when in the throes of a fit, that male spectators soothed their agony by standing on their stomachs or pressing their breasts? The *convulsionnaires* were not divinely inspired but lower-class women of

[76] For a typical 'enlightened' response to the *convulsionnaires*, see Voltaire, *The Age of Louis XIV* (London, 1961), pp. 438–9.

[77] Anon. [Ph. Hecquet], *Lettres d'un medecin de Paris à un medecin de province sur le miracle arrivé sur une femme du Faubourg S. Antoine* (n.p., 1725). There are two letters, one dated 19 July, the other 6 Aug. 1725.

[78] Anon. [Ph. Hecquet], *Le Naturalisme des convulsions dans les maladies de l'epidémie convulsionnaire* (Soleure [Paris?], 1733), p. 1.

[79] *Ibid.*, p. 139. Hecquet's hostility to the *convulsionnaires* probably accounts for the fact that his death in 1736 went unrecorded in the underground Jansenist periodical *Les Nouvelles Ecclésiastiques*. Certainly he lost a number of his Jansenist friends because of his position; see Saint-Marc, pp. 78–81.

dubious virtue gaining an easy subsistence by tricking respectable Jansenist clerics into giving them money.[80]

In the second place, Hecquet's love of order bridled at the subliminal feminism that surfaced when the *convulsionnaires* went into fits. They not only played the role of the physician by pretending to cure the sick, but turned the world completely upside down by pretending to be priests:

L'un[e] s'est cru[e] Pape ou Evêque, de sorte qu'[elle] passoit la mitre en tête donnant ses béndictions au peuple. Les figures faisoient rire, mais celles des filles qui disent la Messe scandalisent les fidèles, deshonorent nos mystéres et dégradent la Religion.[81]

It was quite impossible, in consequence, to suppose that God approved of the *convulsionnaires'* activities. The Paris theologians who defended the godliness of the movement were betraying their Jansenist predecessors, who would never have allowed themselves to be associated with such immodest behaviour.[82]

Hecquet was convinced that the convulsions, even if a divine chastisement, were naturally caused.[83] In fact, they were nothing other than a severe attack of the vapours. Relying closely on the writings of the Halle professor, Hoffmann, he insisted that the convulsions were the result of abnormally vigorous contractions of the muscular fibres, which in turn were the product of retained lymph. Such retention was commonplace in girls in their late teens, especially in the lower abdomen, because it was the lymph that provided the nourishment for babies in the womb. The extraordinary behaviour of the *convulsionnaires* in the grips of their fit was therefore nothing novel. Hoffmann in his study of the vapours gave an account of patients whose ecstasy caused them to crow like a cock or moo like a cow.[84] The erotic side of the malady, too, was well documented. The cure, as a result, was simple:

Que les opulentes bourses qui se cotisent depuis des années pour l'entretien de ces créatures à rien faire que scandaliser la religion et la raison, fournissent des dotes pour

---

[80] Anon. [Ph. Hecquet], *Réponse à la lettre d'un confesseur (touchant le devoir des médecins et des chirurgiens, au sujet des miracles et convulsions)*, 15 May 1733 (n.p., n.d.), p. 8.

[81] Hecquet, *Le Naturalisme des convulsions*, p. 104.

[82] Hecquet, *Réponse à la lettre d'un confesseur*, pp. 25–6.

[83] Interestingly, Hecquet never suggested the women were demonically possessed. Indeed, he does not seem to have recognized the possibility of possession at all. Significantly, he judged earlier cases of mass convulsions as also naturally caused, including the notorious incident in the Richelieu era involving the Ursulines of Loudun. See Anon. [Ph. Hecquet], *Reponse des medecins au défi que leur font les convulsionnistes* (n.p., 1736), p. 1.

[84] See, in particular, Anon. [Ph. Hecquet], *Lettre sur la convulsionnaire en extase ou la vapoureuse en rêve* (n.p., 1736). Hecquet does not cite the works of Hoffmann that he has used, and merely refers to the results of the Halle professor's investigations into cases of ecstasy.

procurer des maris à ces filles, et bientôt vous verrez vuide les Auberges des Convulsionnaires.[85]

Hecquet, however, was not content to deploy his science to demonstrate merely the naturalism of the *convulsionnaires'* contortions. He felt it necessary if the movement was to be totally discredited, to show that the cures the women claimed to have undergone and to be capable themselves of procuring were also naturally explicable. Both claims, he agreed, might be bogus but this could not be ascertained until the women had been properly investigated by professional physicians. As this had not been permitted so far (in 1736), for the *convulsionnaires* performed their miracles in private, the best that could be done was to take them at their word but show that they were deluded in believing themselves the beneficiaries of a special divine intervention.[86]

Hecquet particularly interested himself in the case of Charlotte de la Porte, the *convulsionnaire* with the highest profile. In his opinion, La Charlotte's claim to have a miraculous sucking powder with which she could heal incurable wounds could easily be explained without recourse to the supernatural. Both Pliny and Plutarch referred to *Les Psylles*, people with a reputation for healing snake bites by suction. Charlotte was simply employing an unusual therapeutic practice, not in her case involving herself in the dangerous task of extracting poison, but merely sucking out the fetid matter from scrofulous wounds. There was nothing mysterious about the process. Suction was a species of attraction, a commonplace natural phenomenon which was of particular importance in the physiology of plants and now well understood thanks to the work of a number of Englishmen: Newton (in the *Opticks*), Freind, Derham and especially Stephen Hales (1677–1761). By sucking the wound, Charlotte drew off the morbid matter and drew into the vessels of the ulcerated part healthy lymph which acted as a 'seve balzamique' and restored the *tonus* of the damaged fibres. 'Et en cela consiste tout l'art d'une cicatrisation qui guérira naturellement les écrouelles. Aussi adieu les miracles de Charlotte.'[87]

---

[85] Hecquet, *Reponse des medecins au défi que leur font les convulsionnistes*, p. 22. The recommended therapy to reduce this plethoric state was phlebotomy.

[86] Anon. [Ph. Hecquet], *Reponse a la lettre d'un docteur en medecine de la faculté de xxx* (n.p., 1736), pp. 15–16. Some physicians did not take kindly to Hecquet's apparent readiness to accept the therapeutic powers of the *convulsionnaires*. At the beginning of this pamphlet Hecquet explains why he has done so.

[87] Anon [Ph. Hecquet], *la Suçeuse convulsionnaire ou la Psylle miraculeuse* (n.p., 1736), p. 14. Hecquet's explanation of La Charlotte's powers was the subject of attack as much as his readiness to credit their reality; see the hostile, Anon., *Lettre d'un docteur en medecine de la faculté de . . . pour servir de reponse à la Succeuse [sic] Convulsionnaire ou la Psylle miraculeuse* (n.p., n.d.), in the Bodleian collection, 3 Delta 525, no. 38.

CONCLUSION: MEDICAL MECHANISM AND JANSENISM IN
EARLY EIGHTEENTH-CENTURY PARIS

The one secure conclusion to this chapter is that the medical and
religious enthusiasms of Philippe Hecquet cannot be neatly separated
into two distinctive views of the world, for they were mutually rein-
forcing. To reiterate, Hecquet was a *Pascalien*. The earlier suggestion,
however, that Hecquet's Jansenism not merely informed, but strongly
promoted, his mechanist interests must remain at the level of a plausible but unproven hypothesis. The fact that many Jansenists were
supporters of the mechanical philosophy and that the two philosophies
were highly compatible is insufficient in itself to posit an ineluctable
connection in this specific instance. Without Hecquet's own account of
his conversion to medical mechanism, the relative weight to be attached to the formative influence of Jansenism in his scientific development can never be ascertained.

On the other hand, further progress might be made if we knew more
about the connection between medical mechanism and Jansenism in
general. We have plenty of evidence (if admittedly not of a statistically
precise kind) of the attraction of mechanism to Jansenist theologians,
clerics and professors of philosophy. But those who have emphasized
the connection between the two movements have said nothing about
its appeal to Jansenist physicians. To the best of my knowledge,
Hecquet is the first French Jansenist and medical mechanist to be
identified and studied. Clearly, it would help in evaluating the specifically Jansenist involvement in his medical philosophy, if the religious
affiliation of other French medical mechanists were to be analysed.

Unfortunately, a rapid exploration of the possibilities of such a
study has not suggested that the approach will prove very productive.
Of the hundred or so members of the Paris faculty in Hecquet's day, it
has been possible to identify a definite clutch of mechanists and
chemists by studying in particular surviving student theses. As the
dissertation record for the early eighteenth century is virtually complete, it would doubtless be possible, in time, to credit the large
majority of the doctors to one or other of the medical schools.[88] It has
proved much more difficult, however, to identify the religious alle-

---

[88] The Bibliothèque de la Faculté de Médecine at Paris possesses two collections of theses from
the early modern period compiled in the middle of the eighteenth century by the Paris physician
H.T. Baron (1707–87): 9 vols. in folio and 16 vols. in quarto. Details are given in N. Le Grand,
*La Collection des thèses de l'ancienne faculté de médecine depuis 1559 et son catalogue inédit
jusqu'à 1793* (Paris, 1913). Le Grand lists the surviving theses from the middle of the eighteenth
century until the faculty was closed by the Revolutionaries. Baron's own catalogue can be
consulted in the British Library under the title: H.T. Baron, *Quaestionum Medicarum, quae*

giance of faculty members. Hecquet was peculiar among early eighteenth-century Paris physicians because of the size of his literary output.
Most of his colleagues wrote nothing at all and even the more famous
académiciens of the faculty produced little beyond narrowly focused
scientific papers. Perhaps only the dedicated iatrochemist, Nicolas
Andry de Boisregard (1658–1745), permits a similar detailed appraisal,
an interesting figure certainly in that he was bitterly critical of
Hecquet. Indeed, his polemics in favour of meat-eating and purgatives
were deliberate ripostes to Hecquet's works.[89]

An analysis of Andry's *œuvre* has not yet been undertaken, but it
could prove instructive. He was almost certainly not a Jansenist for he
not only did not turn up at the faculty on that fateful day when the
doctors backed the appeal against *Unigenitus*, but at a later date,
according to the Jansenist periodical the *Nouvelles Ecclésiastiques*, he
apparently worked to have the decision revoked.[90] On its own, however, a knowledge of Andry's medico-religious universe would take us
little further. What is desperately needed is some way of identifying the
religious temper of the faculty *tout court*.

In the absence of the most obvious approach, a less satisfactory but
conveniently rapid alternative is to use the information provided in the
record of the faculty's appeal to the General Council. The forty-six
doctors who turned up to support the appeal were presumably staunch
Jansenists, committed enough to brave the wrath of establishment
opinion. Among the doctors who stayed away, of course, there may
have been other followers of the movement too faint-hearted or too
dependent on the establishment to risk coming out into the open. But at
least the list provides us with the names of a sizeable Jansenist coterie.
The game can then be played the other way round. Instead of fitting a
religious identity to mechanists or chemists, the Jansenists can be
provided with a medical personality.

So far the philosophical allegiance of only ten out of forty-six has
been positively identified, but the tally should improve when further
work is done on the surviving dissertations. Of the ten, eight were

---

*circa medicinae theoriam et praxim, ante duo saecula, in scholis Facultatis Medicinae
Parisiensis, agitatae sunt et discussae, Series Chronologica; cum doctorum praesidium, et
Baccalaureorum propugnantium nominibus* (Paris, 1752). This is a simple chronological list
and does not reveal the format of individual theses.

[89] N. Andry, *Le Régime du caresme* (Paris, 1710); N. Andry, *Remarques de médecine sur
differents sujets, principalement sur ce qui regarde la saignée, la purgation et le boisson* (Paris,
1710). Biographical details in *Dictionnaire biographique française* II, pp. 1013–15. On the
Hecquet–Andry quarrel, see Saint-Marc, pp. 32–3, 61; they were apparently reconciled in the
1720s.

[90] *Table raisonée des Nouvelles Ecclésiastiques*, 4 vols. (Paris, 1803), IV, pp. 919–20.

mechanists and two chemists, including the *académicien*, Etienne-François Geoffroy (1672–1731).[91] Significantly, a number of definite iatromechanists are missing from the list. When Hecquet published his monograph *De la Digestion* popularizing Baglivian mechanism in 1712, twelve faculty doctors gave the book their written testimonial. Only five of these, however, joined the appeal in October 1718.[92] Does this mean that they were opponents of Jansenism or weak-kneed supporters too timid to appear? Interestingly, four of the absentees were *académiciens* and consequently dependent on royal favour – A. Littré (1658–1725), J.B. Winslow (1664–1760), J.G. Du Verney (1648–1730), and Louis Lemery (1677–1743).[93] Unfortunately at present the question remains unanswerable for only Winslow's religious allegiance has been even partially identified. Like Andry, Winslow was almost certainly an anti-Jansenist. A protestant convert from Denmark, instructed in the catholic faith by the Augustinian but orthodox bishop, J.B. Bossuet (1627–1704), Winslow according to the *Nouvelles Ecclésiastiques* was a supporter of the revocation of the appeal in the 1720s.[94]

To date, therefore, it would appear that there was some connection between medical mechanism and Jansenism in early eighteenth-century Paris, but the relationship is only a tentative one. It was quite possible to be a Jansenist and an iatrochemist and it was equally possible to be an anti-Jansenist mechanist. The exact influence of Jansenism in Hecquet's medical development must in consequence remain a mystery. All that can be said until further research enlightens the enquiry is that his religious affiliation may have helped but certainly did not inevitably determine his conversion to medical mechanism. To that extent his religious and scientific development must be taken as being biographically separable, if in the mature man his Jansenist and mechanist enthusiasms were continually overlapping.

[91] The figure is derived from the information I have to hand about the content of Paris theses in the early eighteenth century drawn from Bibliothèque de la Faculté de Médecine, Paris, *Theses Medicae Parisiensis*, in fol. 10, vols. VIII–IX, (1663–1724).

[92] Hecquet, *De la Digestion*, frontispiece.

[93] If so, then three of their colleagues had more pluck; besides Geoffroy, the *académiciens*, Antoine de Jussieu (1686–1758) and Michel Louis Reneaume de la Gareene (1675–1739) were among the appellants. The list also included the *médecin ordinaire du roi*, J.B. Chomel (1671–1740). Otherwise physicians reliant on royal patronage are noticeably absent from the list.

[94] *Table des Nouvelles Ecclésiastiques*, IV, pp. 919–20. In the course of a graduation ceremony in 1734 Winslow purportedly delivered an oration objecting to the faculty's appeal to a General Council.

8

Isaac Newton, George Cheyne and the 'Principia Medicinae'

ANITA GUERRINI

The emergence of Isaac Newton as an intellectual force, as a patron and as a focus for social and political ideas strongly affected both medical theory and the medical profession. The influence of Newton's ideas, particularly his theory of matter on physiological theory, recast iatromechanism. Their effects ranged from chemical notions based on attracting atoms earlier in the eighteenth century, to attempts in the 1730s to resolve the mind–body relationship by means of a Newtonian ether.

The Scottish physician Archibald Pitcairne (1652–1713) and his students and disciples at Edinburgh, Leiden and Oxford envisaged a medical theory on the same level of certainty as Newton's theory of the world, which they referred to as a 'principia medicinae theoreticae mathematicae'. Indeed, they considered the two systems to be strictly analogous. Their work stemmed from the atomistic theory of matter Newton had outlined in the essay 'De natura acidorum' and from queries added to the 1706 Opticks. In 1713, the year of Pitcairne's death, the second edition of Principia appeared, with hints of a change in Newton's thoughts. This change became far more apparent in his 1717–18 revisions of the Opticks, in which Newton's previous reliance upon atomistic explanations of chemical and related phenomena shifted towards a theory relying upon various 'subtle fluids' or 'ethers'. This change, which appeared fundamental to observers although it may not have seemed so to Newton, quickly manifested itself in works on medical theory, often by the same men who had written thoroughly atomistic treatises some twenty years earlier. By the 1740s, however, mechanistic, materialistic explanations of physiology based on Newtonian natural philosophy faced challenges from

This material is based upon work supported by the National Science Foundation under Grants no. SES-82-04747 and SES-86-19503. I also wish to thank Michael A. Osborne and Andrew Wear.

several fronts, and Newton's direct influence on medical theory becomes more difficult to trace.[1]

Equally as important as Newton's intellectual influence in this period was his role as a patron, and also the emergence of a 'Newtonianism', now historically defined as an ideology of wider impact than on the scientific community alone.[2] The politics, religion and careers of self-professed 'Newtonian' physicians illustrate Newton's influence in this wider realm. A broad range of medical practitioners invoked Newton's name, in varying contexts, as the relative homogeneity of the Pitcairne group gave way to a more disparate and scattered community. The impulse toward professionalization among medical men in the eighteenth century, lately discussed by Geoffrey Holmes, becomes in this later period a central consideration both in the adoption of Newtonian ideas, and in changes in medical practice.[3]

In the following pages I shall discuss some of these Newtonian physicians, with particular emphasis on the life and career of the Scot George Cheyne (1671–1743). Cheyne's central role among Newtonian physicians has been noted often, but seldom discussed. His long and productive career, spanning the years 1700 to 1742, and his close attention to Newton's thought and its philosophical and religious implications, make him an especially good case-study of the relationship between Newtonianism and medicine.

[1] On Newton's theory of matter, see Robert E. Schofield, *Mechanism and Materialism* (Princeton, 1970); Arnold Thackray, *Atoms and Powers* (Cambridge, Mass., 1970); A.R. and M.B. Hall, 'Newton's Theory of Matter', *Isis*, LI (1960), 131–44; R.H. Kargon, *Atomism in England from Hariot to Newton* (Oxford, 1966). Newton's influence on medical theory is discussed in Theodore M. Brown, *The Mechanical Philosophy and the 'Animal Oeconomy'* (New York, 1981); Lester S. King, *The Philosophy of Medicine: The Eighteenth Century* (Cambridge, Mass., 1978); Anita Guerrini, 'Newtonian Matter Theory, Chemistry, and Medicine, 1690–1713' (University of Indiana, Ph.D. thesis, 1983). The following articles came to the author's attention after the completion of this paper: Jonathan Barry, 'Piety and the Patient: Medicine and Religion in Eighteenth-Century Bristol', in Roy Porter (ed.), *Patients and Practitioners: Lay Perceptions of Medicine in Pre-industrial Society* (Cambridge, 1985), pp. 145–75; G.S. Rousseau, 'Mysticism and Millenarianism: "Immortal Dr. Cheyne"', forthcoming in Richard Popkin (ed.), *Millenarianism and Messianism in the Enlightenment* (Berkeley).

[2] See Margaret C. Jacob, *The Newtonians and the English Revolution, 1689–1720* (Ithaca, 1976); John Gascoigne, 'Politics, Patronage and Newtonianism: the Cambridge Example', *Hist. J.*, XXVII (1984), 1–24; Stephen Shapin, 'Of Gods and Kings: Natural Philosophy and Politics in the Leibniz–Clarke Disputes', *Isis*, LXXII (1981), 187–215; Frank E. Manuel, *A Portrait of Isaac Newton* (Cambridge, Mass., 1968); Larry Stewart, 'Samuel Clarke, Newtonianism, and the Factions of Post-Revolutionary England', *J. Hist. Ideas*, XLII (1981), 53–72.

[3] Geoffrey Holmes, *Augustan England: Professions, State and Society, 1680–1730* (London, 1982); N.D. Jewson, 'Medical Knowledge and the Patronage System in Eighteenth-Century England', *Sociology*, VIII (1974), 369–85; Harold J. Cook, *The Decline of the Old Medical Regime in Stuart London* (Ithaca, 1986).

Dissatisfied with both mechanical and chemical explanations of animal function, Archibald Pitcairne turned to the works of Newton for a new approach. Trained at Edinburgh and Rheims, Pitcairne had been a founding member of the Royal College of Physicians of Edinburgh in 1681.[4] In 1687, the newly widowed physician was lodging with his good friend David Gregory (1659–1708), professor of mathematics at the University of Edinburgh and correspondent of Newton.[5] Pitcairne had probably studied mathematics with the late James Gregory, David's uncle and predecessor in the mathematics chair. Both Pitcairne and Gregory welcomed the arrival, in the later summer of 1687, of a copy of Newton's newly published *Principia*.[6] Pitcairne had already been studying the works of Borelli and Bellini, and with the arrival of Newton's work, he set himself the ambitious task of devising a new theory of medicine based on mathematics. The usefulness of the *Principia* to this programme lay less in its theory of attraction than as a model of mathematical precision, a crucial tool in the campaign Pitcairne wished to mount against qualitative, inexact chemical theories of function. In his published works, his strongest obloquy is directed not against the Cartesians (whom he also criticizes), but against the Helmontian chemists.[7]

Newton made an important contribution to this campaign with his essay 'De Natura Acidorum', which he gave to Pitcairne during the latter's visit to Cambridge in 1692. In a few pages Newton put forward the essential premises of his theory of matter: the world, he said, consisted of atoms endowed with a short-range attractive force analogous to gravity. He reaffirmed Boyle's assertion of a 'single catholick matter' in the universe, and outlined a hierarchical structure of visible matter based on invisible corpuscles of this single matter. These statements, coupled with Newton's strong affirmation of the analogy

[4] See Anita Guerrini, 'Archibald Pitcairne and Newtonian Medicine', *Med. Hist.*, XXXI (1987), 70–83; Brown, *Mechanical Philosophy*, ch. 4; Andrew Cunningham, 'Sydenham versus Newton: the Edinburgh Fever Dispute of the 1690s between Andrew Brown and Archibald Pitcairne', *Med. Hist.*, suppl. 1 (1981), 71–98.
[5] Richard Mead, *Of the Influence of the Sun and Moon on Humane Bodies* (London, 1712), pp. 43–4. For Gregory, see Anita Guerrini, 'The Tory Newtonians: Gregory, Pitcairne and their Circle', *J. Brit. Stud.*, XXV (1986), 288–311; Christina M. Eagles, 'David Gregory and Newtonian Science', *Brit. J. Hist. Sci.*, X (1977), 216–25; P.D. Lawrence and A.G. Molland, 'David Gregory's Inaugural Lecture at Oxford', *Notes and Recs. Roy. Soc.*, XXV (1970), 143–78.
[6] Gregory to Newton, 2 September 1687, in H.G. Turnbull, J.F. Scott, A.R. Hall and L. Tilling (eds.), *The Correspondence of Issac Newton*, 7 vols. (Cambridge, 1959–77), II, p. 484. Hereafter cited as Newton, *Correspondence*.
[7] Guerrini, 'Pitcairne and Newtonian Medicine'.

between the microcosm and the macrocosm in 'Hypothesis III' of the *Principia*, provided Pitcairne with a compelling mode of explanation for vital phenomena. Over the course of his two-day visit to Newton, Pitcairne asked several questions on points of physiology, particularly on the topic of secretion. Following his visit, Pitcairne sent copies of Newton's essay, and notes of their conversations, to Gregory and possibly to others. For the next two decades, secretion provided the paradigm case of Newtonian explanation in physiology.[8]

Pitcairne discussed this topic in public 'dissertations' delivered during his sojourn as professor of the theory of medicine at the university of Leiden in 1692–3.[9] In one of these lectures, 'On the circulation of the blood through the minutest vessels of the body', Pitcairne attacked conventional mechanical and chemical explanations of secretion on methodological and theoretical grounds introduced by Newton. Without fully adopting Newton's own explanation, based on the attractive forces between the secreted fluid and the secreting vessels, Pitcairne proposed another mechanical scheme based on the sizes and shapes of fluid particles and corresponding vessels. To him, Newtonian attraction seemed as methodologically suspect as the theories of the despised chemists.[10]

Despite his qualified Newtonianism, and a relatively small number of publications, Pitcairne strongly influenced a subsequent generation of physicians as a teacher in Leiden and Edinburgh. Members of this group included William Cockburn (1669–1739), Richard Mead (1673–1754), George Cheyne and George Hepburn (?1670–1759). David Gregory moved from Edinburgh to Oxford in 1692 and there led more students into the Newtonian fold, including John Freind (1675–1728) and the Scottish brothers James (1673–1719) and John Keill (1671–1721). Known primarily as a mathematician, Gregory held strong interests in medicine and several of his medical notebooks survive in manuscript.[11]

[8] Isaac Newton, 'De Natura Acidorum', in Newton, *Correspondence*, III, pp. 205–14; the notes, pp. 212–14, detail Pitcairne's visit. Gregory's copy of the manuscript is Royal Society, Gregory MSS., fos. 17, 64–5. Other copies are at Christ Church, Oxford and the Royal College of Physicians of London.
[9] G.H. Lindeboom, 'Pitcairne's Leyden Interlude Described from the Documents', *Ann. Sci.*, XIX (1963), 273–84.
[10] Archibald Pitcairne, *Dissertatio de Motu Sanguinis per Vasa Minima* (Leiden, 1693), translated in Archibald Pitcairne, *The Works* [trans. George Sewell and J.T. Desaguliers] (London, 1715), pp. 29–61.
[11] Gregory's medical notebooks include British Library, Add. MS. 29, 243; University Library Edinburgh, MS. DC.1.62, 'Praxeos Pitcarnianae Specimina'. Gregory appears to have treated patients in Oxford: Pitcairne to Gregory, 20 February 1701, in W.T. Johnston (ed.), *The Best of Our Owne: Letters of Archibald Pitcairne, 1652–1713* (Edinburgh, 1979), p. 35. Hereafter cited as Pitcairne, *Correspondence*.

Together, the British students of Pitcairne and Gregory formed an intellectual circle focused on Isaac Newton. These men emerge as a specific group from the wider circle of Newton's followers for several reasons, which I have described in detail elsewhere.[12] Kinship and community relationships, as well as shared intellectual interests, unified this group. Most of its members were Scots; and in this era of the Glorious Revolution and the resurgence of the presbyterian Kirk, these men were neither presbyterian nor whig, but episcopalian and tory. Pitcairne, a vocal Jacobite, remained in Scotland after his brief stay in Holland, but Gregory and their students left Scotland for the more hospitable land to the south. Newton's rise to prominence, made manifest by his move to London in 1696, provided another compelling motive for these ambitious young men to take up residence within his proximity.

Between 1695 and 1713, members of this group followed Pitcairne's lead in several works on matter theory, medicine and physiology. Prominent among this group was George Cheyne, whom Pitcairne especially promoted.

Cheyne was born in 1671 in the episcopalian northeast of Scotland, the son of a clergyman. He studied at Marischal College, Aberdeen, and at the University of Leiden, where he probably met Pitcairne. We know nothing of his career until 1701, when he received his M.D., like many others, from the University of Aberdeen. The degree proclamation indicated the high hopes which rested on Cheyne's broad shoulders; the university waived the usual fee, it stated,

because he's not onely our owne countreyman and at present not rich, but is recommended by the ablest and most learned Physitians in Edinburgh, as one of the best Mathematicians in Europe and for his skill in Medecine he hath given a sufficient indication of that by his learned tractat *De Febribus*, which hath made him famous abroad as well as at home, and he being just now goeing to England upon invitation from some of the members of the Royal Society, in all probability he may prove ane ornament to our Nation as well as to our Society.[13]

Soon after, Cheyne made his way to London, armed with a letter of recommendation from Pitcairne addressed to Hans Sloane. Pitcairne described his protégé as 'a knowing man & good mathematician', adding, 'he is very desirous to be knowne to you a patron of learn'd men'.[14]

---

[12] Guerrini, 'The Tory Newtonians'.

[13] Henry Viets, 'George Cheyne, 1673–1743', *Bull. Hist. Med.*, XXIII (1949), 435–59; Lester S. King, 'George Cheyne: Mirror of Eighteenth Century Medicine', *Bull. Hist. Med.*, XLVIII (1974), 517–39; *Life of George Cheyne M.D.* (Oxford, 1846). The degree proclamation is in P.J. Anderson (ed.), *Officers and Graduates of University and King's College, 1495–1860* (Aberdeen, 1893), p. 124.

[14] Pitcairne to Sloane, 29 September 1701, Pitcairne, *Correspondence*, p. 37.

Cheyne's *New Theory of Continual Fevers*, referred to in his degree proclamation, was published anonymously in 1701. As another sally in Pitcairne's protracted dispute on fever therapy with the Royal College of Physicians of Edinburgh, its authorship was obviously an open secret; Pitcairne himself had thrown broad hints to his London colleague Robert Gray, adding, 'I'l answer for it, sufficientlie'.[15] Cheyne's particular antagonist in this round of the fever debate was Charles Oliphant, who also happened to be David Gregory's brother-in-law, and Gregory's lifelong hostility to Cheyne undoubtedly stems from this event. Moreover, Cheyne's *New Theory*, printed in Edinburgh but sold in London – at Pitcairne's instigation – by the Scottish *émigré* George Strahan, brought the debate before the Royal Society, a new and potentially more favourable audience than the Edinburgh College of Physicians. Pitcairne's gamble paid off; within six months of arriving in London, Cheyne was elected to the Royal Society.[16]

A New Theory of Continual Fevers could hardly have been better designed to appeal to Newton and his contingent at the Royal Society. Aggressively mathematical in format, it presented Pitcairne's qualitative ideas on secretion in elaborate geometrical proofs of fluid dynamics, closely approaching his ideal of 'iatromathematics'. Cheyne then briskly arrived at his less than earth-shattering 'general proposition': 'The general and most effectual Cause of all Fevers, is the Obstruction or Dilatation of . . . the Glands'.[17] He elaborated this theme with frequent reference to Borelli, Bellini and Pitcairne, and went beyond even the latter in his scorn for chemical explanations. Like Pitcairne, Cheyne demonstrated his knowledge of Newton's works, including 'De Natura Acidorum'; but, as Pitcairne had done, he stopped short of fully acknowledging Newton's concept of short-range attractions.

Shortly after his election to the Royal Society, Cheyne published a second edition of his *New Theory of Continual Fevers*, prefaced by an *Essay Concerning the Improvements in the Theory of Medicine*. Here

---

[15] Pitcairne to Robert Gray, 27 November 1700, Pitcairne, *Correspondence*, p. 34; Johnston has transcribed 'I'l answer for its sufficiencie'. On the fever dispute see Cunningham, 'Sydenham versus Newton'.

[16] Gregory mentioned his marriage to Elizabeth Oliphant in a letter to Arthur Charlett, 26 September 1695, Bodleian Library, MS. Ballard 24, f. 38. Pitcairne wrote to Robert Gray that 'De febribus 300 copies are sent to Mr Strachan', asking that he not tell Gregory: 27 February 1701, Pitcairne, *Correspondence*, p. 36.

[17] George Cheyne, *A New Theory of Acute and Slow Continu'd Fevers – the structure of the glands and the manner and laws of secretion – to which is prefix'd, An Essay Concerning the Improvements of the Theory of Medicine*, 3rd edn (London, 1722), pp. 40–6. This edition does not differ significantly from the first, *A New Theory of Continual Fevers* (London, 1701).

Cheyne made his loyalty to Newton explicit, in an essay strongly reminiscent of Pitcairne's inaugural lecture at Leiden ten years earlier; both compared the sorry scientific status of medicine with more exact sciences such as astronomy, and both suggested that the reform of medicine lay in the mathematical methods of those sciences. With greater detail than Pitcairne, Cheyne went on to outline a scientific medicine. The body, he said, consisted of fluids and canals which were eminently quantifiable, and could be analysed according to the laws of physics and geometry.[18] Like many of his contemporaries, Cheyne believed that diseases in his time were both different and more virulent than those of the ancients, and therefore required new therapies, developed with modern scientific – that is, mechanical – theory.[19] I shall say more below about the millenarianism his comment implied.

Cheyne listed four requirements for the improvement of medicine: a more thorough knowledge of anatomy, a 'Compleat History of Nature', a 'Compleat System of Mechanick Phylosophy', and the composition of a 'Principia medicinae theoreticae mathematicae'. Should the reference to Newton be unclear, he went on to note that 'a compleat System of Mechanick Phylosophy, i.e. an Account of all the Visible Effects of Nature upon Geometrick Principles' had in fact been formulated by 'that stupendiously Great Man, Mr *Newton*'. A *Principia* of medicine, he went on, would consist of Newtonian principles applied to 'the more minute . . . Appearances of Nature'.[20]

Cheyne reiterated these themes in another work written in the same year, 1702, his *Remarks on two Late Pamphlets Written by Dr Oliphant*, yet another round in the fever dispute. Cheyne's pen was at its sharpest in this defence not only of Pitcairne but of his own programme for the reform of physic. 'It is very hard,' he noted, 'to apply *Geometry* to *Physiology* . . . *Medicine* and *Philosophie*,' but a good physician would make the effort: 'A *Mathematician*, who besides the *Practice*, understands the *Theory*, will find *Expedients* for all *Emergencies* . . . this is one principal *Difference* . . . between a meer *Mechanick* and a true *Philosopher*, who can both think and act.'[21]

Cheyne's appropriation of the Newtonian banner for himself and

[18] Cheyne, *New Theory*, pp. 7–8. Originally published in Edinburgh, 1702. Cf. Archibald Pitcairne, *Oratio, qua Ostenditur Medicinam ab omni Philosophorum Secta esse Liberam* . . . 26.4.1692 (Leiden, 1692), in Pitcairne, *Works*, pp. 7–24.

[19] Lloyd Stevenson, '"New Diseases" in the Seventeenth Century', *Bull. Hist. Med.*, XXIX (1965), 1–21.

[20] Cheyne, *New Theory*, pp. 21–32; quoted passage, pp. 23–4.

[21] George Cheyne, *Remarks on two Late Pamphlets Written by Dr Oliphant, against Dr Pitcairn's Dissertations* . . . (Edinburgh, 1702), preface, pp. 8–9.

Pitcairne enraged Gregory, whose protégé John Keill similarly sought to establish himself within the Newtonian orbit.[22] By the end of 1703 Pitcairne asked his friend Colin Campbell to 'take notice that Dr Gregorie and Dr Cheyne are not indissoluble friends, tho both are mine'.[23] Keill had followed Gregory to Oxford in 1692. Gregory promoted him with as much zeal as Pitcairne did Cheyne, wangling him a 'Scotch exhibition' at Balliol, and then importuning the university to accept Keill's Edinburgh M.A. as sufficient for the granting of an Oxford M.A., which would allow Keill to compete for university posts. Like Gregory, Keill found a niche in the high-church tory community centred around Henry Aldrich at Christ Church. In his first publication, *An Examination of Dr Burnet's Theory of the Earth* (1698), Keill avenged the wits of Christ Church, wounded in the *Phalaris* debate, with a critique of the ideas not only of Burnet but of William Whiston, a Cambridge crony of Richard Bentley, the *Phalaris* antagonist. Keill attempted to best the Bentleyites at their own game by claiming that his explanation, rather than Whiston's, was the most in accordance with Newton's aims.[24]

Keill was suitably rewarded with an appointment in 1699 as deputy to the ageing Sedleian professor, Thomas Millington. He took his duties seriously, seeing his lectures as an opportunity to establish his scientific, and Newtonian, credentials. These credentials were enforced by his election to the Royal Society at the end of 1700. His lectures, published in Oxford in 1702 as *Introductio ad Veram Physicam*, increased his reputation, even though the lectures were less than the simplified *Principia* they professed to be.[25] Keill's brother James, a physician, meanwhile secured enough connections to be able to leave public dissecting in Oxford for a lucrative medical practice in Northampton by 1703.[26]

Others however, followed Cheyne's lead to jump onto the Newtonian bandwagon. Richard Mead, an obscure dissenting physician in Stepney, published his *Mechanical Account of Poisons* in 1702, pre-

---

[22] For Keill see Guerrini, *Tory Newtonians.* Gregory's feelings may be seen in his memoranda: W.G. Hiscock (ed.), *David Gregory, Isaac Newton and their Circle* (Oxford, 1937), p. 15 and *passim.*

[23] Pitcairne to Colin Campbell, 1 October 1703, Pitcairne, *Correspondence*, p. 39.

[24] David Kubrin, 'Providence and the Mechanical Philosophy: the Creation and Dissolution of the World in Newtonian Thought', (Cornell University Ph.D. thesis, 1968), pp. 318–34. For another view of Keill's role in the cosmogony debate, see James Force, *William Whiston, Honest Newtonian* (Cambridge, 1985), pp. 60–2.

[25] John Keill, *Introductio ad veram physicam* (Oxford, 1702).

[26] Frances Valadez and C.D. O'Malley, 'James Keill of Northampton', *Med. Hist.*, xv (1971), 317–35.

senting it as a small contribution toward Cheyne's *Principia Medicinae*. He mentioned Bellini, Pitcairne and Cheyne in his preface, and asserted, somewhat naively, that the identical attractive force acted between atoms and between heavenly bodies: 'this Mr. *Newton* has demonstrated to be the great Principal of Action in the Universe'.[27] By the next year he had obtained a position as physician-in-ordinary at St Thomas's Hospital in Southwark and election to the Royal Society. Although there is no evidence of Newton's direct involvement in these appointments, the connection between Newtonian science and professional success was an easy one for contemporaries to make.

Acting, according to Gregory, on a suggestion from Cheyne, Mead published in 1704 a work even more literally Newtonian, his *De Imperio Solis ac Lunae*. Although Gregory claims that Halley found 'not one right or sensible word' in Cheyne's original paper, Halley none the less later published an English translation of Mead's version in his *Miscellanea Curiosa*. In this short book Mead claimed that Newton's theory of the tides applied equally to the air, with obvious physiological consequences.[28] Cheyne later cited these arguments to explain the periodicity of gout.[29]

Having extolled the value of Newton's fluxions for the reform of medicine in his *Essay Concerning the Improvements in the Theory of Medicine*, Cheyne could not resist publishing on that topic himself, in his next work, *Fluxionum Methodus Inversa*, published in 1703. His motives can only be guessed: certainly he wished to demonstrate his mathematical prowess, thus showing himself to be the kind of philosopher–physician he extolled. Since Newton's own writings on the calculus remained unpublished, this would also be an opportunity to show how close Cheyne sat to the throne. In his letter to Gregory on the publication of this work, *Fluxionum Methodus Inversa*, he pleaded disingenuously that Pitcairne had 'press'd' him 'very often' to write out his ideas on fluxions, and 'some of my friends thinking it will contribute toward my interest to print it', he was 'forced . . . to let it go'. Newton, Cheyne added, 'thought [his treatise] not intolerable', and

---

[27] Richard Mead, *A Mechanical Account of Poisons in Several Essays* (London, 1702), pp. 13–14; see also William Coleman, 'Mechanical Philosophy and Hypothetical Physiology', in Robert Palter (ed.), *The Annus Mirabilis of Isaac Newton* (Cambridge, Mass. 1970), pp. 322–32.

[28] Hiscock, *Gregory*, p. 19; Edmond Halley (ed.), *Miscellanea Curiosa . . . the second edition, to which is added A Discourse concerning the Influence of the Sun and Moon on Humane Bodies, by R. Mead*, vol. 1 (London, 1708). See Edmund [*sic*] Halley, 'The True Theory of the Tides, extracted from that admired Treatise of Mr. *Isaac Newton* . . .', *Phil. Trans.*, XIX (1697), 445–57.

[29] George Cheyne, *An Essay on the Gout, with an account of the nature and qualities of the Bath waters. Intended for Richard Tennison, Esq.*, 3rd edn (London, 1721), pp. 9–10.

indeed Westfall has argued that Newton offered to pay for its publication. Cheyne delicately noted to Gregory that he had used one of his methods of expansion, with due acknowledgement; he also asked for Gregory's comments, but Gregory's reply is not known.[30] In the following year, 1704, Gregory noted in his memoranda the rebuke to Cheyne's mathematical pretensions delivered by the Huguenot mathematician Abraham de Moivre.[31]

But Cheyne was flying high. By January 1705, Gregory reported that 'Dr Cheyne braggs that next summer he is to goe to Scotland, and together with Dr Pitcairn settle all the Practice of Physick, and publish unalterable Principles thereof'. The *Principia Medicinae* was at hand. Cheyne was in fact working, as Gregory knew, on a book on religion, his *Philosophical Principles of Natural Religion*, perhaps in an attempt to capitalize on the success of the Boyle lectures, several of which had been delivered by members of the Cambridge Newtonian circle. To mollify Gregory's evident unhappiness over his book on fluxions, Cheyne, using John Arbuthnot as an intermediary, asked Gregory to read the new book and note its errors.[32]

Gregory commented that Cheyne was rumoured to have 'stoln a great deal of his book of Religion from Dr Bentleys Sermons preached at Mr Boyles Lecture'.[33] As Bentley had attempted to demonstrate the existence of God by the works of nature, in particular by Newton's system of the world, so in the *Philosophical Principles* Cheyne made a similar demonstration with examples drawn mainly from physiology and the microcosm. God had revealed the 'Secrets of Nature' to a corrupt generation to persuade it anew of his existence. Like Bentley, he argued that the amazing contrivance of the Newtonian cosmos could not have arisen by chance; it begged for a Creator.[34] In his 1702

---

[30] Cheyne to Gregory, 20 January 1702[/3?], printed in Hiscock, *Gregory*, pp. 43–5. The original is pasted to the inside back cover of Gregory's copy of Cheyne's *Fluxionum Methodus Inversa* (London, 1703), at Christ Church. R.S. Westfall, *Never at Rest* (New York, 1980), p. 639.

[31] Hiscock, *Gregory*, p. 15.

[32] *Ibid.*, pp. 24–5; as Hiscock notes, the '429 errors' – mostly typographical – which Gregory found were in the *Philosophical Principles*, not in *Fluxionum Methodus Inversa*. The latter claim is made by T.M. Brown in C.C. Gillispie (ed.), *Dictionary of Scientific Biography*, 14 vols. (New York, 1970–1980), III, p. 244 and by Geoffrey Bowles, 'Physical, Human and Divine Attraction in the Life and Thought of George Cheyne', *Ann. Sci.*, XXXI (1974), 477, n. 17. See also Christ Church, Gregory MS. 346, fo. 101: 'Dr Cheyn librum scribit de existentia Dei . . . Edidit, 10 Febr 1703/4, Addenda et Adnotanda (verius Emendanda) ad Fluxionem Librum'.

[33] Hiscock, *Gregory*, p. 25.

[34] George Cheyne, *The Philosophical Principles of Natural Religion* (London, 1705), preface. See Richard Bentley, *A Confutation of Atheism from the Origin and Frame of the World*, parts II and III (London, 1693), reprinted in I.B. Cohen (ed.), *Isaac Newton's Papers and Letters on Natural Philosophy* (Cambridge, Mass. 1958), pp. 313–94.

Remarks on Two Late Pamphlets, he had asserted that Pitcairne's collected essays, which had just been published, 'serve to demonstrat the *Infinit* wisdom of the CONTRIVER of the *Universe*'. This wisdom assured that 'the same laws of *Mechanism* are observed in the lesser, as in the greater Bodies of this *System*'. The reduction of life processes to mechanics demonstrated this.[35]

The *Philosophical Principles* expanded on this theme. Animals were indeed mere machines, and could be analysed as such; but men could not therefore make a machine that would act like an animal. The immense and minute complexity of animal form, as well as the non-mechanical interaction of mind and body, indicate that 'the Production of an Animal is altogether *immechanical*', calling therefore for a creator.[36] Unlike Bentley, Cheyne injected an apocalyptic note into his discussion. Drawing upon Newton's comments on the nature of light in the recently published *Opticks*, Cheyne speculated that 'the Quantity of Heat and Light in the *Sun* does daily decrease . . . our *Atmosphere* and all the Bodies on our Globe are *saturated* at all times with Rays of Light which will never return again to their Fountain'. Optimistically, he calculated that this decay was imperceptible; the particles of light were so small that the amount emitted over years may only equal a grain of sand.[37] In his refutation of the eternity of the world, he briefly returned to the theme of dissolution, but he did not elaborate on its implications until much later.[38]

On the whole, Cheyne's *Philosophical Principles* adhered closely to Bentley's reasoning. Its physiological examples came from such upright mechanists as Bellini, Pitcairne, Cockburn and James Keill. His God, like Bentley's, was a clockmaker who acted through the non-mechanical principle of gravity, yet Cheyne derived no moral precepts from this activity. But his views soon began to change. Geoffrey Bowles has described the physical and spiritual crisis Cheyne underwent after the completion of the *Philosophical Principles* in 1705, and Cheyne himself discussed his case in 1733 in *The English Malady*. As a result of this crisis, Cheyne left London and the fashionable life which had, he believed, brought on his ill-health, for Bath. There he treated 'low and nervous *Cases*' who visited the spa.[39]

He did not leave the project of a *Principia Medicinae* to others,

[35] Cheyne, *Remarks on Two Late Pamphlets*, p. 2.
[36] Cheyne, *Philosophical Principles*, part II, pp. 22–4; cf. Bentley, *Confutation of Atheism*, part III.   [37] Cheyne, *Philosophical Principles*, I, pp. 95–6, 98.   [38] *Ibid.*, II, pp. 40–55.
[39] Bowles, 'Physical, Human and Divine Attraction', *passim*; George Cheyne, *The English Malady* (London, 1733), pp. 325–52.

although there were others, including John and James Keill and John Freind, who continued the enterprise. During the period between the appearance of the Latin *Opticks* in 1706 and 1710, the Keills and Freind described a Newtonian theory of matter based on attracting atoms, following the hints Newton had given in query 23. The force acting between these atoms was analogous, but not identical, to gravity. Cheyne had hinted at this in the *Philosophical Principles* when he noted that the attractive force between particles, as opposed to larger bodies, could not be as the square of the distance, because the distance between particles was so much smaller.[40] John Keill outlined this theory in thirty axioms, published in the *Philosophical Transactions* for 1708. As he noted, this theory was especially applicable to physiological problems, and almost immediately his brother James published an essay on animal secretion which made explicit use of this theory to explain the problem which had so vexed Pitcairne. Freind followed closely with a book on Newtonian chemical principles in the next year, 1709.[41]

Cheyne took the enterprise in quite a different direction, emphasizing the close interconnections between matter and spirit. Pitcairne wrote to Gregory in 1706, 'I am clear that metaphysics can never prove a Deity, and therefor think our churchmen here have no ground not to be Atheists'. Cheyne felt uncomfortably the truth of this assertion in his own case. He realized, he later wrote, that he had derived his Christianity from '*abstracted* Reasonings, as well as from the best *natural philosophy*', but he now began to question the adequacy of this as a basis for belief.[42]

Political considerations may also have begun to weigh upon him. In a memorandum written at the end of 1704, Gregory cryptically referred to an 'intrigue betwixt My Lord Roxburgh, Dr Pitcairn, Dr Cheyn, &c of reforming Colleges, &c in Scotland'.[43] Pitcairne used his contacts with his patient the earl of Mar, one of the secretaries of state for Scotland and a strong Jacobite, to influence appointments to the various professorships in mathematics at the Scottish universities. Pitcairne favoured Thomas Bower, formerly Cheyne's tutor at Marischal, for the Aberdeen professorship over Gregory's brother

---

[40] Cheyne, *Philosophical Principles*, I, pp. 110–17.
[41] John Keill, 'Epistola .. in qua leges attractionis', *Phil. Trans.*, XXVI (1708), 97–110; James Keill, *An Account of Animal Secretion* (London, 1708); John Freind, *Praelectiones Chymicae* (London, 1709). See Anita Guerrini, 'James Keill, George Cheyne, and Newtonian Physiology, 1690–1740', *J. Hist. Biol.*, XVIII (1985), 247–66.
[42] Pitcairne to Gregory, 25 February 1706, Pitcairne, *Correspondence*, p. 43; Cheyne, *English Malady*, p. 330.   [43] Hiscock, *Gregory*, p. 21.

Charles, but recommended Charles for the St Andrew's chair. Both appointments were made as he recommended.[44] Was this the 'intrigue' to which Gregory referred?

Cheyne tutored the young John Ker as early as 1690, perhaps on the recommendation of his kinsman Gilbert Burnet.[45] Ker succeeded to his brother's title of Earl of Roxburgh in 1696. Cheyne dedicated the *Philosophical Principles* to Roxburgh, who had recently been named one of the secretaries of state for Scotland, claiming that the book grew out of his 'discourses' with the earl – whether in the 1690s or at some later date is not known.[46] As part of the *squadrone*, a splinter group of the whig 'country' faction in Scotland, Roxburgh was involved in the negotiations which led to the Union of 1707, a project in which David Gregory was also active. For his role in promoting the Union, Roxburgh was named first duke of Roxburgh in 1707. At least for moderate Scottish tories such as Gregory, the union seemed preferable to an independent Scotland dominated by presbyterians.[47] Pitcairne, on the other hand, was a vocal and apparently unrepentant Jacobite; in 1699 he had served a term in the Tolbooth, and paid a fine of two hundred pounds, for a libellous anti-government letter to his friend Robert Gray. Yet he too declared himself in favour of the Union in 1706.[48] Cheyne did not reveal his own political leanings in his writings, but as another episcopalian émigré, his position probably resembled Gregory's.

Other Newtonian physicians were equally involved in current political affairs; connections with Robert Harley figure especially prominently by the end of the first decade of the eighteenth century.[49] John Freind accompanied Peterborough to Spain from 1705 to 1707 as his physician, and wrote a defence of the earl's actions upon his return. Peterborough later became part of Harley's circle.[50] In 1712, Freind served the duke of Ormonde – described by J.P. Kenyon as a 'High Tory and a crypto-Jacobite' – in a similar capacity in Flanders.[51]

[44] Pitcairne to John Erskine, earl of Mar, 1706–8, Pitcairne, *Correspondence*, pp. 43–6, 52–5.
[45] Viets, 'George Cheyne', pp. 435–9; for Roxburgh, see *Dictionary of National Biography* (hereafter referred to as *D.N.B.*), XI, pp. 50–1; P.W.J. Riley, *The Union of England and Scotland* (Manchester, 1978), pp. 75–102 and *passim*.
[46] Cheyne, *Philosophical Principles*, preface.
[47] Riley, *Union*, p. 10 and *passim*. For Gregory's involvement, see his correspondence with Arthur Charlett, Bodleian Library, MS. Ballard 24.
[48] Extracts of the 1699 proceedings are in Pitcairne, *Correspondence*, pp. 25–32; Pitcairne to Mar, 28 May 1706, Pitcairne, *Correspondence*, p. 44.
[49] See Guerrini, 'Tory Newtonians', 308–11.
[50] John Freind, *An Account of the Earl of Peterborow's Conduct in Spain* (London, 1707); Geoffrey Holmes, *British Politics in the Age of Anne* (London, 1967), pp. 127, 226.
[51] Freind's letters from Flanders to his friend Henry Watkins are in the Royal College of Physicians of London. J.P. Kenyon, *Stuart England* (Harmondsworth, 1978), p. 266.

William Cockburn, physician to the Navy since 1695, continued to have an exclusive contract with the admiralty for provision of his anti-dysentery 'electuary'.[52] His friend Jonathan Swift shifted toward Harley around 1710, about the time John Keill put himself at Harley's service in the matter of the Palatine refugees.[53] By the time Keill became Savilian professor of astronomy in 1712, he was listed as one of the Queen's 'decypherers'.[54] Pitcairne himself wrote a poem in praise of Harley in 1712.[55]

In view of these connections and activities by Cheyne's associates, we should, I think, take Cheyne's retreat from the world produced by his post-1705 breakdown, relied upon by Bowles in his assessment of the development of Cheyne's thought, with a grain of salt. The breakdown did occur, and the solitude it enforced led Cheyne to a period of introspection in which he closely examined his religious faith. Yet he did not thereby abandon his study of Newton or the successful medical practice he began to build in Bath, then just begin-ning its fame. Beau Nash moved to Bath in 1705, and the first pump room for medical treatments was built in the following year. The patronage of Anne as princess and then queen, who visited Bath for her gout, led to the emergence of the town as a fashionable spa of the early years of the eighteenth century; soon Swift could comment, 'Everyone is going to Bath.'[56] Cheyne's retreat to Bath, therefore, was less monastic than he pretended. By 1709 he had removed there perma-nently. He had already begun revising his *Philosophical Principles*, but the revised edition did not appear until 1715, ten years after the first issue.[57]

If Cheyne had changed his mind over these ten years, so, apparently, had Newton. In 'De Natura Acidorum', finally published in a trun-cated version in John Harris's *Lexicon Technicum* in 1710, Newton reasserted the matter theory of query 23 of the 1706 *Opticks*, in which particles of matter were 'endued' with an 'Attractive Force; in which their Activity consists'.[58] But a few years later, in the second edition of the *Principia*, Newton hinted at the existence of a 'certain most subtle spirit', tentatively identified with the nervous spirits or animal fluid,

[52] Guerrini, 'Tory Newtonians', 303–4, 309; Brown, *Mechanical Philosophy*, pp. 239–48.
[53] Guerrini, 'Tory Newtonians', 309; papers regarding Keill's activities with the Palatine refugees in 1709–11 are in Cambridge University Library, Lucasian MSS.
[54] Thomas Hearne, *Remarks and Collections*, ed. C.E. Doble et al., 11 vols. (Oxford, 1885–1921), IV, p. 69.
[55] Pitcairne to Robert Ramsay, 1 September 1712, Pitcairne, *Correspondence*, p. 68.
[56] David Gadd, *Georgian Summer: Bath in the Eighteenth Century* (Park Ridge, N.J., 1972), pp. 19–27.   [57] Bowles, 'Physical, Human and Divine Attraction', 477–8.
[58] Isaac Newton, 'De Natura Acidorum' and 'Some Thoughts on the Nature of Acids', in John Harris, *Lexicon Technicum*, II (London, 1710), reprinted in Cohen, *Papers and Letters*, p. 257.

which could cause a variety of phenomena, including gravity. Newton's intention in this reintroduction of an ether has been the topic of much historiographical dispute, which is beyond the scope of this paper.[59] It is enough to say that Cheyne saw in Newton's 1713 statement, and his more explicit espousal of an ether in 1717, sanction for the introduction of spirit into his natural philosophy.

Cheyne profoundly revised the *Philosophical Principles*, as indicated by its new title, *Philosophical Principles of Religion, Natural and Revealed*. Not only did he add a long second section on revealed religion, but he also rewrote his original account of natural religion. In both cases, the role of spirit became overriding. Cheyne expanded his earlier millenarian hints in a decidedly neoplatonic account of cyclic decline and regeneration fuelled by active principles generated by God's love. Earthly attractive forces were merely copies, in a platonic sense, of divine love. This equation also had its moral side; for as humans were imperfect copies of God, so human love reflected that of God, and the best human laws reflected the laws of nature given by God – and shown to us by Newton. Newton's 'arithmetick of infinites' demonstrated that the whole of nature formed a continuum of steps between matter and spirit, with the ether acting, literally or figuratively, as the intermediary. In the method of analogy, as detailed by Newton in his third 'Rule of Reasoning' in the *Principia*, Cheyne found the expression of God's design in the great chain of being.[60]

From such lofty realms Cheyne soon descended again to earthly ailments. Bowles surmises that Cheyne continued to struggle with his tendency to excess in food and drink, and to suffer from ill health, until the later 1720s.[61] Beginning in 1720, however, until his death in 1742, Cheyne produced a steady stream of popular works on medicine which enjoyed immense commercial success. Probably the best known was his *Essay on Health and Long Life*, first published in 1724, which

[59] Isaac Newton, *Principia*, trans. Andrew Motte, rev. Florian Cajori (Berkeley, 1934), p. 547. See Henry Guerlac, 'Newton's Optical Aether' *Notes and Recs. Roy. Soc.*, XII (1967), 45–57; Joan L. Hawes, 'Newton and the "Electrical Attraction Unexcited"', *Ann. Sci.*, XXIV (1968), 121–30; J.E. McGuire, 'Force, Active Principles, and Newton's Invisible Realm', *Ambix*, XV (1968), 154–208; J.E. McGuire and P.M. Heimann, 'Newtonian Forces and Lockean Powers', *Hist. Stud. Phys. Sci.*, III (1971), 233–306.

[60] George Cheyne, *Philosophical Principles of Religion: Natural and Revealed* (London, 1715), 'Preface to the second part'; Newton, *Principia*, pp. 398–400. See also the poem 'Platonick Love', attributed to Cheyne, British Library Burney MS. 390, fo. 8b. I am grateful to Simon Schaffer for this reference. For fuller accounts, see Bowles, 'Physical, Human and Divine Attraction', 478–88; Guerrini, 'Keill, Cheyne, and Newtonian Physiology', 260–62; Helene Metzger, *Attraction universelle et religion naturelle chez quelques commentateurs anglais de Newton* (Paris, 1938), part III, pp. 140–53.

[61] Bowles, 'Physical, Human and Divine Attraction', 475–6.

reached a tenth edition by 1745. Meanwhile his fellow Newtonians in London had been enjoying great success as practitioners among the fashionable population, demonstrating the usefulness of a scientific reputation, and Newton, as William Harvey had been for a previous generation of practitioners, became the symbol of a profession.

John Freind and Richard Mead, close friends despite their political differences, became fellows of the Royal College of Physicians of London on the same day in 1716. In the following year they demonstrated their classical knowledge with the publication, in Latin, of nine commentaries by Freind on Hippocrates' accounts of fevers in his *Epidemics*, addressed to Mead, and including his response. Freind discussed the various methods of evacuation of current therapeutics, with numerous case histories and classical references. The physiology he described was mechanistic, but not especially Newtonian.[62] In the next year, however, John Woodward, head of an anti-Newtonian faction at the Royal Society, criticized Freind in *The State of Physick: and of Diseases*. Woodward's motive stemmed in part from his jealousy at the success of the Newtonian coterie. His work set off a pamphlet war which involved Woodward and John Harris on one side against Freind, Mead and John Quincy (d. 1722).[63] Quincy had studied with Pitcairne at Edinburgh and had translated his lectures, and had written extensively on Sanctorius and his 'statics', a popular topic among Newtonians. His edition of Sanctorius, with extensive commentary, was republished in 1720 with the addition of James Keill's *Medicina Statica Britannica*.[64]

Keill, who died in 1719, published a second edition of his *Account of Animal Secretion* in 1717 under the title of *Essays on Several Parts of the Animal Oeconomy*. The edition included two new essays on the velocity of the blood and the force of the heart, in which he attempted to quantify some aspects of his secretion theory, using his brother's lecture on hydraulics. As mathematical exercises they were interesting, but far from conclusive, as James Jurin (1684–1750), another rising young physician, pointed out in his criticisms of Keill in the *Philosophical Transactions*.[65] Keill's medical practice in Northampton continued

---

[62] John Freind, *Commentarii Novem de Febribus* (Amsterdam, 1717).
[63] John Woodward, *The State of Physick: and of Diseases* (London, 1718). On the dispute, see Lester Beattie, *John Arbuthnot, Mathematician and Satirist* (Cambridge, Mass. 1935), pp. 242–62.
[64] See *D.N.B.*, XVI, pp. 555–6; John Quincy, *Medicina Statica* . . . *The 2d ed. To which is added, Dr Keil's Medicina Statica Britannica* . . . (London, 1720).
[65] James Keill, *Essays on Several Parts of the Animal Oeconomy* (London, 1717). His exchange with Jurin is in *Phil. Trans.*, XXX (1717–19).

to be successful, with such patients as Lord Leominster and the Walpole family. The fortune he amassed passed at his death to his brother John in Oxford, who himself died in 1721."

In 1717, Newton commenced a new edition of his *Opticks*, which completed publication in the next year. Its most important revision consisted in the addition of eight new queries, numbered 17 to 24, between the original sixteen and the seven added in 1706. The new queries made explicit Newton's reassessment, and renewed commitment, to an ether. This ether, 'exceedingly more subtile than the Air, and exceedingly more elastick and active', acted as a medium for the transmission of light, as well as providing a mechanical cause of gravity by its varying density in space.[67] In query 24, he suggested that his ether could also be the cause of animal motion, not in the crude mechanical sense of a nervous fluid in tubular nerves, but in terms of vibration along solid nerves.[68]

Newtonian physicians, many of them now established in highly profitable practices, took notice of these changes only gradually. The discussion in Richard Mead's treatise on plague of 1720, as well as Cheyne's work on gout of the same year, (discussed below), rested on Newton's earlier theory of particulate matter and short-range forces. Mead repeated the statements in his *Mechanical Account of Poisons* on the infective action of 'fermentative particles'.[69] But in his next work Mead fully acknowledged the change in Newton's thought, and decisively shifted the focus of Newtonian physiology from secretion to the nervous system. In 1724, he joined Henry Pemberton in issuing a new edition of William Cowper's *Myotomia Reformata*, a work on muscle anatomy first published in 1694.[70] Pemberton, a young physician, had studied medicine with Boerhaave in Leyden and had insinuated himself into Newtonian medical circles. His success at this was such that Newton chose him to edit the third edition of the *Principia* in 1726. Pemberton's editorial contributions were few, but he parlayed his connection with Newton into a long, if not very productive, career.[71] Mead and Pemberton Newtonized Cowper's book with a long intro-

[66] Valadez and O'Malley, 'James Keill'; Hearne, *Remarks and Collections*, VI, pp. 273–4.
[67] Isaac Newton, *Opticks*, 4th edn, 1730 (rpt. New York, 1952), pp. 349–51.
[68] *Ibid.*, pp. 353–4.
[69] Richard Mead, *A Short Discourse concerning Pestilential Contagion*, 6th edn (London, 1720).
[70] William Cowper, *Myotomia Reformata . . . To which is prefix'd An Introduction concerning Muscular Motion* (London, 1724). Hearne, *Remarks and Collections*, VII, p. 271: 'this Book will be the most Beautiful Book . . . ever printed in England'.
[71] D.N.B., XV, p. 725–6; *Dictionary of Scientific Biography*, X, p. 500–1. R.S. Westfall comments in the latter that Pemberton's lack of activity 'suggests how deadening the role of sycophant can be' (p. 501).

duction, filled with mathematical diagrams, in which they rejected various mechanical explanations of muscular motion. Their own explanation, no less mechanical, concluded that 'the Fluid contained in the Nerves is probably no other than part of that subtle, rare, and elastic spirit [Sir Isaac Newton] concludes to be diffused throughout the Universe'.[72] Although this was not exactly what Newton had said, it appeared to pass muster.

In writing more popular works, Cheyne departed from the scholarly world of other Newtonian physicians, who retained the close ties to the Royal Society which Cheyne had allowed to lapse. The appearance of learning remained an important item in the physician's armoury, and here Cheyne was no exception, although his works largely lack the abundant classical references of Freind or Mead. But his emphasis on self-help portended a new direction for academic physicians, increasingly in competition with apothecaries and surgeons for clients. Learning would no longer be enough; effectiveness had to be proved.[73] The espousal by learned physicians of such doubtful expedients as Joanna Stephens's lithontriptic in the 1730s may have been induced by this need to seem effective next to the impressive technical skill of Cheselden and other surgeons, and the increasing mastery of the pharmacopoeia by apothecaries. In addition, by eschewing the fashionable life in London for a plainer, though by no means ascetic, provincial existence, Cheyne consciously provided an example, both physical and moral, to those who had wearied of worldly pleasures. His message, as we shall see, was not lost upon his readers.

Yet Cheyne's loyalty to Newton's ideas, at least by his own interpretation, never wavered. Into his popular works Cheyne injected his new-found spirituality, alongside his mechanico-Newtonian physiology and admonitions to temperance. This odd but effective mix first appeared in his *Observations Concerning the Nature and Method of Treating the Gout* in 1720. In his preface, dated July 1719, Cheyne indicated his reformed personality; in contrast to his earlier argumentative self, he now asserted that he would not defend himself if disputed. But he was not above self-aggrandizement, noting that God had conveniently provided Bath-waters 'as the most *Sovereign Restorative* in all the Weaknesses of the *Concoctive Powers*'.[74] Gout was endemic among Cheyne's class of patients, and given the vividness of his descriptions of its symptoms, the doctor himself was probably a sufferer. He explained its occurrence entirely in mechanical terms. The

[72] Cowper, *Myotomia Reformata*, p. lxxii.   [73] Holmes, *Augustan England*, 204–5, 234–5.
[74] Cheyne, *Essay on the Gout*, pp. vi–vii.

sufferer from gout, he said, must have capillaries which are 'narrower and more stiff' than those of a normal person. Coupled with 'the Abundance of Tartarous, Urinous, or other Salts, introduc'd into the Blood by the Food', a gouty attack resulted. Thus Cheyne gave equal measure to natural temperament and the effects of over-indulgence in rich food and drink.[75]

Cheyne, hardly originally, recommended Bath-water as a cure for the gout, and moderation in food and drink as its prevention. Bath-water, he said, contained an efficacious mixture of steel and sulphur. He drew his account of sulphur and its effects largely from Newton, both the *Opticks* and 'De Natura Acidorum'. The particles of sulphur, said Cheyne, were especially small and active, and could thus insinuate themselves into small clogged vessels. In addition, '*Sulphurous* Bodies will readily unite with and destroy the Effects of all *Saline* Particles, but especially those of the acid kind'.[76] His book closed, however, on the hectoring note of a preacher: gout, he said, afflicted chiefly 'the *Rich*, the *Lazy*, the *Voluptuous*', and he obviously included himself among these. 'TEMPERANCE only', he concluded, 'Divine, Innocent, Indolent and Joyous *Temperance* can Cure or effectually Relieve the *Gout*'.[77]

This tendency to preach, coupled with the use of his own case as an example, was especially prominent in his next work, *An Essay of Health and Long Life*. It struck a chord among much of the public, reaching seven editions in its first two years of publication. The young John Wesley, then a student at Christ Church, recommended the work to his mother at the end of 1724: 'I suppose you have seen the famous Dr Cheyne's Book of Health & Long Life . . . He refers almost everything to temperance & exercise'.[78]

Cheyne had just endured another bout of ill-health, and considered the *Essay* his swan song. He prefaced it, therefore, with a long apologia for his life and works. He criticized, but did not wholly reject, his earlier works, written under Pitcairne's influence. He mainly regretted that science did not teach him humility; but he carefully avoided condemning the scientific enterprise or indeed the content of his own works. With his works from the *Philosophical Principles* onward he remained well content.[79]

[75] *Ibid.*, pp. 2–3.   [76] *Ibid.*, pp. 32–7.   [77] *Ibid.*, pp. 96–8.

[78] John Wesley to Susanna Wesley, 1 November 1724, John Telford (ed.), *The Letters of John Wesley* (London, 1931) I, p. 11.

[79] Bowles, 'Physical, Human and Divine Attraction', 475–6; George Cheyne, *An Essay of Health and Long Life*, 8th edn (London, 1734), preface. His opinion of his earlier works may be indicated by the reissue of his first two works, *A New Theory of Fevers* and *An Essay on the Theory of Medicine*, in 1722. See also M.C. Jacob, *The Radical Enlightenment* (London, 1981), pp. 96–7.

The *Essay of Health and Long Life* followed a familiar genre of commentary on what were commonly known as the 'six non-naturals'.[80] 'Most of my Arguments (as they needs must) have risen out of animal Functions and Oeconomy', he noted; and indeed they fall within the conventional mechanico-Newtonian framework of attracting particles, though with Cheyne's distinct brand of moral exhortation superimposed.[81] As Wesley noted, and as in his work on gout, he recommended moderation in diet, exercise and good humour as the keys to health. Unfortunately, the doctor himself followed his own precepts only infrequently.

The exception to Cheyne's conventional arguments was his remarkable chapter on the passions, in which he reiterated the arguments of the 1715 *Philosophical Principles* to explain the specific case of the mind–body relationship. Cheyne conceived of mind and body as distinct, but strictly analogous. As God has established laws of nature which we know of by observation and experiment, so too are there laws governing spirit, which we can only discern by their effects.[82] But if bodies are 'purely *passive*', spirit, on the other hand, is innately active, having its origin in God. As such, it provides the basis for all motion; for this point Cheyne cited Samuel Clarke's letters to Leibniz. As in bodies there is gravity, so the analogous principle in spirits, as Cheyne had explained in the *Philosophical Principles*, was love. God had implanted love in individuals, that is, 'an *infinite Tendency, Bent and Biass* . . . towards *Himself*' and each other, to counteract the pernicious tendencies of other passions.[83]

Divided roughly into good and evil, the immaterial passions strongly influenced material bodies. Cheyne explained these effects in a conventionally mechanical way:

As the *Passions*, when *slow* and *continued, relax, unbend*, and *dissolve* the *Nervous* Fibres; so the sudden and violent ones *screw up, stretch*, and *bend* them, whereby the Blood and Juices are hurried about with a violent *Impetuosity*, and all the *Secretions* are either stopp'd . . . or at least dispose[d] toward *Inflammations, Fevers* or *Mortifications*.[84]

Diet, exercise and finally physick may help in such cases. But if the passions persisted in gaining the upper hand, with 'tumultuous, overbearing *Hurricanes* in the Mind', only God could affect a cure. All other passions must be drowned in the love of God.[85]

Contemporaries were less spiritual in their account of the mind–

[80] See L.J. Rather, 'The "Six Things Non-natural"', *Clio Med.*, III (1968), 337–47.
[81] Cheyne, *Essay of Health*, p. xv.   [82] *Ibid.*, pp. 146–7.   [83] *Ibid.*, pp. 150–1.
[84] *Ibid.*, pp. 158–9.   [85] *Ibid.*, pp. 161–2.

body relationship and its effects on physical and mental health. Nicholas Robinson (?1697–1775), a protégé of Mead, published *A New Theory of Physick and Diseases, Founded on the Principles of the Newtonian Philosophy*, in 1725. His language was Newtonian, and his ideas of physiology were predictably mechanical. Robinson drew his account of secretion from James Keill's Newtonian work of 1708. He conceded that one problem in physiology could not be solved by means of attracting particles: the influence of the mind on the body.[86]

Robinson explored this relationship in 1729 in *A New System of the Spleen, Vapours and Hypochondriack Melancholy*. Again, he described the body in mechanico-Newtonian terms as consisting of fluids and fibres, both in turn composed of attracting particles. The variable attractions between particles made these fibres more or less springy.[87] Springy fibres formed vivacious, lively personalities; but too much elasticity could lead to biliousness or even madness. Slack fibres, on the other hand, caused a melancholy individual. Other mental afflictions were attributed to 'a clog of matter in the brain', which prevented animal spirits from freely flowing through the tubular nerves. This followed conventional theories of disease, which postulated noxious matter in the blood vessels as a cause.[88]

To explain the mind–body relationship, Robinson introduced the concept of a self-moving soul, rather as Cheyne had proposed. Like gravity and God, the soul did not change; only the body did. Robinson then added a fillip to this spiritual action-at-a-distance, proposing the existence of an 'animal ether' which would fill the gap between soul and body just as Newton's ether filled the gap between force and matter. He equated this material ether with the passions, which as Cheyne had noted, could not be accounted for mechanically. This ether caused the animal spirits to move through the nerves, but did not affect the material causes of insanity. As a purely physical affliction, insanity had no connection with the soul or, apparently, with this ether. Only material means of cure would help those with mental diseases. By Robinson's concept, the soul, like the God of the deists, was left with little room for manoeuvre.[89]

Cheyne answered what he viewed as the pernicious materialism of

[86] Nicholas Robinson, *A New Theory of Physick and Diseases founded on the Principles of the Newtonian Philosophy* (London, 1725), p. 10. See *D.N.B.*, XVII, p. 36. For a fuller account of the following, see Anita Guerrini, 'Ether Madness: Newtonian Ideas of Insanity', forthcoming in Stephen G. Brush (ed.) *Newton's Principia, 1687–1987* (Princeton University Press).
[87] Nicholas Robinson, *A New System of the Spleen, Vapours and Hypochondriack Melancholy* (London, 1729), pp. 2–4, 15–17.   [88] *Ibid.*, pp. 18–23, 66–7.
[89] *Ibid.*, pp. 27–30, 35–42, 78–9.

such works as Robinson's in *The English Malady*, published in 1733. In this extended discussion of mental function, he used his own case to show the nature of mental illness and the central role of the soul in its onset and cure. His account begins mechanically enough: 'the Human Body is a Machin of an infinite Number and Variety of different Channels and Pipes, filled with various and different Liquids and Fluids'. Nervous diseases arose from weakness in the solids, especially the nerves.[90]

His discussion of nervous function, however, is highly critical of other accounts of Newton's ether. In 1732, an Irish physician named Bryan Robinson (1680–1746; no relation to Nicholas) published *A Treatise of the Animal Oeconomy*, in which, like Mead and Pemberton, he identified Newton's ether with the nervous fluid.[91] Cheyne rejected this explanation. No material fluid was rare enough to cause muscular motion, he claimed; moreover, the vulgar notion of tubular nerves was not supported by anatomy. Cheyne returned to Newton's image, in query 24, of solid nerves along which a vibrating motion is communicated by the ether. Cheyne again used an analogy to music which he had used in the *Essay*: the brain is the conductor, and the music flows along the nerves. Since the nerves were not tubular, mental illness could not be caused by blockages in them, although Newton had suggested that 'obstructions' in the nerves, by breaking the vibrating motion, 'create Palsies'.[92]

But was this ether material or immaterial? Cheyne returned to his earlier arguments on the nature of spirit, and elaborated them. The ether which caused cohesion and other functions must itself be made of particles; must we then postulate other ethers to explain this one, or must we 'allow Particles of Matter impress'd with these Qualities in their Creation immediately by the *Supreme Being*'? Obviously, Newton's intent, believed Cheyne, was to demonstrate the direct activity of God in the universe, and his ether was an intermediary between God and nature, as Cheyne had explained in the *Philosophical Principles*. Unlike Nicholas Robinson and his 'self-moving' soul, Cheyne explicitly involved God directly. Always the platonist, he indeed postulated a hierarchy of 'Intermediates between *pure, immaterial Spirit* and *gross Matter*'.[93]

To substantiate this central role of the spirit in mental function and

[90] Cheyne, *English Malady*, pp. 4, 14.
[91] Bryan Robinson, *A Treatise of the Animal Oeconomy* (Dublin, 1732). See *D.N.B.*, XVII, p. 4–5.
[92] Cheyne, *English Malady*, p. 69; Newton, *Opticks*, p. 354.
[93] Cheyne, *English Malady*, pp. 85–9. See Metzger, *Attraction universelle*, part III.

mental illness, Cheyne turned to his own case, describing his illness of
1705–6. His health, he claimed, could not sustain the fast lane of
fashionable London life, and he experienced a severe breakdown, with
feelings of vertigo and nausea as well as a severe depression. He retired
to the country sorely melancholy, and began to contemplate his faith.
But the comfortable latitudinarianism of the 1705 *Philosophical Principles* provided little comfort, and he recognized the worth of Pitcairne's
comment that 'metaphysics can never prove a religion'. As we have
seen, this realization led to his greater emphasis on the role of God and
spirit in the 1715 *Philosophical Principles*.[94]

In his country retirement, however, the weakness of his faith made
Cheyne even more depressed, and he sank into a religious melancholy,
a near relative of religious enthusiasm, its opposite. He dealt with his
physical illnesses by his usual methods of diet and exercise; but this
moral illness could only be dealt with by spiritual means. This was not
a mere clog of matter in the brain. He read theological works and
gradually strengthened his faith, which in turn strengthened his mental
state; by contemplating the love of God, he learned to love himself.[95]

Cheyne was not alone in rejecting an established church increasingly
based on '*abstracted* Reasonings, as well as . . . the best *natural
Philosophy*'.[96] John Wesley, who had so admired Cheyne's *Essay*,
made a similar spiritual journey in the late 1720s to a more direct and
emotional relationship with God. By the time *The English Malady*
appeared, the methodists were well known in Oxford; and in that same
year, 1733, the first extended account of methodist views appeared in
The Oxford Methodists. This work has been attributed to William
Law, whom Cheyne certainly knew; he introduced Law to the works of
the German mystic Jacob Boehme.[97]

By the later 1730s, Cheyne and Wesley were well acquainted, and
they mutually influenced each other.[98] Wesley borrowed much of the
methodist regimen from Cheyne's *Essay*, while Cheyne, in later works,
continued the attempt to integrate Newtonian science with the life of
the spirit. He commenced his *Essay on Regimen* (1740) with a comment that could have been written by Wesley: 'the true Reason of the
present *Darkness*, both in *Providence* and *Revelation*, is the Difficulty
of recovering this *Purity* of *Heart* and *Life*'. In this work and his last,

---

[94] See Guerrini, 'Ether Madness'; Cheyne, *English Malady*, pp. 325–52.
[95] Cheyne, *English Malady*, pp. 325–52; see also Cheyne, *Essay of Health*, pp. 165–6.
[96] Cheyne, *English Malady*, p. 330.
[97] *The Oxford Methodists* (London, 1733); see *D.N.B.*, XI, 677–81, s.v. 'Law, William'. See also
     V.H.H. Green, *The Young Mr. Wesley* (London, 1961), p. 200.
[98] See Guerrini, 'Ether Madness'.

The Natural Method of Cureing the Diseases of the Body (1743), he reiterated his now familiar themes.[99]

With Cheyne, we seem to travel the full distance from strict mechanism to deep mysticism. Yet the distance between these two points may not have been as great as it now seems. While I would not go as far as a recent characterization of eighteenth-century Britain as a confessional state,[100] we should not need to be reminded that religious motives remained compelling for a very long time. Science did not displace these concerns, but recast their expression.

By the 1730s, physicians who professed to be Newtonians formed a far more heterogeneous group than the Pitcairne circle of the turn of the century. Pitcairne and Gregory had espoused Newtonianism as a fruitful intellectual path. The motivations of their followers, however, were more complex. While the Keills and other Scots found in Newton an intellectual model, they were not immune to the blandishments of fame and fortune which discipleship increasingly offered. In this they followed the example of David Gregory, who had used Newton's recommendation in 1691 to obtain the Savilian professorship of astronomy at Oxford. Richard Mead proved to be a particular beneficiary of the Newton connection, and he in turn acted as an important patron for younger physicians such as Pemberton and Nicholas Robinson.

For the third generation of physicians who came of age in the 1710s and 20s, Newton was a given in the scientific world. Certainly not all young physicians therefore professed themselves to be Newtonians, but those who did seemed guaranteed of success in the elite circles to which scientific respectability was important in a physician. Freind, Mead and Cheyne demonstrated the lucrative potential of the scientific reputation. If Cheyne took Newton off into mystical realms, Mead remained firmly grounded in the real world, to the extent of revising his atomistic works in the 1740s to conform to the new Newtonian orthodoxy of ethers.

While not quite all things to all men, Newtonianism could be a remarkably flexible doctrine among physicians. Men of widely varying political and religious views comfortably coexisted as disciples at Newton's Royal Society. I would not deny the evident connection made by contemporaries between Newtonianism and the whig state, but it seems to me that this connection needs to be examined much more critically than it has yet been. If such men as Cheyne are to be considered good Newtonians, our categories need to be redefined.

[99] George Cheyne, *An Essay on Regimen* (London, 1740), preface, p. vi.
[100] J.C.D. Clark, *English Society 1688–1832* (Cambridge, 1985).

9

Physicians and the new philosophy: Henry Stubbe and the virtuosi-physicians

HAROLD J. COOK

Where Practitioners of Physick are altogether illiterate, there oftentimes Specificks may be best met with.

Robert Boyle, *The Usefulnesse of Experimental Naturall Philosophy*[1]

That reasoning [is] equally absurd, which pleads for the Empericks to be countenanced as if their experimentings might very much further this pretended Reformation in Physick.

Nathaniel Hodges, *Vindiciae Medicinae et Medicorum*[2]

As the new philosophy gained in popularity and persuasiveness in England in the later seventeenth century, London physicians became embroiled in a number of disputes. Various aspects of the new philosophy challenged parts of the established outlook held by university-trained physicians. The disputes in which physicians became engaged concerned both intellectual and professional issues, for they involved arguments about both the intellectual foundations and the practice of academic physic. The arguments cannot be characterized simply as quarrels between physicians and their medical rivals, be they apothecaries, chemists, or virtuosi, for the physicians themselves as well as their opponents were divided in their opinions about how they ought to respond to the challenges of the new philosophy. Some physicians vigorously touted the advantages of the new philosophy, while others pointed to the dangers of moving too far from the established ways that made physicians different from other medical practitioners. Because

For helpful suggestions on an earlier version of this chapter I would like to thank the discussants at the Cambridge conference, and William Coleman, David Lux, Michael Mac-Donald, Ronald Numbers and Nicholas Steneck.
[1] Robert Boyle, *Some Considerations touching the Usefulnesse of Experimental Naturall Philosophy* (Oxford, 1663), part II, p. 221.
[2] Nathaniel Hodges, *Vindiciae Medicinae et Medicorum: Or an Apology for the Profession and Professors of Physick* (London, 1666), p. 6.

the intellectual issues were so important to the profession of physic, quarrels among physicians and between themselves and others undoubtedly would have arisen in a wide range of circumstances. But in restoration England, a variety of institutional issues complicated the arguments. As it happened, the various opinions might have been set out in more muted tones had it not been for the ways in which the London College of Physicians seemed to be losing institutional prestige to the newly established Royal Society. In untangling the arguments over physic and philosophy of the later 1660 and 1670s, then, we can understand better the precise challenges raised by the new philosophy for a group of well-educated men sensitive to the implications of intellectual change. We can see how it threatened to change the intellectual foundations of a profession.

While the medical disputes of the restoration raised fundamental questions about the kind of knowledge physicians ought to pursue, there were limitations to the arguments. None of the physicians took issue with the new physiological discoveries of William Harvey and his adherents, which have received so much attention from historians. Nor did any of them completely reject the new philosophy or its branches, such as chemistry. Rather, the physicians struggled with the fundamental problem of precisely what aspects of the new philosophy were worth incorporating into the arsenal of learned physic. The consequent debates among physicians therefore grappled with questions about the intellectual foundations upon which their profession ought to rest, and hence about what kind of a profession it would be. To suggest that the medical debates in the period of the 'scientific revolution' were merely about physiology or curative techniques misses the central problem facing physicians in the period. It distorts our view about the kind of learning upon which the physicians' reputations rested.

In the seventeenth century, university-trained physicians still studied 'physic', which was divided into both theoretical and practical parts. The theoretical was divided into a knowledge of the naturals, non-naturals, and contra-naturals; the practical part was divided into the five institutes: physiology, pathology, semiotics, hygiene and therapeutics. Both parts were grounded in the study of natural philosophy, even the therapeutic part of 'practice' requiring a firm knowledge of Latinate grammar, logic and philosophy. Physic not only enabled a physician to restore health to the ill, it enabled him to preserve health by prescribing a regimen; and it enabled him to do both by offering learned advice. Physicians prescribed therapies when necessary, but ideally did so only after all other advice and counsel failed. However, the virtuosi (or promoters of the new philosophy, people we sometimes call 'scientists') saw the purpose of physic as above all medical: to prescribe therapy rather than to offer learned counsel. The virtuosi argued that physicians must know details about nature, for such a knowledge in natural history rather than sophistication in natural philosophy led most quickly and certainly to new therapeutic discoveries. But trimming learned physic back to merely therapeutic medicine could too easily lead to a belief that simple experience with natural things might suffice for medical knowledge. To some physicians' minds, therefore, the virtuosi's interests strengthened the arguments of medical empirics and undercut the need for physicians to be deeply educated in natural philosophy.

The learned members of the London College of Physicians were divided on their interest in and assessment of the new philosophy. While a number of College physicians actively promoted the new philosophy, some Fellows of the College worried about its implications for their profession. Physicians intrigued by the new philosophy argued that as men educated in applied natural philosophy, they ought to lead the new explorations in natural history, and that discoveries in natural history would uncover new and better methods of treatment. On the other hand, those physicians who saw themselves as scholars of physic (and of the natural philosophy upon which physic had been built) tended to see the promoters of the new philosophy as people who threatened to undercut the prestige of learned physic. They thought that if the virtuosi had their way, the profession of physic might be transformed into the practice of mere medicine: that the university-inculcated discipline of physic might become a merely curative art based upon empirically discovered therapies. Such a transformation threatened to break down the division between the learned physicians and their unlearned rivals.

The arguments of those physicians who saw the new philosophy as encouraging philistinism were presented most forcefully in the pamphlet war in which Henry Stubbe fought vigorously: in 1670 and 1671, Henry Stubbe, practising physic in Warwickshire, published four books attacking the virtuosi and the Royal Society. This pamphlet war has been disassociated from its context by most historians: those who have seen in Stubbe only a reactionary enemy of the Royal Society, those who see him as a radical, those who have seen the surrounding debates only in light of an 'age-old' controversy between physicians and apothecaries[3] and those who have discerned the medical debates primarily as a conflict between chemists and Galenists. As we shall see, while the arguments swirled around a number of parties, at root they centred upon the question of the kind of knowledge best suited for medical practice. Because the Stubbe controversy flowed from a large set of problems, Stubbe explicitly brought some of these other controversies into his exposé of the dangers of the new philosophy.

Stubbe himself has been commonly portrayed as a unique individual whose works caused a stir but were of little consequence. Orthodox opinion views him as an 'ancient' fighting the 'moderns',[4] and as a splenetic and venal penman.[5] The suspicion of many contemporaries and most historians has been that Stubbe was a paid hack for Dr Baldwin Hamey, the younger, or other members of the London College of Physicians. Yet this might mean only that Stubbe was a trimmer who got out of hand, running well beyond his charter due to his choleric temper. To supporters of this view, Stubbe's works are of little consequence for suggesting differences between the virtuosi and the physicians. Hamey's biographer, for example, decided that Hamey's '"Champion" far exceeded his mandate';[6] and Sir George Clark's history of the London College of Physicians raised doubts about any connection between Stubbe and Hamey, further declaring that even if a member of the College did hire Stubbe, it was done privately and had nothing to do with the College itself.[7] A. Rupert Hall, following Clark's lead, also dismisses Stubbe's views as peculiar and private, arising from individual spleen.[8]

[3] See Charles F. Mullett, 'Physician vs. Apothecary, 1669–1671: An Episode in an Age-Long Controversy', *Scientific Monthly*, XLIX (1939), 558–65; C. Wall, and H.C. Cameron, *A History of the Worshipful Society of Apothecaries of London*, ed. E.A. Underwood, vol. I: *1617–1815* (London, 1961), pp. 114–20, 356–7; Sir G.N. Clark, *A History of the Royal College of Physicians of London* (Oxford, 1964), I, pp. 342–4.

[4] Richard Foster Jones, *Ancients and Moderns: A Study of the Rise of the Scientific Movement in Seventeenth-Century England* (1st edn 1936; 2nd edn 1961; reprint, 1975), pp. 238, 244–63. But because he exhibited some 'modern' interests, for Jones, Stubbe was 'really confused about the issue' of ancients and moderns (p. 245).

[5] R.H. Syfret, 'Some Early Critics of the Royal Society', *Notes and Records of the Royal Society*, VIII (1950), 20–64, esp. 20–42; R.H. Syfret, 'Some Early Reactions to the Royal Society', *Notes and Records of the Royal Society*, VII (1950), 207–58, esp. 255–6.

[6] John Keevil, *The Stranger's Son* (London, 1953), pp. 178–80.

[7] Clark, *History of the Royal College*, pp. 311–12.

[8] A. Rupert Hall, 'Medicine and the Royal Society', in A.G. Debus (ed.), *Medicine in Seventeenth Century England* (Berkeley, 1974), pp. 421–52, esp. 421–3. Also see Harcourt Brown, *Scientific Organizations in Seventeenth Century France (1620–1680)* (Baltimore, 1934), pp. 255–7, who writes that 'Stubbs [was] a pamphleteer of no consequence, hired by a jealous supporter of an older institution' (p. 257). However, note that Sir Hans Sloane was asked to send a copy of one of Stubbe's tracts to Spain, even in 1735: Brit. Lib., Sloane MS. 4026, 'Sloane to Monsieur Buriet, Medecin de la Chambre du Roi D'Espagne, Oct. 2, 1735', fo. 320.

Most recently, James R. Jacob has attempted to reverse the ideology of Stubbe, while still retaining the view that he was unique. Jacob argues that Stubbe's attack on the Royal Society had its origin in the 'radical' ideology of Hobbes he imbibed during the revolutionary period.[9] Although forced into outward conformity by the reactionary atmosphere of the restoration, Stubbe's language veiled a hidden message about the dangers of the new philosophy and its supporters, according to Jacob: Stubbe found the Royal Society to be promoting an ideology of materialism and capitalism, while he held out for a free-thinking brotherhood. Stubbe thus becomes the first in a continuous line of underground radicals who appear in the open only in the years following the Glorious Revolution of 1688. Jacob's argument does have the merit of examining Stubbe's pamphlets against the Royal Society in the light of his writings of the late 1640s and the 1650s. But Jacob follows the interpretation of Stubbe's position first developed by his opponent, Joseph Glanvill, and does not pursue Stubbe's career or work beyond the time of his first tracts against the Royal Society. Jacob thus paints Stubbe as a renegade, never even examining the question of whether Stubbe had patrons, when it is clear from Stubbe's own statements that during the restoration the very royalist Drs Thomas Willis and Alexander Fraizer aided Stubbe, and that probably Hamey did as well. Moreover, it is doubtful whether Hobbseianism was fundamentally 'radical': while espousing an unorthodox corpuscul-arianism, Hobbes nevertheless also argued for very strong royal autho-rity.[10] In short, Jacob's argument about Stubbe being an isolated figure and a radical during the 1660s is not persuasive.

Most historians, then, have agreed that Stubbe's publications do not signify anything other than the private views of a peculiar individual, prefering to assume that there was no serious conflict between physi-cians and virtuosi. There is an alternative view, however, one that provides the starting point for this chapter: a view that takes the debates about the new philosophy in which Stubbe became engaged as indeed pointing to fundamental issues. The new philosophy was, after all, new in some important ways; it did have intellectual potency; and it therefore gave real cause for concern to established scholars in physic

---

[9] James Jacob, *Henry Stubbe: Radical Protestantism and the Early Enlightenment* (Cambridge, 1983).

[10] For a recent examination of Hobbes's ideology, see Steven Shapin and Simon Schaffer, *Leviathan and the Air Pump: Hobbes, Boyle, and the Experimental Life* (Princeton, 1986); see also Quentin Skinner, 'Thomas Hobbes and the Nature of the Early Royal Society', *Hist. J.*, XII (1969), 217–39.

as well as in church and university.[11] Stubbe's tracts therefore provide a focus for an investigation of the wider cultural context of restoration London, in which the profession of physic was in turmoil, caused in part by the implications of the new philosophy.

PHYSIC AND THE VIRTUOSI

At the time that Henry Stubbe took up his pen against the virtuosi he was not a London physician. He possessed only an M.A., but he had been a member of the circle of physicians and virtuosi at Oxford during the interregnum as well as second library-keeper at the Bodleian. He had gone on to practice physic at Stratford-upon-Avon; after the restoration he entered upon a practice in the king's service in Jamaica; and then upon returning to England in the middle of the 1660s, he practiced again, this time in Warwick and around Bath. He had friends at court (as his later works of propaganda against the Dutch show), among them Sir Alexander Fraizer,[12] the king's first physician and the person who (with Thomas Willis) secured him his post in Jamaica; and according to a later account, Stubbe had friends among the members of the London College of Physicians.

As Stubbe explained, he was forced to take up his pen against the virtuosi after he heard about the disparaging remarks on physic published by Joseph Glanvill. Those remarks came to Stubbe's attention as he sat at the dinner table of an unnamed person of honour, a person who shared Glanvill's opinion because the virtuosi declared it to be true. The impetuous young minister Glanvill had recently published a book defending the new philosophy: begun as a defence of his intellectual interests against the charges of atheism levelled at him by his clerical colleagues,[13] Glanvill's *Plus Ultra* became transformed into a defence of the Royal Society, or the 'Royal Colledge of Philosophers' as he called it.[14] In his enterprise of detailing the new philosophy he had

---

[11] See esp. Michael Hunter, *Science and Society in Restoration England* (Cambridge, 1981), pp. 136–61.

[12] Unfortunately, very little can be discovered about Fraizer's views on physic, medicine, or the new philosophy, although it is clear that when elected to the Royal Society he never came to it to be admitted: Michael Hunter, *The Royal Society and its Fellows 1660–1700: The Morphology of an Early Scientific Institution* (Chalfont St Giles, Bucks., 1982), pp. 186–7.

[13] Nicholas H. Steneck, '"The Ballad of Robert Crosse and Joseph Glanvill" and the Background to *Plus Ultra*', *Brit. J. Hist. Sci.*, XIV (1981), 59–74.

[14] Joseph Glanvill, *Plus Ultra: Or, the Progress and Advancement of Knowledge Since the Days of Aristotle* (London, 1668), p. 1. Further details on tracts published between 1668 and 1673 are included in the appendix to this chapter.

the encouragement of Henry Oldenburg, John Beale and possibly other virtuosi.[15]

According to Glanvill's words, the Royal Society explicitly disavowed philosophical discussion in favour of practical knowledge of benefit to mankind. In the course of introducing this argument, Glanvill made many remarks about how the new philosophy would transform physic for the better, including the remark that Stubbe's host soon reported to Stubbe as a simple fact:

> the *Modern Experimenters* think, that the *Philosophers* of elder Times, though their wits were excellent, yet the way they took was not like to bring much *advantage* to *Knowledge*, or any of the *Uses* of *Humane life* . . . And the *unfruitfulness* of those *Methods* of *Science*, which so many *Centuries* never brought the World so much *practical, beneficial* knowledge, as would help towards the *Cure* of a *Cut Finger*, is a palpable Argument, That they were *fundamental Mistakes*, and that the *Way* was not *right*.[16]

Here was a very direct attack on university-taught physic. If one believed Glanvill, the medical knowledge possessed by the physicians was virtually useless because it inculcated a sophistication in natural philosophy derived from the ancients rather than a practical course of curing. Only the new programme promoted by the Royal Society, which dealt with useful rather than argumentative knowledge, could chart a course to remove physic from its slough of ignorance to the firm rock of curative experience.

Whether by design or simplicity, Glanvill's remarks could not have been better calculated as a frontal attack on the intellectual training of university-educated physicians. Moreover, if one is to believe Stubbe, Glanvill's words were read and repeated by laymen to their physicians. Therefore, because of the incident at the dinner table, and that 'sense of *Injury* I supposed to be done *to me* and all other *Rational Physicians*, by this *barbarous Opiniatour*', Stubbe

> determined to avenge *my Faculty* [the learned physicians] upon Mr. *Glanvill* . . . and by *sacrificing* that *Virtuoso* to publick *Obliquy*, thereby to establish (if possible) our *general repose* and tranquillitie, that *we* might not (as I observed *we* were) be troubled in *all Companies* and Assemblies, with *Extravagencies of this kinde*.[17]

Stubbe's own book therefore tried to set the public straight about Glanvill's claims, especially about the mistakes Glanvill made in his chapter on medicine.

For after a general prefatory chapter, Glanvill's book had taken up

---

[15] *The Correspondence of Henry Oldenburg*, ed. A. Rupert Hall and Marie Boas Hall (Madison, Wisc., 1966–70), vols. III–VII, letters no. 672, 873.   [16] Glanvill, *Plus Ultra*, pp. 7–8.
[17] Henry Stubbe, *The Plus Ultra Reduced to a Non Plus* (London, 1670), preface, pp. 1–2.

matters that concerned physic. Chemistry and anatomy were some of his favourite examples for showing the usefulness of the new philosophy to life. Glanvill dismissed phlebotomy with contempt as an outmoded practice of physicians while arguing that chemical medicines, discovered by the new experimenters, resulted in pure and effective drugs. Glanvill also claimed that anatomy was pioneered by the virtuosi and led to such matters as transfusions, which would also much improve the health of men.[18] He clearly found medicine important only in so far as it could cure diseases, and he also clearly found learned physic's abilities in that department sadly lacking. In short, Glanvill argued that the virtuosi of the Royal Society were overthrowing all the old, useless ways and finding new methods to promote useful knowledge, in physic as in all other subjects.

Stubbe set about composing a vigorous rebuttal to Glanvill by early 1669; at the same time, there threatened to be proceedings brought against the Royal Society in the House of Commons.[19] As Stubbe soon explained to his patron Lord Arlington, to his acquaintance Robert Boyle, and to the public, the attack of the virtuosi upon philosophy was dangerous because so much of the established order was rooted in philosophical traditions. When virtuosity threatened the traditional underpinnings of intellectual life it therefore threatened to undermine the established church, the established polity, the universities, and the London College of Physicians.[20] But the virtuosi fought back against Stubbe by spreading rumours about him at court, and they initially stopped him from getting his works into print.[21]

When Stubbe's three works finally appeared in the spring of 1670, the first of them directly rebutted Glanvill. Stubbe tried to correct Glanvill's errors and to temper Glanvill's too head-strong enthusiasm for the new philosophy with a knowledgeable respect for the natural philosophy of the universities. Like other physicians of his time, Stubbe criticized Glanvill for his ignorance of chemistry while praising

---

[18] Glanvill, *Plus Ultra*, ch. 2, pp. 9–19.
[19] See Stubbe's letter to Boyle, in Boyle's *Works*, ed. Thomas Birch (1772; reprinted Hildesheim, 1965), I, pp. xc–xci; *Correspondence of Oldenburg*, letters no. 1222, 1248, 1374, 1380, 1477, 1481, 1482, 1504, 1603.
[20] Letter to Boyle, Boyle's *Works*, pp. xc–xci; Stubbe's letter of 18 May 1670 to Lord Arlington, *Calendar of State Papers, Domestic Series, 1670 with Addenda, 1660 to 1670* (London, 1895), pp. 224–6.
[21] *Correspondence of Oldenburg*, letters no. 1150, 1156; letter of Stubbe to Boyle, Boyle's *Works*, pp. xcii–xciii; Stubbe, *Plus Ultra Reduced*, preface; 'A Reply unto the Letter', in Stubbe, *A Censure Upon Certain Passages contained in the History of the Royal Society* (Oxford, 1671), pp. 13–32; Nicholas Steneck has also told me of an unpublished letter of Stubbe's in which he details how the virtuosi had tried to block his works from reaching print.

the subject for having brought much good.[22] Stubbe showed that the
credit for advances in anatomy should go to the university-trained
physicians and not to the virtuosi,[23] and that transfusion experiments
were first done in Paris and Oxford rather than at the Royal Society (as
he also demonstrated that they were without therapeutic value).[24]
Stubbe argued generally that it was best to rely upon experienced
methods in physic rather than new and untried cures.[25] In short, in the
course of correcting Glanvill, Stubbe demonstrated his own knowledge of both physic and the new philosophy while defending the
intellectual foundations of learned physic. Stubbe continued this
theme in his other works. In his reply to Thomas Sprat's *History of the
Royal Society* of 1667, for example, Stubbe remarked that while the
virtuosi's arguments were often taken to support empirics and new
methods of medical practice, the therapies of learned physic were still
valid: the 'most that the *Novellists* have done, is to find out *new
reasons* for an *antient practice*'.[26]

   Glanvill's comments suggested, then, that even a minister educated,
like him, in a university, could draw conclusions from the new philosophy that menaced established learning. For many physicians,
Glanvill's book was another instance of a point of view growing in
influence, which favoured new experiments over natural philosophy.
It suggested that such a point of view might encourage untamed
medical empiricism, an empiricism that would focus wholly on the
therapeutic part of physic to the exclusion of the other parts. Moreover, since Glanvill seemed to be speaking with at least the complicity
of others, the professional dangers inherent in his intellectual position
seemed to receive the endorsement of the virtuosi. Baldwin Hamey's
nephew may therefore have been right to suggest that his uncle
patronized Stubbe.[27] Hamey had been a powerful and conservative
member of the London College of Physicians, although he had just
been voted out of the offices of *consiliarius* and Treasurer in favour of

---

[22] Stubbe, *Plus Ultra Reduced*, pp. 50–70; in fact Stubbe was a good chemist, but Glanvill was
   not: see *ibid.*, pp. 135–53 for Stubbe's analysis of the mineral water at Bath, and his 'Directions
   for drinking of the Bath-water, and *Ars Cosmetica*', published in John Hall, *Select observations on English bodies*, 3rd edn (London, 1683), while Glanvill importuned Oldenburg to
   have Boyle advise him on how to analyse mineral waters: *Correspondence of Oldenburg*,
   letters no. 813, 821, 957.   [23] Stubbe, *Plus Ultra Reduced*, pp. 71–115.
[24] Stubbe, *Plus Ultra Reduced*, pp. 116–35.   [25] Stubbe, *Plus Ultra Reduced*, postscript.
[26] Stubbe, *Legends no Histories* (London, 1670), sig. *1v.
[27] Ralph Palmer, 'The Life of the Most Eminent Dr. Baldwin Hamey', 1733 (Royal College of
   Physicians, MS. 337). My examination of the manuscript finds that the passages referring to
   Hamey's patronage of Stubbe (page inserted between pp. 90 and 91) is not a forgery, being in
   the same hand and ink as the rest of the manuscript (in which it is common to find inserted
   pages).

men who followed the new philosophy. Physicians of the College usually refused to defend themselves in print as something beneath their dignity, but they did employ others to defend their interests.[28] It may indeed have been that, as he claimed, Stubbe exploded with anger at the virtuosi after hearing of Glanvill's remarks; but he was also encouraged to go forward with his public arguments by receiving protection, favours, and possibly the promise of an introduction into London circles (which would help him set up a practice there) from some of the physicians of the College. The rewards offered by Hamey and others may well have encouraged Stubbe to put his views into print.[29] Stubbe certainly could have used the protection of influential men, for Glanvill defended himself by tarring Stubbe with the brush of sedition;[30] Stubbe did his best to defend himself by counter-attacking.[31] But as we shall see, whether Stubbe came to the controversy with Glanvill and the virtuosi as a recruit or a volunteer, the opinions he expressed were not unique.

Glanvill's remarks were not just offensive to many physicians and apparently persuasive to hosts of dinner parties, they came at a moment when the learned members of London College of Physicians felt particularly vulnerable. Glanvill's book was published just three years after the bitter controversy of the College of Physicians with the chemists that almost resulted in the chartering of a Socety of Chemical Physicians apparently with the backing of some of the virtuosi and courtiers;[32] at the same time as the Royal Society was planning to erect a 'College' of its own;[33] and immediately upon the heels of an election in the College itself that replaced many of the philosopher–physicians such as Hamey with physicians who were also members of the Royal

[28] For example, William Johnson, the College's chemist, had earlier defended the College (Johnson, *Short Amimadversions* (London, 1652) and *Agurto-Mastix* (London, 1665), and Hamey's protégé Charles Goodall later promised Richard Boulton that he would get him into a London practice in order to get Boulton to defend the College from attack (Boulton, *A Letter to Dr. Charles Goodall* (London, 1699).

[29] Stubbe did receive the gift of some silver plate from an Oxford don: *Correspondence of Oldenburg*, letter no. 1539.

[30] Glanvill, *A Praefatory Answer to Mr. Henry Stubbe* (London, 1671), preface, pp. 7–192 *passim*. Glanvill's argument is the one that Jacob takes seriously, almost word for word, and despite the evidence that Glanvill rather than Stubbe may have been a former puritan: see Jacob, *Henry Stubbe*.

[31] Stubbe, 'A Reply unto the Letter', appended to his *A Censure Upon Certain Passages contained in the History of the Royal Society* (Oxford, 1671); Stubbe, *The Lord Bacons Relation of the Sweating-Sickness Examined* (London, 1671), pp. 6–32.

[32] Harold J. Cook, 'The Society of Chemical Physicians, the New Philosophy, and the Restoration Court', *Bull. Hist. Med.* LXI (1987), 61–77.

[33] Michael Hunter, 'A "College" for the Royal Society: The Abortive Plan of 1667–1668', *Notes and Records of the Royal Society*, XXXVIII (1984), 159–86.

Society.[34] These institutional threats appeared to be even more significant in that Glanvill's arguments echoed the opinions of some members of the College of Physicians themselves who were virtuosi, just
then publishing their own tracts arguing that the therapeutic part of
physic should be made pre-eminent and reformed experimentally.

THE PHYSICIANS AND THE MAKING OF MEDICINES

The virtuoso Fellow of the College of Physicians who argued most
forcefully for the importance of the new philosophy to physic was
Christopher Merrett. He and some other physician members of the
Royal Society published several treatises in the later 1660s that appeared to be attacks on the apothecaries, but which were in truth more
significantly about the usefulness of the new philosophy to medical
practice. Merrett's works in the dispute with the apothecaries clearly
exhibited his belief that only if he and his physician colleagues became
better acquainted with the experimental details of medicine could they
withstand the inroads apothecaries and other empirics were making
into medical practice: the physicians had to become virtuosi.

Merrett, like Stubbe an Oxford man (M.D. 1643), had been an
original member of the Royal Society. At Oxford he had been part of
William Harvey's circle; when he moved to London he took part in the
'1645 group' of natural philosophers and then, from its founding until
the end of the decade, actively participated in the Royal Society.[35]
Merrett's book on natural history was among the 'exceptional books
by English authors' according to the Italian visitor Lorenzo
Magalotti.[36] Merrett also published a translation of Antonio Neri's

[34] Harold J. Cook, *The Decline of the Old Medical Regime in Stuart London* (Ithaca, N.Y. 1986),
pp. 162–4.
[35] Robert G. Frank, Jr., *Harvey and the Oxford Physiologists: Scientific Ideas and Social
Interactions* (Berkeley and Los Angeles, 1980), pp. 74–5; letters of John Wallis about the
background to the Royal Society, reprinted in Sir Henry Lyons, *The Royal Society 1660–1940:
A History of its Administration under its Charters* (Cambridge, 1946), pp. 8, 11; Hunter, *The
Royal Society*, pp. 162–3. Merrett participated frequently in the early meetings of the Royal
Society: see Thomas Birch, *The History of the Royal Society of London* (London, 1756), vols. I,
II.
[36] W.E. Knowles Middleton (ed. and trans.), *Lorenzo Magalotti at the Court of Charles II: His
Relazione d'Inghilterra of 1668* (Waterloo, Ontario, 1980), p. 149; Christopher Merrett, *Pinax
Rerum Naturalium Britannicarum, Continens Vegetabilia, Animalia, et Fossilia, In haec
Insula reperta inchoatus* (London, 1667). For a modern evaluation of Merrett's book, see
Charles E. Raven, *English Naturalists from Neckam to Ray: A Study in the Making of the
Modern World* (Cambridge, 1947), pp. 305–38. Merrett's book may have been stimulated by
the fact that the Royal Society '"desired [him] to prosecute his collection of the curious things
of nature to be found in England, and to present the society therewith"': quoted in K.
Theodore Hoppen, 'The Nature of the Early Royal Society', *Brit. J. Hist. Sci.*, IX (1976), 5.

The Art of Glass, how to colour Glass in 1662, to which he added his own *An Acount of the Glass-drops*; he had his work on cold published as an appendix to Robert Boyle's *New Experiments touching cold* (1665); he presented at least six formal papers on natural history to the Royal Society;[37] and he headed the Society's committee on the history of trades.[38] But Merrett was not only an active member of the Royal Society. He became an active member of the College of Physicians as well. After enrolling as a Candidate (1648) and a Fellow (1651), he served as Gulstonian lecturer for the College (1654) and as a Censor (1657 to 1663 except for 1659, and again in 1670). He also resided in the College as Harveian Librarian, a post he obtained upon Harvey's own recommendation when the Harveian Museum and Library opened in 1654. Most important, Merrett threw himself into the campaign during the restoration to re-establish the College's prestige and authority over other practitioners,[39] and into both the disputes between apothecaries and physicians and the controversy between Stubbe and the virtuosi.

For physicians like Merrett, who were active members in both the Royal Society and the College of Physicians, the new philosophy and physic complemented each other. The definition of a physician's task that Merrett later gave is therefore telling:

The word Physician, derived from the Greek *pusikos*, is plainly and fully rendred by the word *Naturalist*, (that is) one well vers'd in the full extent of Nature, and Natural things; hereunto add the due, and skilful preparation and application of them to Mens Bodies, in order to their Health, and prolongation of Life, and you have a comprehensive Definition of a Physician.[40]

To preserve health and prolong life, Merrett and others wrote, the physician needed to know all about natural things (that is, natural

[37] Merrett, 'A Paper Concerning the Mineral Called Zaffora by Dr. Merrett found amongst Dr. Hook's papers by Mr. Waller'; 'The Art of Refining Lead'; 'Some Observations Concerning the Ordering of Wines' (later published at the end of Walter Charleton's *Discourses on the Wits of Men* [1692]; 'A Table to find when the Washes begin to be Fordable'; 'An Account of the Tynn Mines and working of Tinn in the County of Cornewall'; and 'Observations concerning the Uniting of the Barks of Trees cut, to the tree itself' (Royal Society, Classified Papers).

[38] Birch, *The History of the Royal Society*, I, p. 439.

[39] Merrett brought out *Catalogus Librorum, Instrumentorum Chirurgicorum, Rerum Curiosarum, Exoticarumque Coll. Med. Lond. quae habentur un Musaeo Harveano* (London, 1660) and *A Collection of Acts of Parliament, Charters, Trials at Law, and Judges Opinions Concerning Those Grants of the Colledge of Physicians London* (London, 1660); he probably also drew up the *Collegii Medicorum Londinensium Fundatores et Benefactores* (London, 1662).

[40] *The Character of a Compleat Physician, or Naturalist*, (London, 1680?), pp. 2–3. This book is ascribed to Merrett by Anthony Wood, *Athenae Oxoniensis*, VI, cols. 430–2; and according to the catalogue at the Wellcome Institute Library the copy in the Bodleian Library is inscribed to John Aubrey from 'Dr. Chr. M'.

history) and how they could be made into medicines. A 'naturalist' physician would be a master of the precise, systematic, empirical details about nature that could establish the physicians' pre-eminence over other practitioners who knew only some things about nature. A studied naturalist might also discover new and beneficial uses for things, leading to new cures for diseases. Merrett's introduction to his book on natural history therefore explains that a full understanding of natural things and their proper names will end the ignorant blathering of the ill-informed and superstitious empirics and chemists against the physicians.[41] A physician ought therefore to be a virtuoso.

Hence, when Merrett launched himself into controversy with the apothecaries, there were far more than parochial conflicts between the London physicians and apothecaries at stake. Merrett and other physicians believed that the apothecaries were cheating the public by selling bad and over-priced medicines, and that they were also cozening the king's subjects by practising medicine themselves. However, the solution offered by Merrett and his two fellow publicists was not to invoke the legal privileges of the College of Physicians to prosecute this activity, but to have the physicians stop sending prescriptions to apothecaries and begin making up the drugs themselves: to become more like virtuosi. That this quarrel touched on more than institutional rivalries between the College and the Society of Apothecaries is also suggested by the fact that three of the six physicians publishing in this quarrel were not Fellows of the College of Physicians; and of the three College Fellows involved, all were *also* Fellows of the Royal Society.

The dispute was begun by three physicians who were natural historians and virtuosi: Jonathan Goddard,[42] Daniel Coxe[43] and Christopher Merrett.[44] They emphasized drug therapy over dietetic advice and, by arguing that physicians should give patients drugs made by themselves, encroached upon the trade of the apothecaries while telling their colleagues to reform their ways. But almost immediately, their arguments grew more complicated due to an anonymous reply

[41] Merrett, *Pinax Rerum Naturalium*. The work contains the lists of names and the definitions of English plants, animals and minerals, as well as various classifications for plants.
[42] [Jonathan Goddard?], *A Discourse Concerning Physick* (London, 1668); Jonathan Goddard, *A Discourse Setting forth the Unhappy Condition of the Practice of Physick* (London, 1670).
[43] [Daniel Coxe], *A Discourse wherein The Interest of the Patient in Reference to Physick and Physicians is soberly debated* (London, 1669).
[44] Christopher Merrett, *A Short View of the Frauds and Abuses Committed by Apothecaries* (London, 1669); *ibid.*, *The Second Edition more correct* (London, 1670); Merrett, *Self-Conviction; or an Enumeration of a Absurdities, Railings against the College, and Physicians in general* (London, 1670).

from the apothecaries,[45] two works defending the virtuosi/physicians by Timothy Clarke[46] and Gideon Harvey,[47] another objection by an apothecary,[48] two further defences of the physicians by a 'C.W.'[49] and Everard Maynwaring,[50] an attempt to reconcile the two sides,[51] and a final booklet by an apothecary.[52]

It is almost a commonplace to note that in the 1660s many members of the College of Physicians were concerned about both the growing institutional strength of the Society of Apothecaries and the apparently increasing boldness of its members to enter into the business of making money by diagnosing and prescribing for patients' diseases. The number of apothecaries in London, as throughout England, was growing rapidly, with the numbers of apothecaries who practiced medicine in addition to (or instead of) dispensing drugs consequently expanding as well.[53] The apothecaries, like other medical empirics, argued that their experiences with medicines made their knowledge therapeutically more useful than a physician's. More particularly, the Society of Apothecaries, as well as the Barber–Surgeons' Company and other groups and individuals, had, in April 1664, blocked ratification in the House of Commons of the new charter given to the College by the king. The new charter would have restored and extended the powers of the College to control medical practice in London, which had been lost in a court case of 1656.[54] The College had therefore suffered a grave blow to its public authority and prestige at a time when the restoration had seemed to promise it renewed institutional strength. It was natural for many physicians to resent the many medical rivals they were now impotent to control, among whom were the apothecaries.

The three physicians who began the dispute by publishing pamphlets in 1668 and 1669 argued that the increasingly bold and numerous apothecaries abused both physicians and patients by falsifying prescriptions and giving medical advice for personal economic gain. Goddard (a Fellow of both the College and the Royal

---

[45] *Lex Talionis* (London, 1670).
[46] Dr C.T. [Timothy Clarke], *Some Papers Writ in the Year 1664* (London, 1670).
[47] Gideon Harvey, *The Accomplisht Physician, the Honest Apothecary, and the Skilful Chyrurgeon* (London, 1670).
[48] *Medice Cura Teipsum! or the Apothecaries Plea* (London, 1671).
[49] C.W., *Reflections on a Libel* (1671).
[50] Everard Maynwaring, *Praxis Medicorum Antiqua et Nova* (London, 1671).
[51] *An Essay for the Regulation of the Practice of Physick* (London, 1673).
[52] C.D., *Some Reasons, of the Present Decay of the Practise of Physick in Learned and Approved Doctors* (London, 1675).
[53] On the rapidly expanding numbers of apothecaries in England, see John Patten, *English Towns, 1500–1700* (Hamden, Conn., 1978), pp. 273, 285.
[54] Cook, *Decline of the Old Medical Regime*, pp. 134–45.

Society) wrote that the lack of university education on the part of apothecaries meant that they necessarily lacked the mental skills possessed by physicians.[55] Coxe (a Fellow of the Royal Society) also spent the bulk of his book condemning the apothecaries: the physicians were apt to suffer from the 'malice or Design of Apothecaries',[56] the apothecaries were ignorant of Latin and therefore made mistakes in filling physicians' prescriptions,[57] they were not well acquainted with *materia medica*,[58] most apothecaries trusted 'to several Compositions, in whom . . . Physicians have little reason to confide',[59] and they substituted simples they had on hand for ones in the prescriptions, acted in other ways to adulterate drugs, and remained ignorant of chemistry.[60] Merrett also condemned the apothecaries for abusing medicines,[61] for abusing patients,[62] and for endeavouring 'to extirpate' the physicians.[63] The apothecaries, Merrett and the others argued, were profiting from the medical abuses they encouraged.[64] The remedy they proposed in such situations, however, was not better regulation of the apothecaries, but economic warfare: to stop sending prescriptions to the apothecaries.

This approach, however, meant that an another level the physicians' pamphlets argued not about how to reform the abuses of apothecaries but rather about how to reform the ways of the physicians. If physicians stopped sending prescriptions to apothecaries and made up medicines themselves, Merrett and the others claimed, the physicians would benefit medicine by learning more about drugs while discovering new cures for diseases. Merrett spent the bulk of his book trying to prove how making their own remedies would improve the practice of physicians.[65] Goddard even argued that the greatest part of the reason why ancient physicians had been such good practitioners was that they had made up their own medicines rather than employed apothecaries.[66] All three urged physicians to become more like virtuosi than natural philosophers, since the former course would lead to better cures, the end of medicine according to them all.

[55] Goddard, *Discourse Setting forth the Unhappy Condition*, p. 12.
[56] Coxe, *Discourse wherein The Interest of the Patient*, pp. 13–16.
[57] *Ibid.*, pp. 16–20.   [58] *Ibid.*, pp. 20–3.   [59] *Ibid.*, pp. 23–9.   [60] *Ibid.*, pp. 29ff.
[61] Merrett, *Short View*, 1st edn, pp. 7–13.   [62] *Ibid.*, pp. 13–18.   [63] *Ibid.*, pp. 19–25.
[64] For example, Merrett, *Short View*, 1st edn: they 'live so high, spend so freely, gain so great Estates, by their return of so little money yearly, which how 'tis done every man may conceive as he list', p. 8. Dr Faye Getz has pointed out to me the very 'Baconian' nature of the three physicians' arguments, but in this case following the Oxonian, Roger Bacon.
[65] Merrett, *Short View*, 1st edn. pp. 25–53.
[66] Goddard, *Discourse Setting forth the Unhappy Condition*, pp. 5–9.

Thus, these physicians were seeking to use the anger some of their colleagues felt towards the Society of Apothecaries to try to convince them that physicians should be more like the virtuosi of the Royal Society. Why otherwise begin a pamphlet war blaming only the apothecaries for the troubles extant in the medical marketplace, when uncontrolled empirics and practising surgeons also threatened the physicians? This was the puzzle that a Londoner, probably an apothecary, set himself to answer in a letter to his friend T.O., an M.D. of Caius College, Cambridge. '[M]ight not all this harangue bene published aswell of the Chirurgions, ye Chymists, ye Mountebanks, and Quacks of all sorts, as well as of them [the apothecaries]? Therefore why is all this against ye Apothecaries done, and singled out from those others?'[67] The author of the letter, A.N., notes that there was so much controversy over the recently published book on the apothecaries,[68] even among 'Persons noble, illustrious, and of ye best and highest quality', that he could not put his ideas about its purposes in writing.[69] A.N. did, however, commit to paper the more general condemnation that the book had four suspicious qualities: firstly, it was innovatory, since it advocated new methods of making up drugs when the old were working reasonably well; second, it was unjust, since it attempted to subvert the rights of the duly incorporated Society of Apothecaries; third, it was indiscreet, since it was in the interest of physicians and apothecaries to unite together against empirics rather than to be divided from one another; and fourth, it was disingenuous, since it had not received any authorization from the College of Physicians.[70] After all, the apothecaries were as deeply threatened as the physicians by the intrusion of unregulated empirics into medical practice: perhaps even more so, since the empirics often sold their own remedies rather than sent their patients to apothecaries. A.N. therefore clearly implied in his letter that the author of at least one of the pamphlets against the apothecaries had a hidden agenda, blaming the apothecaries for all the physicians' troubles when the author's real purpose was otherwise: to make physicians into virtuosi.

---

[67] Brit. Lib., Sloane MS. 631, 'Letter from A.N. to T.O., M.D. of Caius College, Cambridge', fo. 174.

[68] The only remark helpful in identifying the book being described by A.N. (other than a general account of its content) is that the author's name was not given: 'A.N. to T.O.', fo. 173. The book in question was therefore either Coxe's *Discourse* or either of Goddard's *Discourses*, all published anonymously. The controversy probably surrounded Goddard's first pamphlet, the first pamphlet in the debate, that reviewed in the *Philosophical Transactions* – see appendix – and if so, A.N.'s comment suggests that it was the furore over this review that caused Oldenburg not to review the other books.

[69] 'A.N. to T.O.', fo. 168.   [70] 'A.N. to T.O.', fos. 169–73.

By arguing that physicians could only overcome their rivals by becoming expert in natural history and the making of drugs, however, Merrett, Goddard and Coxe played a dangerous game. They were taking up themes long argued by the physicians' professional rivals: that the end of medicine was curing by therapy rather than preserving life by dietetic regimen, and that only by personal and direct experimentalism could medical practitioners learn the best remedies and hence improve their practices. Particularly strong were the resemblances of their arguments to those made just four years earlier by the chemists and the virtuosi.

In that struggle in the spring of 1664, which occurred in the wake of the College's failure to obtain its charter in parliament, a bitter pamphlet war had emerged between the College of Physicians and the proposed Society of Chemical Physicians. The chemists had declared that their medical practices were far superior to those of the College physicians because as chemists they knew the composition of the medicines they gave, having firsthand experience with their manufacture. Almost as bad, perhaps, was the support these medical empirics seemed to receive from the virtuosi and those circles at the royal court in which leading aristocrats, including the duke of Buckingham, the duke of York and even the king himself, took a lively interest in experimentalism and the Royal Society.[71] Additionally, one of the books published in the midst of the debate between the physicians and the chemists bluntly told the College that if it wished to defeat the new Society it would have to reform itself along lines similar to the Royal Society: it must become an experimental society in which the physicians would make their remedies themselves rather than sending to apothecaries. The recent defeat of the College's charter in parliament, the author of this latter work maintained, had been in part because the College seemed so old-fashioned in defending 'rational' physic rather than promoting 'experimental' medicine. The author, 'T.M.', had also introduced the argument that ancient physicians had not employed surgeons or apothecaries to do part of their business (a legacy of the 'dark ages'), but had united head and hand in a unified medical practice.[72] This was the argument that Goddard took up explicitly, and

---

[71] On the controversy between the College of Physicians and the Society of Chemical Physicians, see Henry Thomas, 'The Society of Chymical Physitians: An Echo of the Great Plague of London', in E. Ashworth Underwood (ed.), *Science, Medicine and History* (New York, 1953), II, pp. 55–71; P.M. Rattansi, 'The Helmontian–Galenist Controversy in Restoration England', *Ambix*, XII (1964), 1–23; Charles Webster, 'English Medical Reformers of the Puritan Revolution: a Background to the "Society of Chymical Physitians"', *Ambix*, XIV (1967), 393–412; and Cook, 'The Society of Chemical Physicians'.

[72] T.M., *A Letter Concerning the Present State of Physick* (London, 1665); also see Cook, *Decline of the Old Medical Regime*, pp. 141–3.

Coxe directly quoted passages from 'the judicious Author', T.M., of the 'late excellent Discourse concerning the State of Physick, and the regulation of its Practice'.[73]

Thus, when someone, probably a physician, began to make notes about what Merrett and Goddard were writing, he first jotted down his opinion of the Royal Society: 'the Royal Soc. countenances Mountebanks O'Dowd [that is, the Society of Chemical Physicians] etc. . . . All, All afairs are in danger of their incroachments. They desire all the secrets of Professions shall fall into their Knowledge . . .'[74] The general purpose of these notes appears to have been to compile information refuting the works of Goddard and Merrett by showing that the professional division between apothecary and physician was ancient and useful, so that if a wedge were driven between the two groups the field would be left open to empirics.[75] But because of the threat from empirics, the author keeps returning to the dangers for physic posed by the virtuosi:

> To Goddard: Did his brethren the Experimentators first disparage ye Ancient practise of Physic as inutile; ye Censure ye Compa[ny] as useless, and advance O'Dowds Colledge. RS they are Common enemy as to all Literature. Twill be Better for a Physician to discover the disease of his Patient, that it is new nor Strange, that others have had ye like before and bin curd by such medicaments and methods wherin this or that hath bin hurtfull and [un]wise[?] . . . then like a virtuoso unaquainted with ye method of Physic and History of Diseases tell him that he hath found out a new preparation of syrup of wormwood etc. more dextrous than any in the shops, . . . it operating God knowes how, he shall find God knowes what.[76]

The manuscript also suggests that the virtuosi wrote their books in order to advertise their practices: 'I suppose Mr. Boyle, Manwaring, and Merret sett out bookes like bills on Posts to tell where you may have Arcanas.'[77] This manuscript also contains phrases that are very similar to some of Stubbe's later remarks.[78]

As a result of these debates between the College and the chemists, and between the physicians and the apothecaries, when Stubbe took up his pen in 1669 he was rebutting far more than Glanvill's remarks alone. Stubbe argued that the virtuosi and the Royal Society had supported the Society of Chemical Physicians and other empirics against the College.[79] He urged Robert Boyle and other gentlemen to

---

[73] That is, T.M.'s *Letter*: Coxe, *Discourse wherein The Interest of the Patient*, introduction.
[74] Untitled notes, B.L. Sloane MS. 1786, fo. 116. These notes are attributed to Stubbe in the printed index to the Sloane manuscripts, but do not appear to be in his handwriting. This suggests that they are notes made by another physician and passed on to Stubbe. But they also do not appear to be in the hands of either Hamey or Fraizer.
[75] *Ibid.*, fos. 116–18, 119–19b, 125b–8b.   [76] *Ibid.*, fo. 118b.   [77] *Ibid.*, fo. 119.
[78] Compare Stubbe's remarks quoted above, and those of Stubbe quoted in Hunter, *Science and Society*, p. 125.
[79] Stubbe, *Campanella Revived* (London, 1670), 'To the Reader'.

withdraw from participation in the Royal Society because it was an institution that supported the enemies of the physicians.[80] Stubbe also claimed some success in helping to cause most of the physicians to leave the Royal Society.[81] Additionally, he argued that the virtuosi were trying to gain the upper hand by ruining both the College and the Society of Apothecaries.[82]

The connection Stubbe made between the virtuosi and the threat to physic from medical empiricism is further demonstrated by the fact that replies to Stubbe came from some of those who had earlier argued for the importance of becoming more expert with medicines. For example, in the midst of the pamphlet war over the making of medicines, Christopher Merrett defended his remarks by supporting the virtuosi. At the same time, he suggested that Stubbe had been the author of the apothecaries' attack on him and the other virtuosi/physicians, going so far as to accuse Stubbe of being 'a brother apothecary'.[83] Stubbe understandably saw this as an attempt on Merrett's part to ruin his reputation with the physicians of the College.[84]

In the final incident of this debate, Stubbe was clearly writing on behalf of some physicians of the College. When the chemist George Thomson, who had been involved in the Society of Chemical Physicians, became bold again in promoting his own secret therapies while attacking those of the physicians (especially the practice of phlebotomy),[85] Sir Alexander Fraizer asked Stubbe to turn his attention immediately to rebutting Thomson.[86] Stubbe's association of Thomson with the virtuosi (like his earlier association of the Royal Society with the Society of Chemical Physicians) underlines the links drawn by some physicians between empirics and the virtuosi.[87] Several Fellows of the College of Physicians caused Stubbe to return yet a second time

[80] Stubbe, letter to Boyle, in Boyle's Works, xcv–xcvi; Stubbe, letter to Merrett, published in Glanvill's A Praefatory Answer to Mr. Henry Stubbe; Stubbe, Legends no Histories, preface.
[81] Stubbe, Campanella Revived (1670), 'To the Reader'; in fact, in the later 1660s and early 1670s the Royal Society did go through a 'crisis' of membership, with many physicians dropping out: Hunter, Royal Society, pp. 36–7.   [82] Stubbe, Campanella Revived, p. 20.
[83] Merrett, Self-Conviction; or an Enumeration of the Absurdities, Railings against the College (London, 1670), p. 1; Merrett, A Short Reply to the Postscript, etc. of H.S. (London, 1670).
[84] Stubbe, Campanella Revived, postscript, pp. 19–22. A work sometimes ascribed to Stubbe (but which I doubt is by him), Medice Cura Teipsum! or the Apothecaries Plea (London, 1671), defends both physicians and apothecaries from Merrett's aspersions.
[85] George Thomson, 'Aimatiasis': Or, The true way of Preserving Bloud (London, 1670).
[86] Stubbe, An Epistolary Discourse concerning Phlebotomy (London, 1671), p. 1.
[87] 'According to the peculiar fate of the modern Baconists, [Thomson] hath either out-lived his learning [in Greek, Latin, and English languages], or never was endued with any': Stubbe, Epistolary Discourse, p. 1.

to the attack against Thomson, Stubbe explaining that 'experiment [is]
a new innundation of Goths and Vandals amongst us . . . outdo[ing]
Theodoric, in that [the virtuosi] promote a licentiousness of Experiments in Physick, which that wise Goth severely forbad, out of tender
regard to the welfare of his subjects'. In short,

The Faculty [of physic] is in danger to be overthrown, and the Nation to be subjected to
all those inconveniences which the defect of able Physicians, and the multiplying of
cheating Mountebanks can introduce . . . All this mischief hath its principle source,
original, and strength from the BACONICAL PHILOSOPHERS.[88]

CONCLUSION

The dispute between Stubbe and the virtuosi ended only when Glanvill
and Stubbe turned their attentions elsewhere in their efforts to advance
themselves. Glanvill finally gave up trying to refute Stubbe directly,
embarking upon other enterprises to demonstrate his piety.[89] And
despite Thomson's reply to Stubbe attacking his character,[90] Stubbe
ignored Thomson, taking up his pen for the court during the third
Dutch war. But the tensions between philosophical physicians and
virtuosi 'naturalists' continued throughout the seventeenth century.
Many physicians in the later seventeenth century who pursued natural
historical endeavours made their entrées into London society first
through the virtuosi, joining the College of Physicians only after they
had been in London as Fellows of the Royal Society for a time.[91] And
institutional jealousies could still erupt, as when in 1696 the College
officers took Hans Sloane to task for placing the imprimatur of the
Royal Society before that of the College on his catalogue of Jamaican
plants.[92] Some members of the College of Physicians even began to
favour experimental medicine so much more than learned physic that
they severely hindered the attempts of the College officers later in the
century to regain institutional authority over other practitioners. As

---

[88] Stubbe, *The Lord Bacons Relation of the Sweating-Sickness*, dedication to the part of the text
against Thomson; and Stubbe's letter to Thomson explaining his reasons for attacking him, in
Thomson's *A Letter sent to Mr. Henry Stubbe*, (London, 1672), pp. 10–13. Also note that
Thomson's *A Check given to the insolent Garrulity of Henry Stubbe* (London, 1671) defends
the virtuoso/physician Merrett, pp. 11–13.
[89] Glanvill, *Philosophia Pia; or, A Discourse of the Religious Temper, and Tendencies of the
Experimental Philosophy* (London, 1671), esp. p. 235.
[90] [Thomson], *A Letter sent to Mr. Henry Stubbe* (London, 1672).
[91] For example, Nehemiah Grew, Martin Lister, Edward Tyson, Walter Needham, Robert Pitt
and Hans Sloane.
[92] Annals, Royal College of Physicians, III, fos. 95b–6a. My thanks to the Royal College of
Physicians for permission to cite their records.

266   HAROLD J. COOK

Joseph Browne explained in his rebuttal of the medicine-oriented
Robert Pitt's attack on the apothecaries, there was nothing in Pitt's
treatise that had not been published by Coxe, Goddard or Merrett
thirty-three years before, except that dissensions within the College
were now much more public.[93]

The learned physicians of the College faced telling problems in the
1660s. In an era of institutional weakness, physicians were vulnerable
to virtually unchecked competition and criticism from practitioners
without university educations. But it was the intellectual fashion for
the new philosophy that complicated their professional problems most
of all, for such a fashion pushed learned physic itself in the direction of
mere medicine. Natural history and natural philosophy might very
well complement one another when pursued by men who shared a
common tradition that valued learning. Men like Stubbe argued that
there might have been changes in some of the details of natural history
and even natural philosophy, such as the importation of 'Democritical
[i.e., atomistic] and Chymical Principles' into natural philosophy. But
yet the

Rules, Methods, and Medicines, which more immediately respect the useful and
practical part[s] [of medicine], are still to be retained, and that they are rather more
reconcileable to the Modern, than they were to the Ancient Hypotheses.[94]

The author of these sentiments, Oxford-educated Dr George Castle,
also demonstrated (as Stubbe would, only two years later) that the
physicians had been great proponents of 'New Improvements and
Discoveries in Physick, and the great Promoters of Experimental
Philosophy'.[95] While the theories of elements, qualities, temperaments
and humours could no longer stand as the ancients had interpreted
them, Hodges still thought that natural 'qualities' still caused diseases,
that terms such as 'temperaments' and 'humours' were still of use, and
that ideas such as critical days and pulse doctrine might still help the
physician treat patients.[96] Even in an era in which some new diseases
had appeared, a rational physician could still make good use of the
rules, methods and medicines of a physic rooted in ancient traditions.[97]

---

[93] Robert Pitt, *The Craft and Frauds of Physick Expos'd* (London, 1702); Joseph Browne, *The
Modern Practice of Physick Vindicated, and the Apothecaries clear'd from the Groundless
Imputations of Dr. Pitt* (London, 1703).
[94] George Castle, *The Chymical Galenist: A Treatise wherein The Practise of the Ancients is
reconcil'd to the new Discoveries in the Theory of Physick; Shewing, that many of their Rules,
Methods, and Medicines, are useful for the curing of Disease in this Age, and in the Northern
Parts of the World* (London, 1667), sigs. A3v–A4.
[95] Castle, *The Chymical Galenist*, sig. A5, pp. 3–30.
[96] Castle, *The Chymical Galenist*, pp. 134–70, 181ff.
[97] Castle, *The Chymical Galenist*, pp. 31–69.

Many university-educated physicians stuck to the essential elements of their traditions: changes in the principles of natural philosophy did not therefore make learned physic useless, nor revoke its long tested rules as handed down from educated physician to educated physician. Nathaniel Hodges, yet another Oxford-trained physician, agreed that many parts of physic had been recently altered,

but yet I cannot allow the inference by some late Writers in favor of the Vulgar Experimenters, from hence deduced . . . [F]or the consequence is altogether illogical, and fallacious to conclude from some particular defects in Physick, that the whole Art is thereupon impleadable of the same misprision of insufficiency and uncertainty.[98]

Cambridge-bred Robert Sprackling offered similar arguments, showing in addition (as Stubbe also would do a few years later) that those who argued for physicians making their own remedies were simply trying to separate those who shared basic mutual interests: the apothecaries and the physicians.[99]

Stubbe, then, voiced opinions shared by many physicians who entered the lists of controversy in the period. Chemistry and the new philosophy produced good things in the hands of knowing men. But the university-bred physicians needed to point out the dangers of unchecked empiricism. To the non-university man, or even to the interested university-trained amateur such as Glanvill, the new natural history appeared empirical, experimental, entertaining and useful, while the old natural philosophy seemed rather bookish, argumentative, difficult and useless. To the Glanvills of the world, the natural historical endeavours offered to cure the world's ills, while the natural philosophical led only to useless intellectual difficulties and resigned shrugs. Should attitudes like Glanvill's prevail, what was to stop the mere medical enthusiast, with his penchant for trying to discover new therapies, from taking the educated physician's place as foremost among practitioners – especially in an era virtually free of regulation? The physicians who replied to the attempts to make physic into merely practical medicine did so in two very different ways. One answer was that of Merrett and his fellow virtuosi/physicians: to harness the interest in natural things to the purposes of physicians by making physicians pre-eminent among the experimenters. The other answer was that of Stubbe and his fellow philosopher/physicians: to caution the virtuosi from becoming too outspoken about the importance of

---

[98] Nathaniel Hodges, *Vindiciae Medicinae et Medicorum: Or, an Apology for the Profession and Professors of Physick* (London, 1666), pp. 5–6.

[99] Robert Sprackling, *Medela Ignorantiae: Or, A Just and Plain Vindication of Hippocrates and Galen from the groundless imputations of M.N.* (London, 1665), pp. 28–30.

experimentalism alone, for that might subordinate the parts of physic to mere medical therapy.

Caution became the watchword among the educated. Otherwise their intramural quarrels might spill into the public arena in such a way as generally to undermine respect for university-inculcated learning.[100] Robert Boyle, ever an opponent of philistinism, noted that he was 'restrained by some justifiable Considerations' from setting down all the chemical experiments of use to physicians, 'especially 'till I see what Entertainment, the things I now venture abroad, will meet with there'.[101] But when he made too enthusiastic remarks about medical empiricism, Dr Hodges

wonder[ed] that the honorable Mr. Boyle should so much favor the practise of Empericks . . . [D]id I not believe that these lines fell as a casual blot from this honorable persons Pen, I should more strictly examine them.[102]

The new philosophy's emphasis on natural history might easily become a mere curiosity about medical novelties, even among the most cautious.

So, too, the Oxonian Stubbe had argued. There is no doubt that Stubbe could be an excitable opponent. But he attacked the virtuosi along lines very similar to those that other physicians had already developed in reply to the empirical critics of learned physic. Drs Castle, Hodges and Sprackling, however, wrote in reply to chemists such as Marchamont Nedham.[103] While Nedham was an educated man, the medical chemists as a group were often divided on intellectual principles, of quite varied social, educational and political backgrounds, and without an institutional home. Stubbe, in attacking one of the more enthusiastic of the virtuosi, attacked a member of a group that had generally higher social positions, better educations and an institutional home in the Royal Society, which in turn had the king's protection. Hence he has commonly been portrayed not as a defender of learned physic but either as a hateful man who held on to outdated ideas against the spirited and rational virtuosi, or as a heroic radical.

The attitudes of the Fellows of the London College of Physicians towards the new philosophy are illuminating, encompassing as they do a variety of viewpoints. Their personal attitudes towards the new

---

[100] Michael Hunter has illuminated the concerns of many other educated men about the implications of the new philosophy in his *Science and Society*, pp. 136–61.
[101] Boyle, *Some Considerations touching the Usefulnesse*, preface.
[102] Hodges, *Vindiciae Medicinae*, pp. 24–5.
[103] M[archamont] N[edham], *Medela Medicinae. A Plea For the Free Profession, and a Renovation of the Art of Physick* (London, 1665) which frequently quotes from Boyle's *Some Considerations touching the Usefulnesse*.

philosophy largely depended upon their individual ideas about the most appropriate intellectual foundations of their vocation, learned physic. Those physicians who believed that they were first and foremost scholars of physic tended to see the virtuosi as gentlemen dabblers who were undercutting the prestige of academic learning. Other physicians were intrigued with the new philosophy's growing social cachet as well as its implications for medical practice. They tended to think of their enterprise as one that ought to try to find quick, new and certain cures. In other words, the individual physician's attitudes towards his own profession conditioned his attitudes towards the new philosophy. The concerns of physicians about the new philosophy indicate the seriousness with which scholars debated the meaning of the new learning, and the future for men like them should the virtuosi succeed in coming to dominate the intellectual world.

APPENDIX: SEQUENCE OF TRACTS DEBATING PHYSIC AND
PHILOSOPHY 1668–73

Joseph Glanvill, *Plus Ultra: Or, the Progress and Advancement of Knowledge Since the Days of Aristotle. In An Account of some of the most Remarkable Late Improvements of Practical, Useful Learning: To Encourage Philosophical Endeavours. Occasioned By a Conference with one of the Notional Way* (London, 1668); the book bears a licence dated 2 May 1668, and was registered with the Stationers' Company on 4 July 1668 (see *A Transcription of the Registers of the Worshipful Company of Stationers, From 1640–1708 A.D.* 3 vols. (London, 1913–14)).
    [Jonathan Goddard?], *A Discourse Concerning Physick, and the many Abuses thereof by Apothecaries* (London, 1668). This volume is no longer extant, but is reviewed in the *Philosophical Transactions*, no. 41 (Nov. 16, 1668), pp. 835–6 and ascribed to Goddard by Anthony Wood, *Athenae Oxoniensis*, ed. P. Bliss (London, 1817), III col. 1029. The review described the contents of the first volume to be quite like Goddard's second (see below), and in his second work Goddard says his manuscript had been prepared five years earlier; I thus take it to be a 'lost' work rather than a 'ghost': cf. Frank H. Eliss and Leonard M. Payne. 'Jonathan Goddard, Discourse Concerning Physick ... A Lost Work or a Ghost?', *Med. Hist.*, VII (1963), 188–90; and R.S. Roberts, 'Jonathan Goddard ... A Lost Work or a Ghost?', *Med. Hist.*, VII (1964), 190–1.
    [Daniel Coxe], *A Discourse wherein The Interest of the Patient in Reference to Physick and Physicians is soberly debated. Many Abuses of the Apothecaries in the Preparing their Medicines are detected, and Their Unfitness for Practice Discovered. Together with the Reasons and Advantages of Physicians preparing their own Medicines* (London, 1669). The book was registered with the Stationers' Company on 11 November 1668, and was also advertised for sale in November 1668 (Edward Arber, *The Term Catalogues, 1668–1709* (London, 1907), I, p. 2)
    Christopher Merrett, *A Short View of the Frauds and Abuses Committed by Apothecaries; As Well in Relation to Patients, as Physicians: And Of the only Remedy thereof by Physicians making their own Medicines* (London, 1669); it was licensed 13

November 1669, registered with the Company 9 December 1669. Merrett's book is couched in terms of defending Coxe's book ('last year a Book was printed on the same argument, by an inquisitive person, now Dr. in Physick' [Coxe had just received an M.D. by royal mandate in late 1669], 1st edn, pp. 6–7).

[Jonathan Goddard], A Discourse Setting forth the Unhappy Condition of the Practice of Physick in London, And Offering some Means to put it into a better (London, 1670); licensed 19 January 1669/70, and advertised in February 1670 (Arber, I, 26).

Christopher Merrett, A Short View of the Frauds, and Abuses Committed by Apothecaries; As Well in Relation to Patients, as Physicians: And Of the only Remedy thereof by Physicians making their own Medicines The Second Edition more correct (London, 1670); it bears a Postscript dated 20 February 1669/70, and was advertised in February 1670 (Arber, I, 26).

Henry Stubbe, The Plus Ultra Reduced to a Non Plus: Or, A Specimen of some Animadversions upon the Plus Ultra of Mr. Glanvill, wherein sundry Errors of some Virtuosi are discovered, the Credit of the Aristoteleans in part Re-advanced; and Enquiries made . . . (London, 1670); registered with the Company 17 April 1670.

Henry Stubbe, Legends no Histories: or, A Specimen Of some Animadversions Upon the History of the Royal Society. Wherein, besides the several Errors against Common Literature, sundry mistakes . . . are detected, and ratified (London, May? 1670).

Lex Talionis; Sive Vindiciae Pharmacoporum: Or a Short Reply to Dr. Merrett's Book; And Others, written against the Apothecaries: Wherein May be discovered the Frauds and Abuses committed by Doctors Professing and Practicing Pharmacy (London, 1670). Sometimes attributed to Stubbe because of Merret's ascription (see next item, pp. 1–2, and Merrett, A Short reply, also below, pp. 27–42), it is clearly written in a different manner from Stubbe's books, and is likely to have been composed by a 'cabal' of apothecaries as argued by Gideon Harvey (see below, pp. 91ff).

Christopher Merrett, Self-Conviction; or an Enumeration of the Absurdities, Railings against the College, and Physicians in general . . . and also an Answer to the Rest of Lex Talionis (London, 1670).

Henry Stubbe, Campanella Revived, Or an Enquiry into the History of the Royal Society, whether the Virtuosi there do not pursue the Projects of Campenella for the reducing England unto Popery . . . With a Postscript concerning the Quarrel depending betwixt H.S. and Dr. Merrett (London 1670; Postscript dated 14 June 1670).

Gideon Harvey, The Accomplisht Physician, the Honest Apothecary, and the Skilful Chyrurgeon, Detecting Their Necessary Connexion, and dependance on each other. Appended is: A Lash for Lex Talionis; or, A just Repraehension of the Practising Apothecary (London, 1670); the book is advertised in June 1670 (Arber, I, 48).

Christopher Merrett, A Short Reply to the Postscript, etc. of H.S. Shewing his many falsities in matters of fact; the impertinences of his promised Answers to some Physicians that have written against the Apothecaries; his conspiracy with Apothecaries to defame them, the R.S. and many learned men of our Nation (London, 1670).

Dr C.T. [Timothy Clarke], Some Papers Writ in the Year 1664. In Answer to a Letter, Concerning the Practice of Physick in England. Published at the Request of a friend and several Fellows of the College of Physicians (London, 1670; licensed 3 August 1670).

George Thomson, 'Aimatiasis': Or, The true way of Preserving Bloud In its Integrity, and Rectifying it, if at any time polluted and Degenerate; Wherein Dr. Willis his Errour of Bleeding is reprehended, and offered to be confuted by Practice and frequent Experiments: And certain opinions of Dr. Betts in Physick rejected (London, 1670).

Medice Cura Teipsum! or the Apothecaries Plea. In some short and modest Animadversions, upon A late tract entituled a short view of the Frauds and Abuses of the Apothecaries by C. Merrett... from a Real Well-wisher to both societies (London, 1671). Sometimes attributed to Stubbe, the pamphlet's sentiments are somewhat similar to his and may be influenced by Stubbe's communications to the Society of Apothecaries; but C.W. (next item, p. 1), an avowed opponent of Stubbe's, declares this work to be by an apothecary with initials I.R. It was advertised in February 1671 (Arber, 1, 65).

C.W., *Reflections on a Libel, Intituled, A Plea for the Apothecaries* (London, 1671).

Everard Maynwaring, *Praxis Medicorum Antiqua et Nova: The Ancient and Modern Practice of Physick Examined, Stated, and Compared. The Preparation and Custody of Medicines, as it was the Primitive Custom with the Princes and great Patrons of Physick, asserted, and proved to be the proper charge, and grand duty of every Physician successively* (London, 1671; licensed 17 March 1670/1).

Henry Stubbe, *An Epistolary Discourse concerning Phlebotomy. In Opposition to G. Thomson Pseudo-Chymist, a pretended Disciple of the Lord Verulam* (London, 1671).

Joseph Glanvill, *A Praefatory Answer to Mr. Henry Stubbe, The Doctor of Warwick. Wherein The Malignity, Hypocrisie, Falshood, of his Temper, Pretences, Reports, and the Impertinency of his Arguings and Quotations in his Animadversions on Plus Ultra are discovered* (London, 1671).

Henry Stubbe, *A Censure Upon Certain Passages contained in the History of the Royal Society, As being destructive to the Established Religion and Church of England. The Second Edition corrected and enlarged. Whereunto is Added The Letter of a Virtuoso in Opposition to the Censure, A Reply unto the Letter Aforesaid, And a Reply unto the Praefatory Answer of Eccobolius Glanvill, Chaplain to Mr. Rouse of Eaton (late member of the Rump Parliament... Also an Answer to the Letter of Dr. Henry More, relating unto Henry Stubbe* (Oxford, 1671).

Henry Stubbe, *The Lord Bacons Relation of the Sweating-Sickness Examined, in a Reply to George Thomson, Pretender to Physick and Chymistry. Together with a Defense of Phlebotomy... in opposition to the same author and the author of Medela Medicinae, Doctor Whitaker, and Doctor Sydenham... and a reply, by way of Preface to the Calumnies of Eccobolius Glanvile* (London, 1671); advertised July 1671 (Arber, 1, 79).

George Thomson, *A Check given to the insolent Garrulity of Henry Stubbe: in Vindication of My Lord Bacon, and the Author* (London, 1671); advertised November 1670 [*sic* for 1671?] (Arber, 1, 55).

Joseph Glanvill, *Philosophia Pia; or, A Discourse of the Religious Temper, and Tendencies of the Experimental Philosophy, Which is profest by the Royal Society* (1671).

[George Thomson], *A Letter sent to Mr. Henry Stubbe, Wherein The Galenical Method and Medicaments, As Likewise Bloudletting in particular, Are offered to be proved ineffectual, or destructive to Mankinde; by Experimental Demonstrations. Also his answer thereunto by letter; On which Animadversions are made By Geo. Thomson, Dr. of Physick, By whom is added A Vindication of his Stomack-Essence, or Alexi-Stomachon, and other really-powerful Remedies* (London, 1672); advertised February 1672 (Arber, 1, 96).

An Essay for the Regulation of the Practice of Physick, Upon which Regulation Are grounded The Composure of all Differences Between Physicians and Apothecaries (London, 1673); advertised May 1673 (Arber, 1, 134).

10

The early Royal Society and the spread of medical knowledge

ROY PORTER

The establishing of the Royal Society promised to be an event of great significance for medicine in England. After all, right from the start, a substantial minority of its inner core included those physicians and inquirers into the economy of life who had made the College of Physicians such a lively body during the interregnum – men such as Goddard, Ent, Glisson and Croune – responsible for what Frank has seen as the Harveian research programme.[1] And, more broadly, medical practitioners constituted easily the largest and most active single occupational group – about a fifth – amongst the early fellows.[2] In his *History of the Royal Society of London* (1667), Thomas Sprat bent over backwards to disarm any hostile critics who might fear that the assimilation of medical men within the Society would prejudice the rights and interests of the College of Physicians;[3] and the fact that some leading College physicians – not least its censor, Thomas Wharton, and its president, Baldwin Hamey, aided by his nephew, the maverick, Henry Stubbe – resented the Society's intrusion and attempted to discredit its pretensions, helps confirm that its foundation was indeed recognized as promising, or rather threatening, a shift in the centre of gravity of medical inquiry and authority.[4]

[1] Robert G. Frank, *Harvey and the Oxford Physiologists: A Study of Scientific Ideas* (Berkeley, 1980); Charles Webster, 'The College of Physicians: "Solomon's House" in Commonwealth England', *Bulletin of the History of Medicine*, XLI (1967), 393–412; Charles Webster, *The Great Instauration: Science, Medicine and Reform 1626–1660* (London, 1975).

[2] See M. Hunter, 'Reconstructing Restoration Science: Problems and Pitfalls in Institutional History', *Social Studies of Science*, XII (1982), 451–66; M. Hunter, *The Royal Society and its Fellows 1660–1700* (Chalfont St Giles, Bucks., 1982); M. Hunter *Science and Society in Restoration England* (Cambridge, 1981); T.P.R. Laslett, 'The Foundation of the Royal Society and the Medical Profession in England', *British Medical Journal* (1960), II, 165–9.

[3] Thomas Sprat, *The History of the Royal Society of London* (London, 1667), p. 67. Sprat nevertheless implied that the Royal Society's business included medical research (p. 83).

[4] Jim Jacob, *Henry Stubbe, Radical Protestantism and the Early Enlightenment* (Cambridge, 1983), p. 82 ff.

There can be little doubt that that actually happened, temporarily at least. The post-restoration College of Physicians underwent, as Cook has recently demonstrated, one of the more traumatic periods of its existence, finding itself uncertain of crown support, challenged by the rival Society of Chemical Physicians, in conflict with the Apothecaries, divided within itself, discredited by the Plague catastrophe of 1665, and robbed of its premises by the Fire of 1666.[5] Perhaps unsurprisingly, under these circumstances, that identification of the College with medical research which had seemed so promising in the 1650s evaporated. By contrast the dice fell right for the Royal Society. It had the aura of novelty, it recruited an estimable foreign membership, it cashed in on the optimism for new learning, experience and experiment associated with Bacon and the moderns. Above all, perhaps – thanks largely to the personal dedication of Henry Oldenburg – the Society was able to articulate enthusiasm effectively for scientific knowledge through a vast correspondence network, and to identify scientific advance with itself through the medium of the *Philosophical Transactions*.[6] In research fields such as human anatomy, respiration, generation, blood, muscle physiology, organic chemistry, animal experimentation, and so forth, the early years of the Royal Society show an impressive collocation of activity, involving links with the best investigators in Europe as well as in Britain, even if on occasion it gave rise to acrimonious episodes, such as the priority dispute surrounding Regnier De Graaf's researches on the anatomy of the testes.[7] In the biomedical sciences, as elsewhere, the evidence fully bears out Rupert Hall's tribute to the Society's 'mass of learned publication devoted to basic science'.[8]

I shall not explore the Society's contributions to anatomy and physiology, however, but shall concentrate on the more clinical and practical sides of medicine. Against a backdrop of Hall's view that one may 'discover in the Royal Society's correspondence a farrago of medical curiosities and chemical wonder drugs . . . triviality and misguided enthusiasm among English medical practitioners of all

[5] H. Cook, *The Decline of the Old Medical Regime in Stuart London* (Chicago, 1986); Sir G. Clark, *A History of the Royal College of Physicians of London*, 3 vols. (Oxford, 1964–72); Charles Webster, 'English Medical Reformers of the Puritan Revolution: A Background to the "Society of Chymical Physitians"', *Ambix*, XIV (1967), 16–41.

[6] Sir Henry George Lyons, *The Royal Society, 1660–1940. A History of its Administration under its Charters* (Cambridge, 1944).

[7] A. Rupert Hall, 'Medicine in the Early Royal Society', in Allen G. Debus (ed.), *Medicine in Seventeenth Century England* (Berkeley, 1974), 421–52.

[8] A. Rupert Hall, 'English Medicine in the Royal Society's Correspondence: 1660–1677', *Medical History*, XV (1971), 111–25.

levels of sophistication',[9] I wish to explore how practical medical matters found a place for themselves in the early Royal Society; in particular I shall survey the role of the Society in collecting, distributing, and authorizing, medical information.

Historians of science and medicine have generally been so preoccupied with 'the anxiety of influence', with 'discovery' and 'originality', that the larger issue of the maintenance of an economy of knowledge has often been largely neglected.[10] Questions of the authorization and circulation of accredited truth are not of course easy to resolve. And that applies particularly within medicine, on account of the extraordinarily heterogeneous nature of the discipline, which mixes the practical and the theoretical, and involves a hierarchy of professional strata and a diversity of points of educational input (university, apprenticeship, etc.). Medical knowledge was traditionally exchanged through a remarkable plurality of channels. Not least, as Nicholas Jewson has rightly insisted,[11] practical medicine always had a cognitive orientation in which 'truth' (obviously paramount within 'pure' science) necessarily had to engage with questions of efficacy and also (at least at a time of imperfect professionalization) with customer power in the relatively free market in medical theories and therapies. Study of one organ which played a substantial part in airing medical knowledge during the eighteenth century, the *Gentleman's Magazine*, has indicated that in both form and content the medical knowledge in circulation responded to such pressures.[12]

In an earlier generation, the Royal Society became a significant medium in the diffusion of medical knowledge ('Communications must run through all ye veines of ye Main worke', John Beale assured Henry Oldenburg).[13] In some respects, the Society served simply as a secondary channel of transmission. Thus, through giving prominence to lengthy book reviews (which largely took the form of substantial

[9] Hall, 'Medicine in the Early Royal Society', 452.
[10] For an entry into 'diffusion' studies, see R.G.A. Dolby, 'The Transmission of Science', *History of Science*, XV (1977), 1–43.
[11] N.D. Jewson, 'Medical Knowledge and the Patronage System in Eighteenth-Century England', *Sociology*, VIII (1974), 369–89.
[12] Roy Porter, 'Laymen, Doctors and Medical Knowledge in the Eighteenth Century: The Evidence of the *Gentleman's Magazine*', in Roy Porter (ed.), *Patients and Practitioners. Lay Perceptions of Medicine in Pre-Industrial Society* (Cambridge, 1985), pp. 283–314; Roy Porter 'Lay Medical Knowledge in the Eighteenth Century', *Medical History*, XXIX (1985), 138–68.
[13] A.R. Hall and M.B. Hall, *The Correspondence of Henry Oldenburg*, 11 vols. (Madison, Wisconsin, 1966–73; London, 1975), I, p. 481. Beale to Oldenburg, 21 December 1662. The best general survey of the Society's role in the transmission of science is Marie Boas Hall, 'The Royal Society's Role in the Diffusion of Information in the Seventeenth Century', *Notes and Records of the Royal Society of London*, XXIX (1975), 173–92.

paraphrase), the *Philosophical Transactions* communicated knowledge of latest publications to a readership which (for the most part) would never have purchased, or had any other access to, the original books themselves. Through such reviews, *Philosophical Transactions* readers had ready and almost instant access to the researches of Steno or Malpighi, just as they could thereby enlighten themselves on more exotic topics such as acupuncture.[14] The part played by the *Philosophical Transactions* in simply broadcasting up-to-date knowledge, speedily and widely, through its numerous and extraordinarily conscientious book reviews deserves close study, but I will hardly touch upon it here.[15]

Rather I wish to sketch how the Royal Society operated as an organ for the *exchange* of medical information, through stimulating communications from fellows and outsiders to the Society, through initiating longer-term chains and networks of correspondents, through establishing certain topics as objects of medical inquiry, and so forth. The Baconian programme promised that knowledge would be advanced, and looked to information collection and exchange as major means towards that end.[16] Dismissing the so-called infallible truths of 'mountebanks, conjurors and peddlars' and the credulity of the 'hoi polloi', Timothy Clarke informed Oldenburg that 'for two thousand years past medicine has grown through experience', and envisaged the gathering and due processing of 'experience' as the royal road forward.[17] So how was medical knowledge transmitted by the early Royal Society? What were the pathways of exchange? How great was the rate of flow? And did it produce any consequences?

There would be no point, I believe, in trying to map out a fixed scheme of trade routes through which medical data flowed into or out of the Society, for each exchange took its own course. Some information exchanges stopped almost as quickly as they began (involving, say, just a letter from a correspondents, followed by an acknowledgement, with thanks, from Oldenburg. Others flourished; letters would be reported to a meeting, possibly being printed in the *Philosophical Transactions*, and would lead to a further proliferation

---

[14] See 'An Account of a Book; viz. Wilhelmiten Ryne. Transisalano Daventnensis. 1. Dissertatio de Arthemde. 2. Mantissa Schematica. 3. De Acupunctura. 4. Orationes tres. sc. De Chymices Botanicae Antiguilate e dignitate De physiognomia. De Monstris. Londini in 8° 1683', *Philosophical Transactions*, XIII (1683), 225–32.

[15] Oddly, the history of the *Philosophical Transactions* has never been fully written. For some wider perspectives see David Kronick, *A History of Scientific and Technical Periodicals* (New York, 1962).   [16] See especially Webster, *Great Instauration*.

[17] Hall and Hall (eds.), *Oldenburg Correspondence*, IV, p. 363: Timothy Clarke to Oldenburg, April/May 1668.

of inquiries and replies. Some contacts, of course, passed between active fellows and/or men acquainted with each other quite independently of the Society. Oldenburg and Boyle, for example, were in communication with each other before the founding of the Society, and so their correspondence cannot simply be seen as indebted to the Society's existence. Even so, it remains true that many of the letters from the indefatigable Oldenburg to the rather hypochondriac Boyle were specifically concerned with the Society, and included much of medical interest, as this report of a Society meeting held on 10 June 1663:

This afternoon we had no ordinary meeting: There were no less yn 4. strangers, two French, and two Dutch Gentlemen; ye French were, Monsr de Sorbière, and Mr Monconis; ye Dutch, both the Zulichems, Father and Son: all foure, inquisitive after you. They were entertained first with some Experiments, wch the bearer hereoff will give you a good account off: and afterwards with good store of occasionall observations, discoursed of promiscuously, pro re nata; wch the strangers (as well as our Company) seemed to be much more pleased wth, yn with set and formall discourses: They were, 1. Of various Petrifactions, even of children in ye wombe; item in ye Lungs; in ye Plexus Choroides, and in all ye parts of human bodis. 2. Of persons altogether moveless, but yt they could speak, and eat and drink whereof one was alleged by Sr R. Moray, seen by himselfe at ye Spaw; out of whose fingers and cheeks also he had observed a chalky matter to issue: another was mentioned by Mr Beale in a letter to me, of his owne kinswoman, yt lived some years as unmoveable as a stone, unable to move finger or toe, yet her mouth she could move, and had a good stomach and was recovered at last by Bathes. I doubt, Sr, here is matter for an occasional meditation.

Next, there were very odde relations made of women, voiding bones, together with their menstrua, every month: of others, bringing away bones of children (they had been severall years afore big off) by seige, or out of their sides.[18]

The Society also played a part in establishing contacts and inaugurating information exchanges. These were communications sent to the secretary or some other fellow of the Society from relatively obscure provincial practitioners, for many of whom (it is safe to say) the founding of the Society was crucial in creating a commerce of ideas between their individual clinical experiences and a wider world of inquiry. In 1669, for instance, the Plymouth physician, Dr William Durston, ventured a communication to the Society. He opened – as he clearly felt necessary – with an effusive apology for his presumption, combined with an attempt to establish his bona fide as a creditable authority:

In obedience to the commands of the Right Honorable the Lord Ambassadour for Barbary, I present your Lordship with a Phænomenon in matter of fact in Nature, which, for its rarity and prodigiousness, may, with a lesser check to me from your Lordship for the presumption, and a lesser regret for the avocation, obtain the favour

[18] Hall and Hall (eds.), Oldenburg Correspondence, II, p. 66: Oldenburg to Boyle, 10 June 1663.

of your perusal. The thing is evident, and shews itself, and can withall be attested by thousands, but above all the rest by his Excellency, the said Lord Ambassadour, why was an Eye-witness of it, and imposed this task on me, of giving your Lordship a perfect Narrative of the wonder.[19]

Durston proceeded to relate the details of the case, a young patient, Elizabeth Travers, whose breasts had swollen to monstrous proportions. What is interesting about Durston's report, which runs to some three hundred words, is its conformity to (and thus familiarity with?) the scientific protocols of the Society, not least in its Petty-like commitment to vital statistics:[20]

	Feet.	Inch.
The Circumference of the right Breast	2.	7
Of the left Breast	3.	X$\frac{1}{2}$.
The length of the right Breast from the Coller-bone	1.	5$\frac{1}{2}$
The length of the left Breast	1.	7$\frac{1}{2}$
The breadth of the right Breast as it lyes	1.	1
The breadth of the left	1.	4$\frac{1}{2}$

Surely (one suspects) Durston had already familiarized himself with the house style of the *Philosophical Transactions* and had chosen to follow it religiously.[21] Further letters were sent by Durston on 17 September and 2 November 1669, the latter reporting the woman's death.[22] When he and other physicians proposed an autopsy, her family objected, but (possibly with his audience of London savants in mind) he pressed ahead, and he remitted his best attempts to make a quantification of her condition at the time of death:

I have sent you inclosed *one* measure, which was the *Breadth* of her two Breasts (as she was layd out on a Table being dead;) I mean, from the further end of the one to the other; which you'l find *three foot two Inches* and *an halfe* and *another* measure, shewing the *Circumference* of the Breasts *long*-wise, *viz. four foot*; and near *four* inches; and a *third*, giving the *Circumference* of the *Breadth, viz. three feet four inches* and *a halfe.*[23]

The correspondence of Oldenburg and the first score or so volumes of the *Philosophical Transactions* are full of comparable cases. Such

[19] 'An Extract of a Letter Written by the Learned Dr. William Durston, Physitian at Plimouth, to the Right Honorable the Lord Vice-Count Bruncker as President of the R. Society; concerning a very sudden and excessive Swelling of a Womans Breasts', *Philosophical Transactions*, IV (1669), 1047–9. Durston (b. 1624), was an Oxford graduate. He was expelled from his college in 1648, and was created M.D. in 1660.
[20] *Ibid.* Durston also enclosed a figure, which was also published in the *Philosophical Transactions*. [21] *Ibid.*
[22] 'An Extract of a Letter Written to the Publisher from Plymouth Novem. 2. 1669, by William Durston Dr. of Physick; concerning the Death of the Bigg-breasted Woman (discoursed of in Numn. 52) together with what was thereupon observed in her Body', *Philosophical Transactions*, IV (1669), 1068–9. [23] *Ibid.*

reports clearly did not contribute, in any tangible way, to medical 'progress', or even to changing the face of medicine. But in an age when none of the medical corporations was encouraging medical record-keeping, a time before the existence of the medical press in any shape or form,[24] the existence of the Royal Society may have been no negligible factor in encouraging a new 'style' of observation and recording in routine, everyday clinical medicine.

Of course, much of the exchange of information took place on a rather more substantial and sophisticated plane. For one thing, the activities of the Royal Society, and of 'sister' societies such as the Oxford Philosophical Society, stimulated fresh contributions from recognized medical figures. Thus it is interesting to find printed in the *Philosophical Transactions* a letter from the celebrated Salisbury oculist, Dr Turberville, on the eye condition, bursa oculi, stating that he had been induced to write because he had heard that the Oxford Society had 'lately received accounts of some unusual Distempers of the Eyes and that more account of this nature will be welcome to you'.[25] Turberville followed up his initial epistle with a further one, also published in *Philosophical Transactions*, which reveals another dimension of the attraction for a practitioner of going into print: its commercial advantages. For the second letter amounts to a not very carefully concealed puff, relating the case of a man with convulsions around his eyes, who had 'used many things prescribed him by *Physicians* and *Chirurgeons*, but to no purpose', but who recovered thanks to the aid of Turberville's special plaster.[26]

Personal profit aside, it is clear that practitioners welcomed the opportunities which the Royal Society provided for the spread of medical news. Oldenburg's correspondence is full of requests, from home and abroad, to be kept abreast of the latest developments, as when Major wrote, from Hamburg in 1664 inquiring after injection therapy experiments:

I have heard in a letter, through the courtesy of a certain noble Senator in my native city of Breslau, that not very long ago Mr. Theodore Jacob, a lawyer, my fellow-countryman, and a friend whom I have valued for many years, spoke to you directly concerning the use, administration, object, and success of a celebrated invention made by someone in your country.[27]

[24] W.R. Lefanu, *British Periodicals of Medicine* (Baltimore, 1978).
[25] 'Two Letters from the great, and experienced Oculist, Dr. Turbervile of Salisbury, to Mr. William Musgrave S.P.S. of Oxon. containing several remarkable cases in Physick, relating chiefly to the Eyes', *Philosophical Transactions*, XIV (1684), 736–7.
[26] *Ibid.*, 'The second Letter'.
[27] Hall and Hall (eds.), *Oldenburg Correspondence*, II, pp. 336–7: Major to Oldenburg, 13 December 1664. Major was physician to the City of Hamburg.

Indeed, news of the pioneering of injections and later transfusions at the Society undoubtedly triggered further experiments across Europe in short order, many of which were communicated to Oldenburg, leading him to this optimistic expression to Boyle:

I must intimate to you, that among ye papers yt come from ye Baltick, I find one, written by a Physirian of Dantzick, relating that there they have cured the Lues Veneres, and Convulsions, by injecting liquors into Veins; wch I intend, God willing, to read at our next meeting, to occasion the Society to urge Dr. Clerks publication of his Experiments of yt nature, though they come short of such effects. As far as I see, both those Experiments, that met wth so much difficulty and contradiction at first (I mean yt of Infusion and Transfusion) may at last prove very beneficiall to the Health of Man. The person, yt hath ye Sheeps-blood in his Veins, is still very well, and like to continue so. If we durst believe him self, who is flatteringly given, he is much better, than he was before, as he tells us in a Latin account, he brought in to ye Society.[28]

It is noteworthy that Oldenburg's correspondents on the subject of blood transfusions constitute a much wider circle than those directly involved in furthering investigations, such as Justel and Denis in Paris and Travagino in Italy.[29] They include 'bystanders', obviously eager to be kept in the picture. Thus minor English figures such as William Neile would write to Oldenburg praising that 'verie usefull experiment', and requesting further details – providing some indication at least that the climate of opinion among the wider ranks of those associated with the experimental learning of the Royal Society was favourably disposed towards forms of experimentation which hardly squared with the priorities of traditional humanistic physick.[30]

MEDICAL COMMUNICATIONS: WHAT DID THEY CONTAIN?

To some degree, the medical interests encompassed by the early Royal Society were shaped from the centre. Problems and topics would be suggested, which fellows and others took it upon themselves to tackle. Thus the *Philosophical Transactions* contain a piece by Dr Fred Slare on the 'calculus humanus' which he states was 'in answer to several Queries proposed by Sir John Hoskins'.[31] Oldenburg himself often

[28] Hall and Hall (eds.), *Oldenburg Correspondence*, IV, pp. 6–7: Oldenburg to Boyle, 3 December 1667.
[29] H. Brown, 'Jean Denis and transfusion of blood, Paris, 1667–1668', *Isis*, XXXIX (1948), 15–29.
[30] Hall and Hall (eds.), *Oldenburg Correspondence*, IV, pp. 8–9: W. Neile to Oldenburg, 5 December 1667. Neile, who studied mathematics under Wilkins at Oxford, was a founder member of the Royal Society as a gentleman scholar. For medical humanism, see Cook, *The Decline of the Old Medical Regime in Stuart London*; J. Keevil, *Hamey the Stranger* (London, 1952) and *The Stranger's Son* (London, 1953).
[31] 'An Abstract Treatise of the Calculus Humanus in answer to several Queries proposed by Sir John Hoskins; by the Learned and Ingenious Fred Slare M.D. and fellow of the Royal Society', *Philosophical Transactions*, XIV (1683/4), 523–5.

spelt out personal 'Queries' to individual correspondents and travellers, either exclusively or partly of a medical nature. Thus he sent Thomas Coxe a slate of questions in 1669 to arm him for his trip to Germany and Hungary, in the hope of putting London in the picture about central European medicine.[32] And, at a more specific level, Oldenburg despatched a series of letters to Martin Lister, the Yorkshire physician and natural historian, asking him to dig out information about certain allegedly extremely long-lived locals. Lister's reply was tailor-made to fit the cognitive requirements of the Society:

> Since my last to you I have been in *Craven*, where I was not unmindful of your Commands; but, indeed, I find it a very hard, and troublesome business to verifie precisely the *Ages* of such Persons, as either affirm themselves, or are believed very *Old*: the best Informations and Reports I could get I send you.[33]

With the aid of Boyle, Oldenburg also inserted more general queries in the *Philosophical Transactions* aimed to stir up medical inquiry. Important amongst these – important because they drew responses – were the 'General heads for a natural history of a countrey' [i.e. county] and 'Articles of inquiries touching mines', both inserted in 1666, with their orthodox Hippocratic interest in the relationship between environment, exhalations, miasma and disease.[34]

Queries of this kind, in the 'Airs, Waters and Places' tradition, stirred responses because they put their finger on areas of interest and

---

[32] Hall and Hall (eds.), *Oldenburg Correspondence*, VI, p. 77: Oldenburg to T. Coxe, 30 June 1669:

> Inquiries for Germany and Hungary
> commended to Mr. Thomas Coxe
> 30 June 1669
>
> 10. Let there be arranged for us correspondence with men in Germany and Hungary who are outstanding in experimental philosophy, in mathematics, mechanics, anatomy, chemistry, and medicine.
> 11. Let it be inquired what books have lately appeared on matters of physic, chemistry, medicine, and mathematics.
> 12 Let men who are notably ingenious and industrious be urged to compile the natural histories of the regions wherein they dwell with the utmost care and reliability; and let medical men particularly, in all parts, be encouraged to commit to paper with accuracy and good faith the histories of diseases, to whose remedy they are summoned.

[33] 'A Letter written to Mr. H.O. concerning some very aged Persons in the North of England, by Dr. M. L.', *Philosophical Transactions*, XIV (1684), 597–8. Lister reports on their alleged longevity, but it is clear he takes it all with a pinch of salt:

> *Robert Montgomery* now being living in *Skipton*, but born in *Scotland*, tells me that he is 126 years of Age; the oldest persons in *Skipton* say, that they never knew him other than an Old Man; he is exceedingly decayed of late, but yet goes about a begging, to which his debauchery (as is said) has brought him.

[34] *Philosophical Transactions*, I (1666), 186–9; I (1666), 330–43. For the Society's key role in directing research in America, see Raymond Phineas Stearns, *Science in the British Colonies of America* (Urbana, 1970).

controversy already current. Thus it is no surprise that the properties of spas and mineral springs show up prominently in Oldenburg's correspondence, in minutes of the Society's meetings,[35] and in the *Philosophical Transactions* (there is a characteristically garrulous piece by John Beale).[36] Closely related, also, and much debated was the issue of climate – a subject Oldenburg particularly commended to the attention of those voyaging overseas. Accounts in the *Philosophical Transactions* of the natural history of the colonies typically involved observations of the effects of weather upon health, as when Dr Henry Stubbe explained how 'the Change of Climat and the effects of it are very sensible to our Bodies, as we approach the *Tropick*',[37] before going on to offer some more general observations on the relations between atmosphere and disease:

And thus we see in Diseases, that it is not the bare alteration of weather, but from some peculiar mixtures in the Air, that incline to, or increase Consumptions and Coughs: since oftentimes the greatest *Raines* are less fatal to such bodies, as *hazy* weather renders dangerously indisposed. All the alteration, our Sweet-Meats, and Lozenges, and Gamons of Bacon, underwent, must be attributed to some peculiar principle in the Air: For, in all our Voyages to the *Barbadoes* we had not one Shower, that I remember. And if any will have the Air moist, whilest a constant *Levant* (that is, a *drying*) Wind fills our Sails, at least during the *long reach*, how comes it to pass, that so much heat joyn'd with moisture doth not occasion *putrid Fevers*? And why in all that Journey, and after in *Jamaica*, when the Glasses for many weekes stood open and uncover'd, did not the *Lixivate* Salts of *Wormwood* and *Ash* contract any moisture?[38]

Beyond issues of this kind to which the Society itself drew correspondents' attention, what other medical matters figured prominently in

---

[35] T. Birch, *The History of the Royal Society of London*, 4 vols. (London, 1756).
[36] 'The Ingenious Reflexions to *Medical Springs* Numb. 52, Considered. The palpable Indications of some Healing Springs remarked, With an account of some such Springs in England, which do confirm the Indications; and of others Obiter; By Dr. J. Beale to the Publisher: Which Discourses were in N. 56, omitted for want of sufficient room; not without injury to the Author, who has designed these Communications for another prop, specifying by manifest observations, how Terrestrial steams may be the Generative Cause, both of Minerals and Metals, and of all the Peculiarities of Springs: And should have immediately followed p. 1134', *Philosophical Transactions*, V (1670), 1154–63. See also Hall and Hall (eds.), *Oldenburg Correspondence*, VI, 4851: Glanvill to Oldenburg, 16 June 1669, and F.N.L. Poynter, 'A Seventeenth Century Medical Controversy: Robert Wittie versus William Simpson', in E. Ashworth Underwood (ed.), *Science, Medicine and History*, 2 vols. (London, 1953) II, pp. 72–81.
[37] 'An Enlargement of the Observations, formerly publisht Numb. 27, made and generously imparted by that Learn'd and Inquisitive Physitian, Dr. Stubbes', *Philosophical Transactions*, III (1668), 699.
[38] 'An encouragement of the observations; formerly published Nº 27 made & generously imparted by that Learn'd & Inquisitive Physitian, Dr. Stubbes', *Philosophical Transactions*, III (1668), 709.

the early Royal Society? The Plague inevitably loomed large.[39] In his
History, Sprat turned the terrible outbreak of 1665 to advantage,
arguing that the celerity with which life had returned to normal in
London after the Plague and the Fire proved that the English were
imbued with that brisk, businesslike attitude to life which augured well
for natural philosophy. Sprat admitted that as yet there were no
successful plague remedies:

> It is true, that terrible *evil* has hitherto in all Countries, been generally too strong, for
> the former remedies of *Art*.[40]

But it was – by implication at least – the job of the Royal Society to
change all that:

> But why should we think that it will continue so for ever? Why may we believe, that in
> all the vast compass of Natural virtues of things yet conceal'd, there is still reserv'd an
> *Antidote*, that shall be equal to this *poyson*? If in such cases we only accuse the *Anger* of
> *Providence*, or the *Cruelty* of *Nature*: we lay the blame, where it is not justly to be laid.
> It ought rather to be attributed to the *negligence* of men themselves, that such *difficult
> Cures* are without the bounds of their *reasons power*.
>
> If all men had desponded at first, and sunk under the burden of their own *infirmities*,
> almost every little wound, or pain of the least *member*, had been as deadly, as the
> *Plague* at this time. It was by much Inquiry, and use, that most of the mildest diseases
> became *curable*. And every first success of this kind, should always strengthen our
> assurance of farther conquests, even over this greatest *Terror* of mankind.[41]

Certainly, Oldenburg was much involved during 1665 in correspondence, from home and abroad, to sound out and to test plague
remedies. For instance, Signor Borrhi sent Oldenburg his 'expulsif'
antidote ('Antiloimoides'), which he then analysed and assessed with
the aid of Boyle and Moray. Oldenburg was enthusiastic:

> I have an opinion, you will be pleased with seeing and examining yt Medicine, wch
> comes from such a man, in such a way, for such an end, and with such a character,
> annexed to it by ye Author, yt, if it were for a King, he know not to give any better, both
> for preventing and expelling ye Plague.[42]

[39] Indeed, the Plague precipitated this announcement in *Philosophical Transactions*, I (1665), 94:

> Advertisement
> The Reader is hereby advertised, that by reason of the present Contagion in London, which may
> unhappily cause an interruption as wel of Correspondencies, as of Public Meetings, the printing
> of these *Philosophical Transactions* may possibly for a while be intermitted; though endeavors
> shall be used to continue them, if it may be.

[40] Sprat, *History of the Royal Society of London*, p. 123.   [41] *Ibid.*, p. 123.
[42] Hall and Hall (eds.), *Oldenburg Correspondence*, II, p. 512: Oldenburg to Boyle, 18 September
1665. Moray answered Oldenburg (II, p. 560, 10 October):

> Mr. Boile thinkes at first as I think he will tell you, that he presumes Treacle is the ground of
> Borrhis Medicament, to morrow when your letter is read wee will set him on to examine it,
> which I think hee hath not done as yet, hee hath read both yours. The Salterius of Medicines
> for the plague is a thing I know not how may be hoped to be done with advantage to the

As this instance suggests, the commitment of the early Royal Society to 'science' certainly did not amount exclusively to 'basic science', stopping short of the more practical aspects of medicine, which might have been regarded as the sole province of the College of Physicians or the Society of Apothecaries. 'Merely' medical books frequently received extensive reviews, as for example Thomas Trapham's *A Discourse of the State of Health in the Island of Jamaica*,[43] and the epistolary intercourse of the secretaries contains lively discussions of the merits of various remedies, therapies and regimens for health. Here idealist concern for medical advance clearly mingled with the personal health worries of the hypochondriacal Boyle and Hooke, and even of Oldenburg, whose health was occasionally 'ticklish'.[44] 'I owe you many thanks for a medicin against violent fluxes', Oldenburg tells Boyle,

but give me leave to ask, whether the hot Cinamon and Nutmeg may not claime as great a share in the effect, as the cold Deadmans skull?[45]

Many of Oldenburg's key correspondents were free in communicating their pet remedies and recipes. John Beale, for example (who on one occasion commended lily of the valley to Oldenburg as 'the cleanser of the head from thummes and dullnes &; the students friend')[46] was invited by Oldenburg to referee William Jackson's account of Cheshire cheese making and discussion of the virtues of cheese for health. 'I return yr Chesshire cheese', he replied, advising non-publication on the grounds that Dr Thomas Moufflet's *Health's Improvement* (1655) had said it all already.[47]

It is, perhaps, unclear how deeply the ruling circles wished the Society to involve itself in the intricacies of pharmacy. But Oldenburg's

maker Nor know I a way to distribute any thing but by employing the Master of the pesthouse. To that purpose if you should write to Borrhi for some quantity for a tryall first, possibly if it prove effectuall profit may be made of it after a tryall *Gratis*.

See also Oldenburg to Boyle, 24 October 1665 (II, pp. 578–9), and for discussion of an antidote, II, p. 481. Borri (d. 1695), was an Italian alchemist.

[43] 'An Account of two Books: a Discourse of the State of Health in the Islands of Jamaica, with a Provision calculated for the same, from the Air, the Place, and the Water; the Customs and manner of Living, &c. By Thomas Trapham M.D. Coll. Med. Lond. Soc. Hon.', *Philosophical Transactions*, XII (1677), 1030–2.

[44] Hall and Hall (eds.), *Oldenburg Correspondence*, II, p. 531: Oldenburg to Boyle, 28 September 1665.

[45] Hall and Hall (eds.), *Oldenburg Correspondence*, II, p. 262: Oldenburg to Boyle, 20 October 1664.

[46] Hall and Hall (eds.), *Oldenburg Correspondence*, I, p. 481; Beale to Oldenburg, 21 December 1662.

[47] Hall and Hall (eds.), *Oldenburg Correspondence*, VI, p. 560: Beale to Oldenburg, 15 March 1669/70.

correspondence leaves no doubt that numerous enterprising operators sent him their potions and nostrums in the hope of achieving some sort of Royal Society imprimatur. In general they met with a cool response. As I shall show below, the Society adopted a sceptical line against the claims of panaceas, and certainly did not want its credit involved with false or exaggerated claims. More importantly, perhaps, the nucleus of the Society regarded the practices accompanying nostrums – the fact that they involved *secret* knowledge, used essentially for private benefit – as radically at odds with the public profession of the Society itself, committed as it was to cognitive openness and the public good. Such a view was clearly stated by Sprat in his *History*:

> For by such concealments, there may come very much hurt to mankind. If any certain remedy should be found out against an *Epidemical* disease; if it were suffer'd to be ingross'd by one man, there would be great swarms swept away, which otherwise might be easily sav'd. I shall instance in the *Sweating-Sickness*. The *Medicine* for it was almost infallible: But, before that could be generally publish'd, it had almost dispeopl'd whole Towns. If the same disease should have return'd, it might have been again as destructive, had not the *Lord Bacon* taken care, to set down the particular course of *Physick* for it, in his History of *Henry the Seventh*, and so put it beyond the possibility of any private man's invading it. This ought to be imitated in all other *soveraign cures* of the like nature, to avoid such dreadful casualties. The *Artificers* should reap the common crop of their *Arts*: but the *publick* should still have *Title* to the miraculous productions. It should be so appointed, as it is in the profits of mens Lands: where the Corn, and Grass, and Timber, and some coarser Metals belong to the *owner*:[48]

and it underpinned Boyle's own practice. For example when the recipe for the Helmontian Laudanum was 'as a great secret communicated to me by an expert Chemist', Boyle remonstrated, saying that he thought 'the Chymist a Benefactor to Physick, if he would have made public, or permitted me to publish the way of making so successful a medicine'.[49] Not all fellows of the Society proved so high-minded (Nehemiah Grew, for example, took out a patent for Epsom salts), but collectively, the Royal Society held firm against secrecy.

A substantial portion of the medical discourse of the early Royal Society centred upon the topics just discussed – drugs, the relation between environment and health, the health risks and benefits of travelling abroad, and so forth. They were clearly matters of concern to laymen as well as to practitioners, and they were sent in by laymen, such as John Beale, as well as by professionals. Indeed, they bear considerable resemblance to the topics commonly dealt with in the

---

[48] Sprat, *History of the Royal Society of London*, p. 75.
[49] 'An Account of the two Sorts of the Helmontian Laudanum, communicated to the Publisher by the Honourable Robert Boyle, together with the Way of the Noble Baron F.M. van Helmont (Son to the famous Johannes Baptista) of preparing his Laudanum', *Philosophical Transactions*, IX (1674), 147–50.

next century in the *Gentleman's Magazine*.[50] It would be misleading, however, to create the impression of a concentrated inquiry around an 'agenda'. Far from it. Most of the items raised in Oldenburg's correspondence (some of which found their way into the *Philosophical Transactions*) are extremely miscellaneous. Some fall into Hall's category of 'triviality and misguided enthusiasm', or in other words, precisely those aspects of 'nature deformed' which Francis Bacon thought so instructive a pathway to understanding the *regularities* of Nature.[51] Prominent amongst these, not suprisingly, were monstrous births. The *Philosophical Transactions* reported Siamese twins from Paris in 1667[52] and from Venice in 1670.[53] Tellingly, the latter report seems to have triggered a further letter from the zealous Dr William Durston in Plymouth, proffering a parallel tale of his own Siamese twins born to the wonderfully named Grace Batter'd ('the wife of a shoemaker, of honest repute'). True, once again, to his grasp of Royal Society protocols, after their death Durston set about a post mortem ('having with some difficulty obtained the Fathers leave to dissect it'), and gave the Society the benefit of the precise dimensions of this monster:

We first weighed this Birth, the weight whereof was *eight* pounds and a *quarter*; the Circumference of the left head was about *eleven* Inches, that of the right being half an Inch less. The Circumference of the Trunk was about *Sixteen* Inches and a quarter; and the length of both, from head to foot, was full *eighteen* inches and *an half*.[54]

Not all the medical correspondence on such 'curiosities' perhaps shared Durston's Baconian highmindedness. Letters to Oldenburg abound with casual references to the medically strange and titillating, as for example Joseph Glanvill's note of the 'labouring man who doth the necessityes of nature at a hole opened in his side, one of his gutts being broken against that place of his belly he tyes it up with a ribbon and untyes it for the occasions of nature',[55] or the report from Nathan-

50 See Porter, 'Lay Medical Knowledge in the Eighteenth Century'.
51 Thus Nathaniel Fairfax's 'Divers Instances of Peculiarities of Nature, both in Men and Brutes', *Philosophical Transactions*, II (1667), 549–51, despite the title, is actually an interesting record of various allergies.
52 'Extract of a Letter, Written from Paris, containing an Account of some Effects of the Transfusion of Bloud; and of two Monstrous Births, &c.', *Philosophical Transactions*, I (1665), 479–80.
53 'An Extract of an Italian Letter Written from Venice by Signor Jacomo Grandi, to an Acquaintance of his in London, concerning some Anatomical Observations and two odd Births: English'd by the Publisher, as follows', *Philosophical Transactions*, V (1670), 1188–9.
54 'A Narrative of a Monstrous Birth in Plymouth, Octob. 22 1670; together with the Anatomical Observations, taken thereupon by William Durston Doctor in Physick, and communicated to Dr. Tim Clerk', *Philosophical Transactions*, V (1670), 2096–7.
55 Hall and Hall (eds.), *Oldenburg Correspondence*, VI, pp. 191–2: Glanvill to Oldenburg, 15 August 1669.

iel Fairfax, the Suffolk nonconformist minister and physician, about a
strange case of hermaphroditism. After the death of her husband in the
Plague, Maria Fisher seduced her maid servant; the servant became
pregnant and blamed it on the widow Fisher; she in turn was hauled up
before quarter sessions, and an anatomical examination revealed that
she was a hermaphrodite. Fairfax related the story to Oldenburg in
Latin because 'some passages may seem too broad in English', a clear
indication that he was aiming for publication in the *Philosophical
Transactions*, an honour he was denied.[56] Yet it would be wrong to
treat a man such as Fairfax simply as a mere prurient 'virtuoso'. Thus
an interesting case history from him to Oldenburg related the 'rude
history' of Mrs Eliot:

> Gw. Eliot of Mendlesham Suffolk a pale, middle-aged, fullbodyed woman, tediously
> afflicted for some years wth a torment of ye bowells, was prevaild wth by a neighbour,
> who had suffered much in the like case, to swallow a Qualiver bullet, whereupon she
> found, (as he before her) present eas, but afterwards her paines returnd & increasd.[57]

Eventually, Mrs Eliot voided the bullet, covered in a chalky incrusta-
tion, with her urine. Fairfax offered the case as warning against this
precursor of the 'magic bullet', which he knew was a common country
remedy, and went on to raise the question of how the bullet had
actually passed down into her bladder (declining to speculate himself,
having, he said, 'mean thoughts of my own reflections on things').
Oldenburg published Fairfax's account,[58] and received a follow-up
mailbag – from Fairfax[59] and from others such as Joseph Glanvill, on
the same therapeutic resort.[60]

How much such correspondence contributed to the 'advancement of
learning' is difficult to say. Other motives than disinterested love of
truth may have been present, not least hopes for personal relief, a
theme commonly present. William Neile's letters to Oldenburg form a
nice coda. Hinting at his own 'Hypochondricalnesse' ('I am not over
merrily disposed'), Neile congratulated the Society on its success with
transfusion experiments, looked ahead to its prospects of taming
diseases in general ('I believe it is possible now you have once begunne

56 Hall and Hall (eds.), *Oldenburg Correspondence*, v, pp. 376–9: Fairfax to Oldenburg, 4
   February 1668/9.
57 Hall and Hall (eds.), *Oldenburg Correspondence*, v, pp. 47–9: Fairfax to Oldenburg, 18
   September 1668.
58 'An Extract of a Letter written by Dr. Nathan. Fairfax to the Publisher about a Bullet voided by
   Urine', *Philosophical Transactions*, III (1668), 803–4.
59 Hall and Hall (eds.), *Oldenburg Correspondence*, v, pp. 284–5: Fairfax to Oldenburg, 28
   December 1668.
60 Hall and Hall (eds.), *Oldenburg Correspondence*, vi, pp. 324–5: Glanvill to Oldenburg c. 22
   November 1669, offering a 'crusted bullett, which I believe . . . may gratify ye inquisitive'.

you might fine the waie to generate most kinds of diseases'), and then broached what was clearly his chief theme, his own plight:

I have of late been something subject to yellowe Jaundies which made mee consider a little what might be the cause of that disease and it seems to mee not so much to be an obstruction of the galle as too great an abundance of it for I could not find anie great signs of obstruction of galle my guts and stomacke seeming rather to be overflowing with it I believe rather that there is too much galle generated and perchance (cheifly) in the stomacke and guts, and it may be those things that cure it worke by correcting the irregular ferment which inclines to too much generation of galle and possibly the Liver and Pancreas may only collect that which was originally generated in the stomacke and guts for the use of digestion. I have been also troubled with the scurvye (that is with a kind of pricking pain in my armes) which I conceive to come from want of concoction which by distributing the ailment too rawe may perchance afterwards cause that vellication but when ever I talke of those kinds of things you must not look for anie foundation of skill of knowledge I only give some loose light conjectures which I hope will be favourablye accepted from Sir

    your assured freind and servant
     William Neile[61]

THE SHAPE OF ROYAL SOCIETY MEDICINE

Rupert Hall has drawn a sharp distinction between the 'mass of learned research devoted to basic science' by the Royal Society in such fields as physiology and anatomy, and on the other hand, the 'farrago of medical curiosities'.[62] Is this not a distinction too sharply drawn? For the great bulk of the correspondence of a medical nature generated by the early Royal Society was undoubtedly struggling to put medicine on a more 'scientific' footing. No anachronistic notion of 'scientific medicine' is here implied (indeed, Hall is correct to note a relative indifference to the kinds of questions of medical aetiology which would preoccupy later thinkers), merely the conscious attempt of many contributors – such as William Durston discussed above – to sort truth from falsehood, to establish standards of accuracy, of trustworthy authority and so on, and the concommitant efforts of Oldenburg and other influential minds to establish precisely what deserved credence.[63] Clearly, the Society's own experiments were in this respect canonical, above all, the transfusion experiments on dogs (replicated soon afterwards in Paris when a madman was injected with sheep's blood to his apparent benefit).[64] The Royal Society had been granted

---

[61] Hall and Hall (eds.), *Oldenburg Correspondence*, IV, pp. 8–9: W. Neile to Oldenburg 5 December 1667.
[62] Hall, 'English Medicine in the Royal Society's Correspondence: 1660–1677'.
[63] For this general problem see Steven Shapin and Simon Schaffer, *Leviathan and the Air Pump. Hobbes, Boyle and the Experimental Life*, (Princeton, 1985).
[64] N.S.R. Maluf, 'History of Blood Transfusion', *Journal of the History of Medicine*, IX (1954), 59–107.

privileges by Charles II similar to those of the medical corporations for dissecting corpses, but the evidence of medical experimentation actually taking place at the meetings of the Society is very slim. On the other hand, experiments relating to health and disease were commonly reported to the Society, as for example in 1668 when Dr William Holder described demonstrations designed to restore hearing to a deaf child 'known to divers of the R. Society'.[65] A similar instance would be the experiments performed by Fred Slare before the Society on the properties of 'sal armoniack', which he believed might explain the operation of the 'Hysterical frigid Paroxysm'.[66]

In cases where first-hand, eye witness reports were unobtainable, Oldenburg and Boyle between them, as the two chief intelligence gatherers, would often take great pains to secure and then appraise information. This happened in the case of Valentine Greatrakes the Irish Stroker.[67] Greatrakes healed by laying on of hands at many sites in England in 1665, though never before the Royal Society, despite Boyle's belief that they were 'the likeliest persons to give a fair account of it'.[68] Medical opinion at large was deeply divided on two questions: did he genuinely possess healing powers? (or was he a failure or a fraud?), and if he genuinely healed, were his healings by regular natural operations, or instead wonders and miracles? Boyle and Oldenburg were, initially at least, both notably sceptical (Boyle was in particular anxious lest excessively naturalistic interpretations of Greatrakes's powers should undermine the idea of providence).[69] Oldenburg's predictable course of action was to write round to his circle of correspondents asking for their opinions and experiences. Some replies came back positive, as this one from John Beale:

Col. Valentine Gratrix hath formally [?] assumed to himself ye healing of all diseases, and has done very much good to several persons, but he has confessed yt formerly he

[65] 'An Account, of an Experiment, concerning Deafness, communicated to the R. Society, by the Worthy and Learned Divine Dr. William Holder, as followeth', *Philosophical Transactions*, III (1668), 665–8. A parallel would be Beale's account of the tubes he had experimentally developed to correct his astigmatism, *Philosophical Transactions*, III (1668), 802; IV, 474–7; V, 64.

[66] 'An Account of some Experiments made at several Meetings of the Royal Society by the Ingenious Fred. Slare M.D. Fellow of the Royal Society, and one of the Colledge of Physitians, with some short applications of them to Physical matters', *Philosophical Transactions*, XIII (1683), 295–7.

[67] On Greatrakes, see in general, A. Brian Laver, 'Miracles no Wonder! The Mesmeric Phenomena and Cures of Valentine Greatrakes', *Journal of the History of Medicine*, XXXIII (1978), 35–46; Eamon Duffy 'Valentine Greatrakes, the Irish Stroker: Miracle, Science and Orthodoxy in Restoration England', in K. Robbins (ed.), *Religion and Humanism* (Oxford, 1981), pp. 251–73; N. Steneck, 'Greatrakes the Stroker. The Interpretations of Historians', *Isis*, LXXIII (1982), 161–85. [68] Quoted in Duffy, *Valentine Greatrakes, the Irish Stroker*, p. 268.

[69] Jacob, *Henry Stubbe, Radical Protestantism and the Early Enlightenment*.

did use charmes, and tis Knowne, yt he did likewise study magick, but as he now sais, he makes use of neither, his manner is, of stroaking ym with his hand on their bare skins extraordinarily hard and wth soe much paine to himself as ye patient and so drives ye distemper from place to place following it until either it evacuates out of ye posteriors or ye eares or ye mouth, several persons of this place have been wth him some are ye better some ye worse, and those yt pretend ymselves heald of their lamenes are to us so still yet have no paine at all. Sr Thomas Dancers Lady was troubled wth ye dropsy and extraordinarily sweled, but I am apt to believe, yt ye jogging of ye couch 28. m. in ye country was as great a means of ye cure as his violent stroaking her naked belley, but perhaps the continuance of his warm hand on a ladies belly for 14 days together wth a strong [illegible] might do much, but befor she was absolutely curd, he was summond before ye consistory of Lismor, and being examined by wt authority he did undertake thes things, he answerd, he had none but only his own strong imagination whereupon Dean Gore indicted him and he gave in security not to proceed any further.[70]

Oldenburg gradually moved from scepticism to conviction, writing to Boyle in October 1665:

By the very last, I receaved this Information, yt a Childe in Dr Beale's neighbourhood is cured of ye stone or other stoppage of Urine, wch came all, as he saith, with horrid paine in threads, or ropy, but now, after ye touch, is very perfectly naturall, and without paine. Having related this, He adds, It cannot be denyed, yt innumerable great cures are done, and 'tis not possible, yt all exspectations should be satisfyed, without a general restauration equivalent to a Resurrection. And yn he concludes, yt ye same must suddenly fall, because 'tis odious to many, and winter hinders the passage, and himself He is tyred with the infinite resorte, and mens expectations.[71]

and six months later,

Greatrix does certainly some cures by his frictions, insinuating (perhaps) some salubrious steams or spirits of his own into sickly people's bodies.[72]

Finally Oldenburg evidently felt sufficiently convinced, of the reality of Greatrakes's cures at least, if not of their mechanism, to warrant an insertion in the *Philosophical Transactions*. The issue for May 7, 1666 carries an item entitled 'Some Observations of the Effects of Touch and Friction', which argues, citing the authority of Bacon, that friction, by imparting warmth and motion, can be highly conducive to good health and long life.[73] Some years later, Oldenburg evidently had not changed his mind about Greatrakes's real powers. Writing to Huet in 1674, he explained:

---

[70] Hall and Hall (eds.), *Oldenburg Correspondence*, II, pp. 496–7: Beale to Oldenburg, 4 September 1665.

[71] Hall and Hall (eds.), *Oldenburg Correspondence*, III, p. 556: Oldenburg to Boyle, 10 October 1665.

[72] Hall and Hall (eds.), *Oldenburg Correspondence*, II: Oldenburg to Boyle, 13 March 1665/6.

[73] 'Some observations of the Effect of Touch and Friction', *Philosophical Transactions*, I (1666), 206–9.

As for that Irishman who seemed to have a curative power in his hands: it did not, from what I could notice, extend beyond tumours and pains in the body, which he chased out by a strong friction. He was a strong man, of a sanguine temperament and very healthy, on which apparently depended the power he had to heal certain diseases.[74]

Greatrakes was a real presence on the English medical scene and there was no shortage of reports about him from credit-worthy testimony. Authentication was far more difficult in other cases. Oldenburg was perpetually receiving letters of this kind:

A Friend of mind, a professed Physitian, hath assured me, that at Montpelier, a German hath discover'd the vessels, which convey the Chyle to the Breasts of Nursing Women; and shew'd, that they do issue out of the Ductus of Monsieur Pecquet. This is a discovery of a thing the *being* of which hath been believed long since, though not made out. Another person hath assured me, that there is certainly another passage of the Urine to the Bladder than by the Ureters; an Experiment having been lately made, whereby the Ureters of a Dog were so carefully tyed up, that nothing could pass that way, and yet the Urinary Bladder was found full of Water.[75]

What credit did such narrations deserve? As always Oldenburg flew the flag for firsthand eye witness, accuracy, exactitude, and scepticism where these were deficient. Faced with improbable or exaggerated medical reporting, he warned, berated and cajoled his correspondents. To Rudbeck he asked for information upon his wife's caesarian operation:

I had asked in my last letter to you that you should write for me the narrative of your wife's Caesarian delivery, in which we understand that you performed the operation yourself with a most fortunate outcome. I am doubtful whether you will have satisfied our importunity already, and I now ask a second time what I sought before. Farewell, and continue to adorn and improve philosophy. London, 23 July 1670.[76]

But first he gave this gentle reading of the epistemological riot act:

It is part of the design of the Royal Society to compile a trustworthy natural history to be executed in the most reliable manner, upon which a solid and fruitful natural philosophy may be erected. You will readily agree that the efforts of all distinguished men, over the whole globe, should be combined for this purpose, and that so great a work should be prepared by their mutual exchanges. We have already inspired several philosophers of other countries to this task. We also believe that in Sweden there are many things very worthy of note.[77]

Likewise, having received Glanvill's account of the cures effected at Bath spa, he thanked him, but with a gentle chiding:

[74] Hall and Hall (eds.), *Oldenburg Correspondence*, XI, pp. 26–9: Oldenburg to Huet, 25 May 1674.
[75] Hall and Hall (eds.), *Oldenburg Correspondence*, VII, p. 205: [?]Justel to Oldenburg, 19 October 1670.
[76] Hall and Hall (eds.), *Oldenburg Correspondence*, VII, p. 96: Oldenburg to Rudbeck, 23 July 1670.   [77] *Ibid.*

It were also very desirable to take great care in observing the effects, it truly and most generally exerts in diseased or distempered bodyes; and to be exceeding cautious in not multiplying or exaggerating ye benefits, it affords above reality.[78]

Oldenburg found himself bombarded with too much information he could not trust. At La Rochelle, he writes to Freiherr von Friesen,

There is one of those people called Adepts who claims to possess the universal medicine, and showed us a fluid with a deep reddish tinge in a hermetically sealed phial as being that medicine; as also his philosophical furnace in which it was made. But I shan't believe his tale until he confirms it by some lasting cures.[79]

In a similar tone he reports to Boyle:

If I had not been afraid of Hudibras, I had seconded Dr Charlton wth ye relation of a certain Apothecary in Ireland, who, as I was assured by a Physitian, yt imployed him there, has also 3. testicles, being excessively given to Venery. There is certainly something as well in ye conformation of ye parts, as in ye temper of animals, yt necessitateth ym (if I may say so) to such and such operations.[80]

Oldenburg evidently felt he could never afford not to look over his shoulder:

I am sorry, ye Dissector of ye Doublechild did not putt his name to ye Account, he gave of the operation; and we must contrive some way or another, to have it yet done, for ye more authenticknes of ye relation, now it is to be recorded by a Royall Society of severe Philosophers.[81]

Oldenburg could not be too careful. Even Nathaniel Fairfax mentioned 'the scandal raised on the Society as too friendly to Quacks' – by which he meant chemical physicians.[82] And sometimes Oldenburg was

---

[78] Hall and Hall (eds.), *Oldenburg Correspondence*, VI, p. 106: Oldenburg to Glanvill, 10 July 1669.

[79] Hall and Hall (eds.), *Oldenburg Correspondence*, I, pp. 236–7: Oldenburg to Freiherr von Friesen, 26 April 1659. See also *ibid.*, p. 241, Oldenburg to Michaelis:
At La Rochelle we found a physician who, having showed us a liquid of a full ruddy color in a hermetically sealed phial, boasted that it was his universal medicine; having at the same time exhibited another glass, in which was some yellowish stuff, he hinted that it was the matter of philosophic gold, the mother of the liquid mentioned just now. Several of the French are fully persuaded that the secretly hidden etherial spirit [. . .] is that panacea which has been sought with such zeal. Here at Paris many are rich in promises, few in performance.

[80] Hall and Hall (eds.), *Oldenburg Correspondence*, II, p. 248: Oldenburg to Boyle, 6 October 1664. Boyle himself was never satisfied with second-hand information. Informed about a man's vein said to contain milk not blood, he replied, 'he was desirous to have it very circumstantially from the said Physitian himself, before he would say more of it': in 'Some Anatomical Observations of Milk found in the Veins, instead of Blood; and of Grass, found in the Wind-pipes of some Animals', *Philosophical Transactions*, 1 (1665), 100.

[81] Hall and Hall (eds.), *Oldenburg Correspondence*, II, p. 309: Oldenburg to Boyle, 17 November 1664. For wider issues of credit in the Royal Society, see Peter Dear, 'Totius in Verba: Rhetoric and Authority in the Early Royal Society', *Isis*, LXXVI (1985), 145–61.

[82] Hall and Hall (eds.), *Oldenburg Correspondence*, V, p. 504: Fairfax to Oldenburg, 30 April 1669.

the one who was seemingly being accused of credulity. As Martin Lister responded to him in 1671,

I did much admire ye Experiment of ye Speedy & sure healing of cut-eyes by ye juice of Celandine; & yet, pardon my diffidence, if I thinke we can scarce be too much cautioned against ourselves, we very often, especially in Medicinall matters, take *non causa pro causa* & it is most certain, though ye Eye be beleeved a very tender part, it will suddainly heale of it selfe, as is frequently observed by Cock-masters but since ye Experiment is reduced to Celandine alone by ye G[erman] P[hilosophers] without ye addition of any Vitriolick misterie, I am in great hopes it is no delusion.[83]

CONCLUSION

There are no clear-cut conclusions to be drawn from this brief survey. Whether the founding of the Royal Society directly or indirectly had any real effect in changing the amount and type of medical knowledge in circulation – amongst physicians, the 'learned' and people at large – is an important question. But the role of medicine within the Royal Society remains seriously unresearched. Even the vast trove of the Sloane papers, covering most of the first half of the eighteenth century, has never been subject to proper analysis.[84] Recent research has argued that the standing of provincial medical practitioners was rising in the community from perhaps the 1690s, and Holmes in particular has contended that this in part reflected their growing professional knowledge and expertise.[85] Certainly, medical men were to be prominent during the eighteenth century wherever provincial scientific interests gelled into clubs and societies, just as of course provincial medical societies themselves began to populate the landscape during that century.[86] At some point in the complex series of imputs and stimuli which gradually forged the links between medical presence and sci-

[83] Hall and Hall (eds.), *Oldenburg Correspondence*, VIII, pp. 212–14: Lister to Oldenburg, 25 August 1671.

[84] Maarten Ultee of the University of Alabama is currently engaged in a study of Sloane's correspondence network. The Royal Society played an active role in the introduction of inoculation into England. See Genevieve Miller, *The Adoption of Inoculation for Smallpox in England and France* (Philadelphia, 1957); and Larry Stewart, 'The Edge of Utility: Slaves and Smallpox in the Early Eighteenth Century', *Medical History*, XXIX (1985), 54–70.

[85] I. Loudon, 'The Nature of Provincial Practice in Eighteenth Century England', *Medical History*, XXIX (1985), 1–32; G. Holmes, *Augustan England. Professions, State and Society* (London, 1982).

[86] See for instance Arnold Thackray, 'Natural Knowledge in Cultural Context: The Manchester Model', *American Historical Review*, LXXIX (1974), 672–709; T. Hunt (ed.), *The Medical Society of London 1773–1973* (London, 1972). There is an important pioneering investigation of the medical research community of late eighteenth-century London in Susan C. Lawrence, 'Science and Medicine at the London Hospitals: The Development of Teaching and Research, 1750–1815' (University of Toronto, Ph.D. thesis, 1985). Lawrence does not find the Royal Society central to medical research.

ence, the energizing and co-ordinating role of the Royal Society probably played its part. Timothy Clarke told Oldenburg in 1668:

It seems to me that no remedies have been *revealed* to men, but all have been given to the world as a result of experiments made in various ways, mutually discussed, compared together, and finally collected by learned men. Today innovators assert unblushingly that they have just discovered some great new remedy (formerly unknown to themselves and every one else), and they immediately predict remarkable powers for it, which no one has ever perceived hitherto. Unless I am mistaken, the older, wiser, and more experienced physician will not believe that he who boldly appeals to experience as demonstrating the infallible virtues of specific remedies, has had long experience of sufferers from many and diverse diseases. Yet one encounters every day certain men who, having heard or read by chance of something new to themselves, which perhaps they don't properly understand, clasp it close to their bosoms merely for the sake of novelty, cherishing it with fancies and striving to puff it up into something considerable by embellishing it with polysyllabic words; then they pass this falsehood off on the world as their own, and at once arrogating themselves the names of authors and inventors, lead the half-learned and gullible tyros into error.

But certainly those who strenuously labor at the promotion of true science behave far otherwise. Nothing should be published that is foolish or ill-digested, and the truth, certainly, and utility of things to be published should long be pondered upon. For if only matter sent to press were submitted to a mature judgment, learned men would not labor under such a great mass of useless books.[87]

The ripples of that kind of impulse were probably recognizable for a long while: only further research on the early collective history of the emergent medical profession will tell.

[87] Hall and Hall (eds.), *Oldenburg Correspondence*, IV, p. 363: Timothy Clarke to Oldenburg April/May 1668.

11

Medical practice in late seventeenth- and early eighteenth-century England: continuity and union

ANDREW WEAR

INTRODUCTION

To argue that medicine did not change, or changed slowly, in the second half of the seventeenth century and the beginning of the eighteenth century may appear perverse. After all, as the chapters in this book demonstrate, change was taking place all around medicine and moreover, the institutions and groupings within medicine were changing. But what of medical practice? Here also the different medical sects, the Galenists, Paracelsians, empiricists, chemists, iatrochemists, iatromathematicians had their own particular theories and remedies. Yet there was underlying unity that implied a lack of change both in medical theory and practice. This unity was the consequence of a need by medical practitioners to be understood by patients, to relate to their expectations and hence to attract their trade. Commerce, in other words, could transcend apparent theoretical or institutional differences.

MEDICAL THEORY

It appears obvious that medicine changed radically in this period. The chemical, corpuscular, experimental and mathematical developments in science came to be united in different ways to provide new theoretical bases for medicine. The non-mathematical, non-mechanical, qualitative–humoral system of the ancients seems to have been replaced. For instance, George Cheyne orders his *New Theory of Continual Fevers* using the language of 'Postulata', 'Lemma' and 'Scholium', and having

I would like to thank the members of the Cambridge conference, Peter Burke and Vivian Nutton, for their very helpful comments, and the Carnegie Trust for Scotland for a grant in aid of this research.

postulated 'that the whole body is nothing but a congeries of canals' he wrote in *Lemma 1*:

Let there be a greater distractile cylindrical canal, whose orifice is ABCD, through which a giv'n quantity of liquor passes in a giv'n time; and a lesser one EFGH . . .[1]

When giving practical advice Cheyne also applied ideas from the corpuscular philosophy, recommending for instance 'a large draught of warm water-gruel, or a warm small Mountain-wine whey, as an antidote against the nitrous effluvia, suck'd into the body'.[2] The contrast therefore seems great between Cheyne and someone like Thomas Venner writing at the beginning of the seventeenth century. Venner used 'common sense' qualitative terms. His description of air contrasts with the apparent hard objectivity of Cheyne:

Therefore touching the knowledge of the goodness of the air, it must be considered that it be not vaporous, moist or putrid, nor too hot, or too cold, nor over-moist, or dry: for a vaporous, cloudy, gross or putrid air doth cause rheums, annoy the lungs, corrupt the humors, infect, the heart, deicet the spirits.[3]

The move from the qualitative, subjective, system of ancient and renaissance natural philosophy to the quantitative and objective world of the seventeenth century has been often and variously retold by historians of science. Yet in the case of medicine there is some doubt that we have the same story. The successes of the mechanical philosophy were rarely practical, and medicine in the end is practical. The mortality rate did not fall dramatically in this period nor can the small and ephemeral rise in the expectation of life after 1690 be attributed to medical advance (or even to increased prosperity).[4] Nor did medicine, through the new science, have any new technical apparatus (apart possibly from the microscope) that gave hope for cure.

The change that occurred, therefore, was theoretical and ideological and other historians in this book have been looking at its details. I want to argue, however, first that the new philosophy (which might have led to changes in practice), despite its empiricism was as speculative as the Aristotelian–Galenic when it came to describing the hidden happen-

---

[1] George Cheyne, *A New Theory of Acute and Slow Continu'd Fevers . . . To which is Prefix'd an Essay concerning the Improvements in the Theory of Medicine*, 3rd edn (London, 1722), pp. 7–8. On Cheyne's Newtonianism and his changes of stance within it see Anita Guerrini, 'James Keill, George Cheyne, and Newtonian Physiology, 1690–1740', *Journal of the History of Biology*, XVIII, 247–66, and her chapter in this book.

[2] George Cheyne, *An Essay of Health and Long Life* (London, 1724), pp. 10–11.

[3] Thomas Venner, *Via Recta ad Vitam Longam: Or, a plaine philosophicall demonstration of the nature, faculties and effects of all such things as by way of nourishments make for the preservation of health . . .* (London, 1628), p. 2.

[4] See E.A. Wrigley and R.S. Schofield, *The Population History of England 1541–1871* (London, 1981), pp. 234–6, 412–17.

ings of nature, for instance the sharp penetrating shape of acid particles, or the workings of a disease or medicine inside the depths of the
body. The need to show oneself as an educated, rational, physician and
to attract fee-paying patients made it inevitable that physicians continued to use what, in terms of the experimental and empirical approach of the late seventeenth century, were essentially speculations.
Medical theory, of whatever type, in its structure often fulfilled the
classical requirements of rational medicine (that is relating effects to
cause or, as in the practice of medicine which forms the second part of
this chapter, paying attention to a patient's constitution, regimen,
indications, changing condition and applying remedies to symptoms in
a rational way). But, as I argue, these, the central ideological defences
of the learned physician against the empiric, cannot always be differentiated from empirical practice.

Thomas Willis in his preface to his work on fermentation compared
the three natural philosophies of his time: the Aristotelian, the 'Epicurean' or mechanical, and the chemical. The first had no 'peculiar
respect to the more secret recesses of nature, it salves the appearance of
things, that 'tis almost the same thing, to say a thing consists of wood
and stones as a body of four elements'. The second:

doth happily and very ingeniously disintangle some difficult knots of the sciences, and
dark riddles, certainly it deserves no light praise: but because it rather supposes than
demonstrates its principles and teaches of what figure those elements of bodies may be,
not what they have been, and also induces notions extremely subtle, and remote from
the sense, and which do not sufficiently quadrate with the phenomena of nature, when
we descend to particulars, it pleases me to give my sentence for the third opinion
before-mentioned, which is of the Chymists . . . affirming all bodies to consist of spirit,
sulphur, salt, water and earth.[5]

For Willis the chemists' philosophy was the *via media*, neither too
obvious nor too far from sense (though he did admit that 'the atomical
and our spagyric principles' could merge, the latter into the former as
long as the atoms or conceptions are real). His principles had to be
apparent to the senses:

I mean by the name of principles not simple and wholly uncompounded entities, but
such kind of substances only, into which physical things are resolved as it were into
parts lastly sensible. By the intestine motion and combinations of these, bodies are
begot and increase.[6]

Despite this protestation of empirical virtue, Willis could not remain
unsullied by the temptations of rationalism (in the general Galenic
sense). He naturally wanted to go from effects to causes. Take the
example of Peruvian bark, the new wonder drug for fevers. He ad-

---

⁵ Thomas Willis, *Dr. Willis's Practice of Physick, Being the Whole Works* . . . (English
translation of Latin original) (London, 1684), p. 2.   ⁶ *Ibid.*, p. 2.

mitted that 'it is not to be dissembled, that 'tis very difficult to explicate the causes of these kinds of effects and the manner of working (of the bark)'. As a clinician he noted that the bark seemed to stay in the blood because, although the first bout of fever might still occur after taking the bark, it often stopped the second or third bout. From this he made up the story (or extremely weak inference) that the particles of the bark produce in the blood 'a certain new fermentation, by which, whilst the particles of the blood are continually agitated, they are wholly hindred, that they cannot heap up any excrementitious matter, or enter into feverish turgescencies'. He also noted that fever could return, because the bark was 'too sparingly given' and the 'venom repullulates, and the old poison, thought to have been exploded, is at length brought into act'.[7]

Despite his wish to keep to observables, Willis inevitably fell back upon his imagination when discussing the hidden happenings of the body. There was little difference in structure between Willis's story of what took place in the body and earlier humoral stories. William Clowes in the sixteenth century wrote confidently of quicksilver and its effect on syphilis:

> But yet this I do know assuredly, that . . . it will resolve and molify: and it openeth the body, and provoketh sweat and emptieth the cause of this disease, sometimes sensible and sometimes insensible, and the blood thereby is purged from infection, and all the parts of the body is cleansed from superfluous humors, so that good humors are bred, and they do return again unto their natural cause and disposition, as we daily see by experience.[8]

The ability to tell the story from the seen (the effects) to the unseen (the causes) was from Greek times and up to and beyond the seventeenth century, the mark of the rational (and expensive) physician whose knowledge of causes set him apart from the crowd of empirics and quacks. As Daniel Coxe, the defender of the London College of Physicians against the apothecaries, wrote, the knowledge of causes was taken to mean better medical practice:

> Then as for the cure of diseases, it seems highly probable that they who are best acquainted with the causes and symptoms of diseases will apply medicines more properly than others that cannot so well distinguish although possessed of the same remedies.[9]

---

[7] *Ibid.*, pp. 72–3.
[8] William Clowes, *A Briefe and Necessarie Treatise Touching the Cure of the Disease Called Morbus Gallicus* . . . (London, 1585), p. 25v.
[9] Daniel Cox, *A Discourse, Wherein the Interest of the Patient in Reference to Physick and Physicians is Soberly Debated, Many Abuses of the Apothecaries in the Preparing of their Medicines are detected* . . . (London, 1669), p. 77. Harold J. Cook writes in *The Decline of the Old Medical Regime in Stuart London* (Ithaca and London, 1986), pp. 167–70 that Cox was one of a group of experimental physicians who were trying to make the College more empirical, his language, nevertheless, often expressed the traditional, rational, virtues.

There was tension between the rational and the empirical even for that most empirical of English physicians, Thomas Sydenham. He was certainly suspicious of theory:

He that in physick shall lay down fundamental maxims and from thence drawing consequence and raising dispute shall reduce it into the regular form of a science has indeed done something to enlarge the art of talking ... And he that thinks he came to be skild in diseases by studying the doctrine of the humors, that the notions of obstructions and putrefaction assists him in the cure of fevers, or that by the acquaintance he had with sulphur and mercury he was into this useful discovery, that what medicines and regimen as certainly kill in the latter end of some fevers as they cure in others, may as rationally believe that his cook owes his skill in roasting and boiling to his study of the elements and that his speculations about fire and water have taught him that the same seething liquors that boils the egg hard makes the hen tender.[10]

Sydenham developed this philosophical position when he tried to study illnesses by observation alone. However, in his practice he made the jump 'into the hidden causes of things'.[11] I will return to this case, but one look at Sydenham's advice to a patient of his, John Locke, shows him as an oldfashioned rationalist.

You may not in the least doubt but that a steady persisting in the use of the following directions (grounded not an opinion but uninterrupted experience) will at last effect your desired cause. First, therefore, in order to the diverting and subduing also the ichorose matter 'twill be requisite to take your pills twice a week as for example every Thursday and Sunday about 4 o'clock in the morning and your clyster in the intermitting days about six, constantly till you are well. In the next place, foreasmuch as there is wanting in bodies broken with business and dispirited upon the before mentioned accounts, that stock of natural heat which should bring the matter quickly to digestion 'twill be highly necessary that you cherish yourself as much as can be going to bed very early at night, even at 8 o'clock.[12]

Sydenham may have known by experience that his method would work (the pills, the clyster, the sleep) but the diverting and subduing of the 'ichorose matter' and the natural heat and its digestive power were hidden, theoretical matters. Nevertheless, patients, even one like John Locke, needed to be given reasons for remedies and what better way of explaining things, honorary virtuoso to virtuoso, than by using the language of traditional humoral medicine.

The problem for physicians who wanted to base their work on experience alone was that they might have ended up like Willis and Sydenham reasoning about events in the body during illness or therapy which often could not be known by observation or experiment. This

[10] In Kenneth Dewhurst, Dr Thomas Sydenham (1624–1689), His Life and Original Writings (Berkeley and Los Angeles, 1966), p. 81.
[11] Ibid., p. 81: 'But proud man, not content with that knowledge he was capable of and was useful to him, would needs penetrate into the hidden causes of things, lay down principles and establish maxims to him self about the operations of nature.'   [12] Ibid., p. 167–8.

was less of a problem for writers like Cheyne who easily moved from general principles (mechanical or chemical) in physiology, pathology and finally to treatment. William Cole's discussion of apoplexy in *A Physico-Medical Essay* (1689)[13] is a good example of this. Cole began with general corpuscular theory mixed with anatomical findings to explain brain function and disfunction; he used the bills of mortality to discover the prevalent seasons for the condition and finally, having arrived at the view that cold changed the brain's tone so that particles in the air could enter it to cause apoplexy, he produced a rational treatment for it. However, as Cheyne acknowledged, the logical progress from fundamentals to specifics could be interrupted, though his certainty in the former remained undiminished:

Perhaps my manner of explaining some great and fundamental truths, and a few of the consequences I draw by my method, may be defective: And perhaps, from some of the links being dropt, and from faults in the wording, the chain of the reasoning may not be always clear and strong; but I am sure the foundation is solid and just.[14]

Whether a physician was an empiricist or rationalist (the latter did, of course, allow empirical data to enter into the argument) there does seem to have been a major difficulty for each in the new medicine of the later seventeenth and early eighteenth centuries. The principles of the new medicine, derived as they were from the physical sciences, were abstract and non-biological as Boerhaave put it:

Nothing is more evident that the general rules which are deduced from mechanical experiments; but nothing is more uncertain than what mechanicians assert from those general rules concerning the human body.[15]

The empiricist needed to give a rational account of the working of an illness or a treatment to satisfy the reader or patient, but in so doing could fall from his philosophical position. Again, as Boerhaave wrote, although reasoning (and here he meant reasoning in the traditional medical sense of describing hidden causes for effects) together with the collecting of facts formed the basis of physic, it was nevertheless suspect:

The art of physic was anciently established (1.) by a faithful collection of facts observed, whose effects were (2.) afterwards explained, and their causes assigned by

---

13 William Cole, *A Physico-Medical Essay Concerning the Late Frequency of Apoplexies* (Oxford, 1689).

14 George Cheyne, *An Essay on Regimen* (London, 1740), Preface, p. vii. Dr John Henry (private communication) suggests that Cheyne may have meant by 'fundamental truths' the findings of the senses, which all proponents of the new science took to be fundamental rather than fundamental, theoretical, ideas. The context of the passage and the first chapter where the body is described as 'an hydraulic machine', as if it was an indisputable truth, inclines me to remain with the latter interpretation.

15 H. Boerhaave, *Academical Lectures on the Theory of Physic*, 6 vols. (London, 1742–6), I, p. 47.

the assistance of reason; the first carries conviction along with it, and is indisputable; nothing being more certain than demonstration from experience, but the latter is more dubious and uncertain; since every sect may explain the causes of particular effects upon different hypotheses.[16]

The tensions produced by the application of the teachings of one sect, those of the mechanical philosophers, to medicine, can be seen in the history of eighteenth-century medicine: the rise and fall of different systems, and descriptions of diseases based upon symptoms rather than causes. Instead of using hindsight and giving as a reason for this the absence from the eighteenth century of organic chemistry, biochemistry, neurobiology, molecular biology and the other disciplines that span the gap between the physical sciences and the body, I want to briefly look at other types of reasons for difficulties faced by physicians in the period of the new science.

If one takes the long view and contrasts the later part of the seventeenth century with the centuries immediately before, it becomes apparent that in certain respects there was no such thing as a new medicine. The picture of the physical world may have been transformed. The same did not happen for medicine despite appearances. The preservation of health was discussed in terms of the six non-naturals both in the renaissance and the eighteenth century.[17] It made sense for both humoralist and mechanist, given the conditions of life, to see health in terms of one's food, drink, exercise and passions. The fact that today this still applies is no reason to be blind to such categories. In disease, the language used to describe the secret happenings in the body was the same for both the late seventeenth century and the period before. Despite the impression of objectivity, the use of analogy and metaphor to create the images of fight, defence, penetration, expressing the movement from symptom to cause – were the same for the two periods. Here is Cheyne on sulphur as a remedy for gout:

By its agreeable taste and lightness on the stomach . . . its tenacity, ropiness and elasticity; the smallness of its parts; their efficacy in destroying the mischief of all saline particles, with their natural warmth, join'd to the activity of its acid salt, (making it a kind of natural soap) it enters the small vessels, where no other dilutent, hitherto known, can come; cleanses their insides from the foulness that sticks to them; imbibes and retains all the gouty salts, and carries them out of the body by perspiration; softens, smooths and relaxes the parch'd and stiffn'd fibres; and by leaving some of its oily parts on their surfaces sheaths and defends them from the points of the salts afterwards introduc'd.[18]

[16] *Ibid.*, p. 42.
[17] On the non-naturals see L.J. Rather, 'The Six Things Non-Natural: A Note on the Origins and Fate of a Doctrine and a Phrase', *Clio Medica*, III, (1968), 337–47; P. Niebyl 'The Non-Naturals', *Bulletin of the History of Medicine*, XLIII (1971), 486–92.
[18] George Cheyne, *An Essay of the True Nature and Due Methods of Treating the Gout* (London, 1723), p. 39.

There are several points to be made about this sort of language. First of all it was qualitative, the only difference is that instead of the humors and herbs of the sixteenth century we have chemicals. A theory, even one as powerful as the mechanical or corpuscular, could not immediately overcome a deeply rooted way of describing substances. (Its practitioners might have stated that they were not yet at the stage where they could dispense with such language.) Sir John Floyer explicitly recognized in *The Preternatural State of Animal Humours Described by their Sensible Qualities* (1696) that the new philosophy, particularly experimental chemistry, still had a place for the perception of qualities and that as the title of another book of his had it, one could discover 'the Virtues of vegetables, minerals and animals by their tastes and smells'.[19] The public had to use their own taste, smell and sight when deciding what was good meat, fish or water. We still sometimes do this today, but public health bodies and scientific methods and analysis have replaced subjective judgement. In the seventeenth and eighteenth centuries the qualities of things were matters of everyday importance. So Cheyne would have been able to take his audience along with him when he wrote:

All other things being equal, vegetables and animals of a strong, poignant, aromatic and hot taste, are harder to digest than those of a milder, softer and more insipid taste.[20]

In the case of illness, patient, relative and doctor also had to use a qualitative evaluation of the state of the patient's body. Cheyne's description of the hidden effects of sulphur on gout was a narrative, a story of courageous deeds in the body, and it was couched in qualitative terms. On both these counts it was accessible to the patient, in fact Cheyne's treatise was ostensibly written for a patient. This accessibility has been discussed recently by Jewson and Porter (and in a forthcoming article by Nicolson).[21] But let me add a caveat before going overboard for the open market-place theory of the medical world of the eighteenth century where patient dictated financially to the doctor and where the latter had to tailor his explanations to the understanding of the former. One can imagine Cheyne giving bits of the above

[19] Sir John Floyer, Φαρμακο-Βαβανος *Or the Touch-Stone of Medicines. Discovering the Vertues of Vegetables, Minerals, and Animals by their Tastes and Smells*, 2 vols. (London, 1687–91).
[20] Cheyne, *An Essay of Health and Long Life*, p. 26.
[21] N.D. Jewson, 'Medical Knowledge and the Patronage System in 18th Century England', *Sociology*, VIII (1974), 269–285; Roy Porter, 'Laymen, Doctors and Medical Knowledge in the Eighteenth Century: The Evidence of the *Gentleman's Magazine*', in Roy Porter (ed.), *Patients and Practitioners. Lay Perceptions of Medicine in Pre-industrial Society* (Cambridge, 1985), pp. 283–314. Malcolm Nicolson, 'The Metastatic Theory of Pathogenesis and the Professional Interests of the Eighteenth Century Physician', *Medical History*, (forthcoming).

explanation when treating a patient with sulphur but, although the explanation in its form and much of its content was accessible to the patient, being part of a common experience (a story structure and qualitative description), the tone of the story presupposes an unravelling, an explanation of complex workings – as such it is specialized knowledged possessed by the physician alone. (There are no contradictions here: just think of the status of the Homeric poet and the popularity of his stories.)

Nevertheless, it was probably the need to be understood by the patient that led to the graphic, qualitative element in medical theory. A part may also have been played by the poorly regulated market composed of wise women, herbalists, empirics, astrologers, apothecaries, chemists, barber–surgeons, physicians, as well as those less clearly defined as practitioners: the self-help patients, family members, neighbours, clergymen. As long as physicians competed in this type of market, they could not afford to mystify their clients by going overboard for chemical or Newtonian medicine. Instead, they had the best of both worlds: the cachet of a fashionable new theory, but expressed in a language which reflected how illness had traditionally been perceived (and still is by many lay people today).

MEDICAL PRACTICE

If medical theory, as it related to illness and therapy, did not change in its basic structure, what of medical practice? Again, at first sight, the answer is easy. If we follow some recent historians who have reflected in their work the 'professional' and occupational divides in medicine, and take at face value the rhetoric of the London College of Physicians against the empirics, or of traditional Galenists against empiricists influenced by the 'new science', then clearly there was great change and disunity in the world of late seventeenth-century medicine, and this had its counterpart in the relatively recent changes in theory (Paracelsian, chemical, mechanical).[22] At one level this picture cannot

---

[22] See, for instance, Theodore M. Brown, 'The College of Physicians and the Acceptance of Iatromechanism in England 1665–1695, *Bulletin of the History of Medicine*, XIVL (1970), 12–30; Theodore M. Brown, 'Physiology and the Mechanical Philosophy in Mid-Seventeenth Century England', *Bulletin of the History of Medicine*, LI (1977) 25–54; Michael Hunter, *Science and Society in Restoration England* (Cambridge, 1981) is wide-ranging and subtle but still gives great emphasis to institutions, especially the Royal Society; see also the valuable new work by Harold J. Cook, *The Decline of the Old Medical Regime in Stuart London*. The large amount of work on the Royal Society and, to a lesser extent, on the College of Physicians has perhaps put too much emphasis on the growth and internal struggles of institutions, and on lines of demarcation.

be denied. But underlying this diversity there was some unity in medical practice (and at this point my focus moves from the question of change to that of its approximate opposite, unity).

Diversity fits a medical market-place where medical authority and licensing was not strong enough to impose uniformity. But a market-place, if it deals in one commodity (here health, or cure of disease) must show not only diversity but unity, the outward differences which make the goods attractive conceal underlying similarities, otherwise how could customers recognize them in the first place and make comparisons? Patients certainly moved easily between different types of practitioner and ignored the rhetoric that sought to demonstrate that the members of a particular group were the sole practitioners of proper medicine. In about 1652 Willis described the case of Mrs White of Pusey who 'has suffered from the spitting of thick and yellow coloured matter in which there were sometimes blood-stained flecks'. He noted that she had dipped into the medical market-place (which by extension included self-help and the family):

She has so far tried many remedies during the summer from her brother, a learned doctor; she also began studying medicine, and recently has taken from empiric women many remedies which are said to be good for phthisis. Since the disease grows worse she begs me and her brother to prescribe some method of cure, if this be possible.[23]

The easy movement of the sufferer from one type of practitioner to another may indicate that the differences between practitioners were more real to the providers of health than to the buyers. Certainly, the patient often was seen as a poor judge of the quality of medical practice. Daniel Turner wrote in *The Modern Quack, or the Physical Imposter Detected* (1718) that his purpose was:

to set before Mens Eyes the great Danger they incur by meddling with any Medicines (let their titles be never so specious) sold in divers Parts of this City at Tradesmens Shops and which are indeed not other than so many *Baits* laid to defraud them farther, that no great or powerful Medicine can be prepar'd but that if taken in this way of publick *Advertisement* in *News-papers*, or distributed by Bills, either given into their Hands, or posted upon Posts, altho' the nicest Directions that can be are delivered therewith, yet will the same be liable to do more Harm than Good.[24]

It was not only the 'Common People' who lacked judgement and had to be warned:

[23] Kenneth Dewhurst, (ed.), *Willis's Oxford Casebook (1650–52)* (Oxford, 1981), p. 147. Dewhurst points out that Willis had mixed views about empirics: he 'warned that a quack's remedies are "like a sword in a blind man's hand"' (p. 41) but he also thought that empirics' remedies could be better than a physician's (p. 50); Willis himself early on worked as a 'piss prophet' or uroscopist at Abingdon market (p. 128).

[24] Daniel Turner, *The Modern Quack, Or the Physical Imposter Detected* (London, 1718), p. a2v.

The Common People did I say? I might, I think, have included all Orders and Degrees
of Men, since we find oftentimes those of great Fortunes, and as great a Share of
Understanding in other Matters, have been in this way impos'd on as much as others.[25]

Rhetoric such as this can bear a different intepretation: it shows that
the buyers of health were not impressed by the differences in medical
practice. If this was the case, what were the common structures in
medical practice that allowed patients to move across different parts of
the market? Clearly it was not a structure based upon theory, at least as
expressed in the different viewpoints of Galenists, astrologers,
Paracelsians, chemists and iatrochemists. Although, as noted above,
underneath the surface of new theories there can be discerned the same
type of qualitative narrative that had helped to make sense of the inner
happenings of the body. There were probably two structures. One is
banal but important. People wanted remedies and all types of practitioners offered them. In the end all practitioners were nostrum pedlers.
The second common structure was the wrapping around the remedies.
Practitioners rationalized about their remedies and made them appear
appropriate and attractive to buyers. How this was done varied in
elaboration, the most expensive and thick wrapping being of the
'rational' physician who tailored the remedy to the niceties of the
patient's constitution, others might imitate the 'rational' physician,
but use less time and care over the fit between remedy and patient or
they might advertise their wares by appealing to experience and
authority. The language in which this was expressed could vary
according to the practitioner's theoretical standpoint. Another way of
putting it is that all practitioners gave out remedies and that the
empiric was a bit of a rationalist and vice versa.

THE PHYSICIAN'S PRACTICE

James Clegg, the dissenting Derbyshire minister and physician, wrote
in his diary on 28 of August 1723 about the case of his daughter
Margaret who on the 19th 'was seized with a violent pain in her
stomach and bowels, which was attended by frequent and painful
vomiting of green and yellow choler, this continued about 3 days'. The
structure of Clegg's treatment is significant. He responded not only to
the general condition, but also to the day-to-day state of his daughter,
and he also tried to foresee complications. He attempted to deal with
both the causes of the illness (clearing the choler and absorbing the
acid) and with its symptoms (settling the stomach, quietening pain):

[25] Ibid., p. a2v.

I endeavoured to clear her stomach of it (choler) by giving her frequently to drink a decoction of camomile and tea, and chicken broth but her pain still continued and vehement sickness. After the vomiting staid, I then gave her a little Diacodium, but very little to compose her spirits, settle her stomach and procure sleep. She rested better but awakened very sick and thus continued two days more. I ordered a cooling clyster for she was very hot and restless her pulse quick, breath very short. The clyster brought nothing away, in the evening I ordered another which gave only one stool, hard greenish and very foetid. Her fever increased, I had before ordered and continued to give her powder of crabs claws, oyster shells and nutmeg with sugar to absorb the acid and sweeten the juices in her stomach. On the Saturday the pain in her belly being violent I gave her about one scruple and a half of Rhubarb in powder in syrup of July flowers to procure a passage and gentle discharge. On the day following she had a stool and found ease but it continued not long . . . her fever increased, her pulse quick, breath short . . . On the Monday morning another stool, loose but not very large, at noon she parted with much wind and found some ease. She was restless and hot and in frequent sweats. I feared a diorrhea and to prevent it gave her the white decoction with tormentil root . . . but on Monday night . . . she grew much worse her tongue faltered her pulse quicker but weaker the phlegm disturbed her she sweat much and slumbered, but awakened sick. Thus she continued til about '6 a clock and then departed.[26]

In some ways this is a very empirical piece of description. It has a Hippocratic air about it, it notes the pulse, breath, stools, etc. as well as the other symptoms. It is rational in so far as there seem to be reasons for the treatment ('a cooling clyster for she was very hot and restless . . .'), and at very stage of the illness Clegg responded with treatment for the changing symptoms. The attempt to give rational treatment, whether in the strong form to causes or more weakly to symptoms, was significant especially in the eyes of physicians. Cheyne praised the 'Medicina philosophica seu rationalis' where the virtues and uses of medicines were known and adjusted to the causes of a particular illness so that 'the best natural philosopher will . . . ever be the best physician'.[27] Whether Clegg was rational in the sense of attacking the causes rather than the symptoms of the illness is a moot question. I am possibly stretching a point by taking choler and acid to be the causes of the illness in Clegg's mind, though I suspect they were.

Clegg could also have been rational in another sense. He may have seen his daughter's symptoms as the indications of her constitution during the illness. Indications were crucial for the Galenic *methodus medendi* and helped to differentiate learned medicine from that of the empirics by stressing that as indications varied from person to person the care had to be tailored to the individual and not to the illness. (The indications would include the patient's normal constitution, the time

[26] James Clegg, *The Diary of James Clegg of Chapel en le Firth 1708–1755*, ed. Vanessa S. Doe, part I, (Derbyshire Record Soc. II, 1978), pp. 19–20.
[27] George Cheyne, *The Natural Method of Cureing of the Diseases of the Body and the Disorders of the Mind depending on the Body* (London, 1742), pp. 64–5.

of year as well as the changing state of the patient.) Richard Browne, a licentiate of the College of Physicians, saw the difference between the ways in which physicians and empirics treated their patients in this way:

their general directions for such their trash ['the pills and elixirs of our quacks'] are sufficiently exploded. For it requires the deliberate and particular consideration of the best physician, whether to purge his patient at all, and (if requisite) with what sort of physic, and when to terminate the dose. Of how many murders then must they be guilty that let fly their poisonous, ill prepared and worse proportioned doses at a venture among the multitude, upon their own and their poor deluded patients small discretion when and how to take them.[28]

Despite such propaganda for the physicians it may not be unfair to compare their practice with that of the empirics. In some ways Clegg was practising as an empiric, as did many other much more learned physicians. What Clegg was doing was to give a nostrum for each particular stage of the illness, just as an empiric gave a single nostrum to cover all the stages of the illness. Moreover, the treatments that Clegg gave at the different stages of his daughter's illness were pretty standard ones – for instance, cooling clysters and testaceous powders. If one looks at his general practice we find him giving similar standard treatments, with little individual tailoring. Clegg's practice was a busy one, he often had to travel miles across country to visit patients and he could not be with them during all the stages of their illness as he could with his daughter. On 24 September 1728 he wrote:

Visited Mrs Waterhouse at Martinside she is afflicted with an hysteric asthma. I prescribed gum ammoniac in Vin(egar) Solu(tion) and spermacelis after bleeding. Visited Mrs Swan at Waley Bridge. She was in an intermitting fever. I ordered an electuary of the bark and a julep. I was called thence to Mrs Barber at Malcoff and found her in a fever, took some blood and gave her a vomit which answered well.[29]

In the following days he saw Mrs Barber again, but gave no details of her illness or treatment. What we have here resembles, in a sense, the practice of a modern G.P., with little time available for patients and a preference for standard treatments.

Some apothecaries apparently argued that they could tell from previous experience of a physician's prescribing practice what he would order for any one case, that in other words, physicians had standard treatments:

I have heard several of the apothecaries confidently (not to say impudently) affirm they were so thoroughly acquainted with such mens practice, naming some eminent

---

[28] Richard Browne, *The Cure of Old Age and Preservation of Youth by Roger Bacon . . . Translated out of Latin; with Annotations . . .* (London, 1683), p. 91.
[29] Clegg, *Diary*, I, p. 42.

physicians that if they knew the case they would lay a wager they did exactly predict before they took pen in hand what they would prescribe.[30]

Daniel Coxe, defending rational medicine wrote, rather unconvincingly:

the knowledge they derive from doctors prescripts is very uncertain, and fallacious: it being absolutely impossible for the best physician to calculate a medicine that shall be proper for all that are, or shall be subject to any one disease, unless he were possessor of the Univeral Remedy. So great is the variety of complexions, so many are the complications of distempers and so infinite the variations of circumstances: all of which the judicious physician attends to, and which few apothecaries are capable of comprehending.[31]

Yet with no statistically-based clinical trials, rational medicine was a lottery, just like the empirics' nostrum. Moreover, the value of particular treatments for particular constitutions would often be a matter of subjective judgement and controversy despite general rules such as the cure by contrary. Clegg illustrated this, and also how the provincial physician could disagree (and be ignored) by his London superiors, when he wrote on 10 September 1725:

I was desired by my dear and good friend Mrs Elizab. Bagshaw to visit her second son Adam then dangerously ill of the small pox in London . . . Found the young man very full of smallpox of a bad kind under the care of a London physician called Knapp. The second fever came on the day after we came there. Dr Mead was called in. Blisters were applied to his arms, unseasonably as I thought, a strangury succeeded. Cordials were given but no sleeping potions were administered, nor could I prevail to have them. The fever continued to rise much on Friday. He had been without stool 12 to 13 days. I urged the necessity of clysters, but no stool could be procured tho' many were administered. On Saturday a delirium . . . and on the 19th Lords day morning . . . he expired.[32]

One can understand why people collected successful remedies and noted the sequence of remedies used in particular cases, (in other words the methods of cure). Traditional rational medicine, which emphasized the individuality of each case, could produce uncertainty; one could not easily use past cases as a guide to future ones as each case was supposed to be unique. But the ties with rational medicine were often broken, if unconsciously. The collections of John Hall and James Cook on successful cases, *Select Observations on English Bodies of Eminent Persons in Disparate Diseases* (1679), were published for instruction and imitation – despite the authors' seeming orthodoxy. Sydenham, of course, saw methods of cure as the solution to the problem of being a rational physician who did not want to go beyond

[30] Daniel Cox, *A Discourse*, pp. 75–6. [31] *Ibid.*, pp. 74–5.
[32] Clegg, *Diary*, I, p. 22.

experience. Sometimes lay people noted down successful cures and remedies. In 1681, William Blundell, who had recovered from a 'violent cold' ordered his servant, Walter Thelwall, to write down all the medicines that he had been given by his doctor and by the 'elder Lady Bradshaigh': After listing the medicines Thelwall wrote:

My master's opinion of these several things in particular is here to be inserted for further use, viz. That the spirits first named, of which twenty-six drops were put into a small cap of barley water and beer or into barley water alone, had no apparent effect, although he doth not much doubt but the secret effect might be good. That the like might be said of the pills . . . although it seemed that they did somewhat assuage his cough, which was extremely violent. The Lohoch, a liquor like a syrup, did apparently bring up phlegm, and was well liked. The lozenges were pleasant and did sometimes stop the cough. Barley water . . .[33]

Here we have less the holistic sense of a method of cure, more that of remedies being sampled one by one, in other words an empirical approach very close to that of the empirics. There is really very little difference between a nostrum touted in an empiric's bill and one of Blundell's remedies:

The elder Lady Bradshaigh sent my master a bottle containing as we guess, about one ounce of balsam, which in her letter she calls (if we read it aright) balsam of sulphur. Her Ladyship then saith that it is an approved cure for a cough; that she had it from Sir Peter Brooks that it had cured him of a most violent cough, and that the Lady Ossory had sent it to him.[34]

Apart from the commercial note the advertisement below had essentially the same message as Lady Bradshaigh's letter:

Doctor John Turner his most excellent lozenges approved by Doctor George Bowls, and many others to excel the best and most approved lozenges which have been heretofore made by any other person whatsoever, for the preventing and curing of consumptions, coughs of all sorts, pthisics, putrified and corrupted lungs . . . You may take two or three of them at night.[35]

In both cases the remedy was to be used regardless of the type of patient (in terms of complexion, way of life, stage of illness, etc.), but they employed a common wrapping, experience and authority ('approved cure', 'approved lozenges', Sir Peter Brookes, Lady Ossory, Doctor George Bowls).

Some historians have presented the rise of empirics in the second half of the seventeenth century as a sudden disjunction in the practice of medicine. Certainly contemporaries were aware of their increase, and historians have rightly emphasized their effect on orthodox physicians and have given increased consumer spending and national prosperity

[33] T. Ellison Gibson, A Cavalier's Note-Book (London, 1880), pp. 245–6.   [34] Ibid., p. 244.
[35] Advertisement in British Library collection of medical advertisements C.112 fo. 9.

as one of the main reasons for the explosion in the numbers.[36] However, empirics had been around from the sixteenth century and before as had physicians' diatribes against them.[37] Moreover, there is no evidence that patients' expectation of treatment underwent a radical change at this time despite what one reads from self-serving defences of the College of Physicians. What is likely, I would argue, is that the medicine of the empirics was acceptable to many patients because this is what occurred in their experience when they were treated by physicians: each stage of their illness was cured by a remedy, (whereas for the physician the treatment was a response to the changing state of the patient), the difference was that the empiric offered to cure the whole illness with one remedy. Empiric medicine was also familiar because it was analogous to the centuries-old practice of offering remedies to family and friends; indeed it is worth remembering that family remedies were sometimes equated with empirical medicine, and that physicians were seen as attacking both. The young law student, Dudley Ryder, noted that his cousin:

talked also about empiric medicines, which he said he begun to have a much better opinion of, for he recovered his daughter by some of them given him by a gentlewoman, after all that the doctor could prescribe had proved useless and ineffectual. But the doctors had made it their business to decry all this kind of receipts which are in the hands of private persons and thereby made persons of good sense and thought afraid to use any of them, though no doubt there may be very good receipts lodged in private hands.[38]

---

[36] See S.H. Holbrook, *The Golden Age of Quackery* (New York, 1959); Eric Jameson, *The Natural History of Quackery* (London, 1961); W.F. Bynum and Roy Porter (eds.), *Medical Fringe and Medical Orthodoxy 1750–1850* (London, 1986). On the increase in consumerism in the eighteenth century see G. Holmes, *Augustan England: Professions, State, and Society 1680–1730* (London, 1982); N. McKendrick, J. Brewer and H.J. Plumb, *The Birth of a Consumer Society* (London, 1982).

[37] For instance, the Frankfurt physician Johann Hartmann Beyer, wrote that 'mad, deaf, toothless witches, priests, barbers, porters, Jews, murderers, and criminals who deserve the cross, and also people who are bereft of reason, are all rich with remedies . . .', in Girolamo Capivaccio, *Pratica Medica* (Frankfurt, 1594) sig. 4v. See also the attack on empirics and uroscopists in J. Langius, *Epistolarum Medicinalium* (Frankfurt, 1589) p. 999; P. Forestus, *De Incerto, Fallaci Urinarium Judicio* (Leyden, 1589). William Clowes, *A Briefe . . . Treatise . . . Morbus Gallicus*, pp. 9–10 writes of how 'in these days, it is the more lamentable to see how so famous an art, and the true professors of the same, are thus spurned at, trodden down, embaced and defaced, through the wicked behaviour and counterfeit gloses of the afore named rude rable of obscure and imperfect experimenters and such prating peasants and ignorant asses'. Specifically, he condemned the 'cosinage and lewd crafts of one Valentine Rarsworme of Smalcade' and 'his adherents commonly called quacksalvers, mountebanks, landlopers, fugitives and other masterless makeshifts, the very spawn and frie of blind boldness and ignorance'.

[38] Dudley Ryder, *The Diary of Dudley Ryder 1715–1716*, ed. William Matthews (London, 1939), pp. 276–7.

I would argue that because there was, and had been for centuries a multiplicity of practitioners of various types, so there were no clearly defined boundaries between rational medicine and that of the empirics. But before discussing this further it is worth saying more about the nature of rational, orthodox medicine.

In a sense, time, rather than education or philosophy, was the criterion that served to distinguish physicians from empirics. The more time one could devote to a patient the more one could be a rational physician. But time was expensive and probably only physicians with rich clients could go into a very great deal of detail and study the patient's way of life and symptoms. However, the practice of John Symcotts and that of the surgeons Joseph Binne and Richard Wiseman shows that ordinary practitioners could give time and consideration to a patient.[39] Sir Edmund King was one such expensive physician, his case-book is full of rich and noble clients. In November 1679 he wrote down the details of a patient: 'A fine young lady aged about 22 florid complexion . . . beautiful and a widow. Had laboured under violent paines in her stomach and sides for a year and a half'. He noted her previous treatments, she had been 'through many courses of physic, with several Doctors, abundance of stools, several waters, without relief also bitter drinks'. He also let her tell him her idiosyncrasies, 'purging made her worse', and on another visit listed what brought on the pain:

1. fasting too long. 2. eating too much. 3. tea after dinner. 4. apple pie or apples. 5. chocolate ill made.[40]

All this information would need time to be elicited, but as the patient could give her views to the doctor she presumably felt happier for the personal attention, the doctor richer, whilst the norms of rational physic would have been fulfilled. Of course, not all physicians would go along with this and the doctor–patient interview has never been the easiest thing to manage even in the early eighteenth century, which recent historical work tells us was a time of patient power. For instance, on 13 June 1716 Dudley Ryder wrote, 'Intended to go to Dr Wadsworth about the pain in my arm, which is not yet gone, and also to talk with him about my whole constitution.' The next day he went to see Dr Wadsworth 'I intended to talk with the Doctor about my whole

[39] F.N.L. Poynter and W.J. Bishop, *A Seventeenth Century Doctor and His Patients: John Symcotts 1592?–1662* (Bedfordshire Historical Record Soc. XXXI, 1950); Joseph Binne, 'Chirurgical Observations 1633–1663', B.L. Sloane MS. 153; Richard Wiseman, *Severall Chirurgical Treatises* (London, 1676).
[40] Sir Henry King, 'Medical Cases and Receipts', B.L. Sloane MS. 1589, fos. 144, 146.

constitution, about the cold bath and Tunbridge and Bath waters. But when I came to talk with him I was at a loss what to say'.[41]

It may be a little unhistorical to talk of patient dominance in the doctor–patient relationship at this time, possibly we may be introducing modern concerns too much into the past. Yet there is no doubt that patients knew about rational medicine and spoke its language (Ryder's 'whole constitution'). A patient wrote to Sir Hans Sloane:

I have been free from that complaint which I made to you at that time but cannot get rid of a very great heat, especially in my hands and feet which is very uneasy to me, and more than all the rest my tongue is grown worse than when I was in town, though not so bad as it has been sometimes, I have taken the bark as you ordered, and now drink the asses milk, I am weak and have very little appetite and no good sleeper. Pray Sir be so obliging as to think over this account of a crazy constitution.[42]

The reference to some of the non-naturals (appetite, sleep, constitution) tells us that patients had also been educated into the ways of rational medicine. The parenthetical and pathetic 'though not so bad as it has been sometimes' also tells us that anxiety and hope do not disappear even when the patient pays the doctor and apparently dominates the relationship (the binary opposition of dominance/subordination seems too simple here, and one can doubt the applicability of the Jewson thesis at the psychological level of the doctor–patient relationship as opposed to its financial and contractual aspects).

The large number of correspondents to Sir Hans Sloane, patients, their relatives and doctors who asked for medical advice seem to speak the language of rational medicine. Lay people used fewer technical terms, but many of the correspondents tried to give an account of the case which included the general condition of the patient and the various stages of the illness and the treatments used at each stage.

A representative example of how an orthodox practitioner saw a case is Charles Kimberley's report to Sloane of his patient, Mr Isted:

I found his blood very firie, his pulse very regular, no thirst, a little clamminess in his tongue, urine good in quantity. His chief complaints were little wandering pains . . . and a great inclination towards sweat. I encouraged a gentle perspiration to the 20th but found no other alteration in any particular than his being tired with his confinement. On the 22nd I gave him a purge with manna, which worked very well, his pains still the same, leaving stiffness behind them. I have debarred him malt liquors and all seasoned meats. His chief drink is wine and Bristol waters and the wood decoction of your prescribing. Upon some little irregularity in the non-nat(ura)ls he has had a looseness, I think, not to his disadvanatage. His appetite is very good and what he eats gives him no uneasiness. His blood is foul and abounds with acid salts. Mercurial

[41] Ryder, *Diary*, p. 256, p. 257.
[42] Sir Hans Sloane, 'Medical Correspondence', B.L. Sloane MS. 4075, fos. 340–1. I am currently researching Sloane's medical correspondence.

purges by breaking the viscid cohaesions of the blood and attracting those salts might
be of great service; but I doubt not you are very well acquainted with the prejudice Mr.
Isted has conceived against them.[43]

The description of pulse, urine, the use of diet as a form of treatment all
point to Kimberley being a rational physician. His description of the
blood and its acid salts and the effect of mercury on them is one of the
infrequent uses in the letters of the new science when rationalizing
about the effects of remedies.

Patients, however, could move easily between rational and empiric
medicine. John Evelyn wrote in 1703 to Sloane about his piles. He
wrote that he was greatly troubled with them though:

Now is being look'd upon as a slight infirmity amongst my visitant neighbours, everyone is ready to recommend their remedies, as ointments of the ashes of oak. The bones
of green fish calcind to a fine powder, and inwardly sulphurous lozenges etc. But none
of these do stay them [the piles] from their periodic descend.

Evelyn then requested from Sloane what was really a nostrum, but he
fully realized that he had to supply the details required by a rational
physician.

If therefore you have any topiq [topical medicine] which might hinder them from
falling down, it would be a mighty soulieyoument [?] to a weary octogenerius: I have
always been naturally costive which by straining I believe irritates: but lenitive
electuary relieves me, when my belly is hard and ponderous. I have in the meantime a
good appetite and eat of everything that is tender; shellfish from the sea weekly, and of
my own ponds. But my ill digestion makes me cautious. My urine which for 3 or 4 years
past was as pale as clear water, is of late come to be of a landuble colour, nor have I
been sensible of nephritic pains. In the morning I now and then drink a glass of meath
made with birch-water: sometimes Grewell.[44]

In his next letter Evelyn discussed the success of Sloane's remedies;
he did not see them as a method of cure but as a separate number of
items which might or might not have an effect. He wrote: 'nor do either
the liniment or sulphur lozenges keep up their swelling at the constant
period', whilst after bleeding 'That night (or evening rather) the piles
descended with great pain'.[45]

So far I have tried to show that, although both patient and doctor
knew what rational medicine entailed, nevertheless, in structural terms
it could appear to merge with the medicine practiced by the empirics. I
now turn to them.

[43] *Ibid.*, fo. 353.   [44] *Ibid.*, fo. 94.   [45] *Ibid.*, fo. 96.

THE EMPIRICS' MEDICINE

Harold Cook has indicated in his recent book how Royal Society empiricists were taken to be close to empirics. Also Michael Hunter has noted how:

Thomas Wharton, Censor of the College . . . fulminated against 'this new upturned brood of Vertuosis' with their 'Jesuitisme and policy, English books, Experiments, and receipts in phisick', who were likely to influence all the families of Note in England'; he linked them with 'the swarmes of quackes, mountebacks, chymists, Apothecares, surgions' who were ruinous to our old and settled and approved practice of physick.[46]

Historians such as Harold Cook, Theodore Brown and Michael Hunter who have concentrated on institutional quarrels and, in this case on the spleen of the old guard in the College of Physicians and on the reform of the College, have given us valuable insights.[47] But it would be a pity if institutional history was our only entry into the world of physicians and empirics, as the recent work of Porter, Barry, Bynum and Loudon on empirics demonstrates there is more to be said than that.[48] My argument is that physicians and empirics were closer than has been suggested (the very fact that they competed with each other is a sign of closeness). I have sketched how the physicians in their rational practice may have been nearer than they thought to empirics. Is it possible to argue that empirics were, at times, approaching the rational practice, or at least, the rhetoric of the physicians?

I do not want to overturn completely the received idea of the empiric. Certainly, if one reads their bills or adverts they made outrageous claims, though so did an orthodox physician every time he undertook a cure. And the stigma of quack or mountebank was so real at the time that empirics sought to avoid it. One bill, headed by a magnificent coat of arms stated: 'There is lately come to London, an Italian Doctor, who never was any Stage-Quack or Mountebanck, who has been very successful in the speedy cures of these following Distempers Viz.'[49] R. Clark, 'Chymist' acknowledged that there was a prejudice against medicines sold by advertising, but he pointed to the similar practice of the College of Physicians:

I am very sensible People are averst against Medicines, that are publish'd by way of Bills, yet several Ingenious Men, and some Colledg Physicians have done, and still do the same by Medicines that have been successful for many years.[50]

---

[46] Hunter, *Science and Society in Restoration England*, p. 138.   [47] See note 22.
[48] See their essays in Bynum and Porter (eds.), *Medical Fringe and Medical Orthodoxy 1750–1850*.   [49] In *Medical Advertisements*.
[50] R. Clark, *Vermiculars Destroyed, With an Historical Account of Worms...* (London, 1690), p. 31.

However, some empirics, men such as William Salmon, 'the Ring-Leader or king of the Quacks', published books and entered the world of learning. Salmon,[51] who began as an assistant to a mountebank, came to practice medicine and astrology at the gate of St Bartholomews Hospital and sold 'an antidote against the plague and all pestilential Venom', 'Family pills' and an *Elixir Vitae*. He was attacked in 1700 in a broadsheet: 'The Churchyards and Burying places are everywhere ample witnesses of your travels.' Salmon published books on herbal remedies, on chemistry for medicine and medical case studies.[52] There was clearly a commercial motive in publishing. His *Medicina Practica: Or the Practical Physitian* (1707) gave his address at the Blue Boar and advertised his 'Balsam de Chili': 'It is an excellent balsam differing from that of Peru ... but no way inferior in virtues and excellency as the several experiments lately made of it by several learned physicians in the curing of diseases have given sufficient proof'. He claimed it cured pains, ulcers, bruises, coughs, epilepsy, apoplexy, convulsions, palsies, it killed worms, cured ruptures, dissolved soft stones, eased colic, griping, provoked menstruation, opened obstructions of the liver, etc.[53] Yet when one comes to the main body of the book it is clear that what we have is rational medicine with a strong commercial pitch. In cases of hysteria he advised:

To quiet the irregular and turbulent motion of the Spirit and hysteric fumes the following things are fit to be done. First the stomach, and whole region of the abdomen are to be bathed with *Powers of Amber*, or *Pennyroyal* ... Secondly, the nostrils are to be often touched with *Postestates Cornu Cervi* ... Moreover, our *Tinctura Hysterica* should be at convenient times given in a little wine ... The third intention of cure, is to sweeten the acid salts and juices of the body, for which purpose there is certainly nothing more powerful and admirable than our *Spiritus Universalis* (which see in our *Phyl Medic Lib.* 2 cap 2) given twice a day ... or instead of this, *Volatile Sal Armoniack* ... Some possibly may prescribe preparations of Pearls, Coral, Amber, Crabs Eyes etc. [often prescribed], but these things (though after a very long using may do some good, yet) being fixt Alcalies, do not immediately enter into the mass of blood, and are therefore to be laid aside ... The fourth indication is to evacuate the morbific cause, or peccant humor, which you may most completely accomplish with my *Pilulae Mirabiles*.[54]

The Latin *Phyl Medic* Lib 2 cap 2 was a nice touch. Clearly Salmon was imitating the rational physicians; he was also using the more up to date reasoning – the acids and alkalies. So here we have a small paradox: an empiric, who employed the new philosophy but who also used the

[51] Daniel Turner, *The Modern Quack or, the Physical Imposter Detected* (London, 1718), p. 79.
[52] C.J.S. Thompson, *The Quacks of Old London* (London, 1928), pp. 126–31.
[53] William Salmon, *Medicina Practica: Or the Practical Physitian* (London, 1707), p. B1V–B2V.
[54] *Ibid.*, p. 62–3.

language of traditional Galenic medicine, 'peccant humour', 'intention' and 'indication' (he was slightly confused about the last) and who gave a story of what was going on in the body to account for the symptoms and to justify the treatment. If profit was really motivating Salmon, then we are being told what, in Salmon's judgement, it was that people wanted to read: a bit of the new (chemistry) and a bit of the old (reasoned medicine). Both theories were mixed at will without contradiction, both provided good advertising copy. Salmon used them to wrap up his remedies for prospective buyers and to describe how the medicines could intervene in the inner happenings of the body (only a College Physician or pedantic historian would point out Salmon's inconsistency in using two apparently different theories – the fact that they could be mixed was a sign of their underlying unity discussed earlier).

Daniel Turner's sour view of the 'learned' empiric betrays the fact that a little learning was good for trade:

You will say probably 'that some of these People who put out Bills and print Advertisements, must surely be able Men, for that they publish Books concerning the Distemper and apply solely or chiefly to the study thereof'. I grant they do indeed put up for Authors, and set forth Books, but were yourselves judges of the Subject they debate you would need no greater Evidence of their Ignorance, as well as evil Design; for tho' they have some tolerable good Books to Steal from or Plunder, yet so wretchedly unskill'd are they in both terms of Art and Method, that they have only jumbled up a heap of incoherent Matter, interlarded with false Latin, flat Nonsense, or Sense inspired, which is only fit to amuse poor ignorant People, who are ready to take for granted, that he who can write a book, must . . . be some great Scholar.[55]

Quacks certainly used the authority of scholarship to sell their wares, but by labelling their works as 'flat Nonsense', Turner side-stepped a major point: the *meaning* of the quacks' books and bills must have appealed to customers and in much the same way as Turner's own learned medicine. R. Clark, 'living at the Golden Ball in Devonshire Street' in his *Vermiculars Destroyed, with an Historical Account of Worms: Collected of the Best Authors, as well Ancient as Modern. And Experiments By that Admirable Invention of the Microscope*, advertised his powder, plaister and ointment. He did so in the context of appearing learned and citing authors in the best text-book fashion, up to date with accounts of microscopical experiments and careful of his readers' healths. On the last he gave full accounts of 'the diagnostic signs of worms', of the 'signs of health', and the following section of his very detailed instructions for taking the 'Pulvis benedictus' might have

[55] Turner, *The Modern Quack*, p. 85.

been approved by a College doctor (though not in all respects, the patient deciding his constitution may have been disagreeable):

So great is the difference in Constitutions, that it is impossible to propose any one Dose for all, though of an age; when a child of five or six years of age will, and do often take three Papers, and shall have with it no more stool than a man that takes the same quantity, therefore I would advise you to begin with a low dose, till you know the strength of your constitution, and keep that dose as gives only two or three stools.[56]

Anthony Daffy, 'student in physick' acknowledged the cultural and theoretical signposts of seventeenth-century medicine: God, experience, Nature, equilibrium of the temperament, the differences in constitutions and noxious humours. Yet, in his advertisement for his 'Elixir Salutatis' he had the best of both worlds, a medicine that could relate to all the above concepts and yet was still a nostrum powerful enough to transcend all the distinctions of rational medicine and therefore was useful for everyone. (This was commercially important, as the drink would not be limited, for instance, to young female phlegmatics, but could be sold to everyone.) Daffy described 'his health-bringing Drink' as:

A famous CORDIAL DRINK, Found out by Providence of the Almighty, and (for above Twenty years) Experienced by myself and diverse persons (whose names are at most of their Desires here inserted) a most Excellent Preservative of Mankind.

A SECRET

Far beyond any Medicament yet known, and is found so agreeable to Nature that it effects all its Operations, as Nature would have it, and as a virtual Expedient proposed by her, for reducing all her Extreams unto an Equal Temper; the same being fitted into all *Ages*, *Sexes*, *Complexions*, and *Constitutions*, and highly fortifying Nature against any Noxious humour, involving or offending the *Noble Parts*.[57]

The surgeon, John Marten who could be called an empiric also advertised his 'anti-venereal pills' in his *Treatise of all the Degrees and Symptoms of the Venereal Disease in both Sexes* (sixth edn 1708?) He titilated his readers with case-histories, but the structure of his treatment (relating it to symptoms and the changing state of the body) was no different from what the College physician would have done in a different disease (venereal disease was often left to surgeons).

The public probably were attracted by some aspects of rational medicine as they were by those of empiric medicine. The need to cater for the public, a desire for status and a belief that their medicines

---

[56] Clark, *Vermiculars Destroyed*, p. 27.
[57] Broadsheet in Wellcome Institute Library, Cabinet of seventeenth-century empirics' broadsheets.

deserved to be used in the best possible way – and this should not be underestimated – were probably all reasons that led empirics towards rational medicine.

The empirical virtuosi, whom Harold Cook has rightly seen as close to the empirics, could also at times approach rational practice. Sydenham, in the letter to Locke mentioned earlier, set out a very traditional and rational view of the case. As well as discussing the cause of the illness, 'the ichorose matter', etc. Sydenham considered:

Your age, ill habit of body and approach of winter concurring, it comes to pass that the distemper you complain of yields not so soon to remedies as it would do under contrary circumstances.[58]

He also discussed what foods and drink Locke should have or avoid. The emphasis on constitution, season, food and drink together with the discussion of the causes of the illness shows that in a case where the physician felt he should talk with, or in this example write to, a patient (and a friend) at length, the old structures of rational, traditional, medicine took over.

Another virtuoso, Robert Boyle, certainly published his favourite remedies and felt that one could learn from the shops of the chemists and from traders.[59] Yet the people who took his remedies wanted instructions if not reasons. Anne Conway in 1664 wrote to her husband that she wanted him to get directions from Boyle as to when one of his remedies should be taken, how long for, how much, and in what 'vehicle' and if it was good for scorbutical distempers as well for her headaches.[60] The need to know the dosage was a direct echo of rational medicine which sought to tailor remedies to the individual's constitution and illness. In today's medical practice the instructions on the bottle of pills, although they may make us feel they are addressed to us as individuals, usually make distinctions only between large groups such as adults or children. However, all types of medical practitioners (Galenists, empiricists, empirics) took some account of the desire of patients to have individualized remedies or at least doses (the special language used to extol 'universal' remedies reinforces the point). One of Salmon's bills advertising his 'family pills' recommended them to

[58] Dewhurst, *Sydenham*, p. 167.
[59] See R. Boyle, *Medicinal Experiments: Or, a Collection of Choice and Safe Remedies; Of the Reconcileableness of Specific Medicines to the Corpuscular Philosophy; The Advantages of the Use of Simple Medicines* in Robert Boyle, *The Works*, 6 vols. ed. Thomas Birch (London, 1772), v; and part 2 of *Some Considerations Touching the Usefulness of Experimental Natural Philosophy*, in Boyle, *Works*, II.
[60] Marjorie Hope Nicolson (ed.), *Conway Letters* (London, 1930), pp. 229–30.

'Travellers, Soldiers, Seamen, and such like who cannot attend a Cure, but are forced to go about their business'. The recognition that people wanted, if possible, the individualized therapy of a 'cure' was paralleled by Salmon's instructions as to dosage. He made them as individualistic as possible by detailing how and when they could be taken, by splitting up the age categories and by giving the patient scope to find his or her own dosage level:

The way of using the Pills. These Pills may either be swallowed down alone, or taken in the Pap of an Apple or Honey, or a stewed Prune, or a little Syrup, or a Water with a little Beer, Ale, Wine, Broth, as every one likes best, and so taken early in the Morning, or late at Night going to Bed, with out Observation of any other Order, only taking heed of Cold. From two years old, to three or four, you may give one Pill: From four Years old to ten, you may give two or three: From ten to sixteen you may give three or four: and from sixteen Years of Age to threescore and upwards you may safely give five or six Pills; you may begin with a little Dose first, and so encrease it as you find the Body is in strength.[61]

Boyle himself used a variety of remedies for the different stages and symptoms of his own illness. The structure of his treatment was probably very similar to that found in King or Clegg. In the Meditation 'Upon his reviewing and tacking together the several bills, filed up in the apothecary's shop' he wrote:

Either my curiosity, Sophronia, or my value of health, has made it my custom, when I have passed through a course of physic, to review the particulars it consisted of; that taking notice by what remedies I found most good, and by what, little or none; if I should fall into the like distemper for the future, I might derive some advantage from my past experience. In compliance with this custom, as I was this day reviewing and putting together the doctor's several prescriptions sent me back by the apothecary; Good God! said I, in my self, what a multitude of unpleasant medicines have I been ordered to take! the very numbering, and reading them, were able to discompose me, and make me almost sick, though the taking of them helped to make me well. And certainly, if when I was about to enter intò a course of physic, all these loathsome medicines, and uneasy prescriptions, had been presented to me together as things I must take, and comply with, I should have utterly despaired of a recovery . . . But then, although I now see these troublesome prescriptions all at once, I did not use them so, but took only one or two harsh remedies in one day, and thereby was enabled to bear them, especially being assisted by moderate intervals of respite, and supported by other seasonable cordials.[62]

It is interesting that Boyle employed, in a very orthodox manner, both doctor and apothecary, who clearly treated him in a step by step way. The empiricist/empiric was also there, taking no risks with empirics' nostrums but learning in the safest possible way (and in the most rational, as well as empirical) – from his own constitution.

[61] Broadsheet in Wellcome Institute Library, Broadsheet Cabinet.
[62] R. Boyle, *Occasional Reflections*, section 2, meditation xv, in *Works*, II, pp. 381–2.

CONCLUSION

The new philosophy did not, and could not, alter traditional rational ways of thinking about illness and the effects of medicines – although the terms in which the explanations were couched, of course, did change radically. Without the ideological force that a successful new philosophy of medicine could exert (as Newton's work did for the physical sciences) in producing uniformity, medicine was free to enjoy all the variations that there could be between rationalism and the practice of empirics. This was no period between paradigms, where a hundred medical flowers could blossom until the new paradigm asserted itself. Variety had been the norm in English medical practice for centuries; it was perhaps heightened by an increasingly commercialized market-place, but the significant point is that people were at ease with the two extremes of the medical market-place. One reason for this is that perhaps they had more in common with each other than we might think.

In some ways this was still the time of the *longue durée* in medicine, despite evidence to the contrary from the other contributions in this book. Although theory changed it was still expressed in such a way that it spoke to patients and so attracted their trade. The warring factions in the medical market-place probably exaggerated their differences; all the groups had in common remedies and some degree of rationale or advertising to justify them. Moreover, we know that patients in actual fact frequently moved with ease from one type of practitioner to another.[63] What change there was came at bottom, not from new scientific theories but from commercial developments in the market. This was a time when Lockyer's Pills were sold wholesale on an organized basis in different towns, and George Jones's 'Tincture of the Sun', his Balsam and Electuary were sold by his 'trusty Friends' such as Mr John Ashtone, postmaster of Warrington, Richard Ballard Esq., mayor of Monmouth, Mr Joseph Russel, postmaster of Arundel, Mr John Holm, barber chirurgeon of Penrith in Cumberland and by many others in over fifty places spread across the country.[64] Given such

---

[63] See the essays in Porter, *Patients and Practitioners*. A typical story of patient mobility is in John Marten, *A Treatise of all the Degrees and Symptoms of the Venereal Disease in Both Sexes*, 6th edn (London, 1708?), pp. 142–3; a gentleman of fifty-four years contracted a gonorrhoea, was treated at a hospital for many weeks but the advice and treatments had no effect. He went to 'an eminent physician' but 'with as little success' and was 'at last recommended to me'. The possibility that the 'history' was made up by Marten, makes it even more typical.

[64] In Wellcome Institute Library, Broadsheet Cabinet. The Jones advertisement was probably written in 1675.

commercial developments, and the growth of an urban group of practitioners centred around the chemists' shops and warehouses, it is not surprising that emphasis was being placed on the remedy rather than the process of cure. But the public, or rather the literate public,[65] still desired the appearance of individualized prescribing. In all this, the new scientific theories formed part of the rhetoric used to differentiate medical groups and served the same function as humoral medicine, to make sense of illness, but in a deep sense they altered little. Change in medical practice in this period was slow, just as change in many of the material practices of life was slow.

[65] Little is known, or can be, of the way in which practitioners related to the expectations of illiterate patients.

Index